Women of Consequence

Women of Consequence

The Colorado Women's Hall of Fame

Jeanne Varnell

FOREWORD BY M. L. HANSON

To *MEL*

From *RACHEL*

Johnson Books
BOULDER

Published in the United States by Johnson Books, a division of Johnson Publishing Company, 1880 South 57th Court, Boulder, Colorado 80301. E-mail: books@jpcolorado.com

9 8 7 6 5 4 3 2 1

Cover design by Debra B. Topping
Cover photographs courtesy of The Colorado Women's Hall of Fame. Helen Bonfils photograph courtesy of the *Denver Post*.

The Colorado Women's Hall of Fame is a registered trademark of the Colorado Women's Hall of Fame.

Library of Congress Cataloging-in-Publication Data
   Varnell, Jeanne.
   Women of consequence: the Colorado Women's Hall of Fame / Jeanne
Varnell: foreword by M.L. Hanson.
      p.   cm.
   Includes bibliographical references and index.
   ISBN 1-55566-213-7 (cloth: alk. paper).—ISBN 1-55566-214-5
(paper: alk. paper)
    1. Women—Colorado Biography. 2. Colorado Women's Hall of Fame.
3. Colorado Biography.   I. Title.
CT3260.V37   1999
920.72'09788—dc21   99-35597
                                              CIP

Printed in the United States by
Johnson Printing
1880 South 57th Court
Boulder, Colorado 80301

 Printed on recycled paper with soy ink

Contents

Acknowledgments

To assemble and write the stories of these fifty-nine extraordinary women, I have received priceless assistance, expertise, and encouragement. I express my gratitude to our children—Jeffrey, Julia, Joel, Jon, and their families—for putting up with me and even egging me on. Julia and her husband, Jim Sarjeant, performed emergency computer resuscitation through a major crisis. My brother, Dr. David Mills, shared recollections and medical advice for the chapter about our late mother, Frances McConnell-Mills. My niece Molly Frauenhoff was invaluable in handling library computers and running down bibliographic information.

My sincere thanks to the following contributors to *Women of Consequence—The Colorado Women's Hall of Fame:*

To Barbara Johnson Mussil of Johnson Books, for believing in a book that honors significant accomplishments of Colorado women. To Johnson's editorial director Stephen Topping, who suggested the book and stood by, bolstered, and advised me from the beginning. To Alice Knight, my friend in the Colorado Authors' League, who advised me regarding the book contract.

A toast to the Colorado Women's Hall of Fame and its "founding mother," M. L. Hanson, for assembling an impressive collection of fifty-nine magnificent women, for endorsing my proposal to write the book, and for sharing the Hall of Fame files. Thank you, M. L., for your inspiring Introduction. The Hall of Fame's Cricket Smith generously supplied me with a complete set of inductees' portraits.

My faithful friends—Aleon Devore, a distinguished writing teacher, and Marilyn Stoddard, a fine writer—met monthly to correct each chapter. Alice Levine then pruned, upgraded, and corrected manuscript errors. Patricia Wilcox, my friend and former Sentinel Newspapers colleague, supplied anecdotes about Caroline Bancroft, shared her knowledge of May Bonfils-Stanton and the Belmar estate, and critiqued the Bancroft and Mary Coyle Chase chapters. My longtime friend Sally Lewis Rodeck, a former State Historical Society curator, reminisced about her late professor and mentor, anthropologist Marie Wormington Volk. A note of sorrow: Sally died suddenly in April 1998 shortly after critiquing the Wormington chapter.

Eva Hodges, former *Denver Post* reporter and columnist, critiqued the Helen Bonfils biography. Betty Stouffer Ondrusek Meir, a girlhood chum, shared her experiences growing up as the daughter of Helen Bonfils's chauffeur, Robert Stouffer. Her fascinating accounts give surprising insight to life inside the Bonfils mansion.

Boots Stockton, daughter of the late Senator Ruth Stockton, met with me and shared her scrapbooks and photographs and then reviewed the manuscript. State Senator Tillie Bishop, who sat next to Stockton in the Colorado Senate, recalled his memories of her. I received personal insights into conductor Antonia Brico from soprano Betty Frandsen. Joanna Palacas, Dr. Brico's assistant, described the late conductor's work, methods, and life; she also lent photographs of Brico and later reviewed the Brico biography.

For the Jane Silverstein Ries profile, her former associate Julia Andrews-Jones described Ries's landscape architecture practice, added delightful anecdotes, and lent me a videotaped interview with Jane Ries. Allen and Barbara Young also contributed to the Ries and Brico chapters. Margaret Taylor Curry's daughter, Rosalie J. Lay, shared her scrapbook and family photographs, which added information and liveliness to Curry's profile.

I used the Denver Woman's Press Club archives for the profiles of Helen Black, Mary Coyle Chase, and Edwina Hume Fallis, past members of the club. Leigh Grinstead, director of the Molly Brown House, discussed many of the misconceptions about Molly Brown and recommended other sources. Elizabeth Walker, museum curator, thoughtfully critiqued the Brown manuscript.

I thank Eleanor Gehres, director of the famous Western History Department at the Denver Public Library, for introducing me to the Colorado Women's Hall of Fame and for her interest in this book. Barbara Walton, acquisition curator, was a great help during my incessant library trips. Especially important to my work were the department's large George Bent collection, Kay Bruyn's research notes on Clara Brown, the Morrison Shafroth and Margaret Tobin Brown papers, the large Caroline Bancroft collection, and rare copies of *When Denver and I Were Young* by Edwina Fallis and *Active Footsteps* by Caroline Churchill.

The Stephen H. Hart Library at the Colorado Historical Society holds clipping files and papers of many women born in the nineteenth century, including Baby Doe Tabor, Eudochia Bell Smith, and the Brown Family correspondence. Norlin Library at the University of Colorado houses the Mary Rippon collection and clippings for Martha Maxwell, Rachel Noel, and Hazel Schmoll. Jody Corruccini at the Carnegie Branch Library for Local History in Boulder helped with information from the library's extensive collection on botanist Hazel Schmoll. The Justina Ford Museum, the Denver home and office of the black physician, supplied information about her life. From the Jefferson County libraries, I checked out many old books still in circulation and used the *Denver Post* index. The Pioneer Museum in Colorado Springs sent useful material from its extensive Helen Hunt Jackson collection.

Silvia Pettem, whose biography *Separate Lives: The Story of Mary Rippon* was released last spring, contributed information and reviewed the Mary Rippon chapter. Betty Moynihan, author of *Augusta Tabor: A Pioneering Woman*, lent her expertise on Augusta for this book. Marilyn Van Brunt Chapman of Wheat Ridge, great-great-granddaughter of Elizabeth Hickok Stone, corrected our misconceptions of "Auntie Stone" and critiqued Stone's profile. I am indebted to Esther Cohen Strauss for her account of the rescue of the Golda Meir duplex and its emergence as a museum.

I had the rare opportunity of interviewing twenty-two living Hall of Fame women before writing their biographies; ten of their interviews are on tape. I met with some in person; other interviews were via telephone. I thank these fifty-nine members of the Colorado Women's Hall of Fame for inspiring us with their courage, perseverance, and extraordinary accomplishments. Their biographies will influence countless generations to come.

To my mother, the late Frances McConnell-Mills,
who inspired me to write this book,
and to my husband, Larry,
for his patience and wholehearted support
during the seemingly endless process

Foreword

M. L. Hanson

It is my pleasure to introduce this wonderful book that highlights the lives of women who have done so much to create and influence the values, community, and culture of Colorado. Their leadership and character have a great impact on many lives and sometimes on nations far beyond the state borders. For their accomplishments, all the women in this book have been inducted into the Colorado Women's Hall of Fame.

I chose Colorado as my home when I moved to Denver in 1972. While working at a bank, I became active in the Colorado Federation of Business and Professional Women (BPW). My involvement with this organization was a great support for my career and also helped me to learn about my new home state. I was impressed with the vitality of the women I met and inspired by the pioneering accomplishments of women in Colorado's history.

During my first few years in Colorado, the professional lives of contemporary American women were changing. Women aspired to assume roles traditionally played by men. Many women of insight recognized that women needed their own organizations, conferences, publications, mentors, and awards if they were to move ahead. Women's Bank and Women's Foundation were founded. Publications were launched: *Colorado Woman, Network Magazine, Women's Point of View,* and *WomenSource.* The Women and Business Conference, Passages, and Woman School provided women with skills and savvy to survive and then succeed. The Women at Work Awards, the AMC Cancer Research Center Women's Event, and the Year for All Denver Women were created. The list of firsts goes on and on. Exciting things were happening for women.

Regardless of the advances women were making, I was frustrated because we relentlessly had to cajole, badger, and remind our bosses, the media, and government agencies that women needed to be included in leadership positions and in dialogues within all organizations. Many of us were becoming the *first* officers in banks, partners in accounting and law firms, starting our own businesses, and being promoted to management ranks at an unprecedented rate. Many of the people with whom I interacted seemed to believe our era was the first in which women had done anything outside of the home that influenced society. This belief seemed unfounded.

In 1983 I was elected state president of the Colorado Federation of Business and Professional Women, which entitled me to a seat on the National Board of Directors. My leadership duties included attending the annual Legislative Conference in Washington, D.C. At the conference we discussed the lack of recognition of the historical contributions of women. It became clear to me that women's historical accomplishments were absent from public school curriculums, state histories, and government memories. Our lives were not on record and had not been preserved by the institutions citizens depended upon to fully document events and personalities. Women in a few states had begun to form halls of fame to address the absence of documentation and recognition of women, but they found the process lengthy and arduous. I returned to Colorado resolved to fill this gap in our state.

In February of 1984, I started to ask people if they thought there was a need for some form of recognition for the contributions Colorado women had made and were making to our world. I asked how the histories of these women could be imprinted on the public mind. I asked mothers, librarians, schoolteachers, and business people. Although I mentioned a hall of fame as an option, I didn't ignore other possible formats. Some alternatives were award ceremonies, publications, museums, or a women's historical society. Not everyone I spoke with was interested or thought it was a good idea, but there were enough people who were at least intrigued and some who were passionate, so I continued to ask questions and collect opinions. In March I convened a meeting of friends and colleagues to discuss the feasibility of proceeding. I drew heavily on close friends, especially those in BPW and the women they recommended for their skills.

At first we met in my living room; later meetings were at the Penrose Executive Club. We talked about our heroines, about how difficult it was for young girls to find stories of women's lives to use in their history classes, and how few women were honored in the state Capitol. Then we decided to organize a women's hall of fame. Our goals were to honor women visibly through an induction event, educate the public through traveling exhibits, and provide role models for girls and women by researching the histories of women who had made significant contributions to the state and territory of Colorado. We wanted to reach people around the state and decided a traveling exhibit and induction ceremony would be the core of our program.

Thanks and credit go to Marcia Sky, who provided the first photographs for the exhibit, and to Cindy Fowler, who videotaped the first living inductees. Dana Shea-Reid was our secretary and later vice president; and Judy Richards, as our treasurer, set up an accounting system and diligently accounted for our funds. I was president of the Board until 1997. We applied for incorporation and for nonprofit status. The project was introduced at the state convention of Business and Professional Women in June 1984, only four months after I began investigating the idea of a hall of fame for women. At the convention I presided as president; Claudette Konola, who was the convention committee chair, orchestrated the inaugural presentation. It was thrilling to witness the emotions of the first inductees and the inspiration of the lives of the inductees on those present. The Colorado Women's Hall of Fame was launched!

In addition to our desire to showcase the accomplishments of women, we wanted the hall of fame to provide leadership opportunities for women. By inviting women to serve on the Board of Directors or to volunteer in other ways, we were able to make that goal a reality. Throughout the years, the leadership of the organization changed, but the core group of founding "mothers," remained. Some leaders came and went; some left and returned. Jan Huebner, Anne Flanigan, Linda Scherrer, Rose Flanigan, Cricket Smith, Marilyn Holmes, and Eleanor Gehres—in addition to the original group—continued to contribute their time and skills.

Over the years we have had many adventures while taking the traveling exhibit to schools, corporations, events, and libraries. We continued to produce the induction event and to select women for induction. Nominations were solicited throughout the state for both contemporary (living) and historical (deceased) candidates. The research was always difficult (so many of the women's stories had been lost); but we knew that difficulty proved the point of having the women's hall of fame. We held garden parties, repaired the exhibit repeatedly, raised funds through events and personal contributions, and started and aborted newsletters, projects, and events. Some favorite fund-raisers have been "Wine, Women and Wit," "Like Women for Chocolate," a house tour, and a walk. We've lost count of the number of mailing parties (affectionately referred to as "lick and stick parties"). Canvas bags replaced cardboard boxes for transporting the exhibit, which grew from fewer than ten to more than sixty pieces. There were never enough of us to do the work we thought needed to be done.

Several years ago it became clear it was time for new leadership and new projects. The hall of fame needed an infusion of energy. We convened everyone from the previous Boards and engaged them in organizing an eighteen-month celebration of the tenth anniversary of the Colorado Women's Hall of Fame. One goal was to recruit more women who would bring in even more women. We suspended holding formal Board meetings in favor of entrepreneurial creative sessions. The series of events revealed the future leaders. Women who were involved included Jennifer Stier, Cris Cardenas, Patsy Fetterolf, Sharon Kemp, Claudette Hamilton, Marcia Johnson, Jo Roll, Pat Booth, Rae Garrett, Valerie Sheffield, and Mary Zabinski.

From the protracted tenth-anniversary activities emerged Jeanne Varnell. After successfully nominating her mother for induction, she approached us with the idea of a book. It was my dream come true. Since the beginning of the project I had wanted a book to be written and published about the women we had inducted. The women featured in this book have left a legacy to all of us. Their lives and gifts are inspiring and humbling. I hope you find a heroine in these pages.

Clara Brown

Born January 1, 1800, near Fredericksburg, Virginia
Died October 23, 1885, in Denver, Colorado

On the first day of the nineteenth century, an African-American baby was born in the Virginia slave quarters of Ambrose Smith. When Clara (as the baby was named) was eighteen, she married Richard, another slave, and they had four children—Richard, Jr., Margaret, and twins, Eliza Jane and Paulina. Strict training and hard work governed Clara's life but she accepted her life as a slave and enjoyed her family.

Clara's first loss came when Paulina drowned at age eight. And when Ambrose Smith died in 1835, Clara's familiar world turned completely upside down. Strangers herded her family onto the auction block. She watched in horror as her husband, son, and older daughter were sold separately to distant owners. As they were led away, the auctioneer turned to eleven-year-old Eliza Jane, who was clinging to her mother's skirts. Never would Clara forget the misery and terror on her child's face as the indifferent new master tore Eliza from her side.

Clara was sold last. Recognizing her strong constitution and native intelligence, George Brown, a Kentucky plantation owner, bid high for her. He was a kind and fair master, whom Clara served for twenty-one years. In 1856, Brown granted her freedom and, in gratitude, Clara adopted his last name.

For the first time in her fifty-six years, Clara Brown was a free woman. But she was alone. She heard that her husband and daughter Margaret died in service. Richard, Jr., had been sold so many times his trail was obliterated. With her freedom assured, Clara vowed to dedicate the rest of her life to finding Eliza Jane, but she had no idea where to start looking for her daughter.

She began her new life as a free woman, which would take some getting used to. She was hired as cook and maid by a family that was traveling to Leavenworth, Kansas Territory, a major jumping-off place for the Pike's Peak gold rush. As she watched throngs of emigrants traveling west from Leavenworth, she wondered if Eliza might be out on the frontier, too.

In early April 1859, Clara approached Colonel Benjamin Wadsworth, leader of a sixty-wagon ox train, who was getting ready to head west. She offered to cook for twenty-six men riding with the train in exchange for her fare and the transportation of her stoves, washtubs, washboard, and clothing box. Wadsworth agreed to take her. The trip began on the Smoky Hill Trail, on a branch of the Kansas River. It was not an easy journey for a widowed black woman, especially when a Southern "gentleman" objected to her presence, saying she was sure to bring bad luck. Whenever he complained, Clara would duck out of sight and keep her silence. After eight weeks of grueling prairie travel through searing sun and wind, they reached Denver City and Auraria on June 8.

Clara soon acquired a one-room log cabin and hired on as a cook at City Bakery in Auraria. On November 6, 1859, she was one of seven who met in the cabin of Methodist Reverend Jacob Adriance to found the nondenominational Union Sunday School. The first few meetings of this first Sunday school in the territory were held in Adriance's humble home, which had a dirt roof and floor, board door, and one small window. A devout woman, Clara was one of the first to support the Reverends Adriance and William Goode, who had been sent west to establish Methodist missions in Central City and Denver. She was happy to offer her cabin for their prayer meetings.

Often, she heard conversations about gold discoveries in the mountains and noticed most of the traffic continued westward. On April 1, 1860, having decided to move west even further, she negotiated a ride in a wagon train, which struggled up the steep mountain trails to Gregory Gulch (later named Central City and Black Hawk). An army of miners was already working mining claims up and down the rocky canyons. Now sixty years old, Clara moved into a mountain cabin and opened the first laundry in Gilpin County while working on the side as a cook and midwife. The miners admired her Christian zeal, industry, and excellence of character. Many of them became her lifelong friends.

Clara lived frugally and invested her savings in mining claims and lots. Within a few years, she had accumulated property worth $10,000.

It was said that eventually she owned seven houses in Central City, sixteen lots in Denver, plus mines and properties in Georgetown, Boulder, and Idaho Springs. Her generous contributions helped the Reverends Adriance and Goode to establish Colorado's first Protestant church: St. James Methodist Church in Central City. Clara always participated in civic affairs and frequently lent a hand or a loan to the many bankrupted miners who appealed to her. With her diligence, wisdom, and kind heart, she earned the affection of the townspeople, who called her "Aunt Clara."

Renewing her vow to find Eliza Jane, Clara launched a letter-writing campaign to search for her. Her literate friends offered to write her letters. In 1866, she cashed in her savings and returned to Kentucky to look for her daughter. Clara failed to find Eliza in Kentucky. But she gathered sixteen of her relatives and friends together, paid their fares, and brought them back with her to Colorado. After they arrived, she saw that they got settled and that they found work. When Central City's high altitude and severe mountain climate began to take a toll on the elderly woman, she finally moved to Denver. One of her friends, who owned a small, white frame house set back from 517 Arapahoe Street, invited her to live there, rent-free, for the rest of her life.

She continually fired off letters to Kansas, Iowa, and Missouri, asking for word of her lost daughter. A break came in March 1882, when a friend in Council Bluffs, Iowa, wrote that she thought she had found Eliza Jane. Clara would have to go to Council Bluffs to meet the woman who might be her daughter. By that time, Clara was an eighty-two-year-old woman whose health was beginning to fail and who had to buy a train ticket. She was desperate to follow this last lead but the obstacles seemed insurmountable. She called on her doctor, her church, and a few old friends. With their help she scraped together enough for a train ticket and departed alone on March 3, 1882.

She was riding on a streetcar in Council Bluffs to meet Eliza when she saw a woman walking up the muddy street. Aunt Clara stepped off the streetcar, hurried toward the woman, and held out her arms. Right there on the street, the mother and daughter held a joyful reunion. Reporting the event on March 4, 1882, the *Council Bluffs Nonpareil* described Clara as "still strong, vigorous, tall, her hair thickly streaked with gray, her face kind."[1] After a long visit, Aunt Clara returned to Denver accompanied by her granddaughter.

Two years later, when Aunt Clara had grown too old and ill to work, her friend A. G. Rhoads wrote in a letter on January 19, 1884: "I saw 'Aunt Clara' last Tuesday Eve and took her some grub. She is not very well this winter but ('Lord bless you Honey') she is ready to meet her Master, she states."[2] As one of the '59ers (those who came west in the 1859 gold rush and settled in Colorado), she had been voted into the Society of Colorado Pioneers. To help their old friend, the Pioneers held a benefit dinner in March 1884 in the lecture room of Denver City Hall. The account in the *Denver Republican* read "Dressed in a neat calico dress, turban, and white apron, Aunt Clara received her many guests. They included once dead-broke miners she had helped and [who had] since become affluent."[3]

Despite her age, Clara was still an interesting subject. The *Denver Tribune-Republican* interviewed Clara on June 26, 1885: "She had a droll way of speaking with frequent allusions to Scripture and exclaiming about the goodness of the Lord. Her ideas were original. She had no fear of Indians, for was she not partly Indian? … She even remembered the War of 1812."[4]

Eliza Jane came to Denver and with her daughter cared for Clara until her death on October 23, 1885. The funeral on October 27 at Central Presbyterian Church was arranged by the Society of Colorado Pioneers. The Zion Baptist Choir provided the music. In one of the eulogies, Clara was described as "the kind old friend whose heart always responded to the cry of distress, and who, rising from the humble position of slave to the angelic type of a noble woman, won our sympathy and commanded our respect."[5]

Clara Brown was buried at Riverside Cemetery, but in 1896, her remains were moved to the family lot of Harriet Mason, a member of a family that Clara had helped. A permanent memorial chair in the Central City Opera House is dedicated to her, and her picture hangs in Colorado's capitol building.

Elizabeth Hickok Robbins Stone

Born September 21, 1801, in Hartford, Connecticut
Died December 4, 1895, in Fort Collins, Colorado

The Stone family wagon rolled to a stop at Camp Collins, Colorado Territory, in September 1864. Elizabeth Robbins Stone looked around at her new home, a military post consisting of tents and a scattering of log cabins near the Cache la Poudre River. As the *Rocky Mountain News* recalled on March 16, 1890: "It was nothing more than a parade ground and flagpole with three log huts on one side for officers quarters, and on the east and west ... log barracks for the men."

There was no other white woman in town. Sixty-three years old, Elizabeth couldn't be called a typical frontier wife and here she was embarking upon yet another career on the western frontier. With her second husband, "Judge" Lewis Stone, she had come to operate the officers' mess for Companies B and F of the Eleventh Ohio Cavalry stationed at Camp Collins. Lewis Stone obtained permission to build a two-story log cabin to serve as their home and the officers' mess. Within a month, the Stones had finished building their cabin and were ready to welcome the officers. Throughout the first year, Elizabeth remained the only woman in town. She was described as being "of a merry disposition" and was a gracious hostess of the officers' mess. The men started calling her "Auntie" Stone.

Disaster struck the Stone family in January 1866 when Lewis Stone died. Widowed for the second time, Elizabeth again became the sole support of her family. Since her first husband's death in 1852, such setbacks had only spurred Elizabeth on to fresh challenges.

⁓

Elizabeth Hickok was twenty-two in 1824 when she married Dr. Ezekiel W. Robbins in New York. She could read and write, rare for a woman of her day. Four years later, the couple moved by wagon with their two babies to the fur-trading town of St. Louis. Dr. Robbins ran a small medical practice and Elizabeth tended a family that grew to eight children. In 1840, the Robbins family moved to Chester, Illinois, where Dr. Robbins founded several public schools, served in the legislature, and helped write the Illinois Constitution. When Ezekiel died on July 25, 1852, Elizabeth still had three teen-aged sons to raise.

She migrated to Minnesota prairie country in 1857 and married a widower, Lewis Stone. After the Sioux Indian uprising in 1862, the couple decided to move again. They hitched their two milk cows to a covered wagon and traveled with their family across Nebraska and up the South Platte into Denver. During their year in Denver, Dr. Timothy Smith told them about Camp Collins, an army post east of LaPorte, built to guard the Overland mail route and protect settlers from unfriendly Indian tribes. The Stones, who had operated a hotel in Denver, moved to Camp Collins to manage the officers' mess.

Shortly after Lewis Stone's death, Elizabeth Stone received a letter from her niece, Elizabeth Keays, with news that she, too, had been widowed. Elizabeth immediately invited her niece and her young son to come West and move in with her. Mrs. Keays' journal of her overland journey (now housed in the Western History Department of the Denver Public Library) included this description of the house: "Auntie Stone has a very comfortable home for this country with three large rooms below and chambers for sleeping rooms." Keays and her son moved into the spare room with its "ingrain carpet, nice bed, window with a nice sunset view." In 1866, Elizabeth Keays started teaching her son his letters and soon opened the settlement's first school in Auntie Stone's upstairs "chambers."

In March 1867, the army decommissioned Camp Collins. Elizabeth opened the town's first hotel in her home and fed and lodged travelers along the Overland Trail. She welcomed newcomers, helped them get settled, and served as the fort's only midwife.

Besides operating a hotel, Elizabeth Stone had formed a business partnership in 1867 with Henry Clay Peterson, a gunsmith in town. She provided the initial ideas and financing; Peterson carried out the projects. After watching the region's burgeoning wheat farms, she decided they needed a flour mill. So the partners built a three-story grist mill—the town's tallest building and the second flour mill in northern Colorado. Stone and Peterson harnessed water from the Cache la

Poudre to power the mill. They began operations in 1869, ran the mill until December 1873, and then sold it the following March. The mill kept operating and changing hands until it burned down around 1885. It was rebuilt and was still in use in 1997, as a feed store. By 1870, Stone and Peterson had turned to brick making. Elizabeth Stone looked at the frame buildings around Fort Collins and decided that brick would give the town a more permanent appearance. So the partners opened and operated the first brick kiln in the region. Elizabeth built the first brick building, which she called the Cottage House, and ran a small hotel in it. In 1873, she bought the older Blake House Hotel and ran that until she was eighty-one. Six years later, in 1885, a Fort Collins *Courier* reporter, who interviewed Elizabeth, wrote: "She walks erect, reads a great deal, and talks sensibly. She curls her hair, wears her watch and chain, and dresses up for the afternoons as if she were yet a belle. In fact, she is a belle."

Elizabeth Stone cast her first vote when she was ninety-three. She died on December 4, 1895, when she was ninety-four. To commemorate her long and productive life, all town businesses closed for two hours. The firehouse bell tolled ninety-four times as she was laid to rest.

Elizabeth Stone's original cabin was dismantled and moved many times. Finally, Pioneer Women of Fort Collins moved it to the enclosed yard of the Pioneer Museum in downtown Fort Collins.

Owl Woman

Cheyenne name: Mis-stan-stur
Date of birth unknown
Died in 1847

The wedding of a Cheyenne princess and an American trader took place near Bent's Fort in 1835. The union not only joined two prominent cultures, it played a strong role in spearheading America's peaceful expansion into the vast central plains.

The story of Owl Woman and William Bent begins in May 1829, when William and his older brother, Charles, left their native St. Louis to drive their caravan of trade goods down the Santa Fe Trail. Charles opened a trading post in Taos, then in Mexico. William went up the Mountain Branch of the Santa Fe Trail and built a fort on the north bank of the Arkansas River (a few miles northeast of present-day La Junta).

Completed around 1832 or 1833, the post became known as Bent's Fort in recognition of William, the twenty-three-year-old builder and proprietor. With its fourteen-foot-high adobe walls and two eighteen-foot towers, Bent's Fort was the largest structure that the plains Indians had ever seen. It stood alone, visible for miles on the rolling prairie and when its heavy gates opened for trade in 1832, Bent's Fort became the first permanent white settlement in the central plains.

William's nearest neighbors, the Cheyennes and their allies, the Arapahos, became his friends. They nicknamed him "Little White Man." As William smoked the peace pipe with the Cheyennes, he perceived that their most influential tribal leader was Gray Thunder, an elderly and powerful medicine man. As the tribe's "Keeper of the Arrows," Gray Thunder's person was considered sacred.

William had been pondering ways of consolidating his friendship with the Cheyennes. At the same time, he was contemplating the obvious pleasures of having a comely wife who would cook for him in his own comfortable quarters. Besides, he needed a hostess to preside over the fort's many activities and entertainments. When Gray Thunder brought his family to the fort to trade, his two pretty daughters, Owl Woman and Yellow Woman, caught William's eye. He focused his attention upon Gray Thunder's first daughter, Owl Woman.

William had observed tribal courtship customs, such as making preliminary inquiries with the prospective bride's father and then exchanging ponies. In the Cheyenne tradition, just "talking to" a girl was equivalent to courting her. When it came time for Bent to call on Owl Woman, she probably dressed in her Cheyenne finery of soft white buckskins and beaded moccasins. She was always chaperoned by her sister, Yellow Woman.

William and Owl Woman were married in a Cheyenne ceremony. Historians date the wedding somewhere between 1835 and 1837, at or near Bent's Fort. During the ceremony, William was initiated into her tribe. Owl Woman—with Yellow Woman—then moved into Bent's quarters at the fort. At the reconstructed Bent's Fort (on its original foundation five miles from La Junta, Colorado), Owl Woman's room is furnished as it was then. The room has no bed because she slept, Indian fashion, on the floor.

During the heat of summer and cold winter months, the Bents often moved to Big Timbers about thirty-five miles below the fort (near present Lamar), to join their in-laws under cool, sheltering cottonwoods. Owl Woman's family also lived for long periods around the fort—a practice that put a crimp in the fort's trading business. Because the Cheyennes were usually at war with the Kiowas, Comanches, and Prairie Apaches, these tribes could not safely camp around the fort. To maintain trade with them, the Bents sent regular caravans of trade goods to the outer tribes. When Owl Woman or her family traveled with the Bent wagon trains, unfriendly Indians often appeared on the horizon. Owl Woman would flash a signal with a small mirror and the horsemen would turn away without intercepting them.

Owl Woman's first child, a daughter, was born at the fort on January 22, 1838. William named her Mary for his favorite sister. Their first son, born around 1840, was named Robert in honor of William's youngest brother, who later was killed near the fort by a Comanche band. George, born July 7, 1843, was named for Bent's brother, George, a partner at the fort until he died of tuberculosis.

The Bents were at Big Timbers in the fall of 1845, when William took ill and was unable to speak or even swallow. According to accounts, Owl Woman pushed a hollow quill down his throat and blew broth through it. She then summoned a medicine man. After peering down the swollen throat, he fetched some sharp sandburs, pierced a small hole in each bur, and tied it to the end of a strong thread. Over the burs, he rubbed a quantity of marrow fat and shoved the burs down Bent's throat with a notched stick. One by one, he pulled out each bur, bringing up a mass of infected matter. Before the medicine man left, William could swallow soup. By Christmas he was well. (The illness sounds like diphtheria.)

During the fort's busiest years, a hundred employees lived there and worked as traders, hunters, herders, teamsters, laborers. Many had children, who were the Bent boys' playmates. They knew famous plainsmen—George Fisher, John Hatcher, Tim Goodale, Tom Boggs, Tom Fitzgerald. Even the legendary Kit Carson often stopped there.

Indian tribes, a dozen at a time, would be camped outside the gate. During the day, when Indian men and their wives filled the trading room, the children played outside. They watched in fascination as war parties danced their tribal dances, accompanied by drums and chants, before they hit the warpath. Often, George, the second son, would see chiefs sitting around a circle smoking with his father. Wagons constantly pulled in from Mexico with cargos of colorful blankets or bars and coins of silver.

William Bent was away in 1847 when Owl Woman gave birth to her fourth child. By the time he reached the fort, she had died in childbirth and her tribesmen had placed her body, Indian-style, on a platform in a cottonwood tree. When William returned, he held their baby in his arms and named her Julia, after his oldest sister.

By all accounts, William had remained faithful to Owl Woman, who had been described as "a most estimable good woman of much influence in the tribe."[1] After her death, William gradually accepted her sister, Yellow Woman, as his wife. Owl Woman's son, George, indicated in a series of letters to historian George Hyde that Yellow Woman was a devoted and caring stepmother. She bore one child, whom William named Charles for his oldest brother. (William's habit of naming his children for his own siblings is confusing to historians and must have driven his contemporaries crazy. Brothers Charles, Robert, and George came west with William.)

On November 29, 1864, Yellow Woman was asleep in her lodge in the camp along the Big Sandy creek with her son, Charley, and stepchildren Julia and George. At dawn, U.S. volunteer troops led by Colonel John M. Chivington attacked the peaceful village. Soldiers captured Charles. George, seriously wounded in the hip, managed to escape, as did Julia and Yellow Woman. A year later, Yellow Woman was killed by Pawnee government scouts in Montana during the Poudre River Campaign against Cheyenne, Arapaho and Lakota warriors.

The once-great trade empire of the Bent brothers dwindled with the coming of white settlers and their military dominance. But as long as the two Cheyenne sisters lived, they bravely stood by William Bent and the five Bent children.

Martha Ann Dartt Maxwell

Born July 21, 1831, in Dartt's Settlement, Pennsylvania
Died June 2, 1881, in Rockaway Beach, New York

Martha Dartt Maxwell—only five feet tall and a lifelong vegetarian—became an accomplished hunter and taxidermist whose work changed the look of natural history museums forever. She was one of the first woman in a field that had been dominated by men, and her collection of Rocky Mountain birds and animals garnered praise from some of the foremost authorities of the time.

Separation and loss marked Martha's early childhood. Because of her mother's continuous incapacitating illness, Martha spent many long periods with her grandmother, Abigail Sanford, who was an independent-thinking woman. Her grandmother exerted a strong influence, taking Martha on long walks in the forest and introducing her to the natural world and to wildlife in the surrounding countryside of northcentral Pennsylvania.

The young girl suffered another blow at two and a half when her father died suddenly of scarlet fever. In 1841, when Martha was ten, her mother married again. Josiah Dartt, Martha's stepfather, recognized and encouraged her enthusiasm for education. Although her parents had limited resources, they managed to send Martha to Oberlin

College in Ohio in April 1851. But the money ran out, and a disappointed Martha had to leave the college in October 1852.

In order to support herself, Martha turned toward teaching, a common profession for women at the time. Several months later, James A. Maxwell, a forty-two-year-old widower with six children, hired her as a companion and chaperone for his two older children who were entering Lawrence College in Appleton, Wisconsin. Martha was thus able to continue her education; she studied natural philosophy, drawing, algebra, and music.

Maxwell soon proposed marriage to Martha and after some consideration she accepted his offer. They were wed on March 30, 1854; Martha was twenty-two. Shortly after the wedding, Martha received a letter from a classmate at Oberlin with whom she had fallen in love. Letters he had written to her after she left Oberlin had apparently never reached her. When she and James returned home after their wedding, there was a letter from him, in which he professed his love. Blanching, Martha crumbled the letter and began her life as Mrs. James Maxwell. Their large family was increased by one in November 1857, when their daughter, Mabel, was born.

In 1860, leaving their young daughter behind with her grandmother, and accompanied by James's son, the Maxwells came to Colorado Territory to prospect at Mountain City (later Central City). Martha operated a restaurant in a mining camp. Later the men set up a sawmill, and with his brother-in-law, Maxwell built the first wagon road up Boulder Canyon.

Martha returned to Wisconsin in 1863 (leaving her husband in Colorado) to tend to her mother, who was ill again. She found her younger sisters studying natural history under Professor E. F. Hobart. Martha helped collect specimens for Hobart's school and at his request mounted two birds appearing to fight over a nest. She became fascinated with the idea of using mounted wild animals to create artistic scenes. Her interest in taxidermy had actually begun in Colorado when a German taxidermist jumped her claim on land south of Denver. Fascinated by the specimens he was mounting, Martha wanted him to teach her the technique. Although he agreed at first, he soon reneged, saying she would compete with him. After the man refused to leave the shanty, which the court had ruled belonged to Mrs. Maxwell, Martha broke into the building and removed his materials—but not before she examined them well enough to get a sense of the process.

Eventually, the Maxwells settled in Boulder with their daughter, Mabel, and Martha's half-sister Mary Dartt. Martha continued her work, frequently camping alone in the mountains above Boulder, observing habits and habitats of birds and animals until she became an expert naturalist. She collected specimens and then sculpted them into lifelike positions and displayed them against backgrounds resembling their natural environments.

In the early years, the Maxwell marriage appeared quite companionable. According to the account her half-sister wrote with Martha's help, James accompanied Martha on many of her expeditions. His "vigor of body and equanimity of mind were seldom disturbed. If the weather was disagreeable and roads almost impassable, he was jolly and smiling. If the team grew fractious and the harness broke ... he whistled, talked to the beasts, and tinkered with the gearing."[1] Sitting atop the wagon beside her husband, Martha wore a "gymnastic suit of neutral tint, substantial shoes, and stockings, a simple shade hat and game bag," and carried her gun.[2] After shooting an animal, she would sit by the road to skin and measure her trophy to help her build up the artificial body over which the skin was to be stretched. She then cleaned and skinned the bones to be preserved. She did all the work herself, so she could study the animal's anatomy and musculature and achieve a lifelike effect.

On a trip through Middle Park, the Maxwells explored Hot Sulphur Springs and Martha shot specimens of chipmunks, squirrels, and birds. Martha had become quite a good marksman. Her earliest experience with a gun occurred when she was about fifteen in Wisconsin. Hearing a sound in an adjoining room, Martha and her mother ran in to find a coiled rattlesnake, ready to strike at four-year-old Mary. Quickly, Martha scooped up her sister, handed her to her mother, and snatched her father's gun. She steadied it, aimed, and fired. Her shot sent the dying snake into the cellar.

James and Martha often took Mabel on their trips but the child disliked every minute of the outdoor experience. Years later, in her memoirs, Mabel recalled the discomfort of getting into cold and wet clothes and shoes and of constantly shivering. Throughout their lives, Martha and Mabel struggled with their conflicting goals and desires. Martha encouraged her daughter to get a good education, follow her feminist lead, and achieve in some field. Mabel wanted a conventional life: a home, a husband, and children. The gulf between mother and daughter widened over the years.

By 1868, Martha Maxwell had amassed a fairly extensive collection of Rocky Mountain birds and mammals. At the suggestions of friends, she opened a museum in Boulder. In it she displayed hundreds of birds and mammals in habitat groupings, a significant innovation at the time. Most museums at that time showed stuffed specimens in rows against plain backgrounds. Among the many visitors who marveled at the museum and the displays was author Helen Hunt Jackson, who then wrote several glowing articles in national publications, praising the natural landscapes and the lifelike animals. Jackson was sure that a little dog near the entrance was real; she waited for it to jump and bark—only to realize a moment later that the pet was stuffed. She was also charmed by a comic display of a group of monkeys sitting around a table, playing poker. In one of her articles, she described Martha as a "wee, modest, tenderhearted woman ... as shy as one of her weasels."[3] Although the museum became known nationwide because of the articles, it earned little money for Martha; the small town of Boulder (a village of 300 people in 1868) could not support it. Martha decided to move the museum to Denver to improve her financial situation, but even there she could not meet the expenses and incurred further debt.

In 1870, Martha Maxwell displayed her work at the Colorado Agricultural Society fair in Denver where it was such a success that she was invited to represent Colorado at the American Centennial Exhibition of 1876 in Philadelphia. Appearing in her hunting costume of heavy, brown-checked cloth, she attracted crowds of viewers. A newspaper reporter who saw her display in the Kansas-Colorado building described her as a classic beauty under five feet tall with gold hair, wide-set eyes, and a beautiful figure, with expertise in natural history, geology, and botany. Another noted that her exhibition displayed remarkable taste and artistic skill, citing the placement of the sheep on the mountain-side and the accurate representation of other animals—an elk, a mountain lion, deer, fox, and beaver. When she was criticized for killing animals for taxidermy, Martha argued that she never took a life for carnivorous purposes because she was a vegetarian. "All must die sometime. I only shorten the period of consciousness that I may give their forms a perpetual memory and I leave it to you, which is more cruel? to kill to eat or kill to immortalize?"[4]

After the exhibition, Martha's husband tried to persuade her to re-turn to Boulder. By then, the Maxwell marriage had hit hard times. Martha had been supporting them, trying to raise money for Mabel's education and her taxidermy; James no longer approved of her work and her absences from home. She moved to Boston, instead, where her sister Mary lived. There she became involved in the women's move-ment and studied biology and chemistry. The relationship between Martha and Mabel, which had always been fraught with difficulty, hit another hurdle. When Martha moved to Boston, she urged her daugh-ter to transfer to Wellesley College to be near her. Mabel preferred to stay at the University of Michigan, but Martha prevailed. Mabel later summed up their struggles, saying her mother "looked upon me as an ugly duckling hatched by a thoroughbred hen."[5] During this period, Mary (with Martha's help) began to write *On the Plains and Among the Peaks, or, How Mrs. Maxwell Made her Natural History Collection,* which was finished in mid-1877.

By early 1879, Martha was in financial straits and failing health. She scraped together enough money to return to Boulder to see her ailing mother. While there, she may have seen James, but the marriage was about over. Martha returned to the East in late 1879 and, with the help of a benefactor, set up a small beachhouse-museum at Rockaway Beach on Long Island. But failing health soon turned into serious ill-ness. In May 1881, Mabel arrived after receiving word that Martha was critically ill. Martha was dying of an ovarian tumor. At her bedside, mother and daughter were finally reconciled shortly before Martha died at age forty-nine.

Martha Maxwell earned accolades during her life and after. In 1876, noted scientist Spencer Baird wrote that she deserves "the highest credit for what she has done in the way of bringing together a complete representation of the mammals and birds of Colorado."[6] Maxine Benson, Martha's modern biographer, praised her as "the first woman field naturalist who went out as men did and obtained and prepared her own specimens and the first woman who had a subspecies she herself discovered named after her."[7] With Benson, we note "the costs she paid, especially in the relationships with her husband and daughter."[8]

Helen Fiske Hunt Jackson

Born October 15, 1831, in Amherst, Massachusetts
Died August 12, 1885, in San Francisco, California

During her lifetime, Helen Hunt Jackson, who lived more than a century ago, was described as the "the most brilliant, impetuous, and thoroughly individual woman in her time."[1] Certainly, she was the most famous woman author of her era to live in Colorado.

Helen's mother died of tuberculosis—the first of many losses Helen suffered in her life. Her father, Nathan Welby Fiske, was an original faculty member of Amherst College and the head of a strict, pious household. But from childhood, Helen demonstrated her own mind as a nonconformist, even a rebel, who was known to laugh in church and pull pranks continually. Orphaned by the time she was fifteen, she was sent to a series of girls' schools. At the Abbott School in New York City, she earned a reputation as a scholar.

When she was twenty-one, she married Captain Edward Hunt, a West Point graduate. The union appeared to be quite happy until tragedy struck. Their first son, Murray, died at the age of one. Her husband was killed in 1863 while testing a marine torpedo he had invented for the navy. A second son, Rennie, died from diphtheria when he was nine. "And I am left, who avail nothing," wrote Helen, in her grief, to a friend. As an antidote to her pain and to supplement her income, she began writing magazine articles and poetry when she was thirty-five. Her first poems were gloomy and sentimental but she kept working and eventually demonstrated that she was a gifted writer. She published her verses unsigned or used "H.H." or "Helen Hunt."

Hunt's early writing was praised for its wealth of imagery, freshness, humor, and deep emotion. Buoyed by the success of her poetry, she began to write in other areas—travel, children's stories, and short novels. Soon, she was selling to popular magazines of the day—*Scribner's Monthly,* and *The Nation,* for example. From girlhood, Helen Hunt was a close friend to Emily Dickinson. Later, traveling widely to gain material for her articles, she mingled with such writers as Louisa May Alcott, John Greenleaf Whittier, Oliver Wendell Holmes, Ralph Waldo Emerson, and Harriet Beecher Stowe.

"H.H." was making a comfortable income by the time a critic called her the most successful, popular, and envied woman writer in America. But "the most successful woman" was driving herself so hard she had to write in bed. She became worn down by a chronic bronchial condition, for which her doctor finally ordered her to take in the "curative air of the Rockies." The doctor and her maid, Emma, accompanied her when she arrived in newly incorporated Colorado Springs— a hamlet of log cabins and plain wooden buildings.

Helen's health quickly responded to the dry, sunny winter days. She began to write again—about the marvelous climate where asthma, throat diseases, and early stages of consumption were cured by the rarefied air. Soon, she was traveling by carriage or narrow-gauge railroad to Colorado's remote regions. In town, she stayed in a boardinghouse on Pikes Peak Avenue, where she met William Sharpless Jackson. An eligible bachelor and a Pennsylvania Quaker, he had moved to Colorado Springs with his sister, Margaret, in October 1871, as the secretary-treasurer of the new Denver & Rio Grande Railway. In addition, Jackson (who had great business acumen) had helped establish the El Paso

Bank and was a founder and trustee of Colorado College. Later, he helped organize the Denver National Bank and International Trust Company of Denver.

When he met Helen, who was plump, bubbly, and vivacious, Jackson was quite enchanted. He admired her dainty hands and feet, light blue smiling eyes, and graying curls that framed her forehead as well as her talent and fame. For two years, Jackson courted Helen, although she was five years older than he. They married on October 22, 1875, in New England. "It was the wedding of a skylark to a turtle," commented Helen's friend Frances Wolcott. Helen, she said, was "unpredictable, pixieish, eccentric, and metaphysical. Jackson, a Quaker, was a matter-of-fact businessman—methodical, conscientious, and humorless."[2]

The newlyweds set up housekeeping in a charming Victorian house at the corner of Kiowa and Weber Streets in Colorado Springs. It is said that mining tycoon Winfield Scott Stratton built the house during his earlier carpentering days. Gossips accused Helen of having the entire house rotated on its foundation until she could see Pike's Peak from her window. She furnished the cottage with Navajo rugs, striped serapes, and a fireplace mantel set with blue and white tiles. In keeping with her love of flowers and wildlife, she decorated the shelves with kinnikinnik, silk thistles, and even a bird's nest. The marriage seemed ideal at first. Helen Jackson took trips with her new husband on his railroad, the D & RG, and wrote observations in her column "Bits of Travel at Home and Abroad."

Despite her upturn in fortune, however, Helen told a friend that she was "homesick as a cat." Every fall, she would go back to New England. In 1879, she attended a reception there for Chief Standing Bear, a Ponca Indian. He described the fate of 800 peaceful Indians of his tribe, who had been forced to move from their land in southeastern Dakota to Oklahoma Indian Territory. Many had died on the journey. He asked the audience to help raise money to restore his people to their land. Moved by his plea, Helen Hunt Jackson immediately fired off furious letters to Washington officials, circulated petitions, and raised money.

The timing was bad. In Colorado, it was the year of the Meeker Massacre, and Coloradans were clamoring for the Utes' removal from their state. Helen Jackson, alone, supported the Utes. She wrote of their plight in 1881 in *A Century of Dishonor,* a book blasting the government's history of handling Indian affairs as "a shameful record of broken treaties, unkept promises, and countless other wrongs." Her book created a national controversy that helped bring about reforms.

To improve conditions for American Indians, Helen Jackson mounted a one-woman campaign. She sent letters to editors, army officers, congressmen, and ministers; she wrote about the Sand Creek Massacre of 1864; and she traveled and spoke wherever she could get an audience. The Indian Commission responded by appropriating funds for the Ponca tribe's resettlement. In 1882, Helen was named a special agent to the commissioner of Indian Affairs and was directed to write a report on the Mission Indians of southern California.

After visiting the missions and making her report, she used her research notes to write her famous novel *Ramona,* a fictionalized dramatization of the Indians' plight. The book, completed in three months and published in 1884, which to a modern audience may read like a diatribe against all Americans and their government, was nonetheless effective. *Ramona* eventually became an American literary classic. By 1939, it had been transformed into three movie pictures, a stage play, and a pageant; it had 141 successive printings.

As she had done previously, she had again driven herself to the point of total exhaustion and suffered two bouts of serious illness. Her doctor advised her to go to California for a milder climate, but she hated to leave her husband. In the summer of 1884, Helen fell in her Colorado Springs home and broke her leg. Although she finally went to California, her leg failed to heal. In her last letter to her husband, she urged him "to quickly remarry [after her death] and enjoy a family life with children," which they had not shared in their ten years together. Specifically, she hoped he would consider marrying her niece Helen Banfield.

Helen Hunt Jackson died of cancer on August 12, 1885, in San Francisco. She was fifty-three. Jackson had arrived in time to spend the last few days at her side. He had his wife's remains buried in a private park above South Cheyenne Falls west of Colorado Springs. Thousands of her fans climbed to place stones on her grave until, in 1891, Jackson moved her body to Evergreen Cemetery in Colorado Springs. Her simple granite gravestone bears the inscription "Helen, wife of William S. Jackson, died August 12, 1885," followed by a line from her poem "Emïgravit." "Oh, write of me, not died in bitter pains, but emigrated to another star."

Jackson did marry Helen Banfield in 1888. He was fifty-four (twenty-three years older than his bride) and embarking upon a new career as stepfather to her six children. They added rooms on to the house so they could keep the H.H. side as it was. The second Mrs. Jackson died not long after their marriage, leaving him to raise six small children.

Isabella Bird

Born October 15, 1831, in Yorkshire, England
Died 1904 in Edinburgh, Scotland

Well-to-do Englishmen of the 1800s habitually visited New York or New Orleans, and then returned to England to generalize about America and Americans. Not so Isabella Bird, daughter of an English clergyman, who spent her life touring foreign countries to escape from—of all things—an aching back. When she was twenty and living in Tattenhall, Cheshire, England, Isabella went to her physician suffering from chronic back problems, insomnia, and depression. Failing to cure her, the doctor prescribed a long sea voyage. Thus, Isabella visited Canada and America as a means of improving her health. While she was on the road, her physical complaints magically disappeared and on her return, she wrote *The Englishwoman in America* in 1856 and *Aspects of Religion in the United States* in 1859. Her books were bestsellers and she became an insatiable world traveler.

Again beset with back trouble at age 40, Isabella set off for Australia and Hawaii. She climbed Mauna Loa, the world's largest volcano, and on her way home from Hawaii she detoured by train through Lake Tahoe and on to Greeley. There, she saw 14,255-foot Long's Peak towering above "Longmount" and vowed to climb to its summit. With this in mind, she joined two men riding on to Estes Park. *A Lady's Life in the Rocky Mountains* describes the event: "Never have I seen anything to equal the view into Estes Park. The mountains are very near now, and the near is more glorious than the far, and reality [more] than dreamland."[1]

Reaching the park entrance on September 28, 1873, they stopped at the cabin of Mountain Jim Nugent. He was famous as a "notorious" mountain man, civil and cultured when sober but a dangerous ruffian when intoxicated. (Miss Bird did not learn of his darker self until after she left Colorado.) One side of his face had been mangled in a fight with a grizzly; the other side was strikingly handsome. Despite his reputation, Nugent would become Miss Bird's literate and chivalrous guide on many breathtaking mountain rides.

A plump woman barely five feet tall, Isabella must have presented an astonishing appearance in her "Hawaiian riding dress ... a half-fitting jacket, a skirt reaching to the ankles, and full Turkish trousers gathered to frills over the boots," which she called "a thoroughly ... feminine" mountaineering costume.[2] An accomplished horsewoman, she surprised the locals by riding astride rather than sidesaddle.

In Estes Park, she rented a rough, two-room cabin. "My door opens into a little room with a stone chimney and that again into a small room with a hay bed, a chair with a tin basin on it, a shelf and some pegs. A window looks on the lake and the glories of the sunrises which I see from it are indescribable,"[3] she wrote in *A Lady's Life in the Rocky Mountains.* She would awake on winter mornings in the unchinked cabin to find her bed coated with snow.

She persisted in her determination to scale Long's Peak. After some negotiations, Nugent agreed to guide her up the craggy heights to the top of the "American Matterhorn." Alas, she had not even imagined the exertions of the climb. In the end, Nugent had to drag her to the summit "like a bale of goods."

Isabella and Mountain Jim—direct opposites in all but their love for the Rockies—developed a close acquaintance. (Many who read her book suspect she had a brief love affair with the sometimes chivalrous, but often intemperate, mountain man.)

Later that year, on October 20, Isabella mounted her mare, Birdie, for a 3,000-mile trip, alone, across the Front Range. Her only confidante was her sister, Henrietta, back in England, recipient of ongoing letters that became Isabella's books. Adventures of the lone woman riding her pony through the wild, sparsely populated Rockies in the dead of an 1873 winter still make exciting reading. *A Lady's Life in the Rocky Mountains* describes people she met: uncouth outlaws and vigilance committees; gracious hosts and pinchpenny families grudgingly sharing their rations. She came across cabins deep in filth and others "neat as a London parlor" and "relentless temperance" colonies next door to booming saloons.[4] Her observations add a unique dimension to early Colorado history. Most delicious are her lyrical descriptions of towering peaks and river valleys that she learned to love during her famous three-month tour of the Rockies.

She then returned to England, learned how to use a microscope, and founded a college for medical missionaries. In 1881, when she was fifty, she married Dr. John Bishop, her sister's physician. The had just six contented years together before his death in 1886.

"I am too old for hardships and great exertions now," wrote Isabella Bird in 1893. Sixty-three and just home from Persia and Kurdistan, Japan, and Korea, she was diagnosed with fatty degeneration of the heart, gout, an infected lung, and spinal weakness. Four years later, however, she rode in regal dignity in a bamboo-roofed boat being towed behind an asthmatic towboat. This exotic journey took her up the Yangtze River for 150 miles from Shanghai to Hangchow. Her Oriental costume consisted of a "large, loose ponjee jacket … having capacious" pockets, in which she carried such travel paraphernalia as a portable oil lamp and a loaded revolver. For her book on this trip, *The Yangtze Valley and Beyond,* she snapped and printed her own fine photographs. Her last overseas fling was to Morocco when she was in her seventies.

She traveled for the pure interest and pleasure of life on the road and avoided florid phrases of the professional world traveler. "It is hard to recall another woman in any age or country who traveled as widely, who saw so much, and who left so perceptive a record of what she saw," wrote Daniel Boorstin in his introduction to *A Lady's Life in the Rocky Mountains.*[5]

In 1892, she was the first woman elected a Fellow of the Royal Geographical Society. On the occasion, she dined with Prime Minister William Gladstone and was presented to Queen Victoria. Despite these honors and others, Isabella Bird, one of the foremost travel writers of all time, remained a modest woman. She died in Edinburgh, Scotland, in 1904 at age seventy-three.

Augusta Louise Pierce Tabor
Born March 29, 1833, in Augusta, Maine
Died January 30, 1895, in Pasadena, California

Augusta Tabor was an unsung heroine of the Pike's Peak Gold Rush. Although she was "a frail, delicate-looking woman,"[1] throughout her life, she exhibited a strength of spirit and body that few women possess.

As a child, Augusta Louise Pierce's health was so fragile that it took all her gumption just to keep going—gumption that would come to her rescue many times on the Colorado frontier. She was the third daughter of a well-to-do building contractor and quarry owner, in a close-knit family of seven girls and three boys. Augusta met Horace Austin Warner Tabor when he came to work for her father as a stone mason. Tabor, who came from a poor Vermont family, was ambitious and willing to gamble on his future. He proposed after a short courtship and they were married on January 31, 1857, at the Pierce home in Maine. Tabor was twenty-six; Augusta, twenty-three.

The newlyweds moved to Zeandale in Kansas Territory, where Augusta recalled their first home as a log cabin that "stood alone and solitary upon an open, wind-whipped prairie."[2] Because of her frail health, Augusta never had done housework. She didn't even know how to cook. But she stoked up the cabin's primitive woodstove and started fixing meals for her husband and their two male traveling companions, who thereupon became permanent boarders. During the day, her only company was the despised snakes that invaded every corner of their cabin.

When it came time for their child to be born, Tabor was away, working at Fort Riley. One of the boarders, Nathaniel Maxcy (also spelled Maxey and Maxie), happened to be at the cabin and helped with the delivery. In appreciation, Augusta named her baby boy Nathaniel Maxcy.

After struggling for two years with the relentless Kansas wind, rattlesnakes, and feeble crops, they got word of gold discoveries at Pike's Peak. On April 5, 1859, the Tabors and their two boarders loaded the wagon, hitched up the oxen, and struck out for Cherry Creek. "What I endured on this journey only the women who crossed the plains in '59 can realize," Augusta Tabor recalled. "My babe was teething and suffering from fever and ague, so he required constant attention ... I was weak and feeble ... My weight was only ninety pounds."[3]

After six weeks, they reached Denver City, a primitive camp of wagons, tents, Arapaho Indian lodges, and scattered cabins. Exhausted, they rested there a week before pushing westward along Clear Creek to the foothills, where they camped near the site of Golden on July 3. To Augusta's horror, the next morning, the men snatched up some blankets and supplies, told her to be good to herself, and started hiking toward Gregory Diggings. "How sadly I felt, none but God ... knew," she recalled. "Twelve miles from a human soul save my [sixteen-month-old] babe and the footsore oxen. Three long weary weeks I held the fort."[4]

The men returned on July 26. They all reloaded the wagon and prodded the oxen up a primitive trail. Often, they had to unload and push the wagon up the steep slopes or else widen the road. In three weeks, they had hacked their way to Payne's Bar (now Idaho Springs). Their wagon was one of the first to get through and Augusta the first white woman to arrive in the camp. The miners built her a small cabin. She tied on her apron, started a laundry, fixed meals, and nursed them through their illnesses. When winter came, the Tabor party moved to rented rooms in Denver.

In February, they headed south over Ute Pass and South Park. Augusta was driving the wagon across the Arkansas River when it foundered in rushing water. In panic, she grabbed an overhanging branch with one hand and held Maxcy in her other arm. By the time the men could carry them to shore, she was unconscious and didn't recover for days. Thus went the Tabors' long odyssey through Colorado's boom-to-bust mining camps. They waded through snow, forded streams, and lost their way. They camped at Salt Creek, Trout Creek, and Cache Creek.

In May 1860, they came to California Gulch, where a gold rush had begun. As usual, Augusta was the first woman in camp and again the miners built her a cabin. She fed boarders, took in laundry, and weighed the miners' gold dust on their scales. Years later, she would remember how happy she was that summer.

Augusta used her profits to finance their trip home to Maine. The next spring, the Tabors brought her sister Lilly and brother Frank for a visit. When they moved to Buckskin Joe, Augusta and Lilly opened a restaurant. Wherever they stopped, the men prospected while Augusta tended Maxcy, fed and clothed the family, and ran a business.

In 1868 they returned to California Gulch with its new town, Oro City, and applied to set up a post office. Tabor became postmaster and Augusta the assistant. By then, the Tabors were well-known gold-rush veterans. Augusta had saved enough to open a well-stocked general store and kept her books at night in the Tabors' rooms at the back of the store.

Miners, who were seeking gold, had been discarding the heavy, bothersome black soil. Then someone realized that black soil meant silver and lead, igniting a silver bonanza. After eighteen years of boom-towns, the Tabors moved two-and-a-half miles away to a new camp that soon became Leadville. Maxcy was old enough to help clerk in their two stores, while Horace willingly grubstaked prospectors, who called him "The Old Man." Horace also did some mining and ventured into community politics. In 1878, he was elected the first mayor of Leadville, and the Tabors were welcomed into Leadville society.

Throughout their mining camp years, Horace's gold mine was Augusta, whose earnings provided most of their income. But resentment was simmering in the Tabor camp. The more freehanded Horace was, the more sharply Augusta tightened the purse strings and scolded over his improvident spending. Who knew better than she the worth of a dollar? Despite it all, she went on loving the good-natured Horace.

In the spring of 1878, a couple of flat-broke prospectors, August Rische and George Hook, walked into the store and hit Tabor for a grubstake so they could sink a shaft on Fryer Hill. To everyone's astonishment, they struck a rich silver vein that soon was producing $10,000 a day. They named their mine the Little Pittsburg, and Tabor, thanks to his $60 grubstake, owned a third of it. The Little Pittsburg made Tabor rich. Horace soon bought out his partners and invested in other mines, real estate, and banks. Augusta's customers and friends honored her as the First Lady of Leadville. In 1879, her modest frame house was moved to Fifth Street. Years later it was turned into a small museum.

Horace became active in the Republican Party. When he was elected Colorado lieutenant governor in 1878, he surprised Augusta with a $40,000, twenty-room house at Eighteenth and Broadway in Denver. She only pursed her lips and fretted over his extravagance.

As Horace's reputation soared, he was seen more frequently at fancy parlor houses and in the company of fast women. Augusta heard about his escapades but made excuses to herself. She continued to disapprove of his high-flying expenditures and they quarreled more and more frequently.

Tabor was in Leadville on business during the fall of 1879, when he first set eyes upon a delectable blonde—Elizabeth McCourt Doe. After that, Augusta and Horace appeared in public at only a few more balls and formal occasions in Denver. He was usually in Leadville, where he had established "Baby" Doe at the Clarendon Hotel. The final blow came for Augusta in January 1881. Horace moved out of their home to a suite at the luxurious Windsor Hotel on Denver's Larimer Street.

Augusta took a long trip in Europe. When she returned to Denver, she was surprised to see the Tabor Grand Opera House nearing completion at Sixteenth and Larimer Streets. She sent Horace a humble note asking to join him at the grand opening on September 5, 1881. But on opening night, the opulent Tabor Box was empty. Baby Doe had taken her place in the audience.

Under constant pressure from Tabor's manager, William Bush, Augusta tearfully granted Horace a divorce on January 2, 1883, in exchange for $300,000 and the Broadway house. At the long court hearing, she sobbed out to the judge that she gave the divorce "not willingly." Only later did she learn the ultimate betrayal: Tabor had arranged an earlier divorce in Durango and had secretly married Baby Doe on September 30, 1882, in St. Louis.

All Denver sided with Augusta in the sorry affair and ignored Tabor's new wife and family. Augusta still loved Horace, and the divorce wiped out all her spark and grit. Pictures of Augusta in her sixties reveal a prim, austere woman wearing pinch-nose spectacles and a severe, unflattering hair style—quite a contrast from the pretty young woman with even features, soft eyes and dark curls framing her face, who had married Horace Tabor.

She continued to live in her Broadway mansion, a wealthy woman frugally keeping as many as fourteen boarders. She often got together with Maxcy and her several brothers and sisters, who lived nearby. With her native shrewdness, she managed her money and investments. She continued to stand by, waiting for Baby Doe to leave Tabor.

Augusta served actively in the Unitarian Church. She hosted fundraising events in her large home and gave to community charities and civic projects. She dedicated herself to the Pioneer Ladies Aid Society, helping pioneer women in need. Augusta Tabor earned the love and respect of everyone in Denver—everyone but Horace.

In the 1890s, when Augusta's health declined, she sold her home and moved into a suite at the new Brown Palace Hotel. Suffering from a harsh cough in the winter of 1894–1895, she went to stay at the Balmoral Hotel in Pasadena, California. She died there on January 30, 1895. She was sixty-one.

Funeral services, held on February 8 in the Unitarian Church in Denver, were crowded with friends and associates who mourned her passing. As Caroline Bancroft wrote in *Augusta Tabor: Her Side of the Scandal:* "The tragedy of her life lay in the fact that, although she was beloved of many, she lost the key to the only heart she wanted."[5]

Caroline ("Kate") Nichols Churchill

Born December 23, 1833, in Pickering, Upper Province, Canada
Died January 14, 1926, in Colorado Springs, Colorado

C. M. (Caroline) Churchill made her mark in the 1870s to 1890s as a Denver author and publisher. On a national level, she ran the country's first all-woman newsroom, published one of the first, if not *the* first, women's emancipation newspaper, and was a leading feminist of her time.

She told her story in *Active Footsteps,* her autobiography, which she wrote in the third person—an ingenious device that permitted her to refer to herself as "Mrs. Churchill" without appearing to boast. She would write, for example, "The beauty of Mrs. Churchill's great work is that she never sought preferment for herself. Self-aggrandizement never formed any part of her policy."[1]

She was born Caroline M. Nichols in Canada, the daughter of American parents. Her family of book lovers encouraged her to read a wide variety of topics and she, too, developed a lifelong passion for reading. Caroline left school when she was thirteen and started teaching in a private school.

While in her early twenties, she married a "Mr. Churchill." The union was so unhappy that she never divulged Churchill's first name, although they remained legally married for eleven years until he died in the 1860s. One wonders if the unpleasant marriage gave rise to her strong feminist outlook and lifelong antagonism to men. When C. M.

Churchill moved to Minnesota in 1857, she took their daughter with her. Her sister apparently adopted the little girl, whom Caroline never again mentioned in her writing.

In Minnesota, she met Jane Grey Swisshelm, editor of the *St. Cloud Democrat,* and an abolitionist and feminist. The editor's philosophy added fuel to Churchill's already pronounced feminist attitudes.

Caroline Churchill, afflicted with sudden coughing fits, moved to California in 1870 to better her "seldom perfect" health. During six years there, she began to write and ultimately completed *Over Purple Hills,* a work about California. She took the manuscript to Chicago and had it published. The *Tribune,* the *Times,* and the *Post* reviewed it and one called it "a sprightly written little work." For two years, she toured Missouri, Kansas and Indian Territory, selling that book and two others she had written and publishing travel sketches.

On her return to California in 1879, Caroline Churchill stopped in Denver. She later noted in her autobiography that Denver had "a good atmosphere for weak lungs … [it is] a good place to come to escape the mother-in-law, or any phantom from which the wicked flee. The population [is] very transient and withal very democratic."[2] Denver of the 1870s, with a population of around thirty thousand, looked like a favorable city in which a woman might own and operate a business. It had, by the late 1800s, become a publishing center, particularly for women. At any rate, Caroline Churchill, now forty-six, sold herself on the high, dry atmosphere and decided to make Colorado her permanent home. After all, she said, "I'm [now] fool proof and man proof."

For years, she had considered publishing a newspaper. It rankled her "that men hold in supreme selfishness all the great avenues of influence, the pulpit and the press." Churchill, a "dear lover of animals," said she named her new monthly literary magazine the *Colorado Antelope* partly because antelopes can run so fast. She called it a "politically Demo-Republican, a Greenback-Know-Nothing" publication that strongly advocated women's rights. For the first issue, Mrs. Churchill wrote travel sketches, poems, and a "humorous history" of Leadville. For all the articles, she used "C. M. Churchill" as her byline.

Despite Denver's extremely limited facilities for getting out a publication in the 1870s, she persuaded a lithographers' firm to produce the first issue in 1879. The first thousand copies were delivered to her office early on a Sunday morning. Caroline then stood on a busy corner and sold all the copies (ten cents each) by noon the first day. A second edition was printed but sales were slow. To stay afloat, she decided she would sell out each issue before printing the next. The *Antelope* acquired a "very fair" subscription list and some advertising. Despite its early success, Churchill worked out of her home to contain the publishing expenses and living costs. Her primary problem was finding a reliable printer. When she was away, the printer often garbled her editorials and altered their intent. She hired a young printer, "who proved to be respectful, trustworthy, polite, and sober," she reported later in her autobiography.[3]

After three years, when her subscribers in the East complained that they disliked the magazine's name, Churchill decided that a traditional weekly newspaper would be more successful than the literary magazine. She renamed the *Antelope* as the *Queen Bee* and produced the first issue of the weekly on July 5, 1882. Caroline Churchill (known as "Kate" among her fellow journalists) *was* the *Queen Bee*. She wrote, edited, published and even peddled the publication. One of the earliest publishers to take up the cause of women's suffrage and temperance, she devoted her columns to feminism and to airing the "unpalatable truth about masculine tyrants." As editor, she tackled temperance, the fight against dance halls, the great Catholic threat, inefficient garbage collection, and the evils of tobacco. She chastised H.A.W. Tabor for abandoning his long-suffering wife, Augusta, in favor of Baby Doe.[4]

She found that a weekly paper fared better in small communities where it didn't have to compete with big dailies. While keeping her headquarters in Denver, she traveled regularly in five western states to sell subscriptions and gather material for feature stories. She hired a "girl printer" to get the paper out while she was on the road. Although the printer praised her employer, saying, "Mrs. Churchill is the most manly woman I ever knew, possessing courage to overcome difficulties of which any man might be proud,"[5] while Churchill was away, she sued her for $12 in unpaid wages, tried to auction off the office equipment, and slandered the publisher to her advertisers and subscribers. When the treacherous plot failed, the printer packed up and moved to California.

Six months later, Caroline Churchill opened her own print shop and hired help. She found some second-hand type and an out-of-work printer. "With great effort and many promises, he kept sober long enough to get the office in shape," she recalled. She gradually acquired an all-woman staff (no more male clatter, she remarked in her columns). The *Queen Bee* came out on Wednesdays from her home at 386 Holliday (now Market) Street. Sometime later, deciding to move her business from the heart of Denver, she bought lots at Eighteenth Avenue and Race Street near City Park and then mortgaged them to build a brick combination home and office.

By 1882, the *Queen Bee* could boast that its circulation had reached 2,500—"the highest for any weekly between Kansas City and San Francisco." For thirteen years, the *Bee* attacked the logic of those opposing equal suffrage and ridiculed Colorado's male editors with biting sarcasm. She accused David F. Day, the anti-suffrage editor of the *Solid Muldoon* in Ouray, of going bald "because his brain could not furnish sufficient vitality or nerve … to sustain the growth of hair."

Churchill was a leader in the first successful national referendum for women's suffrage; her paper gained a reputation as the nation's first emancipation newspaper. On November 29, 1893, the front page headlined the victory of women's suffrage in Colorado: "Western Women Wild With Joy Over Colorado's Election."

For eighteen years, Churchill published the *Queen Bee* without missing an issue, "but at a vast outlay of most splendid energy." This accomplishment she credited to her genes and to Colorado's climate. The *Queen Bee* announced it was closing down on September 11, 1895, for "repairs and different arrangements due to use of machinery in printing and general cheapening of literature."

Caroline Churchill soon joined her sister, who had moved to Colorado Springs. From there, she continued to publish the *Queen Bee* for a time and also published *Active Footsteps,* her autobiography, in 1909. She died in Colorado Springs on January 14, 1926, at age ninety-two.

In her own opinion, Caroline Churchill allowed that she was eccentric: "She could never be induced to wear kid gloves, because it took too much of her valuable time to put them on and off." She described herself as having "very brown hair, not very abundant; study ever caused it to fall. … Eyes an intellectual gray, with drooping lids … great animation in countenance when talking." In characteristic fashion she wrote: "Mrs. Churchill has performed a wonderful work under most difficult circumstances. It is not at all likely that another woman on the continent could under the same conditions accomplish as much."[6] One of Colorado's most durable editor-publishers, she maintained a successful career for fifty-seven years.

Chipeta

Translation of Ute name: White Singing Bird
Born June 10, 1843; place unknown
Died August 1924, Bitter Creek, Utah

In 1843, a traveling Tabeguache Ute band came upon a burned-out Kiowa village. As the Utes rode into camp, one of the men heard a baby crying. He found a small child crawling, alone and bewildered, through the deserted tepees. Her parents, they surmised, were dead, apparently killed in the recent Indian raid.

The Utes rescued the child and named her Chipeta, Ute for White Singing Bird. They raised her in their own tribe. As she grew up, she differed noticeably from Ute women with her tall, slender figure and straight, even features. She was endowed, too, with rare intelligence, wisdom, and sound judgment. Although she was born a Kiowa Apache, she became known as "Queen of the Utes" because of her beauty.

Chipeta knew Ouray, the tribe's respected hunter and warrior, his wife, Black Mare, and their baby, Queashegut, whom they called Paron.

After Black Mare died in 1859, Chipeta cared for the son and came to love him as her own. When Chipeta was sixteen and had been managing Ouray's household for some time, he proposed to her. Ouray may have given Chipeta a pony and left a fresh-killed deer outside her lodge. Courting couples sometimes were "smoked," which meant sitting together in a smoke-filled tepee for several hours without dissension—a test of a couple's compatibility. They were considered to be married in 1859, when Ouray was twenty-six and Chipeta was about sixteen.

Ouray had a Jicarilla Apache father and Tabeguache Ute mother. Born in 1833 near the Taos Pueblo, he spoke Spanish and Apache and later learned Ute and some English. He was known as a ferocious warrior who could ride, run, shoot, and use a knife better than anyone in his tribe. No Ute dared to cross Ouray, a subchief of the Tabeguache, or Uncompahgre, Utes. Surely, Chipeta felt honored to become his wife.

Ouray, Chipeta, and his warriors were hunting north of Denver in 1860 when they were attacked by 300 Arapaho warriors. With his thirty men, Ouray held them off all day while Chipeta and Paron hid in the tepee. During the battle, five-year-old Paron slipped out to run after the Ute warriors and disappeared in the confusion. Ouray and Chipeta searched for years, but never found him. Later, the couple adopted three Ute children.

By the early 1860s, white miners and settlers numbering in the thousands were invading the Utes' hereditary lands in the Gunnison and Uncompahgre River valleys. Observing their great powers and numbers, Ouray and Chipeta agreed that no number of Indian arrows could turn back the hordes of white men. Ouray argued that the Utes' only hope for the future would be to take a middle position—to befriend the white people and settle their differences through treaties. Chipeta understood and strongly supported his policies.

Ouray persuaded the Ute council to let him work out a treaty with the U.S. government. With the help of scout Kit Carson, he set up a series of treaties that would guarantee specified boundaries for the Tabeguache and Mouache Utes in return for outlying Ute lands and gov-

ernment gifts of money, food, and supplies. Chipeta accompanied
Ouray for the negotiations and the signing of the first treaty of Cone-
jos, Colorado, in 1863 and also for the treaty signed in Washington,
D.C., in March 1868 and for the amendment dated August 15, 1868.
Washington political leaders who met Chipeta at that time were impressed with her beauty and dignity. She was admired and respected
for her wisdom and good judgment and was the only woman ever permitted to sit on Ute tribal councils.

Ouray came to be called the Peace Chief because he used patience,
diplomacy, and his commanding personality to accomplish his objec-
tives. By then, the government recognized him as chief of the Utes although not all Tabeguache groups accepted him as such. Other chiefs,
especially among the Northern Utes, were jealous of Ouray's authority
and blamed him when the whites broke his treaties.

In 1872, Chipeta and Ouray were en route to Los Pinos Indian
Agency, unaware that Chipeta's stepbrother, Sapovanero, and four
Tabeguache subchiefs were there plotting to kill Ouray. At the last
minute, all the chiefs backed out except Sapovanero, who waited and
hid in the agency blacksmith shop. Unaware of the plot, Ouray led his
horse across the plaza and was tying it to the hitching post when the
blacksmith gave a warning sign. Ouray jumped to one side just as
Sapovanero ran out and hurled his ax, missing Ouray's head by inches.
Ouray threw Sapovanero into a ditch and grabbed his throat. Then
Chipeta risked her own life by jumping between them and snatching
Ouray's knife from its scabbard. Her action saved her stepbrother and
averted a dangerous split between the chiefs.

Ouray and Chipeta lived happily for twenty years on their comfortable 300-acre farm near Montrose on the Uncompahgre River. It was
considered the region's prime farm, with its rich pastures, efficient irrigation system, and fifty acres of crops, vegetables, and hay. In return
for Ouray's friendship, the government guaranteed his title to the farm
plus $1,000 a year as long as he remained chief of the Utes. To set an
example for other Utes, Ouray and Chipeta adopted the white men's
attire and customs. Chipeta, a good housekeeper, furnished their six-
room adobe house with iron beds, a table, chairs, rugs, a piano, and

stoves. It was a decided departure for a woman who always had lived in a skin lodge. Chipeta liked to entertain their white friends. She had a Mexican servant and served meals on fine china; she learned to play the guitar and sing. She joined the Episcopal Church, and Ouray later became a Methodist.

Western photographer William H. Jackson arranged to photograph Chipeta and Ouray at Los Pinos Indian Agency around 1874. According to Jackson, Chipeta "was that day about the most prepossessing Indian woman I ever saw and Ouray was immensely proud of her. She evidently had prepared with care for this event, yet at the last was very timid. ... She sat down ... full of dimpling smiles. ... The doeskin of ... her dress was almost as white as cotton ... [with] a pretty trimming of beadwork and porcupine quill embroidery."[1]

Their peaceful life changed in 1879. Among White River Utes, strong resentment was growing against the new agent, Nathan Meeker, who misunderstood the Ute culture and insisted upon turning the Utes into farmers and ranchers. When he went so far as to plow up Ute Johnson's pony pasture and racetrack to plant crops, it triggered a fatal Ute uprising. Meeker had to send for troops. On September 29, Major T. T. Thornburgh was en route to the agency with 178 men. He was met by Chief Colorow, Chief Jack, and Sowerich and was warned not to cross Milk Creek. Thornburgh continued, nevertheless, and was ambushed by 100 Utes in Red Canyon. In the attack, Major Thornburgh and thirteen soldiers, including his officers, were killed. A few hours later, Chief Douglas and twenty Utes marched to the agency. They murdered Meeker, eight employees of the agency, and three other white men. Douglas then took three white women and two children hostage and held them at a mountain camp, where they reportedly suffered from exposure for twenty-three days.

When news of the massacre reached Los Pinos agency, Chipeta sent a runner to notify Ouray, who was hunting. She begged Ouray to appeal for peace. He sent a message to the White River Utes ordering them to back down and signed it "Ouray, head chief of the Utes." When Colonel Wesley Merritt arrived with reinforcements on October 5, the Utes were dispersing in response to Ouray's order. A delegation of government officials and Ute chiefs was dispatched with Ouray's message that if the women weren't released immediately and delivered to Ouray's home in Montrose by October 24, all other Ute bands would come after them. This escort delivered the hostages after a six-day ride to Ouray's farm at Los Pinos agency.

Josephine Meeker wrote later that Ouray's wife "did everything to make us comfortable. We were given the whole house and found carpets on the floor, lamps on the tables, and a fire burning brightly in the stove." Flora Pica, who was with them, described how Chipeta's "motherly face, dusky but beautiful with sweetness and compassion, was wet with tears." The Ute uprising against Meeker sealed the fate of the Colorado Utes, who (despite Ouray's further efforts) soon after were removed from Colorado.

In 1880, Chipeta and Ouray were summoned again to Washington for the writing of the final treaty. President Rutherford Hayes called Ouray "the most intellectual man I have ever conversed with." They were entertained and feted, and Chipeta, with her native charm and dignity, became the darling of Washington society. She was dressed in Victorian finery and given valuable gifts of silk dresses, millinery, gloves, and silver pieces for her home.

Upon their return, Ouray began suffering acutely from rheumatism and nephritis. But Ouray had one more mission in mind. Despite his illness, accompanied by Chipeta, John McCook, and other Utes, he rode to the Ute agency at Ignacio to induce the Southern Utes to sign the final treaty. Chipeta and Ouray had pitched their camp outside Durango, north of the agency on the west bank of the Pine River. Will Burns, an interpreter, went to see Ouray in his lodge. He lay on his blankets, wearing only a breechcloth, leggings, and moccasins. Burns fetched the agency doctor, who in turn sent for Dr. Lacey, Ouray's physician from the Uncompahgre reservation, and a consulting doctor. They examined the feverish Ouray, by then in severe pain, his stomach distended with Bright's Disease.

Ouray, great chief of the Utes, died in his tent on August 24, 1880, on the west bank of the Pine River. Chipeta summoned a small escort of chiefs. According to Ute custom, they quickly wrapped his body, tied it on his horse, and rode in secret procession to a remote mountain canyon. Ouray's body was seated on his saddle and buried in a deep crevice. Then five of his horses were shot. Chipeta kept his grave site a secret until she died.

Without Ouray, Chipeta lost her power. When a Dutch prospector filed a claim for Chipeta's farm, the government acceded to his demands and offered Chipeta a better home if she would move to Utah. In 1881, when the government removed the Uncompahgre Utes to Ouray, Utah, Chipeta joined the forced march led by the U.S. army. But in Utah, her "better home" was an unplastered, two-room building without furniture. Her tiny plot was arid, without enough water for stock or crop irrigation. The *Denver Republican* reported in 1888 that she married Toomuchagut, a Ute with many sheep. But the union did not last. Disillusioned by the whites, she gave away her fine gifts and money, abandoned her American dress and ways, and reverted to her early lifestyle.

Chipeta's situation declined until she was living with nomadic Ute herders at the head of Bitter Creek on the Book Cliffs. In her final years, she underwent two unsuccessful cataract surgeries. When she was totally blind, her relatives stretched a rope from her shed into the bushes so she could relieve herself in privacy. She died in August 1924 (some say August 9; others say August 16 or 27) at Bitter Creek and was buried in a shallow ravine. A year after her death, five of the Ute chiefs who had been present at Ouray's burial were persuaded to divulge the location of his grave. In March 1925, the towns of Ignacio and Montrose began squabbling over the bones of Ouray and Chipeta. His body was disinterred and moved to Ignacio. Her remains were taken to a tomb near her Montrose farm, where the Colorado Historical Society erected a museum in her memory. Her spirit was captured by poet Eugene Field.

> She rode where old Ouray dare not ride—
> A path through the wilderness rough and wild—
> She rode to plead to woman and child,
> She rode by the yawning chasm's side.[2]

Frances Wisebart Jacobs

Born in 1843 in Harrodsburg, Kentucky
Died November 3, 1892, in Denver, Colorado

On a cold, rainy night in 1892, Frances Wisebart Jacobs trudged through the mud and debris of a shanty town that spread along the Platte River west of Denver. It had become a colony of sick and indigent immigrants. Families of Russian Jewish refugees huddled together in squalid shacks. Tuberculosis victims, who had come to Colorado for their health, lay freezing in their flimsy tents. On this rainy night, Frances Jacobs—herself feverish with a cold—was delivering medicine to a sick baby, not an unusual mission for the thin, gentle Jewish woman. She had ministered to Denver's sick and penniless populace for twenty years.

Her brother, Jacob Wisebart, had arrived in Denver in 1859 with Abraham Jacobs, who opened a store for miners there. As partners, Abraham and Jacob opened the O.K. Store in 1861 in Central City. By 1865, the partners had clothing stores in Denver and Central City. They also played significant roles in politics. Jacob Wisebart was Central City's fifth mayor. Abraham Jacobs helped draft Denver's first "people's constitution" and served on the City Council. In 1863, Abraham returned to Cincinnati to marry Jacob's sister Frances. A schoolteacher, she came from a family of six daughters and one son. The newlyweds crossed the plains by wagon in the winter of 1863 and settled in Central City, Colorado Territory.

Abraham and Jacob ran the store while Frances cared for her family that soon included two sons and a daughter. Abraham also organized and managed the Denver and Santa Fe Stage Line running from Denver to Trinidad until the operation became unprofitable in 1869. Then two major fires caused a downturn in Abraham's fortunes. First, the "great fire" swept through Denver's business district on April 19, 1863, and did serious damage to his Denver store. Then a fire in Central City destroyed the Wisebart Store, hitting the owners with a $50,000 loss. Within a year, the Jacobs family moved to Denver, where Abraham also owned the

O.K. Clothing Store on Larimer Street. But in 1885, this store went out of business. In a final blow, one of Frances and Abraham's sons died.

At the same time, Denver's Jewish community was being deluged with Russian Jewish refugees as well as critically ill Jewish consumptives. An early president of the Hebrew Ladies Benevolent Society, Frances Jacobs began quietly visiting their squalid shacks and tents along West Colfax Avenue and the Platte River banks. Her colleagues criticized her for personally looking into every case, but she went on cleaning them up, carrying in kettles of soup, and summoning doctors. At home, she kept busy collecting and disbursing used clothing.

Frances Jacobs no longer could ignore the suffering that engulfed all of Denver's needy and ill. It became evident to her that the problem extended far beyond the Jewish population and that it was more than one woman, or even Denver's small group of Jews, could shoulder. She organized the nonsectarian Ladies' Relief Society in 1874 and thereafter served as an officer. Soon, the Society became a leading force in Denver's charity work. As vice president, she started to speak about a concerted community effort. Frances became an unusually persuasive public speaker, often called upon to address public meetings.

About that time, Reverend Myron Reed, a Protestant minister, and Father William O'Brien, a priest, approached Mrs. Jacobs to help them consolidate Denver's charity groups. They recruited Dean H. Martin Hart, an Episcopalian, and another Catholic priest. After months of discussion and planning, these five leaders formed Denver's Charity Organization Society (COS) in 1887. It was the nation's first successful, federated charitable organization. For the rest of her life, Mrs. Jacobs served as its secretary.

The COS grew until it combined Denver's twenty-three major charity groups into one powerful organization. (One of the charter organizations was the Hebrew Ladies' Benevolent Society.) The Society adopted an innovative fund-raising system, recruiting teams of volunteers to solicit businesses and citizens once a year for sufficient funds to reach one over-all goal. The Society, the vision of one woman and four clerics, was so successful that it evolved into the nationwide Community Chest in 1922 and eventually became the United Way.

Frances Jacobs, who was described as a frail woman with an unfailing sense of humor, became a passionate and eloquent speaker for many causes. As president of the Ladies' Relief Society, she brought public attention to the plight of homeless women, urged improved standards for all working women, and fought until prisons provided separate quarters for women with female matrons to attend them.

As a member of the National Conference of Charities and Correction, Frances Jacobs spoke at the national convention in San Francisco. While there, she happened to visit the Golden Gate kindergarten. She was so impressed that the day she returned she started a campaign for free kindergartens in Denver. With her persuasion and influence, she organized the Free Kindergarten Association and opened Denver's first kindergarten at the Stanley Public School, 1301 Quebec Street.

Frances Jacobs continued her daily rounds to visit the sick and poor. One day, she came upon a man coughing up blood on the street. She summoned her doctor to treat him at her expense. She had seen sick consumptives often enough, but the image of this man remained with her. In the nineteenth century, tuberculosis was rampant throughout the world; starting in the 1860s, it invaded Colorado. As Ida Uchill noted in her book *Pioneers, Peddlers and Tsadikim,* "on the heels of the goldseekers came the health seekers."[1] When physicians in the East failed to cure their patients, they habitually offered them a one-way ticket to Colorado. The number of "lungers" in the state multiplied until the situation became alarming. Denver newspapers reacted by refusing to mention two words: consumption and tuberculosis. They thought that any publicity would add to the unending stream of indigent and consumptive newcomers to Denver.

Frances Jacobs sponsored a hospital benefit in 1883. Meanwhile, the Charity Organization Society and private philanthropists were grappling with the need to build a hospital for consumptives, even though no one spoke the forbidden words. Temple Emanuel's congregation proposed that the Jewish community build a hospital for the "Jewish sick of the Unites States" and in November 1889 congregants organized a Jewish Hospital Association. After extensive fundraising, planning, and construction, the hospital building was about to be dedicated in 1892.

Then the unimaginable happened. On that rainy night in 1892, when Frances Jacobs delivered medicine to a sick child, her cold turned into pneumonia. After a three-month illness, she died on November 3, 1892, at Marquette Sanitarium in Denver. She was forty-nine. More than 4,000 mourners, of all races, classes, religions, and incomes, attended her funeral services at Temple Emanuel, in one of Denver's largest funerals. A memorial service at First Congregational Church a week later was filled to capacity. The governor, mayor, community leaders, clergy, and friends read eulogies in her memory.

Her co-worker, J. S. Appel, said, "For long years she gave her time and her services to the practical work of charity, and looked more poor and wretched people in the face than any other person in Denver. ... The keynote of her character was ... her great fund of humor that made her see the bright side of everything, that enabled her to devote her life to the work of saving and uplifting humanity. ... This love of humor was the safety valve that kept her heart from bursting at the sorrows and miseries she beheld." The Jewish Hospital Association then read a resolution to name the new Jewish hospital The Frances Jacobs Hospital. Soon after, the name, in gold letters, was mounted above the entrance of the building.

But in the wake of the financial panic of 1893, the hospital had to close for lack of money to buy equipment and furnishings. The Jewish community struggled to raise more money, until in desperation the Denver B'nai B'rith lodge turned over the hospital venture to its national organization. In 1899—seven years after its dedication—the hospital opened, fully furnished and equipped. It had a new name: the National Jewish Hospital for Consumptives. As a nonsectarian institution, it accepted only destitute tuberculosis patients from throughout the country—the first hospital of its kind in the world. The only condition was that when leaving the hospital, the patient would not become a charge upon the Denver community. At its opening in 1899, the National Jewish Hospital (NJH) accommodated 65 patients and planned to expand to 135. The hospital has grown into the world-famous National Jewish Center for Immunology and Respiratory Medicine. Its motto continues to be: "None may enter who can pay;

none can pay who enter." A bronze sculpture of Frances Jacobs stands in the lobby of the hospital's Cohen Clinic.

When Colorado's state capitol was being built in 1899, the board of managers began selecting sixteen outstanding pioneers who best typified Colorado's founding and development. The members of this Hall of Fame would be portrayed in stained glass windows in the capitol dome. The board finally narrowed down the hundreds of nominees to fifteen men to represent the state's great builders. But no one could ignore the unparalleled contributions of one woman: Frances Wisebart Jacobs. Her stained-glass portrait still glows in the Colorado capitol dome.

Nearly a century later, Frances Wisebart Jacobs was inducted into the Colorado Women's Hall of Fame; and in 1994, she was installed in the National Women's Hall of Fame in Seneca Falls, New York. A visionary whose life ended so prematurely, she continues to inspire everyone who knows her story. Her gifts to Denver have developed into ongoing bequests to the world.

Mary Rippon

Born May 25, 1850, in Lisbon Center, Illinois
Died September 9, 1935, in Boulder, Colorado

Mary Rippon had lofty ambitions for a young woman born in 1850. She had just graduated from the high school of Illinois State Normal University, and had inherited a $3,500 trust fund from her father. She was ready for college. Then she learned that the University of Illinois did not accept women. In fact, it was rare for a woman even to think of going to college. But Mary Rippon was determined to advance her education, so she went to Europe. For the next five years, she studied languages and traveled in Germany, France, and Switzerland. When she returned, she accepted a job teaching German in a Detroit high school.

In September 1877, a former university teacher, Dr. Joseph Sewall, who had become president of the new University of Colorado in Boulder, sent Mary an invitation to join the faculty. He may have been seeking, in addition to a fine teacher, a proper role model for the first women students who would be admitted into the freshman class. Mary, who had already signed a contract to continue teaching in Detroit, found another teacher to take over her position and agreed to come to Boulder at the beginning of the university's second term. Mary had been influenced by an article by Helen Hunt Jackson describing Colorado's wildflowers; in addition, she had learned that a fund had been established to start a library at the university.

Mary's train pulled into Boulder, Colorado, on a moonlit January evening in 1878. As she stepped from the Pullman car, Dr. Sewall hurried forward to greet her. He hoped that this small, pretty woman would be content to join a two-man faculty at a new university in a rough prairie town. But when the twenty-seven-year-old teacher gazed up at the jagged Flatirons silhouetted against the evening sky, she was reminded of the Alps on a winter night. She was immediately sold on Boulder and its new university.

On her tour of the "campus" the next day, she learned that Colorado had achieved statehood fewer than two years earlier. Boulder was twenty years old and the first term at the University of Colorado as a preparatory school had just ended. The campus consisted of Old Main, a lonely, three-story building on a hill overlooking the town. To reach Old Main, she went up the hill, climbed over a stile in a cattle fence, and crossed a ravine. The two faculty members were Dr. Sewall, who doubled as president and professor of botany and chemistry, and Justin Dow, professor of Latin and Greek. Fifty-five college prep students made up the student body. Mary Rippon came to teach French and German, but for the first year agreed also to teach mathematics and English grammar. Her salary was $1,200 a year. She was the university's third teacher and the first woman faculty member.

During her second year, the Board of Examiners observed her class work and reported that she "did praiseworthy work in teaching the French and German languages. The tact and zeal she displays in her vocation deserve ... acknowledgment," noted the examiners.[1] With this endorsement, Mary Rippon was made a full professor of French and German in 1881—perhaps the first American woman to become a full professor at a state university. At the same time, she was named chair of the Department of Modern Languages. In 1891 she was promoted to chair of the Department of Germanic Languages and Literature.

Until 1901, Mary Rippon also served as acting dean of women. Working with women students was a priority for her. She formed women's leagues (which later evolved into the YWCA) to promote social graces. Despite her meager salary, she managed to share it with needy women students and always was ready to counsel those with personal problems. A member of her second graduating class described her as "a quiet, low-voiced, attractive young woman full of efficient energy and wholly devoted to her work."[2] Another woman student wrote: "Beautiful Mary Rippon was like a piece of Dresden, but she must have had a stern jaw ... to be dean of women in those early days."[3] She sent newspapers, booklets, and study guides to women isolated on remote ranches and in mining camps to give them an opportunity to learn. On campus, Mary organized fund drives for the university library and planted trees and shrubs throughout the grounds.

At first, Mary roomed at the American House and then she lived as a boarder with several families, including that of Dean J. Raymond Brackett. In 1896, she bought a Victorian cottage at 2463 Twelfth Street, where she resided for the rest of her life. Mary occasionally traveled to Europe to study art and maintain her foreign language skills. A practiced speaker, she presented lantern slide shows (predecessor of slide shows), portraying European art and culture, when she returned home to Boulder.

Yet something may have been missing from Mary's active life; at thirty-seven she was unmarried. Dedicated to her career, she had few single men in her life—except for one, a good-looking former student, Will Housel. The son of a prominent Boulder judge, he was twelve years younger than Mary. He wrote poetry and after acquiring a degree at another college, he returned to Boulder and enrolled in Mary Rippon's German class. She may have been tutoring young Housel when the teacher-student acquaintance flowered into a full-blown love affair.

In April 1888, the unthinkable happened. Mary Rippon was pregnant. They made plans. In June, Mary and Will met in St. Louis to marry in secret. But her dilemma was just beginning. Popular opinion did not favor married women professors taking positions that could be filled by family men. Certainly, Victorians did not hold with single women having babies. Above all, Mary Rippon wished to keep her job. She asked for a year's sabbatical and then sailed in July to Germany. Her daughter, Miriam Edna Housel, was born in Stuttgart in January 1889.

The particulars blur at this point and details vary according to the source. All agree, however, that after graduating from the University of Colorado, Housel attended graduate school in Germany. The couple apparently remained together with their child for a while. Then Mary placed Miriam (who grew up thinking of Mary as her aunt) in an orphanage. Mary paid for her daughter's care and for Will's tuition in graduate school nearby—and then returned alone to Boulder. In December 1891, Will returned to Boulder, leaving Miriam overseas. He and Mary continued their marital relationship for two years while living apart to preserve her secret. "We had long, sad talks but my job—and secret—were secure," she wrote in her diary several years later.[4] Mary Rippon never commented publicly about her romance and lost family life.

Housel eventually took up farming in Ann Arbor, Michigan. In "A Forbidden Love," her article about Mary Rippon, Silvia Pettem noted that Housel married again and fathered another four children. "Whether out of love or guilt, [Rippon] financially supported Miriam and all of Housel's second family," Pettem wrote.[5]

Miriam Housel followed Rippon's footsteps. She studied foreign languages, married, had a son, Wilfred Rieder, and divorced after a turbulent marriage. In 1920, Miriam and young Wilfred moved to Boulder, where she became a professor of Romance languages at the university. It is possible that they moved to Boulder so Miriam could be near her mother and Wilfred could be near his grandmother. But they called themselves "dear friends." The relationship of Miriam and her son to Mary Rippon was not revealed.

Until 1890, Mary Rippon was the only woman on the faculty. She retired in 1909 after thirty-one years of teaching. She died in 1935 in the Victorian cottage in which she had lived for forty years. She was eighty-five years old. Rippon's obituary noted that she was survived by a nephew in Wichita and by "her dearest friends, Miriam Rieder and Rieder's son, Wilfred, her protégé." She was buried in Columbia Cemetery in Boulder.

With the help of alumni, faculty, friends, and a government grant, Mary Rippon's former students conducted a drive in 1936 to finance the building of the Mary Rippon Memorial Theatre on campus. The beautiful Roman-style amphitheater, with twenty rows of sandstone benches, was dedicated on Alumni Day. It is the scene of university events, including some commencements and most notably the Shakespeare Festival. Her classroom in Old Main is part of the Heritage Center, a museum depicting the history of the university. Her house on Broadway still stands—virtually unchanged, despite its use as a hair salon.

Mary Rippon may have been the first American woman to teach men at a state university and may have been the first woman professor at any state university. Certainly, she was a pioneer woman educator. Despite her having studied Romance languages in Europe for five years, no record has ever been found of a college degree. In 1998, Silvia Pettem asked the University of Colorado to grant Mary Rippon an honorary doctoral degree.

Elizabeth Nellis McCourt Doe Tabor

"Baby Doe"
Born September 26, 1854, in Oshkosh, Wisconsin
Died February 21, 1935, in Leadville, Colorado[1]

A kaleidoscope of legends surrounds the second wife of Horace Tabor, "Baby Doe," whose amazing riches-to-rags life story was immortalized in an opera. Because of her passion for a man who was already married and her steadfast devotion to him, most of society shunned her. A few admired her.

In Oshkosh, Wisconsin, Lizzie Nellis McCourt was born fifth in a line of fourteen children of Peter and Elizabeth Nellis McCourt. Her father was a successful clothing store owner and civic figure in Oshkosh, but a succession of fires that wiped out his stores eventually depleted his wealth.

Lizzie's Irish Catholic parents doted on her. She was closest to her older brother James, whom she most nearly resembled and who first called her "Babe" or "Baby." She kept scrapbooks, in which she pasted romantic poems and her own verses, recorded extravagant compliments from admiring beaux, and wrote of her conquests. Rarely did she refer to girl friends, as if she disliked members of her sex. Nonetheless, she had a full social calendar during her later teens. She possessed a natural vitality, strong constitution, charm, and astuteness—but also flirtatiousness and vanity. She was, indeed, the Belle of Oshkosh.

She first met William Harvey Doe, Jr., on the street and set her cap for him. Despite his mother's fierce opposition, Lizzie and Harvey were married June 17, 1877, in Oshkosh. She was twenty-two and he, twenty-three. They promptly moved to Central City where he managed the Waterman Mine, a wedding gift from his father.

Troubles soon developed at the mine. Lizzie watched, outraged, as her husband left the Waterman and worked as a mere laborer at the Bobtail Mine until he was fired. Afterward, he idly frequented town saloons. The Does moved to Black Hawk into smaller and cheaper rooms. When bills came due, he mortgaged the couple's assets. According to some accounts, Harvey had vanished when Lizzie, alone and penniless, gave birth to their stillborn son. Her only friend was Jake Sands, a kind admirer, who paid for a midwife. When Jake moved to Leadville, he suggested Lizzie might go into business with him in his new clothing store and offered to pay her fare, too.

Lizzie learned that Harvey ("Mama's Boy," she called him) had returned to his parents' home in Denver. She went there, intending to ask for a divorce. He wanted to patch things up, but she was through with him and they quarreled violently. He threatened to go to a brothel and she dared him to go ahead, then secretly followed him to Lizzie Preston's place on Market Street. When he entered, she fetched a policeman to raid the brothel and get evidence for a divorce. A judge granted the divorce on March 19, 1880.

In late 1879, Lizzie arranged to leave Central City. She probably got a ride to Georgetown and boarded a stage for the 56-mile run to Leadville. She must have felt terrified, yet invigorated as the coach climbed precarious switchbacks over 13,207-foot Argentine Pass and swept along Ten-Mile Creek. She was embarking upon a new life as a divorcee. She even took on a new name. In Black Hawk, miners (like her brother James) had called her Baby because she had the personality of a "babe." Lizzie settled upon the name Baby Doe McCourt, in keeping with her new life in Leadville.

She put her unfortunate marriage and wretched years in Central City firmly behind her as the stage neared Leadville. She must think about earning a living now, but what training and experience could she offer? Her greatest asset was her striking beauty, curly, red-gold hair, wide-set eyes of a startling blue, perfect white teeth, and a creamy complexion.

Jake met her at the station in Leadville. As he checked her into a room at the Clarendon Hotel on Harrison Street, he told her she would never see a more exciting city. Topping 10,000 feet in elevation and guarded by Mounts Massive and Elbert, Leadville was called Cloud City. With its coming-and-going population exceeding 15,000, Leadville by 1880 was Colorado's second largest city. Already, it boasted six banks, thirteen hotels, three newspapers, and eighty-two saloons. Half the men in town were in mining.

As she explored the town, she learned about Leadville's former mayor and most favored son, Horace Tabor. The more she heard, the more she wanted to know. He and his wife, Augusta, had come to California Gulch, near the site of Leadville, in 1860 when it was a gold camp and had returned in 1868 at the start of the silver boom. Wherever they lived, the Tabors ran a miners' store.

Tabor was lucky at poker and luckier at mining. In 1878, he acquired the Little Pittsburg mine that paid up to $10,000 a day. Later, he sold the Little Pittsburg and bought a fleet of investments, including the rich Chrysolite and Matchless mines plus real estate, adding up to a $9 million fortune. To improve the town, he established the Bank of Leadville and helped build an opera house and hotel. Baby Doe heard talk about Augusta, the allegedly prim and sharp-tongued New Englander who carped at her husband over the smallest extravagance. Folks said that when Tabor struck it rich, he rebelled against Augusta's constant nagging. Never in her wildest dreams did Baby Doe believe she would meet this famous man.

One evening she was waiting in the Clarendon lobby for Jake to finish work when in walked two men followed by a retinue of laughing people. With a thrill, she recognized Bill Bush, former proprietor of the Teller House in Central City. He told her Tabor had come to Leadville that evening for the grand opening of the Tabor Opera House next door to the Clarendon. The next thing she knew, Bush was introducing her to his tall friend—Horace Tabor—and inviting her to join them at dinner. Baby Doe always maintained she fell in love the minute their eyes met. A charming, outgoing man, he was at the crest of his career.

At dinner, Tabor ordered champagne and he and Baby Doe quickly became acquainted. Tabor literally swept her off her feet, although he was forty-nine to her twenty-five. Soon, he was offering to pay Baby Doe's debts to her friend Jake. When he moved her to a luxurious suite at the Clarendon, news of their affair spread like a forest fire through Leadville and set Denver gossips' tongues wagging. After Tabor returned to Denver, he and Baby Doe moved into a lavish suite at the Windsor Hotel. To him, this marked the close of his marriage to Augusta. He instructed his theater manager, Bush, to talk to Augusta about a divorce.

Tabor's business interests had multiplied along with his growing millions. He had completed a six-story Tabor Block on Larimer Street in 1880 and was building his grandiose, $750,000 Tabor Grand Opera House. He involved Baby Doe in selecting finishing touches for the opulent theater. Denver society was agog over its ornate architecture, lavish furnishings, imported carpets from Brussels, French brocades, and cherry paneling.

At the grand opening on September 5, 1881, the Tabor family box, festooned with roses, was unoccupied. Baby Doe sat in a back seat of the parquet, veiled and inconspicuous amid the glittering audience. On stage, the hand-painted curtain was inscribed with a Charles Kingsley verse that some said was prophetic: "So fleet the works of men, back to the earth again. Ancient and holy things fade like a dream."

Civic leaders proclaimed that Tabor's many investments in the city and state ushered in an era of building and culture. He also gave generous support to the Republican Party, especially in the senatorial campaign where he, himself, was a candidate.

As Augusta continued to resist a divorce, Tabor became preoccupied with getting his freedom to marry Baby Doe. At her suggestion, he went to Durango, where he owned a mine, and procured a one-sided divorce. Then Tabor arranged a trip to St. Louis. He and Baby Doe traveled separately and were married secretly on September 30, 1882, by a justice of the peace. The Tabor divorce suit raged on in the court. At last, on January 2, 1883, Augusta testified, sobbing, that she gave the divorce "not willingly." In return for the decree, Tabor gave her $300,000 and the twenty-room Broadway house they had moved into after he was elected lieutenant governor in 1878. The newspapers and all Denver sided with Augusta, the deserted wife.

The timing couldn't have been worse for Tabor's struggling political career. Once a popular contender for Senator Henry Teller's Senate seat (vacated after Teller was appointed to President Chester Arthur's cabinet), Tabor was forced into a runoff in the legislature. The legislature elected Tabor only to finish the final thirty days of Teller's term. (He lost his bid for the Senate seat by one vote in the next general election.)

Baby Doe, meanwhile, was preparing for their wedding in Washington. She sent invitations with silver borders, inviting President Arthur, the entire Colorado delegation, and many other congressmen and their wives to a spectacular wedding and dinner at the Willard Hotel in Washington, D.C. on March 1, 1883. Wives of the Colorado delegation shunned the event in support of the deserted Augusta. But Baby Doe's family came from Wisconsin for the wedding and her father arranged for a Catholic priest, P. L. Chapelle, to officiate. Tabor gave his bride a $75,000 diamond necklace and she wore a fur-trimmed, white satin gown costing $7,000. President Arthur and many gentlemen friends did attend, despite the absence of congressional wives.

The Tabors were officially married but the scandal continued to grow. Amid much publicity, Father Chapelle returned the wedding fee, saying he had been duped by the bride's father into marrying two divorced persons who were already secretly married. Denver society continued to snub Baby Doe, although she donated office space in the opera house to the women's suffrage movement. She provided uniforms for local volunteer firemen that she, herself, had designed—in blue fabric to match her eyes!

Baby Doe met Augusta twice. Augusta Tabor unexpectedly called on her at the Windsor Hotel suite before the wedding. She began by enumerating Tabor's philanderings. When Baby Doe didn't respond, Augusta begged Baby Doe to give Tabor up. At that, Baby Doe dismissed Augusta Tabor, who "left with her ramrod gait," as Baby Doe recalled. Their other meeting, which was uneventful, was at the wedding of Tabor's son, Maxcy.

In 1886, Tabor paid $54,000 for a pretentious mansion at Thirteenth Avenue and Sherman Street. The grounds covered a city block, requiring a staff of five. The Tabors maintained three carriages and six horses. The estate was notable for its nude statues on the lawn, which brought complaints from the neighbors. Their first child, Elizabeth Bonduel Lillie Tabor, was born on July 13, 1884. A son lived only hours after his birth. Then a daughter, Rose Mary Echo Silver Dollar Tabor, joined the family on December 17, 1889. The older daughter, Lillie, was as fair as Silver Dollar was dark and the doting parents lavished on them everything money could buy. During the next decade, they lived in wealth, fame, and opulence. But never did Baby Doe gain a woman friend in Denver society.

Tabor's fortune showed signs of crumbling by 1885, when high-grade ores in Leadville mines started playing out—all but the Matchless, the only major mine Tabor owned entirely. Most of his mining properties were the object of prolonged, expensive litigation. He continued to invest heavily—in mines, banks, a newspaper, railroads, real estate, an illuminating company. All were depleting his fortune by 1893, when President Cleveland signed legislation demonetizing silver. Overnight, Tabor's mines became worthless. He retained only the Matchless, which flooded.

Desperate to save the opera house, Baby Doe turned to her brother, Peter McCourt, who had accumulated a fortune as Tabor's assistant. Peter turned his back, as did other Tabor beneficiaries. Financial reverses had a domino effect, one property mortgaged to save another until nothing remained. Tabor and Baby Doe were carrying candles through an empty mansion and hauling water from the Old Courthouse pump. Then they lost the house. Tabor, an old man at sixty-five, was working for $3 a day as a mine laborer in Leadville when Senator Ed Wolcott arranged to have him appointed Denver postmaster at $3,500 a year. Through the hard times, Baby Doe kept their spirits up and worked to feed and clothe the girls. Then Tabor's health failed.

In April 1899, he was diagnosed with appendicitis but was too weak to undergo surgery. As Baby Doe tended him day and night, he told her she had been the most beautiful thing in his life. Augusta, who thought Baby Doe would abandon Horace if he became ill, had been wrong. Baby Doe stood by her husband until he died on April 10 of a ruptured appendix. Condolences poured in from public officials down to prospectors. Flags flew at half-mast and Tabor's body lay in state at the capitol rotunda. Mourners from across Colorado turned out for Tabor's funeral and then escorted his body to Calvary Cemetery.

Afterward, Baby Doe and the girls lived in rooms in Denver and spent summers in Leadville. Adversities continued. Lillie grew increasingly estranged from her mother and sister and finally moved to Chicago to live with McCourt relatives. Their estrangement was sealed when Baby Doe learned that Lillie had married a cousin. Silver Dollar,

Baby Doe's dearest joy as a pretty and sweet-tempered child, also moved to Chicago to seek a writing and theatrical career. Years later, Baby Doe's heart was broken when she read in a newspaper that her dearest child had been scalded to death in a cheap rooming house.

By then, Baby Doe was living year-round in the Matchless shaft house on Fryer Hill above Leadville—the only mine Tabor had retained. At first, she climbed up and down the ladder hoping to run the mine on her own. But the mine shaft, 365 feet deep, was flooding deeper and deeper. One morning, Leadville residents saw smoke billowing up from the Matchless smokestack. A small crowd ran up the hill. Baby Doe had lit a fire to build up steam in the boiler, not realizing that the governor controlling the steam pressure was rusted and frozen. When townspeople arrived, pressure had built until the boiler was on the verge of exploding. The men quickly blew the boiler and banked the fire so Baby Doe could not repeat her operation.[2]

Baby Doe was not friendless in Leadville. The Patrick Hart family of the P. F. Hart Mercantile Company befriended her. (A later Patrick Hart, descendant of the Leadville merchant, recalled seeing her walking through the snow to her weekly dinner at their house. She was dressed in rags, her feet bound in gunny sacks.) But she sternly maintained her independence. Neighbors left packages of canned food, gloves, and boots on her doorstep, but she returned them. A few close friends kept a lookout for smoke coming from her smokestack on frigid, snowy days. Often, her best friend, Sue Bonnie (also known as Naomie Pontiers), climbed Fryer Hill to visit her.

On the coldest winter day, Baby Doe sat alone amid her dusty and aging finery, a few calling cards, invitations, a lock of hair, and her scrapbooks. Her death is listed as February 21, 1935—thirty-five years after Tabor's death. Bonnie and Tom French broke into the shack and found his still-grieving widow starved and frozen to death. No one knew how long she had been dead.

She was buried at Calvary Cemetery. Later both Baby Doe and Horace were moved to side-by-side graves at Mt. Olivet Cemetery. Baby Doe's story lingers on in the opera, *The Ballad of Baby Doe*, by John Latouche and Douglas Moore, which is frequently performed at the Central City Opera House, in a town where Tabor first mined.

Mary Hauck Elitch Long

Born in May 1856, in Philadelphia, Pennsylvania
Died July 16, 1936, in Denver, Colorado

Happy days followed Mary Hauck Elitch Long, despite heartbreaking personal losses that would have defeated less durable women. As a founder and guiding angel of Denver's beloved Elitch Gardens, she brought fun, flowers, and culture into the lives of countless Coloradans, who returned summer after summer to Elitch's.

She was born Mary Elizabeth (Lydia) Hauck in Philadelphia and soon after her birth, her family moved to San Francisco. When Mary was sixteen, she eloped with John Elitch, Jr., who, at twenty, was an athlete, actor, and restaurateur. The couple opened a restaurant in Durango in 1880; then moved to Denver in 1882, where Elitch opened another restaurant, the Tortoni, on Arapahoe Street. With the idea of growing vegetables for the Tortoni, the young couple bought the sixteen-acre Chilcott Farm at Thirty-eighth Avenue and Tennyson Street.

The property included a farmhouse, groves of shade trees, and an apple orchard that bloomed profusely every spring. As the Elitches added shrubs and flower-lined paths, they became intrigued with the idea of turning their orchard into a pleasure resort. Elitch set up entrance gates next to the old Berkley Motor line (Denverites called it a streetcar) to attract passengers riding out from the city.

At that time, P. T. Barnum, the circus baron, wintered his animals near Sloan Lake. He gave extra young animals to John Elitch to begin what became a respectable menagerie of dancing bears, lion cubs, goats, and ostriches. Soon a sign was placed above the gates: Elitch's Zoological Gardens.

The park opened to the public on May 1, 1890, with several added attractions: band concerts, a miniature railroad, and a steam calliope. For the opening, Denverites streamed out on the Berkley Motor and many friends of the Elitches' arrived from out of town. Celebrities included the H.A.W. Tabors, P. T. Barnum, and Mr. and Mrs. Tom Thumb. After serving everyone a picnic lunch, the Elitches launched their new theater with a vaudeville program of ten acts—introduced by three masters of ceremonies: Denver Mayor Wolfe Londoner, Senator Ed Wolcott, and the poet-journalist Eugene Field. The first summer season was an undisputed success. John Elitch was so excited about the Gardens Theater, he decided to devote himself to managing it.

The next spring, Elitch used their $36,000 in profits to take his Goodyear, Elitch and Schilling Minstrels touring in California. The tour ended in tragedy when John contracted pneumonia at the Alcazar Theater in San Francisco where the group was performing. Mary was with him when he died in San Francisco on March 10, 1891.

Elitch's thirty-four-year-old widow was left alone with an amusement park to run. She recalled later that she cried and cried, having no idea how she could possibly carry on. Then she wiped her eyes and started looking around. She fixed a few broken flower pots and made a few plans. Lacking the previous year's income, she had to sell a majority of the Gardens' stock to some Denver investors but she stayed on to manage the company. Three years later, she repaid the investors to resume ownership.

Elitch's Zoological Gardens was the only zoo between Chicago and the West Coast. Mary loved the animals. A favorite was her "very intelligent ostrich, which [she] trained to harness."[1] Denverites often saw the ostrich speeding along country roads, drawing a rubber-tired sulky with Mary in the driver's seat. Well accustomed to having Mary in their cages, the animals knew and trusted her. Many had been born in the Gardens and raised by her hand. Photographs show Mary—tall and slender with wide-set eyes and a gracious smile—a celebrated Denver beauty, playing with Sam, a pet bear. She kept a pair of lion cubs in her home, bottle-feeding them until they approached adulthood. The lioness was named Anna Schilling for Mary's sister. Another grown lioness was christened Sarah Bernhardt. Peacocks, a water buffalo, elephants, rattlesnakes, and later a camel also populated the zoo.

Some of Mary's creatures enjoyed the limelight. Sam, the bear, danced with her to entertain visitors. A curious monkey named Dude, who once slipped away while his cage was being cleaned, suddenly appeared at center stage in the middle of a rehearsal as stars, stand-ins, stagehands fled to the wings. Mary kept the menagerie until City Park Zoo opened.

Mary continued the vaudeville acts for a while and then ventured into light operas and plays. After two years, she decided to organize her first stock company and concentrate on quality drama. Every year when the Gardens closed for the winter, Mary would go to New York to recruit acting talent for the next season. Countless actors and actresses got their start—or early push—at Elitch's.

One summer morning, as the theater was preparing for a performance of a Shakespeare play, a boy of about twelve appeared at the stage. He asked the janitor if he could do some work to earn a ticket. His mother had read all of Shakespeare's plays with him, he said, and he greatly admired the Bard. The janitor said he didn't have any extra work for him. But the boy walked out on the stage, looked it over, and suggested a good scrubbing might help its appearance. He scrubbed the rough boards and the janitor gave him a ticket. The boy became a student of Margaret Fealy, a well-known drama teacher. In a few years, he made his next appearance on the Elitch stage as an actor in *Cousin Kate*. His name was Douglas Fairbanks.

The hundreds of other famous stars included Harold Lloyd, also of Denver. Frederic March spent an entire summer with the company at $60 a week. In 1906, Mary Elitch signed Sarah Bernhardt to play *Camille* at a matinee and *La Sorcier* in the evening. The two performances were rare and magical. Elitch playbills featured David Warfield, Helen Hayes, Douglas Fairbanks, Sr. and Jr., Gloria Swanson, Vincent Price, Ginger Rogers, Lana Turner, Myrna Loy, Grace Kelly, Debbie Reynolds, and many others. Local talent filled the lesser roles. Marquee-sized portraits of these stars and other greats who performed there were displayed in the theater lobby.

Always a major attraction, Elitch's Theater has been acknowledged as the nation's oldest summer stock repertory theater. For fifty years, Mary Elitch's home in the Gardens was a gathering place for the world's great dramatic stars. After several years, Mary signed Helen Bonfils, well known to Denver and New York City audiences, to manage the theater.

Marching brass bands enlivened early attractions at the park. From the 1890s until 1914, Elitch's brought in symphony orchestras and presented operas, "both grand and light." Mary signed Italian conductor Raffaelo Cavallo to conduct outdoor classical concerts (soon moved indoors by popular demand). During the 1940s and 1950s, big-name dance bands at The Trocador were the biggest draw at Elitch's.

Through the years, Elitch's became a fixture in the lives of generations of Denverites. Adults dined at the Orchard Cafe before taking in the theater. Young parents looked forward to starting out their toddlers behind the wheel of the pint-sized roadsters in Kiddieland, a fairyland of small-fry rides. Young couples danced at "The Troc" to the music of nearly all the Big Band greats—the Dorsey brothers, Sammy Kaye, Frankie Carle, Duke Ellington, Stan Kenton, Lawrence Welk, Les Brown, Freddy Martin, and on and on. Their dance steps marked the decades, from Viennese waltzes to the Charleston to the jitterbug.

During ballroom intermissions, younger dancers would test their courage on the Wild Cat and later, Mister Twister, Elitch's blue-ribbon roller-coasters. Kids of all ages lined up for the ferris wheel, the antique carousel, the bumper cars, the Old Mill, the airplane. Families brought their basket lunches to secluded picnic alcoves that bordered the park. No one could contest the slogan: "Not to see Elitch's is not to see Denver."

Mary always loved children, although she had none of her own. She began a custom of admitting children from the many North Denver orphanages to "free day" in the Gardens. Later, she invited parents to leave their children at the gate every Tuesday for Children's Day. Mary personally welcomed them to a full day of dancing lessons, pageants, folklore classes, games, contests, and tours through the zoo.

Mary Elitch married her long-time assistant, Thomas Long, in 1900. They took a world tour together, then instituted new features at the Garden. But after a few years, Long died. Again, Mary had to carry on alone. As she grew older, the business end of Elitch's started to slide, particularly payments of taxes and bills. By 1916, Elitch's was in financial trouble. Seeing Mary's dilemma, a group of businessmen persuaded John Mulvihill (who was in charge of credit and collections at the Denver Gas and Electric Company) to go over the books. Mulvihill eventually bought the Gardens and continued to run it just as Mary had done.

The Mulvihills invited Mary to stay in her fairy-tale cottage on the grounds. After a few years, when the house began to deteriorate, they built her a large, brick home. She continued living there until she moved in with her sister, Mrs. Will S. Arnold, at 4567 West Thirty-Eighth Avenue, where she died July 16, 1936. She was eighty.

The Lady of the Gardens had become Denver's sweetheart, beloved for her kindness to children and animals, her ever-blooming flowers, and her contributions to the city's culture. Nationally, she was the first woman to own and direct an amusement park and zoo—a powerful role model for girls and young women.

Sarah Sophia Chase Platt-Decker

Born in 1856 in McIndoe Falls, Vermont
Died July 7, 1912, in San Francisco, California

Public service was a cornerstone of Sarah Sophia Chase's family. Her mother was a descendant of the Adams family of Massachusetts; her father, known as "The Fighting Deacon," was an outspoken prohibitionist.

Sarah was born in McIndoe Falls, Vermont, and married early. When her husband died after two years, she soon learned that women had no legal rights. Her own possessions, which she had inherited from her mother, were divided up among members of her husband's family. Only a third were returned to her. She was so disheartened that she permanently dropped his last name. From this unhappy experience, Sarah would become a lifelong suffragette and supporter of equal rights for women.

Sarah entered public life in Holyoke, Massachusetts, as a member of the board of trustees administering funds for the poor. She steeled herself to face the seamy side of life without shrinking and to balance a sympathetic heart with a sound head. As a trustee, she developed a rare and valuable skill for a woman of her day: working on an equal basis with men. Sarah also began to study the causes and effects of social unrest and struggle, and to seek remedies. Throughout her life, she pursued solutions to these problems.

In 1884, she moved to Queens, New York, to work with the orphans' home and child welfare movement. Soon after, Sarah Chase married Colonel James H. Platt, director of the Mineola Children's Home. A Civil War veteran, Platt, who was trained as a physician, had served four terms in Congress. The couple relocated to Denver in 1887. Platt managed the Equitable Accident Insurance Company, and Sarah concentrated on raising her daughters. Together they became involved in Denver politics. In 1890, James and Sarah invested $357,000 in a new Denver paper mill, which Platt was trying to establish. Before he could complete the project, he drowned while fishing at Green Lake near Georgetown, on June 14, 1894. Platt Park in Denver was named in his memory.

Sarah was spurred into public life after the Panic of 1893, when Congress repealed the Sherman Act and removed U.S. currency from the silver standard. Colorado, with its reliance on silver mining, was especially hard hit. Silver mines shut down, many banks closed, and thousands of families were ruined. Coxey's Army of unemployed men was sweeping across the country from east to west and 2,000 of these angry, hungry men congregated in Denver. The city provided a tent camp for the homeless along River Front Park. Sarah Platt led a large relief effort to assist unemployed silver miners and other victims. She also presided at a mass political rally in the Denver Coliseum for William Jennings Bryan, the first silver presidential candidate. She was so effective that soon she was in demand as an organizer and speaker.

Sarah Platt's influence was extending rapidly into nearly every social and political arena. She became the first woman to serve on the state board of pardons. In 1898, Governor Alva Adams appointed her to the Colorado Board of Charities and Corrections, which had general supervision over all Colorado's penal and reformatory institutions as well as the State Civil Service Board. A powerful advocate for women's suffrage, she was a frequent speaker on the subject. "To Mrs. Platt-Decker belongs a great share of the credit that Colorado became the first state in the Union to realize the political rights of women."[1]

Given her stressful and active existence, it is somewhat surprising that romance again entered the life of Sarah Chase Platt, the activist. On December 4, 1888, she married Judge Westbrook S. Decker. Born in 1839, the prominent Denver judge was seventeen years older than Sarah. He had been seriously wounded in the Battle of Gettysburg during the Civil War and spent five months in a hospital. After he recovered, Decker earned a law degree at the University of Michigan. He practiced law in Illinois, although his health still was seriously affected by his army service. Eventually, he moved to Colorado to recuperate. President Grant appointed him the first U.S. District Attorney for the Colorado district. Later, Decker was elected a district judge. Still suffering from his Civil War wounds, however, he retired to practice law. Judge Decker died in 1902. The Decker Branch Library in Denver is named for him.

During this period, Sarah Platt-Decker was an organizer and first president of the Denver Women's Club—one of the many organizations that were active in community affairs in that era. She began to see that her greatest effectiveness and influence would derive from her women's club work. She led the Denver Women's Club in sponsoring a vegetable garden to feed the poor, created the State Home for Dependent Children, and lobbied at City Hall for the women's club's causes.

In 1904, at the national convention of the Federation of Associated Women's Clubs in St. Louis, Sarah Platt-Decker was nominated for president of the entire federation. Just before the vote, her opponent accused her of being "one of these mannish women who insist upon voting." At this, a little old lady from the audience boldly announced, "Well, any woman who has been married three times must have something of the feminine about her!"[2] Buoyed up, Sarah Platt-Decker gave a ringing response and was elected to the office.

During her four-year term as national president, she perceived that the General Federation of Women's Clubs could become a mighty factor in women's national struggle for the right to vote. To this purpose, she traveled thousands of miles, made hundreds of speeches, and converted voters to the cause of suffrage.

Coloradans were urging her to run for the U.S. Senate and even proposed her as a possible presidential candidate. She was a powerful and magnetic speaker, but it was her lively sense of humor and common good sense that powered her through life. Her serenity never became ruffled. Three times a widow, she overcame personal grief in the larger and nobler interests of humanity. Her personal motto was: "Never frown, never sigh, and keep step!"

Sarah Platt-Decker was in San Francisco attending the 1912 convention of the General Federation of Women's Clubs when an old kidney and stomach ailment abruptly recurred and she collapsed. She was immediately hospitalized and underwent surgery, but failed to respond. Her family was with her when she died a week later. Funeral services and burial were in Denver.

Denver's front page headlines announced Sarah Platt-Decker's death and praised her as "Colorado's foremost woman citizen and the real leader of the suffragette movement in the United States."[3]

From her home in Denver, Sarah Platt-Decker's influence had extended far beyond Colorado. A former Denver mayor, learning of her death at fifty-six said, "Her name heads the honor roll among women of the world as a distinguished club-woman, leader of suffrage, philanthropist, and tireless worker in every movement for the public good."[4] "She was, first of all, a woman, motherly, sisterly, in every respect ... a personality of most direct and vivid charm. ... Her public interest and unselfish service assured and preserved [her] leadership," noted Mrs. Edward P. Costigan, Denver Women's Club vice president.[5] At the same time, Sarah enjoyed life as a noted storyteller and one of few people who could enjoy a joke at their own expense. Her body lay in state in the Colorado Capitol with flags lowered to half-mast in recognition of her leadership in state reform and her contributions to the women's club movement.

Mary Florence Lathrop

Born December 10, 1865, in Philadelphia, Pennsylvania
Died October 18, 1951, in Denver, Colorado

In her eighty-five years, Mary Florence Lathrop racked up two successful careers and many significant "firsts"—first as a newspaper and
magazine reporter; next, as a lawyer. She was one of two first woman
members of the American Bar Association and the first woman to try
a case before the Colorado Supreme Court.

At age nineteen, five-foot, hundred-pound Mary joined the staff of
the *Philadelphia Press,* where her first assignment was to report on political news and labor conditions in Pennsylvania fabric mills, at which
time she campaigned for child labor laws in Pennsylvania. Samuel S.
McClure soon saw her stories and lured her over to *McClure* magazine,
which sent her West to cover gold mines, range wars, Indian disputes,
and a labor riot in Cripple Creek. She went to San Francisco in the
1880s to write about attacks on Chinese laborers. Her articles were so
effective that the Chinese government commended her for helping put
a stop to the attacks. So McClure sent her to China.

But *McClure*'s brand of whirlwind journalism was taking its toll on
tiny Mary Lathrop. She came down with pneumonia that developed
into tuberculosis in the 1890s. Like many other easterners, she and her
mother came to Colorado to recover her health. In Colorado, Mary decided that law would be a less hectic career than journalism and she
enrolled at the University of Denver School of Law. Eighteen months
later, in 1896, she graduated with a bachelor of law degree. She went on
to take a special course on probate law in Philadelphia and immediately passed the Colorado bar examination.

Then she hung up her degrees in a one-room office in the Equitable
Building, which had been built in 1890 at Seventeenth and Stout
Streets in downtown Denver. Later, she expanded into three rooms.
Despite Mary Lathrop's distinguished credentials, hurdles loomed. For
the next decade, many male colleagues refused to admit a woman
lawyer into their ranks. One attorney actually refused to try a case

against her client. Behind her back, male lawyers called her "that damn woman."

One of Lathrop's first cases, *Clayton v. Hallett,* was her most significant. George W. Clayton, a prominent Denver pioneer, had willed $2.5 million to found a college for orphaned boys. The will was contested by T. S. Clayton, apparently an heir. The trial dragged on for two years, during which Miss Lathrop researched decisions going back to the Louisiana Purchase and wrote all the briefs in the case. Clayton's will finally was supported in the lower court and district courts. She then argued the case before the Colorado Supreme Court and won the decision in 1898. *Clayton v. Hallett* established Colorado's law of charitable bequests. Mary Lathrop's specialty became probate and real estate issues. In addition, she worked on laws benefiting women and children.

Despite her successes, Mary Lathrop faced much opposition. In 1898, U.S. District Judge Moses Hallett refused to admit Miss Lathrop to federal practice because he did not believe women should practice law. The Colorado and Denver Bar Associations did invite her to become a member in 1901 but she hesitated, fearing she would be blackballed because of her gender. Finally, in 1913, she accepted their unanimous invitation to become the first woman admitted. She also was the first woman allowed to practice before the U.S. Supreme Court and joined the American Bar Association in 1917, where she later became a vice president.

In the tough world of men's law, Mary Lathrop never lost her femininity. A lively, dark-haired, dark-eyed woman, she went to court hearings "wearing a long-suited skirt with a full front of silk, high button shoes, and a hat with bright flowers above the little curls across her forehead."[1] Mary had saved a beautiful lace robe that her mother had worn years before when she was presented to the French Emperor Maximilian and Empress Carlotta of Mexico. Mary wore the same robe for her own presentation to King George V and Queen Mary, when she attended the American Bar Association meeting in London.

A caring and patriotic woman, Lathrop entertained soldiers from seven military installations in the Denver area. During World War II, she began taking a dozen soldiers at a time to dinner at Denver's Cosmopolitan Hotel. At Thanksgiving and Christmas, her guest list expanded to one hundred soldiers. When the war ended, the Veterans of Foreign Wars presented her with the Distinguished Citizenship Medal for entertaining 14,000 GIs.

In later years, further honors poured in: Business and Professional Women's Woman of the Year, Denver's First Lady of the Year, an honorary doctorate in law from the University of Denver, and in 1951, the Founder's Day and Evans Awards from D.U. Always active in professional organizations, she belonged to the Denver Woman's Press Club, the American Society of International Law, the French Society of Advocates, and the International Law Association.

Mary Lathrop lived in a townhouse at 522 East Eighteenth Avenue, Denver. She spent her professional life working from her Equitable Building offices, where she provided old-fashioned rocking chairs for the comfort of her clients and visitors—or for piling up her legal papers. She always wore a lacy apron when she did her legal work. Mary Lathrop continued to work eight hours a day, six days a week in her office until she was stricken with a heart attack and died a week later on October 18, 1951. She was eighty-five.

Margaret ("Molly") Tobin Brown

Born July 18, 1867, in Hannibal, Missouri
Died October 26, 1932, in New York City, New York

"Molly Brown" was not Molly Brown—not in her lifetime. She was born Margaret Tobin, although family and friends may have called her Peggy or Maggie. After her marriage, she used her formal name: Mrs. J. J. Brown. "Molly" didn't make her debut until the 1960s in the hit Broadway musical and movie *The Unsinkable Molly Brown*.

A true heroine of her time, she made international headlines for adventures at least as exciting and dramatic as any fictionalized accounts of her life. Margaret's lively imagination and theatrical flair were evident from girlhood; as a born storyteller, her own anecdotes added to the mystery and confusion surrounding her life.

Margaret Tobin was born July 18, 1867, into an Irish-Catholic family in Hannibal, Missouri, a lively Mississippi River town and jumping-off place for people heading west. Her father, John Tobin, a laborer with Hannibal Gas Works, barely made enough to feed a family that included, at various times: his wife, Johanna, and her daughter Mary Ann by an earlier marriage; his daughter Katie, of a deceased wife; and John and Johanna's children—Daniel, Margaret (Maggie), William, and Helen, the youngest. They lived in a small house at Butler Street and Denkler Alley in Hannibal. Maggie finished eighth grade and then went to work in a tobacco factory. She was waiting tables at the Park Hotel when, as legend has it, she overheard the famous Hannibal author, Samuel Clemens, discussing silver strikes at Leadville, Colorado.

In 1886, Maggie followed her older brother, Daniel, to Leadville, where they lived at the home of her half-sister and brother-in-law, Mary Ann and Jack Landrigan. Soon, she was sewing draperies and selling carpets at Daniels, Fisher, & Smith's—a dry goods store. She was attending a Catholic picnic with friends when she caught the eye of another Irishman, twenty-nine-year-old James Joseph Brown. A buxom, high-spirited girl with wavy auburn hair, Maggie Tobin easily attracted attention. At nineteen, she had little interest in a man twelve years her senior. But J. J. Brown was tall, handsome, and blue-eyed. He had a red-head's temper like Maggie's and a reputation for "having a way with women."

J. J. had worked through the West as a miner, moving up to foreman, and, eventually, mine manager. With his genius for recognizing and evaluating ore lodes, he was recognized as one of the best "metal men" in the country. He courted her persistently until she accepted his proposal. James J. Brown and Margaret Tobin were married September 1, 1886, at Church of the Annunciation in Leadville. They moved into a two-room cabin on Iron Hill near the Louisville Mine where he was foreman.

The Browns' son, Lawrence Palmer, was born August 30, 1887, and Catherine Ellen (they called her Helen) followed in 1889. By this time, the Browns were living in a comfortable home in town. Four more Tobin brothers and sisters had settled in Leadville, making these happy years for Maggie.

J. J. was advancing in his profession, too. In 1891, a mine owner named John Campion (known as the original "Leadville Johnny") headed a group of mining men, who combined their mining properties into the Ibex Consolidated Mining Group. J. J. owned one-eighth of the company stock and in 1892 joined the board of directors. Amid the Panic of 1893, Leadville's silver mines were shutting down. U.S. currency went off the silver standard and demand for silver plunged nationwide; even banks were closing. One day, as manager of the Ibex company's silver mine, the Little Jonny, J. J. was improving the mine shafts when he unexpectedly struck a rich vein of high-grade gold and copper. The Little Jonny *gold* mine was a prize that eventually brought in $20 million. In the midst of a state financial panic, J. J. Brown suddenly was rich.

Befitting their new station in life, the Browns moved to Denver and in April 1894 bought a three-story house on Denver's Capitol Hill. Termed a "Queen Anne street house," it was constructed between 1887 and 1889, of rhyolite, a volcanic stone, and sandstone with a wide front veranda, five bedrooms ("chambers"), and an important address: 1340 Pennsylvania Avenue (later Street). Mrs. Brown furnished it with rich oriental carpets, Victorian furniture, exotic statuary, and gold-framed paintings, making it a showplace in its day.

Margaret and J. J. began their prominence in Denver social and business circles. Margaret had a passion for extravagant gowns and jewelry, lavish entertaining, and charitable functions.

The Browns bought a Jefferson County farm, originally 320 acres, now at 2690 South Wadsworth Boulevard. In 1897, they added a summer home, a plain two-story brick house. Maggie, who named their summer retreat "Avoca" (pronounced A-vok´-a), gave large parties there. J. J. became a gentleman farmer. He grew hay, timothy, and rye, planted a fruit orchard, and raised thoroughbred horses and cows. When Maggie hitched up her buggy to drive to Denver, Bancroft School let the children out to watch her go by.

In 1894, Margaret Brown became a charter member of the Women's Club of Denver, and when the General Federation of Women's Clubs held its convention in Denver, she invited the officers to a luncheon at Avoca. (Apparently, more attended than expected and the food ran out before everyone was served, according to a gossip column written by *Denver Post*'s Polly Pry.) Five years later, in 1906, the Browns sold Avoca. The building still stands a century later. (Under a porch at a corner of the house was a cornerstone inscribed "J. J. Brown" and "1897"—the year it was built.)

The popular notion that socialites ignored her invitations is far from true. In fact, the list of Denver's elite who attended her extravagant functions is long. However, society doyenne Louise Hill, who governed Denver's Sacred Thirty-six—the name given to Denver's prominent families—never invited the J. J. Browns to her exclusive bridge parties and dinners. But newspaper society columnists recounted Margaret Brown's social events of 1900 in detail. The *Denver Times* noted that opera-goers avidly watched the Browns' box every night at the Silver Slaves' Ball and the first night at the opera, where her guests included some of the smartest-gowned women in Denver. An accompanying picture shows Margaret's "famous gilt lace gown described in the Parisian press as one of the most elaborate gowns ever created by handiwork of the French Modiste; [it took] three months [to weave] the lace, [which was] then spangled and embroidered in gold; with it she wore a lace opera cloak lined in ermine … that presents a pretty penny for style." The writer added: "Mrs. Brown's vivacity and merry disposition is a most refreshing trait in a society woman of her position, for in the smart set, any disposition to be natural and animated is quite frowned upon. … Mrs. Brown's gowns are as original as her ideas and that's interesting, too. [Her gown] came from Venice, one of the handsomest … and most unique gowns in all that assemblage of fashion."[1]

In November, Margaret Brown was chosen to head the prestigious Catholic Ball. The *Times* noted: "The Catholic Fair promises to be a great event … with Mrs. Brown's indomitable pluck and energy at the head, [it is] certain to be a great social and financial success. One of the most interesting events will be the doll booth. Mrs. Brown has written prominent people across the country asking for doll donations. … Mrs. Roosevelt sent a black and violet gowned lady doll sure to be a great attraction, as Mrs. Ted [sic] made the little garments and dressed the doll. Mrs. McKinley and Mrs. Bryan dolls are on the way. … Seldom is so much unsolicited interest shown for an affair."[2] The story listed many prominent Denverites involved in the preparations. The *Times* exulted November 25, 1900: "All the world visited the Catholic Fair. No one wore a happier smile than Mrs. J. J. Brown, the woman who possesses the button that controls the entire fair. … [She has] an astonishing ability to be everywhere at once. No one to have seen her, debonaire and mischievous, would have dreamed that it was long past midnight."[3]

Society notices mentioned that Margaret enrolled her daughter in an eastern school in September 1902, and gave a dancing party for her in January 1903, followed in August by a house party for boys and girls at Avoca. Margaret also cared for her aging parents in her home until their deaths in 1899 and 1905. But life inside the Brown House in Denver was not always sweetness and light. J. J. far preferred a quiet, modest home life to the social whirl. During Margaret's parties, he was said to retreat to the basement to smoke cigars and drink. He made frequent trips to Leadville but its high altitude and cold aggravated his arthritis and heart trouble. After his stroke in 1899, which caused temporary paralysis, he quit active mining.

Obviously, the Browns were drifting apart. According to servants and neighbors, J. J. and Margaret, both of Irish tempers, had loud fights in which objects were thrown. J. J. spent more and more time pursuing business interests in Arizona, Utah, California, and Cuba—warm climates were kinder to his arthritis. Margaret stayed in her cottage in Newport, Rhode Island, for long periods.

Helen later wrote in a family letter that the widening gulf between her parents "was the tragedy of my childhood." She said her mother's pursuit of fame and social position caused the gulf between them. J. J. was difficult, bad tempered, and hard to please. Besides, there was J. J.'s drinking and philandering. In 1904, Harry D. Call sued him for $50,000, for alienating the affections of his young wife, Maud. Margaret and J. J. separated officially in 1909. J. J. provided a generous monthly settlement for her maintenance and they rarely (if ever) met face-to-face again, although they often referred to each other in family letters. From 1910 to 1912, Mrs. Brown lived mostly in the East or in Europe. Their son, Larry Brown, who had married Eileen Horton in 1911, was struggling to launch his career. Helen, who had grown into a beautiful redhead by 1912, was completing her studies in Europe.

A front-page story in the *Denver Times* on April 15, 1912, reported that Mrs. Brown had joined the John Jacob Astor party, which was spending the winter in Egypt. With the party, she arranged passage for herself and her daughter to return to New York on the *Titanic*. Mrs. Brown described the voyage in the April 30 *Times:* "All day Sunday, bitter cold shafts from ice fields swept the decks, yet the ship was plowing ahead at ... 23 knots per hour. Most passengers were in their cabins or salons. The great floating palace was still." She was lying in her berth when the ship struck an iceberg beneath her stateroom at 11:40 P.M. on April 14, 1912. In the corridor, passengers and sailors appeared unconcerned. Finally, she was told to dress warmly, to put on a life belt, and to bring her possessions to the deck. At first, she noticed scarcely a flicker of excitement on board. Then the *Titanic*'s plight rapidly deteriorated. In the chaos, Mrs. Brown helped women and children into life boats. As the last boat, No. 6, was being lowered, two powerful men picked her up and dropped her into the boat. Just sixteen people were in No. 6, she recalled. The "quartermaster [on board] was the most craven of cowards. ... All night he sat shivering in the prow ... muttering in a sing-song voice that we were lost, lost, at the mercy of the waves. I threatened to throw him overboard and for a moment he was silenced. For hours, we rowed through the bitter cold and darkness toward a phantom light ... far out on the great deep.

"When we were some nine miles from the wreck, the phantom ship [disappeared]. We started rowing back to the grave of the *Titanic*; signals flashed from sixteen lifeboats. ... We came across a stoker [boiler room worker], black and almost frozen. We pulled him into our boat. I wrapped him in my sables and set him to rowing.

"Just as dawn flashed over the sea, the rescue ship, *Carpathia*, loomed on the horizon. Never was sight so dear as that ship bringing us life. ... The courage and endurance of those women during the long night ... was almost supernatural."[4]

After six hours on the icy waves, No. 6 was the last lifeboat rescued—with all passengers alive. Mrs. Brown cited the heroism of men who went down with the *Titanic* so women and children could be saved, but challenged the wisdom of separating men from families who would later be unable to support themselves. A newspaper story reported that Helen Brown, first listed as lost, was safe in Europe where she had decided to remain to complete her studies. (A year later, in 1913, Helen married New Yorker George Benziger. Like her father, she preferred a quiet, inconspicuous lifestyle.)

On the *Carpathia*, Margaret Brown found plenty of work to do. The ship's lounge had been converted into a makeship hospital, where nearly 700 survivors—most of them women—huddled, shivering, on deck. For four days and nights, Margaret nursed and comforted steerage passengers and sent word ahead to notify families and friends. On shipboard, she organized a drive that raised $10,000 to tide over passengers stranded in New York. When they reached the New York dock, a mob of reporters surrounded the survivors. Someone asked Mrs. Brown how she came through. She replied, "It was typical Brown luck. I'm unsinkable." Headlines hailed her as Lady Margaret, but the name that stuck was the Unsinkable Mrs. Brown.

Margaret Brown's finest moments came during the *Titanic* disaster and her grandest years came in its wake. A *Times* headline on May 1, 1912, heralded, "*Titanic* Heroine at Last Breaks into 'Sacred 36': Mrs. J. J. Brown Realizes Ambition; Is Guest of Mrs. Crawford Hill at Luncheon. ... From now until her departure for the East, she will be wined and dined from morning until night by Denver's exclusive circle," the reporter added.[5]

There were other instances in which Mrs. J. J. Brown demonstrated she had "a heart as big as a ham," as she claimed. After the Ludlow coal mine disaster in 1914, she went immediately to the scene and contributed generously to needy families of striking miners. She helped orphans of World War I soldiers and later worked for Judge Ben B. Lindsey's Juvenile Court in Denver. In a singular political endeavor, as a strong supporter of women's suffrage, she ran unsuccessfully for the U.S. Senate on the National Women's Party ticket in 1914.

Margaret Brown became increasingly eccentric and erratic after suffering a series of strokes that may have caused her later mood swings and affected her mental stability. Pictures from that period show her walking with a tall cane—to support her fallen arches, she said.

J. J., whose mining investments had made him a wealthy man, lived frugally. He gave Lawrence and Helen comfortable homes and monthly financial support. His health was failing rapidly by 1921 and he went to live with Helen's family in Hempstead, New York. He died alone on September 5, 1922, at Flushing Hospital in New York. Mrs. Brown was living at her Newport cottage and traveled all night to attend his funeral.

The disposition of the estate, which consisted of $206,000 plus Ibex stock and bonds, caused a serious rift between Margaret and her children. J. J. had written two wills but never signed them; however, it was understood he wanted Margaret to have half the estate and Lawrence and Helen would split the remaining half. By this time, Margaret's handwriting had supposedly deteriorated to a barely legible scrawl, and her sentences were rambling and disconnected. Lawrence finally told her that Helen and he considered her incapable of managing her own finances. As a result, Margaret brought suit against her children for her share of the estate, which further strained their relationship. When the estate was finally settled, it was divided equally as J. J. had intended but the wealth had been severely depleted.

Mrs. Brown undertook her final Denver project in 1928. She loved the poems Eugene Field wrote while he was managing editor of the *Denver Tribune* in the early 1880s. "Little Boy Blue," in memory of his son, had been written in a bedroom of his frame house at 315 West Colfax Avenue. In 1927, when the American Penwomen asked Margaret Brown to help save Field's house from demolition, she rented it for two years as the Eugene Field Memorial and then bought it for $350. She campaigned successfully to have it moved to Washington Park, where for years it was the tiny Eugene Field Library; then it became headquarters for the Park People. Her rescue of Eugene Field's house was Denver's first preservationist endeavor.

Margaret Brown was living with her nurse at the Barbizon, a women's hotel in New York City, when she died abruptly on October 26, 1932. She was sixty-five. She was buried beside J. J. in Holy Rood Cemetery on Long Island in New York.

The Brown's house on Capitol Hill, which Margaret had furnished so lavishly, changed hands and deteriorated over the years. In 1969, it was rescued from a rooming-house existence when Denver's first preservation group (later called Historic Denver, Inc.) raised money to buy it and restored the interior to match photographs taken during Margaret's heyday. Still guarded by stone lions, it became the Molly Brown House Museum, which is visited by more than 40,000 people a year.

With her wit, charm, outspoken manner, and flair for the dramatic, Mrs. Brown was years ahead of her time. It was fitting that Maggie Tobin Brown's fame was revived in the 1960s when composer Meredith Willson brought her to life again in his hit Broadway musical *The Unsinkable Molly Brown.* Her popularity rebounded in 1998 with the Molly Brown role in the blockbuster film *Titanic.*

Emily Griffith

Born February 10, 1868, in Cincinnati, Ohio
Died September 19, 1947, in Pinecliffe, Colorado

Emily Griffith stood before her class of eighth graders at Denver's Twenty-fourth Street School in the city's poorest neighborhood. Some of the children stared back at her, empty-eyed. Others were downright hostile. Many were recent immigrants, whose foreign languages created an impenetrable barrier.

The year was 1908 and Emily Griffith had been teaching for twenty-six years. But the problems in this classroom discouraged her. In desperation, she went to visit the families of truant and dropout children. She found squalid conditions, and she met parents who barely spoke English and lacked basic skills. They were embarrassed to see their children learning what they did not know. A mother shyly confided that she wished she could read the Bible. Several fathers expressed the need to acquire skills so they could work as craftsmen and figure their bills.

Emily Griffith became convinced that the children never would learn until their parents acquired a basic education. She began tutoring her pupils' families at night in the old, abandoned Longfellow School. She decided the adults also needed skills that would allow them to get jobs and merge into society. She studied their needs and developed an unorthodox concept that someday would open an entire new field of education: free adult education in all areas for those who wished to learn.

Adapting her teaching methods to pupils' needs was an old habit for Emily Griffith. Born in Cincinnati in 1868, Emily completed her elementary grades there. When she was thirteen, her father, John Griffith, moved his wife and four children to a 160-acre farm near Broken Bow, Nebraska. Charles was the Griffiths' first child; then came Emily, Florence (who some people thought was simpleminded), and Ethel, the youngest. Emily, and probably her sisters, enrolled in a one-room sod schoolhouse where all eight grades were taught.

When the teacher left the little school to marry a Nebraska bachelor,

Emily, who was one of the pupils, stepped in as the only possible successor. The young girl quickly learned to deal with unruly older boys,
although she had to struggle to stay a step ahead of more advanced students. The next year, when she was fourteen, she applied to the superintendent of county education for a regular teaching assignment and
passed the examination.

John Griffith, who was lame, proved to be no farmer. So Emily, with
her meager salary, became the main financial support for her family of
six. The Griffiths moved to Denver in 1895, and Emily soon became a
substitute teacher in the Denver Public Schools. At the same time, she
attended Denver Normal School. Although she never went to college,
she started teaching sixth graders and worked her way up to eighth
graders.

As busy as she was, Emily Griffith always worked with her pupils in-
dividually and encouraged them, saying, "You can do it." And they did.
Before long, the educational hierarchy noted her inspired teaching and
in 1904 appointed her to the post of state deputy superintendent of
schools with an office in the capitol building. But Emily missed her
pupils, so she returned to teaching in 1908 at the Twenty-fourth Street
School, where she was to face her greatest challenge: meeting the needs
of the parents as well as the children. In night classes at the Longfellow
School building, she assured her adult students that with proper training, they could earn a living. Their enthusiastic response convinced her
of the need for a free public school where adults could learn marketable skills and trades that would make it possible for them to fit into
society. This conviction became her crusade.

In 1915, she appealed to the Denver School Board for permission to
open a revolutionary school that would provide a free education for
any adult who needed a second chance—the handicapped, dropout,
immigrant, unemployed, the down-and-out of society. Students could
start whenever they wished, study what they wanted, attend day or
night, and proceed at their own pace. The Denver school superintendent gave her permission to resuscitate the abandoned, thirty-three-
year-old Longfellow School building at the corner of Thirteenth and
Welton Streets. In the face of strenuous opposition from some board

members and administrators, she carried her campaign to business-men, women's clubs, and the Denver newspapers. Frances Wayne of the *Denver Post* took up the cause and later helped keep the school going.

At last, the school board agreed to allot her two classrooms and five assistant teachers and it appointed her as principal at a salary of $1,800 a year. She chose the name Opportunity School, and some of her former students, by then at Manual High School, painted a sign and mounted it over the entrance:

PUBLIC OPPORTUNITY SCHOOL
FOR THOSE WHO WANT TO LEARN

Emily Griffith arrived early on September 9, 1916—the opening day for the world's first school geared to provide basic adult education and training in marketable skills. The idea and curriculum were so novel, she must have felt apprehensive. She hoped that 200 adults would enroll during that first semester. To her delight, 2,389 signed up for classes.

Opportunity School became a lifeline for thousands who received training in shoe repair, cosmetology, auto mechanics, mathematics, and English. If necessary, the school would provide even more than classes. A boy who fainted in class one day was found to be suffering from malnutrition. In a few days, a notice on Emily Griffith's blackboard read, "A bowl of soup is served in the basement from 5:30 to 7:30—free. This will save you time." Emily's mother made the soup and her sister Florence lugged it to school on the streetcar—every day for two years.

News of the innovative Opportunity School spread all over the world. Requests poured in for Emily Griffith to establish similar schools in foreign countries, but she chose to remain in Denver. Honors came her way. She became the only honorary woman Kiwanian; she was given a seat on Colorado's Child Welfare Board and awarded an honorary masters of education degree from the University of Colorado; she was named president of the Colorado Education Association and Woman of the Year by the Business and Professional Women's Clubs.

An exceptionally pretty woman, Emily Griffith indulged her fondness for wide-brimmed hats, ruffled blouses, and elbow-length kid gloves. Of her many suitors, she came close to marrying one of them. But in the end, she remained true to her career.

Her students and colleagues were stunned in December 1933 when she abruptly retired as principal of Opportunity School. She would say only that she was tired. No one knew that when she moved to Denver, Emily Griffith had lopped twelve years off her age by changing her birth date from February 10, 1868, to February 10, 1880, possibly to refute any semblance of spinsterhood.

Four months later on March 14, 1934, the Board of Education renamed her school the Emily Griffith Opportunity School and offered her a comfortable pension. But Griffith would accept only the teacher's $50 a month stipend—a penurious income that was to provide for *two* women. Since girlhood, she had cared for her sister Florence, who had epilepsy. Emily, who always knew instinctively what her students needed, shortchanged herself.

A year before her retirement, Emily Griffith had asked Fred W. Lundy, one of the teachers at the Opportunity School, to build a cabin for her sister and herself in Pinecliffe, a mountain hamlet above Boulder. A devoted friend, Lundy moved to a house nearby so he could look after the sisters, do their odd jobs, and run errands for them.

In the summer of 1937, Denver School Superintendent Charles E. Greene, with his family and a friend, visited the sisters in Pinecliffe. The cabin door, just a step from the roadside, opened into the kitchen where Emily and Florence received the visitors, whom they greeted warmly. The sisters wore long, dark skirts and shirtwaists—possible holdovers from World War I days.

The four-room building—spartan even for a summer cabin—was the Griffiths' year-round residence. The interior was scrubbed and tidy, yet it gave visitors an eerie feeling of stepping back into an earlier era. Wood was piled beside the cookstove. There was no kitchen sink—a basin and pitcher set on a table beneath the window served for washing utensils. A few kerosene lanterns were ready to be lit for the evening. Florence Griffith was serving lemonade and pie to the guests, who were seated around the kitchen table covered with oilcloth, when their friend Lundy dropped by to say hello to the superintendent. Lundy, still a kindly and devoted friend, had continued to do odd jobs around their house and to drive the sisters to do their errands.

Ten years later, on June 19, 1947, the Griffith sisters were still living in their humble Pinecliffe home. Emily, seventy-nine, was failing rapidly and struggling to look after Florence. That evening, the youngest sister, Ethel Griffith Gurtner and her husband, Evan, stopped by the cabin to check on her sisters. No one answered their knock. The Gurtners obtained a key and returned at 7:30 the next morning. Evan entered first and almost stumbled over Florence, lying in her bedroom face down in a pool of blood, a .38-caliber bullet embedded in the back of her head. Emily, in the other bedroom, had also been shot in the back of the head.

The Gurtners tried to notify Lundy, but he was missing. After searching through the surrounding mountains, police found his car abandoned beside South Boulder Creek and later recovered his body downstream. A letter with instructions for his burial and disposal of his small estate was on the car seat beside the murder weapon. The killings were never conclusively solved. Friends believed that Lundy, in poor health, could not bear to watch Emily's failing condition. He had been heard to comment that Emily had lived a "martyr life in caring for her sister." Police termed the two deaths a mercy killing. Friends wondered about a possible suicide pact.

Hundreds of Coloradans attended their funeral services at Central Presbyterian Church in Denver. Emily and Florence were buried side by side at Fairmount Cemetery. Emily's estate was valued at $2,500 in real property and $9,500 in personal goods.

A stained-glass portrait of Emily Griffith in the Colorado Capitol Building shows a pretty, petite woman with penetrating blue eyes, wearing one of her outrageously flamboyant hats. Emily Griffith's unorthodox Opportunity School still stands—as it has for more than eighty years—on the same street, offering training and opportunity for "those who want to learn."

Justina Ford

Born January 22, 1871, in Knoxville, Illinois
Died October 14, 1952, in Denver, Colorado

A rundown, turn-of-the-century brick house at 2335 Arapahoe Street in Denver's Five Points district was scheduled to be demolished in 1983. Built in the late 1880s, of Italianate architecture, the handsome nine-room house had been the home and office of Justina L. Ford, M.D., Denver's first black woman physician. When historical preservationists and black community groups learned of plans to tear down the house, they quickly marshaled their forces to save it. After restoring the building as a museum, the preservationists moved it to 3015 California Street and had it listed on the National Register of Historic Places.

For fifty years, Dr. Justina Ford had her office and examining room on the first floor and lived upstairs. Medicine had been her passion since she was a small child. Justina Laurena Ford was the seventh child in her family. Her mother was a nurse, and from the time the family moved to Galesburg, Illinois, little Justina loved to play "hospital"— and always, she played the doctor. She didn't know medical terms for medicines or diseases, so she prescribed "tobacco pills" for every complaint and made up names for illnesses. In a 1950 interview with *Negro Digest*, she said, "I used to dress the chickens for dinner so I could get in there and see what the insides were like."[1] In that way, she could study the heart, lungs, and eyes.

She received her medical degree from Hering Medical School in Chicago in 1899. For the next two years, she directed a hospital and was a doctor at a state school in Normal, Alabama. Because of her race and gender, however, the community did not accept her as a physician and she decided to practice where blacks constituted a more substantial part of the community. She chose Denver. Her great-nephew, Gene Carter, said that when she set out for Colorado in 1902, she thought she was going to "the wild, wild west," but the possibility of harsh environment did not deter her. She was intent upon setting up her obstetrics practice where she thought people might be more accepting of a black woman doctor.

Upon arriving, she faced great obstacles, but "I fought like a tiger against those," she recalled. The first thing Dr. Ford learned was that Denver General Hospital did not accept black patients or black physicians. So Dr. Ford took her practice on the road. Among her patients were Spanish, American Indian, Chinese, Greek, Japanese, "plain whites," and "plain colored" people. "Whatever color they show up, that's the way I take them," she often said.[2] (Black babies comprised 15 percent of her deliveries.) She learned to speak and understand enough of seven languages to diagnose illnesses, prescribe medications, and write out dosage directions in her patients' dialects.

Many immigrant parents were afraid of hospitals and wanted to have a woman at their children's births. Dr. Ford was the answer to both needs. If patients couldn't get to her Arapahoe Street office, Dr. Ford went to their homes—first traveling by horse and buggy, later by bicycle, then on a streetcar or in a taxi. Ottawa Harris, interviewed for the Denver Public Schools' Justina Project, recalled that Dr. Ford could just pick up the phone, give her name, and the cab would show up without charge. Dr. Ford never drove, but she did own a car when she was older. When neighbors saw her long, black automobile (driven by her husband or her nephew) pull up, they knew that another baby was on its way.

A Five Points neighbor, Agneda-Lopez Stoner, noted that "when it came time to deliver a baby, [Dr. Ford] removed her street clothes and delivered the child in her slip or a gown" to protect it from germs that might be on her street clothes.[3] During long labors, Dr. Ford would sit in a rocking chair and drink tea until it was time to deliver the baby. Her husband would wait in the car. She would send him away to eat but she never left before the birth, Stoner said.

She concentrated her practice in obstetrics and believed strongly in natural childbirth. In answer to critics, she said, "The babies were probably conceived at home and have nowhere else to be born but at home."[4] Dr. Ford's fees were more than reasonable: $15 to $20 for pre-natal care and delivery. Some patients couldn't pay even that amount in cash so she would accept payment in produce, chickens, household items, or whatever people could exchange for her services. She later gave most of the items to charity. She was generous to all but particularly with poor people; she was known to send half a ton of coal or a bag of groceries to the homes of cold or hungry patients. Wendell T. Liggins, pastor of Zion Baptist Church where Ford worshipped, recalled that her patients knew they could go to her even when they had no money. Years later, as race and gender issues receded, Dr. Ford was admitted to practice at Denver General Hospital and became a full member of the Denver, Colorado, and American Medical Societies.

Justina's first husband was a minister in Zion Baptist Church. When he was transferred to a church in Florida, she refused to leave Denver with him. After his death, she married Alfred Allen, who often drove her on house calls and did the couple's housework.

Dr. Ford was feisty all her life, as many who knew her testified. When she was eighty, she told Mark Harris, in an interview with *Negro Digest,* that she still enjoyed her hobby. "I like to ride ninety miles an hour in an ambulance. To me, that's good fun."[5] Harris described Dr. Ford as a tiny, round, gray-haired woman. A former patient recalled that she had "a spiritual quality about her and it showed through her eyes." Magdalena Gallegos, writing in *Urban Spectrum,* saw Justina as "a stern-visaged woman whose unmistakable authority was sharply defined."[6] Other people found her active and brisk-mannered but also good-hearted. Dr. Ford's eyesight began to fail and she became ill in the fall of 1952. On October 14, two weeks after treating her last patient, she died at home. She was eighty-one.

In her fifty-year career in Denver, she had delivered 7,000 babies. Many of those "babies" organized community support in 1983 and joined the efforts of Historic Denver and the Black American West Museum to save Dr. Ford's home from the wrecker. The house became the Black American West Museum and Heritage Center.

Honors continued to come to Colorado's first black woman physician. At the hundredth "birthday" of Justina Ford's house, the Colorado Medical Society passed a resolution honoring her "as an outstanding figure in the development and furtherance of health care in Colorado and as a Colorado Medical Pioneer." In 1975, Warren Library in East Denver was renamed the Ford-Warren Library. A group of black health professionals at the University of Colorado Health Sciences Center organized the Justina Ford Medical Society to hold free health screenings and seminars in the basement of her old office.

In the summer of 1952, two months before her death, Dr. Ford defined her philosophy to reporter Gallegos: "When all the fears, hate and even some death is over, we will really be brothers as God intended us to be in this land. This I believe. For this I have worked all my life." She succeeded in living her philosophy in her life and medical practice. "Dr. Ford wasn't concerned about money," said Pastor Liggins. "She was more than a great physician. She was a great American."[7]

Florence Rena Sabin

Born November 9, 1871, in Central City, Colorado
Died October 3, 1953, in Denver, Colorado

A simple inscription, "Doctor of Medicine," is written beneath Florence Rena Sabin's statue in Statuary Hall in the nation's Capitol. But even a hundred words could not describe the magnitude of Dr. Sabin's contributions to her native Colorado and to the world of science.

The distinguished woman physician was born in Central City, Colorado, far from any medical or academic center. Her father, George Sabin, had studied medicine and even left his native Vermont to be a "horse and buggy doctor" in Missouri. But before he realized his dream, he was bitten by gold rush fever and by December 1860, he was prospecting around Black Hawk. Seven years later, he met Serena Miner, a schoolteacher from his home state. They married in 1868 and settled in nearby Central City.

The Sabin's first child, Mary, was born there in 1869 and her sister, Florence, in 1871. Sabin moved his family to Denver around 1875 but continued to manage several mines around Central City. Two younger sons died in infancy.

The girls' mother died on Florence's seventh birthday in 1878—a loss that changed the direction of the girls' lives. George Sabin found he could not run a mine while caring for his daughters, so he enrolled them in Wolfe Hall, a private Denver boarding school. Already close as sisters, Mary and Florence learned to lean on each other for support.

Then Sabin decided to send his girls to live with his brother, a teacher living in a Chicago suburb. They were warmly welcomed into the musical household of Uncle Albert, Aunt Margaret, and their son, Stewart Sabin. During four happy years there, they attended private school. Florence's genius must have become evident by 1883 when Uncle Albert took the sisters to live with their grandparents on a farm in Rockingham, Vermont. Grandfather Sabin told them about their father's abortive attempts to study medicine and about uncles and ancestors who were physicians.

Mary and Florence attended a fine girls' school, the Vermont Academy, which had recently opened in nearby Saxton's River. Mary graduated with high honors, then went on to Smith College in Massachusetts. Florence followed her two years later. At Smith, Florence's fascination with and genius for science was leading her toward medicine and laboratory studies. In this significant period of her life, Dr. Preston, a woman dean at the college, became Florence's mentor and counselor. Impressed by Florence's academic record and hard work, Dr. Preston urged her to become a physician—despite the fact that American medical schools were not accepting women.

Florence graduated from Smith as a Phi Beta Kappa in 1893 and returned to Denver, excited to share her plans with her father and sister. But Colorado was in the grip of a crippling silver panic. Mines were shutting down throughout the state. Many banks and businesses were bankrupt. Her father explained that even if she could get into medical school, he would be unable to pay her way.

Mary, who was teaching mathematics at East Denver High School, urged her younger sister to go into teaching. So Florence taught for two years at her old school, Wolfe Hall, then became a biology assistant at Smith. She developed a rare gift for inspiring and instructing younger students. And she saved every cent she could. Meanwhile, in

Baltimore, three wealthy women agreed to help finance a proposed medical school at Johns Hopkins University *provided* the school would accept women. Florence learned of this opportunity and in 1896 she was among the first sixteen women to enter Johns Hopkins School of Medicine.

In her first year, she signed up for a class in histology (the study of organic tissues). As she peered through the microscope, she got her first close-up look at animal cells and bacteria, which opened a fascinating new world to her. After that, she spent every possible minute in the laboratory. Her professor, Dr. Franklin Paine Mall, assigned her to make a model of a newborn baby's brain stem. He brought her the tiny brain of a deceased baby and after three weeks of laborious study and copying, she completed a beeswax model. Professor Mall was so impressed with its accuracy and beauty that he arranged for her to take it to Germany to have copies made. Florence Sabin's model of the newborn's brain has been used by generations of medical school neurology classes.

Dr. Florence Sabin graduated with high honors from Johns Hopkins in 1900 and served her internship there, with emphasis on laboratory research. She then was awarded a fellowship by the Baltimore Association for the Promotion of University Education for Women, which financed her research to find the origin of the lymphatic system. Her groundbreaking work eventually would demonstrate that the lymphatic vessels develop from a special layer of cells in certain fetal veins. Some claim that her lymphatic system study was her most significant scientific achievement. In 1901, she published her *Atlas of the Midbrain and Medulla,* which has been used widely as a valued medical text.

As a teacher, she worked patiently with medical students, instilling them with her enthusiasm for science. They kept coming back to her long after their classes had ended. Johns Hopkins promoted her to anatomy assistant in 1902 and gave her a full professorship in histology in 1917. She became the first woman professor at the medical school.

Florence believed that "women get exactly what they deserve in this world and needn't think they are discriminated against; they can have whatever they are willing to work for."[1] Her theory soon would be tested in the real world. When her mentor and teacher, Dr. Mall, died in 1917, Dr. Sabin was next in line to head the anatomy department. To the dismay of her colleagues, Johns Hopkins gave the post to a man. The decision severely tested Florence's theory on gender bias.

While at the university, she became active in the National Women's Party and rose to the office of chairman. Florence also was the first woman elected president of the American Association of Anatomists and the first women member of the National Academy of Sciences.

After twenty-nine years in Baltimore, she moved to New York in 1924. Dr. Simon Flexner, chief of the Rockefeller Institute for Medical Research, invited her to set up and head the institute's Department of Cellular Studies—and to become the first woman as a full member in the institute.

At the Rockefeller Institute, she did a cooperative study of the blood in relation to the pathology of tuberculosis. Working with her were twenty-one universities, research institutes, and pharmaceutical companies. She developed a new tuberculosis treatment and discovered origins and development of blood, blood vessels, and blood cells. Wherever she worked, she taught and encouraged younger associates, not only by her brilliance but with her smiling manner, personal philosophy, and enthusiasm for the work. The head of the Rockefeller Institute called her the "leading woman scientist in the world."

Florence was sixty-seven in 1938 when she retired and returned to live with her sister in an apartment at 1333 East Tenth Avenue in Denver. (Mary had retired after a long teaching career at East Denver High School.) Dr. Sabin's retirement lasted only six years.

At the close of World War II, Colorado's governor, John Vivian, was appointing committees to prepare the state for returning veterans. *Denver Post* reporter Frances Wayne noticed that the governor's committees were all headed by men and she hounded him to appoint women, too. Governor Vivian retorted there were no qualified women, and Frances Wayne reminded him that the nation's foremost woman scientist was living in Denver. After some reflection, the governor agreed to have the nice, retired lady doctor head the state health subcommittee.

Dr. Sabin responded swiftly to the call. In October 1946, at age seventy-three, she embarked upon her most gratifying mission—revising

Colorado's health laws, which, she said, had not been updated since Colorado Territory became a state in 1876. To diagnose the state's current health, she toured each of the sixty-three counties. In one county, Dr. Sabin's hostess met her at the train station and asked what she would like to see first. "The sewage disposal plant," Dr. Sabin answered. The woman asked her husband where that would be and was directed to "take her down to the river."

To her horror, Dr. Sabin found that Colorado, paragon of sunshine and fresh air, was one of the sickest states in the union. It had one of the highest infant mortality rates, ranked fifth in diphtheria incidence, third in scarlet fever deaths, and it lacked uniform regulations for pasteurizing milk. "We think of our state as a health resort," she announced. "Yet we're dying faster than people in most other states." She originated a slogan, "Health to Match Our Mountains," to launch a spirited but much-disputed campaign for reform. She then proposed eight Sabin health bills, which included removal of the health department from politics; pasteurization of all milk in the state; inspection of all milk cows; control of sewage; provision of health education; and establishment of local boards of health throughout the state. Dr. Sabin lobbied the legislature and stumped counties throughout Colorado to promote her bills. But the legislature failed to pass Dr. Sabin's public health program in 1946.

The next governor, Democrat Lee Knous, supported Dr. Sabin's reforms and asked her to direct his new State Board of Health. In 1947, the 36th General Assembly passed her health bills. Thus, the nice, retired lady doctor had revised Colorado's health statutes for the first time in seventy-one years and had shaken up the entire state health department.

In 1946, the Denver County Medical Society had demanded the reorganization of Denver's health department. The next year, Mayor Quigg Newton appointed Dr. Sabin as manager of the Denver Department of Health and Charities. Within two years, she began a city-wide X-ray program to diagnose tuberculosis. She launched a crusade to remove rats from city alleys and dumps and to offer vocational training for the poor. Denver's tuberculosis death rate dropped from 54.7 to

27 persons per 100,000. Through it all, she donated her salary to Colorado General Hospital for research.

Dr. Florence Sabin retired permanently in 1951 when she was eighty. An avid baseball fan, she was at home listening to the World Series on October 3, 1953, when she suffered a heart attack and died instantly. She was eighty-two.

In her distinguished career, she had received honorary degrees from fifteen universities. She was awarded a cash prize for the "most distinctive contribution made by an American woman to American life" in 1931. *Good Housekeeping* named her one of America's twelve greatest women. At the University of Colorado School of Medicine, the Sabin Building for Research in Cellular Biology was named for her. She is one of two outstanding Colorado citizens whose likeness stands in Statuary Hall in the nation's Capitol. Coloradans conducted a drive for contributions and then commissioned sculptor Joy Buba of New York to create the life-size statue of Dr. Florence Sabin as Colorado's permanent representative, the third woman accorded this honor.

At her death, the *Denver Post* quoted Mayor Quigg Newton: "Dr. Sabin was one of the greatest persons I've ever known. I will all my life treasure the time I was privileged to spend with her. She was learned, she was wise, she was humble. She loved the world and every living creature in it. With the death of Dr. Sabin the people of Denver have lost a famous citizen and devoted, selfless public servant."[2]

Edwina Hume Fallis

Born November 15, 1876, in Denver, Colorado
Died September 14, 1957, in Denver, Colorado

Edwina Hume Fallis was born in a large brick house at West Fourteenth and Acoma Streets, site of the present Denver Public Library and Art Museum in Denver's Civic Center. Her maternal grandfather,

Daniel Hurd, was a pioneer Denver grocer who served as president of the Denver school board. With such a grandfather, it was not surprising that Edwina Fallis became an exemplary Denver Public Schools product, an outstanding teacher, and a creator of story book characters and story books that enriched many children's lives.

After graduating from East Denver High School and earning a degree from Colorado State College of Education, she attended the University of Denver and Columbia University. She then studied advanced teaching in Chicago. Back in Denver, she went to work as an assistant in a kindergarten. Her official career as kindergarten teacher began in the Gilpin School and continued at Whittier and Lincoln Schools. A dedicated teacher, she taught many pupils who later became city and state leaders.

In "Tell Me a Story," an article that appeared in June 1941 in *Page,* the Denver Woman's Press Club publication, Edwina Fallis wrote that it was her job as a teacher to help children listen to and tell stories. This task was easy if there were only a few children, if they had been read to since babyhood, and if they came from homes where books were as common as bread, she noted. But unless the weather was inclement or many children were ill, her kindergarten group was never that small. There were always some children (especially those standing in the back or those unfamiliar with books) who could neither understand the story nor relate it back to her. Edwina decided to devise toys that would help those children visualize the story.

To help kindergartners imagine the happenings in "The Three Billy Goats Gruff," for example, Edwina Fallis lifted the three goats, the troll, and the bridge off the printed page and made toys of them. The figures and the bridge were made out of three-quarter-inch wood so the children could grasp them easily. Then she mounted them on firm stands so a child with poor coordination could place and move them easily. A child could stand Gruff on the bridge long enough for the troll to challenge him and for Gruff to "knock the sassy troll into the middle of next week," according to Edwina Fallis.

Working with the toy characters, the child created a story that may—or may not—have been the author's intention, which gave the teacher a good idea of the pupil's comprehension. The story toys were so popular that Edwina Fallis added figures from "Goldilocks and the Three Bears," "Chicken Little," "The Three Little Pigs," and other children's classics.

Kindergartners soon were mixing figures from several stories, and then creating stories of their own, which gave her the idea of adding figures of wild animals and their young, wagons, automobiles, trains, airplanes. Eventually, there were eighty different figures illustrating more than twenty-five stories. When she was convinced of their educational value, she decided to put her story toys on the market.

With financing from her family, Edwina and her sister, Belle Fallis, opened the Fallis Toy Shop. Edwina decided which toys to make and Belle designed them. But manufacturing the toys proved arduous and costly. So Edwina Fallis wrote *The Child and Things,* a book that featured their story toys. She took a copy to a convention of the Association for Childhood Education in Milwaukee. There, a manufacturer of educational toys saw the book and contracted with the Judy Company of Minneapolis to manufacture the toys and pay royalties to the Fallis Toy Shop of Denver.

As an educator, Edwina Fallis wrote textbooks and articles for teachers. After forty-two years as a kindergarten teacher, she retired and turned to writing children's stories for *Child Life* magazine. She published 100 poems, some of them selected for anthologies. Edwina Fallis was recovering from a heart attack when she began writing *When Denver and I Were Young,* a charming children's book in which she related her memories of growing up in Denver. The narrative covers the years from 1876 to 1890, when irrigation ditches watered wildflowers growing in vacant lots throughout the city. It depicts typical happenings in the everyday life of a middle-class Denver family living in a big house on Acoma Street.

Edwina described how as a child she got around town by taking horse-drawn cars, hitching rides on the family grocery wagon and, of course, on foot. She recalled the old gravity streetcar, the first gas illumination and electric lights in town, Hangman's Tree in Valverde, River Front Park along the South Platte River, and the opening of

Elitch Gardens. Of particular appeal to children is her portrayal of close-knit family life in early Denver and her accounts of women preserving locally grown fruits and vegetables and patching their clothes until they wore too thin even for patches. In one episode, Edwina relates her encounter, when she was a schoolgirl, with Baby Doe, the second Mrs. Tabor, at McNamara's Store on California Street.

> When Edwina reached McNamara's Store with her grandmother and aunt, she called their attention to a beautiful carriage all lined with baby-blue.
>
> "That's Baby Doe's carriage. She's probably in McNamara's Store now. We'd better not go in, had we?" whispered Aunt Carrie.
>
> "If I want anything in this store I'll not let that woman keep me out. Edwina's grandmother stuck her nose up, lifted her long skirts, and swept into the store.[1]

In her story, Edwina wrote that she hung back to see the "beautiful golden-haired lady," who wore baby-blue satin that matched the lining of her carriage parked out in front of the store. Baby Doe held a baby girl wearing a long dress "made of real lace." According to the story, Grandmother marched Edwina outside and she wondered aloud why Grandmother lifted her skirts as she swished past Mrs. Tabor—after letting them drag over the filthy sidewalk. Her story inadvertently reveals Old Denver's attitude toward the famous belle who won Silver King H.A.W. Tabor from his popular first wife, Augusta.

Edwina's book quickly sold out and went through a second edition. Another of her books, *The Coverlet,* is about a quilt that her grandmother made and brought with her by covered wagon into the western frontiers of Ohio and, eventually, to Colorado. Many of her poems have been published in anthologies. She wrote *Poetry to Read Aloud,* a book for teachers; a filmstrip put out by the Society for Visual Education; and a book published in Braille.

Always active in public life, Edwina Fallis served on the Fox Street Community Center Board, where she instituted "Gollywoggle Sales" for children. She was a president of Denver Woman's Press Club and also belonged to the Colorado Author's League, the Territorial Daughters of Colorado, and the Colorado Historical Society.

Edwina Hume Fallis never married. She died September 14, 1957, at her Denver home and was buried at Riverside Cemetery. She was eighty. After her death, Denver named the Edwina Hume Fallis Elementary School after her as a tribute to her contributions to education.

The Bonfils Sisters

As heirs to the *Denver Post* fortune, May and Helen Bonfils (pronounced Bon´-fees) were among the richest women in the West. They lived in the same house, same city, and received similar educations. Yet no two sisters could have been more different.

May, six years older than Helen, studied art and music in Europe. She shunned the local limelight in favor of annual treks abroad, where she bought priceless antiques and art works. In Lakewood, she secluded herself in her estate—a replica of Le Petit Trianon—which she named Belmar, and surrounded herself in luxury. In her will, she made generous bequests to Lakewood and Colorado.

Helen, popularly called "Miss Helen," lived in the family mansion at Tenth and Humboldt Streets until 1947. She inherited the *Denver Post* and took a strong role in its management. Quite the opposite of her sister, Helen was drawn like a moth to the footlights. She acted and produced plays in two Denver theaters, where she was well known and well liked. Whereas May said, "The Twentieth Century doesn't exist,"[1] Helen was a dominant force in twentieth-century Denver.

Nevertheless, some aspects of their lives were surprisingly similar. Late in life—May was 73, Helen was 47—both women married men who were years younger. Neither sister had children. As a result, Denver and Colorado became their beneficiaries. Today, the Bonfils sisters are celebrated for their priceless and enduring gifts to their city and state.

May Bonfils Stanton

Born April 30, 1883, in Troy, Missouri
Died March 11, 1962, in Lakewood, Colorado

May Bonfils was about twelve years old when the Frederick G. Bonfils family moved from Missouri to Denver. The year was 1895 and Bonfils and Harry Heye Tammen had just bought a small Democratic newspaper, which they renamed the *Denver Post.*

The Bonfils family lived in a somber stone mansion at 1003 Corona Street. May attended St. Mary's Academy and the Miss Wolcott School. Bonfils' wife, Belle, was a strict Catholic, who raised May and Helen accordingly. Papa Bonfils was a tyrant, particularly with his elder daughter, May. He discouraged both sisters from going out with young men because, he said, the boys were only after their money. After May's graduation from Brownell Hall in New York City, her father took her to Europe, where she studied French, art, and music, and became an accomplished pianist and composer. Her father's claim that the Bonfils family was distantly related to Napoleon Bonaparte became a lifelong fascination for her.

Tight paternal reins may have been a factor that prompted May to elope in 1904—all the way to Golden, with a non-Catholic sheet music salesman named Clyde Berryman, who worked for the Wells Music Company. It was rumored that Papa Bonfils was so outraged that he refused to release her belongings and threatened, unless she divorced Berryman, to reduce her inheritance by half. From that time on, May's relationship with her family grew increasingly strained. Younger sister Helen, fifteen, was said to have aggravated the rift, which had long-reaching consequences. May and Clyde Berryman later separated and May paid him a salary to stay away, but it was not until 1947 that she went to Reno, declaring cruelty, nonsupport, and desertion as grounds for a quickie divorce. May even had her maiden restored, but her family never forgave her.

Frederick Bonfils died in 1933, followed two years later by Belle. They left a trust for May, with provisions for her to live on its $25,000 annual income. But Helen inherited millions of dollars plus her father's *Denver Post* stock. Devastated by this glaring snub, May sued the Bonfils estate for her share of the inheritance. After a long trial, she won half of Belle's $10 million estate, 15 percent of the newspaper stock, some cash, and some real estate. Helen, who controlled the *Post*, then decreed that May's name be banned from the newspaper's pages except for uncomplimentary remarks. By the trial's end, the sisters' estrangement was beyond repair.

In Denver, May Bonfils seldom was seen in public. She had her friends, but one writer called her capricious, self-centered, and strong-willed. Virtually a recluse and certainly a woman of mystery, she also was devoutly religious and philanthropic. The family chauffeur, Robert Stouffer, saw a softer, gentler side of May's personality.

May Bonfils had inherited 10 acres near what is now Kountze Lake at Wadsworth and Alameda boulevards in Lakewood. Through the years, she increased that holding into a 750-acre estate. Some say it was after she had been ostracized by Helen and Denver society that May decided to build a lavish home to outshine their Denver mansions.

She engaged the Beaux Arts architect Jules Jacques Benois Benedict to design a replica of Le Petit Trianon Palace (built by Louis XV at Versailles in France). Work got under way in 1937 on May's white, twenty-room Carrara marble palace. She named her million-dollar estate Belmar by combining her mother's name, Belle, and Mary, from which her own name, May, is derived. The approach to Belmar's entrance was a long, straight drive west from Wadsworth Boulevard. A tall, antique fountain gurgled near the entrance. (The fountain can be seen today at Hungarian Freedom Park along Speer Boulevard east of Broadway.) Inside, just off the Carrara marble foyer with its curving staircase, was May's pink marble chapel, where she often prayed and meditated. Presumably, she had her teeth cleaned in the fully equipped dental office, also near the foyer.

To furnish Belmar and add to her collections, she made annual trips to Europe where she toured palaces and museums and shopped at galleries for antiques, art treasures, rare dolls, and fabulous jewelry. She brought back a Marie-Antoinette bed, a piano said to have been played by Chopin, and a gold chair bearing Queen Victoria's crest.

The estate was a private paradise. Swans floated on Grassmere Lake, peacocks paraded on the lawns, and herds of sheep and deer grazed behind the barns. She raised prize Suffolk and Hampshire sheep and kept pet dogs. A caretaker's house was south of the big house. May Bonfils rarely left home, but entertained her friends at small dinner parties. Rather uncharacteristically, she would take her chauffeur to sip a Coke at the Lewis Drug Store, 8490 West Colfax (no longer in existence), while she checked out the latest cosmetics.

When May Bonfils was involved with the Central City Opera Company, she set up a fund to care for the little garden next to the Teller House. At that time, she met Charles E. Stanton, the interior designer and architect who was restoring the Teller House. After a long friendship, May proposed to Stanton, reportedly so he could help her manage Belmar. She added that he would have to marry her to keep Helen from getting any of her estate. They married in the spring of 1956 in ceremonies at Presentation Catholic Church in Denver. He was forty-six; she was seventy-three. When the Stantons were in Rome in 1961, they renewed their vows and received the Pope's blessing.

Many stories have been told of the Stanton's legendary lifestyle. In 1959, the Stanton garage boasted a new $20,000 Rolls Royce, the costliest car ever sold in Colorado. It took six months to build the car—an exclusive Silver Cloud model—which was shipped from England through Mexico to Denver. May owned one of the finest jewelry collections in the nation. Her 70.2-carat diamond, the Idol's Eye, was one of the world's great diamonds. (After her death, it was auctioned for only $375,000.) One of her great delights was her exquisite doll collection.

During May's later years, the Stantons drew up arrangements for the Villa Italia Shopping Center on their land east of Wadsworth. Stanton later donated 1.5 acres east of the shopping center for the Bonfils-Stanton Library (now Villa Library). Still more of her land would be used for Belmar Museum and Belmar Park. In a final transaction, almost a vendetta, May sold her *Denver Post* stock holdings on June 9, 1960, to newspaper magnate Samuel I. Newhouse for a reported sum of $3,533,765. She stipulated that the stock never be sold to her sister. The unexpected stock sale set in motion a series of costly lawsuits as Newhouse maneuvered to gain control of the *Post*.

On March 11, 1962, after a three-week illness, May Bonfils Stanton died at home in the bed where Marie-Antoinette once slept. She was almost seventy-nine. In accordance with her will, she was buried in the Bonfils family mausoleum at Fairmount Cemetery. Then a codicil to the will was found, directing that she be buried at Mt. Olivet Cemetery, and her remains were moved there.

The *Post* mentioned her passing only in a terse funeral notice. She left a $13 million estate, half of it going to Stanton. This included the Belmar mansion plus 10 surrounding acres—unless he remarried; in that case, it would go to the Denver Catholic Archdiocese. Stanton soon found the upkeep and handyman work, which he did himself, to be more than he could handle. He handed Belmar over to the Church. But the Church could not find a use befitting the terms of the will. May Bonfils Stanton's exquisite Belmar was turned over to the wreckers in the fall of 1970.

May Bonfils gave generously from her personal inheritance to charitable and civic causes almost beyond count. The list includes the creation of the Clinic of Ophthalmology at the University of Colorado Medical Center, the library and auditorium of Loretto Heights College, the Bonfils Wing at the Denver Museum of Natural History, and the interior decor of the Catholic Chapel at the U.S. Air Force Academy. Before her death, May Bonfils had been a generous contributor to St. Elizabeth Catholic Church in Denver. In her will, she left half of her estate in trust for the church's Franciscan Religious Order, with proceeds to be spent in Denver "for schools, hospitals, and any comfort to the sick or poor."

After May's death, her sister had to join the *Post* in a long court fight against Newhouse to retain local control. In December 1972, the court ruled in their favor. But the twelve-year trial had drained away funds necessary for the newspaper's continued operation. The *Denver Post* was sold in December 1980 to the Times-Mirror Company.

The Bonfils-Stanton Foundation was incorporated by Stanton, his brother, Robert, and Albert Zarlengo. After Charles Stanton's death, his inheritance was added to the foundation and by 1997, its value had grown from $6.5 million to $44 million. Among the Foundation's beneficiaries were the purchase of the land for Lakewood Municipal Center, the Lakewood Arts Council, Red Rocks Community College, Hospice of St. John, Cenikor, the Boy Scouts, the Girl Scouts, the Eleanor Roosevelt Institute for Cancer Research, and countless charities.

The tragedy of the Bonfils sisters lies in their years-long estrangement, sparked decades earlier by the senior Bonfils's anger over May's elopement and perpetuated by the sisters' rivalries. In the end, as lonely old women in wretched health, the sisters denied themselves the comfort and support they otherwise might have received from one another.

Helen Bonfils

Born November 16, 1889, in Peekskill, New York
Died June 6, 1972, in Denver, Colorado

Helen and her older sister, May, ranked among the richest women in the West. Their seemingly inexhaustible fortune was an inheritance from their father, Frederick Gilmer Bonfils, co-founder and considered by many, ruthless editor of the *Denver Post*.

The Bonfils family moved to Denver in 1895, after F. G. and his partner, Harry Heye Tammen, bought a shaky Democratic sheet, the *Denver Evening Post*, on October 28, 1895. The partners quickly developed the weak weekly into one of journalism's most flamboyant and, eventually, most influential dailies.

At the start, it was not all reflected glory for Bonfils's daughters, Helen and May. From their first home at 1003 Corona Street, the girls attended the Miss Wolcott School, an elite private girls' school. Helen, a bright, pretty girl with blonde hair, was often snubbed by her classmates, whose fathers had been burned in business dealings with her father. She went on to finishing school at the National Park Seminary in Maryland.

Helen, later the favored daughter, inherited her father's keen business sense and determination. Often, she was referred to as Papa's Little

Girl. Bonfils, however, was unreasonably strict with the girls, especially May. They were not allowed to date because, as Papa said, the boys were only out for their money. When they did get to leave the house, they had orders to be home by nine o'clock. In 1904, when she was only twenty-one, May eloped with Clyde Berryman, a non-Catholic sheet music salesman. Her family never got over it, even after the Berrymans separated and finally divorced. May was deeply hurt by the family estrangement, which sister Helen tended to aggravate.

The Bonfils family moved in 1918 to the Leopold Guldman mansion at the corner of Tenth and Humboldt Streets. Bordering Cheesman Park on the west, it was the most graceful house on a street of imposing residences. The household was maintained by a cook and a laundress; Nelson, the yard man; Fannie, Helen's maid; and Robert Stouffer, the chauffeur, who was on call twenty-four hours a day and whose family lived in four rooms above the garage. His daughter, Betty Stouffer, remembers how beautiful and lavish the Bonfils house was. Goldfish swam in their pond in the solarium. Helen's bedroom at the top of the great staircase was ornately furnished (as were all the bedrooms). In the basement were a swimming pool, bowling alley, and a theater with a miniature stage and piano, where Helen loved to present plays for friends and neighbors. A dark, spooky tunnel with dirt walls connected the house and garage.

Betty had the opportunity to see the family from a unique perspective. She thought Frederick Bonfils was a startlingly handsome man. The family charmer, with his rich, mellow voice, he caused heads to turn whenever he entered a room. He was kind to the servants and loved dogs. Belle, his wife, was very retiring, meek, and less polished. "She lived in his shadow. We never got to know her well," Betty said.[1]

Betty always liked May. "She was kind and gentle, and she gave so generously of own inheritance money to many charities. Miss Helen, as she liked to be called, was sad inside, even bitter," Betty recalled. "But she was close to Robert, often confiding her dreams of being in the theater. A statuesque blonde, she was quite glamorous in her theatrical makeup, spike heels, elaborate hats, and stage clothes."[2] Helen and her mother, Belle, often entertained celebrities who came to town, but otherwise they did not mingle much in Denver society.

At his death in 1933, Bonfils left Helen $14 million. He also left the Frederick G. Bonfils Foundation for the Betterment of Mankind. Two years later, when Belle Bonfils died, Helen came into yet another $10 million plus the *Denver Post* stock, the Bonfils's Humboldt Street mansion—in any era, an inconceivable fortune. May was devastated to learn she had been virtually excluded from the will except for a $25,000 annual allowance. She sued the estate in a bitter, three-year trial. At its conclusion, May received some cash from F. G. Bonfils's estate, $5 million from Belle's estate, 15 percent of Bonfils's newspaper stock, and some real estate. The trial widened the sisters' early rift to a chasm and they stopped speaking to each other.

When Helen Bonfils gained control of the *Denver Post*, she took over the management as secretary-treasurer. William Shepherd, editor until 1946, was followed by editor and publisher Palmer Hoyt. In 1966, she was named president and later chairman of the newspaper.

But Helen's first love was the theater and all Denver was her stage. She graduated from her little plays in the basement to an acting career with Elitch Stock Theater. She also was active in the Civic Theater, then at the University of Denver.

In 1934, Helen Bonfils launched what became one of her favorite projects: *Denver Post* open-air, summer performances of Broadway hits or light operas. She chose the Cheesman Park Pavilion, with its incomparable scenery, for the setting. She recruited Broadway stars to play lead roles and locals to fill other parts for the one- or two-week runs. As many as 20,000 Coloradans attended each performance, free. The *Post* continued this annual event until her death.

A tall woman with a husky voice, Helen was theatrical, aggressive, intelligent—and rich. On October 14, 1953, the $1.25 million Bonfils Memorial Theatre opened at Colfax at Elizabeth Streets. Built in her parents' memory as the new home for the Denver Civic Theatre, it could seat up to 550 at plays, operas, movies, concerts, lectures, and television productions. Bonfils Theatre gained a reputation until 1984 for presenting the best drama in Denver. Helen played many roles there and also on the New York stage, where she was most successful as a theatrical producer. Denver dancer Cleo Parker Robinson, who "grew up" backstage at the Bonfils Theatre, where her father was manager for many years and her mother made costumes, remembers Helen as "The Star. She was wonderful—everyone loved her!"[3]

Later, Helen assumed management of Elitch's Theater and it was on stage at little Elitch's where Helen met George Somnes, the new Elitch producer, when she was forty-seven. They became co-producers and Helen played supporting roles. She had great fun supplying her own clothing, furs, and jewelry as costumes. Her carpets and furniture became props. In fact, her costumes and props were in more plays than she was. Helen and Somnes were married in November 1947.

She sold the Humboldt Street mansion around 1947 and they moved to the Wood-Morris House, a fifteen-room French Mediterranean mansion at 707 Washington Street. The couple always was referred to as Helen Bonfils and George Somnes, in that order. Although Helen was years older than Somnes, they appeared to be contentedly married until his death less than nine years later, on February 8, 1956. After Somnes's death, Helen was so lonely that she took up with her chauffeur, Edward Michael "Tiger Mike" Davis. On April 2, 1959, the sixty-nine-year-old heiress married the chauffeur who was then twenty-eight.

Helen's sister, May, would have the last word in their bitter, years-long feud. On June 9, 1960, May sold her *Denver Post* stock to newspaper magnate Samuel Newhouse. The only stipulation was that Newhouse would never sell May's stock to Helen. With that, Newhouse started maneuvering to take over the paper. Determined to keep the *Post*'s ownership local, Helen took Newhouse to court. She hired scores of lawyers and hung on through a bitter, twelve-year court battle.

Yet another lawsuit awaited Helen. After twelve years of marriage to Tiger Mike, she reluctantly obtained a divorce in 1971—concerned, perhaps, over what rights Michael Davis might have to her estate. She got her own name back. He got her Washington Street mansion and other benefits.

Helen's health was failing. She spent most of her last six years at St. Joseph Hospital, where she took over the entire top floor. She died on June 6, 1972. She was eighty-two.

Six months after her death, in December 1972, the U.S. Court of

Appeals overruled the district court, ending Newhouse's efforts to control the newspaper. The final verdict awarded Helen Bonfils a "victory" that cost $5 million in attorneys' fees. Helen Bonfils had been a powerful and able leader for the *Post*. Ironically, it was the sisters' feud that would break the Bonfils's newspaper dynasty. The Newhouse legal battle had impoverished the *Post* beyond recovery. In June 1980, the newspaper was obliged to negotiate its sale to the Times Mirror Company of Los Angeles for $95 million. The sale was completed in December 1980.[4]

Helen Bonfils's will provided an enormous legacy for Denver. "Helen Bonfils wanted to create a foundation to finance a theatrical center," said her attorney, Lester Ward, who helped set up her estate. "She brought Donald Seawell to Denver to run the *Post* and also to create a plan for concentrating the family foundations to create the Denver Center for the Performing Arts [DCPA]."[5] Eventually, it would be a cultural complex covering four square blocks in downtown Denver, a leading force in the city's downtown revival. By the 1990s, the performing arts center, connected by a high, overarching glass roof, consisted of eight theaters with a total of 9,000 seats—the nation's largest performing arts center in terms of venues, with the country's finest repertory theater. In 1998, DCPA was awarded a Tony for being the nation's greatest regional theater complex.

Monumental as the center is, it hardly surpasses the value and importance of the Belle Bonfils Blood Bank, which Helen endowed on February 28, 1943, in memory of her mother. Now self-supporting, the blood bank supplies life-giving blood on a 24-hour basis to people in the Rocky Mountain region. Her foundations also supported the University of Denver, the Denver Symphony Orchestra, and many Catholic churches.

The Bonfils sisters had no heirs to inherit their wealth. In the end, they bequeathed their inheritance to their city in the form of farseeing investments that continue to flower and grow. Denver and Colorado will remember Helen Bonfils for her generosity and wise planning, which endowed scholarships, built churches and hospitals, supported countless charities, and created great theaters for the performing arts.

Josephine Aspenwall Roche

Born December 2, 1886, in Neligh, Nebraska
Died July 29, 1976, in Bethesda, Maryland

Josephine Roche was born with a steel spoon in her mouth. Some considered her a radical, but many others thought of her as a reformer. Her lifelong passions never strayed far from labor politics and America's emerging Progressive Movement.

By the time she was twelve, she showed signs of becoming an independent thinker. As the story is told, she went with her father, John J. Roche, a wealthy banker and investor, to inspect a coal mine owned by the Rocky Mountain Fuel Company, of which he was treasurer. Josephine wanted to go into the mine shaft, but her father said, "No! It's too dangerous." "Then how is it safe for the miners?" she asked, with a child's logic. He did not answer. Roche, who had moved to Denver in 1906, was—like the other mine owners—strongly pro-management and militantly anti-union.

Josephine entered Vassar in 1904 and spent her summers volunteering for the New York juvenile court. She went on to earn a master's degree in social work at Columbia University in 1910. Her thesis, "Economic Conditions in Relation to the Delinquency of Girls," was a preview to her lifelong political philosophy. Josephine was studying for finals when a letter came from George Creel, a *Rocky Mountain News* reporter who was serving as Denver city commissioner at the time. He offered her a job as Denver's first police woman. Specifically, she would serve as "inspector of amusements," a fancy job title for walking the night beat to oversee Denver's dance halls and protect children on the streets and in movie houses from prostitution. The Denver of 1910 gave the appearance of a beautiful, prosperous city; but hidden away from the public eye were decaying neighborhoods, back streets of prostitution, and neighborhoods where poverty-stricken immigrants died of illness. Denver politics was dominated by bosses and rings "out for the buck," while infighting was hamstringing the Progressives.

In 1911, Thomas Patterson, owner of the *News*, assigned Creel to publicize a newspaper campaign to clean up Denver. Creel then organized a task force headed by the "kids' judge," Benjamin Lindsey, and including Edward P. Costigan (later a U.S. senator), writer William MacLeod Raine, and Josephine Roche. Their immediate objective was to dethrone Denver Mayor Robert W. Speer in the coming election. The *Denver Post* and wealthy Colorado corporations fought the Creel slate, but the Progressives still managed to unseat Mayor Speer. They surprised everyone by installing Speer's former lawyer Henry J. Arnold in his place as mayor. Patterson's liberals succeeded in shutting down the houses of prostitution on Market Street and Creel ran out the prostitutes. Then the Progressives' new Mayor Arnold fired George Creel in 1913.

Officer Roche was still working to remove the entertainment district's "entertainment." Apparently, she was too successful. The Fire and Police Board terminated her contract two months later, saying she was bad for business. She went before the Civil Service Commission to contest her dismissal and won back her job. The next day, she resigned to become a probation officer under Benjamin Lindsey, who had acquired an international reputation for his work with young offenders.

Hardly bigger than "a kid" himself (he was five feet, five inches tall and weighed 100 pounds), Ben Lindsey devoted himself to working with juveniles. He had originated Denver's Juvenile Court in 1899. The first of his kind, Judge Lindsey's court was recognized nationally and has continued in Denver for a century as a separate court system, where youngsters are tried as juveniles, not as adults. As a probation officer, Josephine Roche dealt with juveniles and underprivileged clients.

Under Judge Lindsey's influence, she eventually settled upon labor politics as her lifelong profession. She got her first bitter taste of labor politics at Ludlow, a coal-mining camp between Trinidad and Walsenburg, which was owned by the Colorado Fuel and Iron Company (CF&I), the largest, most powerful coal company in the state. The treatment of miners and other workers brought on a strike in 1910, which died down and then flamed up anew in April 1914. To control a volatile situation, the governor called out the National Guard. But young National Guard recruits fired on striking miners, destroyed their tent colony, and killed miners, women, and children.

Josephine Roche hurried to Ludlow to assist the miners' grieving families. She recruited a group of CF&I miners' wives and escorted them to New York City to testify before the U.S. Industrial Relations Commission. The Ludlow Massacre, as it became known, created a scandal that never faded from Colorado history. The only positive result was that CF&I and its coal producers instituted better conditions for workers and fostered a period of labor-management peace.

During World War I, Josephine Roche was called to Washington and assigned to England as special agent for the Belgian Relief Committee. Next, she organized a Belgian relief drive in New York, New Hampshire, and Vermont under Herbert Hoover (who was director of President Woodrow Wilson's Food Administration). In her next assignment, she created the Foreign Language Information Service, which supplied accurate American news translated for the American foreign language press. In 1922, she was the editor of the U.S. Children's Bureau in Washington. On behalf of the Russell Sage Foundation, she campaigned against child labor in the sugar beet industry.

Josephine Roche returned to Denver in 1925 because of her father's declining health. As president of Rocky Mountain Fuel Company (RMF), John Roche had been a "hard-bitten, union-hating man." But when it came to Josephine, he was surprisingly liberal. The two always kept in close touch until his death in 1927. Nonetheless, Josephine must have considered it ironic when she inherited her father's minority stock in RMF. At forty-one, she had become a leading Progressive Liberal and labor advocate in Colorado. Her work in behalf of labor was well known in the east. Suddenly she was sitting on the management side of the bargaining table. She saw the situation as an extraordinary opportunity to put her labor beliefs into practice.

Roche deplored the company's policies of low pay, deteriorating company housing, company stores, and poor sanitary conditions. She resolved to institute a more cooperative management and to improve the treatment of employees. She hoped to avoid conflicts like the one that occurred in November 1927, when state troopers were called in during an RMF miners' strike. In the skirmish, troopers killed six miners and wounded sixty.

Although she did not own a controlling interest and the board disagreed with her labor views, she got the company to hire her liberal colleague, Merle Vincent, as manager. She quietly bought up company shares and, by March 1928, she owned sufficient stock to control RMF. To the horror of other mine owners, she named Vincent president of the company, brought in a labor organizer as vice president, and invited the United Mine Workers (UMW) to unionize her mines. RMF was the first western coal company to sign a union contract and pay its miners an unheard of $7 a day. Under her management, RMF began to flourish until it had moved to second place among Colorado coal producers.

But RMF's competitors, led by John Rockefeller's giant CF&I, started a price war to drive RMF out of business. As they cut their prices below cost, RMF sales plunged. Roche's miners came to her rescue and lent her $80,000 to keep operating. The miners demonstrated with signs and banners that said, "Buy Josephine's Coal." In return, she gave them surface land above the mines, on which they could grow crops to feed their families. Other forces joined the conspiracy against RMF. The depression caused all coal prices to drop. Then a ready supply of natural gas entered the market, heralding even harder times for coal mining. During those years, Roche did not take a salary.

But if one opportunity lagged for her, a new one always surfaced. Her former ally, Edward Costigan, was elected to the U.S. Senate and Roche figured the time was ripe for her to challenge Governor Ed C. Johnson. She ran on the slogan "Roosevelt, Roche, and Recovery!" but she lost to Governor Johnson in the bitter Democratic primary of 1934. Three days after the election, President Franklin Roosevelt invited her to serve in his cabinet as assistant secretary of the Treasury and to oversee the U.S. Public Health Service. Josephine Roche and her Vassar friend, Secretary of Labor Frances Perkins, were among the first women to serve in a presidential Cabinet.

Back in Colorado, the Rocky Mountain Fuel Company was continuing to decline. The United Mine Workers lent her $450,000 to stay afloat and RMF hung on until the 1940s, when the company went into trusteeship. Roche was named an assistant to John L. Lewis, head of the UMW, in 1947. Until she retired, she was a director of the UMW welfare fund.

Josephine Roche returned once more to Colorado to organize her personal papers, which she donated to the University of Colorado's Norlin Library. She lived her final years in a Washington, D.C., apartment and died in Bethesda, Maryland, on July 29, 1976, at age eighty-nine.

In her almost ninety years, Josephine Roche, whom an interviewer once described as "a tiny wisp of a woman whose eyes snap behind tinted glasses and whose face mirrors an ever-changing series of moods," accomplished much. She was the first policewoman in Colorado, the first woman to run a major coal company, and the second woman to serve in a presidential cabinet. Among a host of honors that came to her, Josephine Roche was named America's most prominent businesswoman. She received many honorary college degrees. Eleanor Roosevelt called her one of America's great women, and she was selected by Chi Omega Sorority as one of the ten outstanding American women of 1936. But no one ever appreciated Josephine Roche more than those embattled Rocky Mountain Fuel Company miners.

Eudochia Bell Smith

Born September 9, 1887, in San Antonio, Texas*
Died September 23, 1977, in Denver, Colorado

Eudochia Bell Smith was successful in three careers during a lifetime that spanned ninety years. In each of these careers—as a newspaper editor, a Colorado legislator, and director of a federal agency, she was always involved in the arena of public affairs.

Eudochia Bell was born on September 9, 1887, in San Antonio, Texas, and attended Ursuline Academy and San Antonio High School. As a popular debutante, she eased into the position of society editor for the *San Antonio Express*. She soon developed into a crack reporter whose feature stories were syndicated. In 1910, she moved to the *Houston Chronicle* as associate editor.

In 1909, Eudochia met Joseph Emerson Smith, who until recently had been a news editor at the *San Antonio Express*. Starting as a cub reporter with the *Denver Post*, he built an illustrious journalism career. He moved to the *Rocky Mountain News* as city editor, and then on to the *Denver Republican* as a writer. As a young reporter, Smith had interviewed such colorful Colorado pioneers as H.A.W. Tabor, D. H. Moffat, and three governors. His Colorado history lectures were in high demand. But by 1911, he was in San Antonio recuperating from overwork.

Smith and Eudochia Bell found they shared many common interests, including a love of writing. They were married February 22, 1911. Because of Smith's affection for Colorado, the couple moved to Denver in 1920. She concentrated on freelance writing until 1926; then she joined the *Rocky Mountain News* as women's department editor. She also taught writing at the University of Denver and founded the Catholic Press Club of Colorado.

One day, she was sent to cover a forum that would change her life. The panel members were discussing revelations of intolerable conditions described by boys who had run away from the State Industrial School in Golden. Bell was horrified by what she heard. "It is a shadow on American life that our delinquent youth must be prisoned in such an unsavory place," she said. "The state must be responsible for a better planned program for their care."[1] When she looked further into conditions at the industrial school, she decided that the drastic changes needed could be made only by the legislature. Eudochia Smith later credited the tragic interviews of her newspaper career with bringing "all those heartaches ... to my stoop" and for goading her into politics. "The germ from a quarter-century newspaper work began marshalling memories before me ... an insistent demand for improvement."[2]

She announced her candidacy for the Colorado House of Representatives on the Democratic ticket. With that, Eudochia plunged into the political world of eight or ten campaign meetings a night. Often she waited through hours of speeches to give her own ten-minute talk. A plump Southern woman wearing saucy hats that she became famous for, she clumped in high heels door-to-door through her Denver district and explained her mandate to enact legislation for an overhaul of the industrial school. In November 1936, Eudochia was elected to the House by a wide majority and the next January she climbed the steps of the state capitol under a new name: Smith of Denver.

She began by inviting Father Edward Flanagan of Boys Town, Nebraska, to investigate the school. Using his findings, she wrote a bill offering a three-point remedy: improve the parole system, institute cottages with a homier atmosphere, and have service clubs appoint a Big Brother for each of the boys. Her new law took a significant first step in dealing with juvenile delinquency. She came to believe that "laws affecting the welfare of women and children need the feel of a woman's handclasp, her guidance and protection."[3] This belief would propel Smith of Denver through four consecutive terms in the Colorado legislature.

In another early effort, she tackled the issue of food service regulations. As a neophyte legislator, she made her maiden speech in its behalf and came up against unforeseen, well-heeled lobbyists. Although restaurants at that time were governed by strict sanitation laws, there were few regulations on lunch counters, makeshift facilities in office building halls, wayside hamburger joints, and boarding houses. Eudochia Smith's proposed legislation would require costly changes in office buildings and other places that served food, especially in regard to sanitary requirements for washing dishes.

Smith recognized her strong opposition. She was a woman in a man's realm. She saw the well-paid lobbyist seated at the back and male legislators reading material other than the restaurant bill. Then she remembered how she handled her husband, not by trying to force him but by using straight talk from the shoulder. Weren't these men, after all, a "collective husband"? She held out her hands, palms up. "I am a good cook," she began in her soft Southern voice. Having caught their attention, she went on to describe big office buildings where meals were cooked in impromptu and unsanitary places (next to elevator shafts and over cigar counters, for example), passersby coughed near food, and cooking smells permeated the buildings. During the debate, protests poured in from powerful constituents and her restaurant bill was hotly opposed. But her bill passed and it set much-needed sanitary standards for small lunch counters.

Smith of Denver co-sponsored Colorado's groundbreaking Smith-Hornbaker Old Age Pension Bill, which would pay $45 a month to eligible, elderly Coloradans. A battery of state lawyers and officials worked with lawmakers for weeks to research and write the bill before it was introduced; then the general public discussed it, pro and con, until it finally passed. Another Smith bill focused on birth certificates that were stamped with the word "Illegitimate," inflicting a lifelong stigma on illegitimate children and anguish to adoptive families. Smith conducted extensive research and then sponsored a bill to remove the stigma of illegitimacy from birth certificates and adoption papers.

Male constituents deluged Smith—the only woman in the House— with pleas to introduce legislation to outlaw frivolous breach of promise suits. Her "heart balm" bill provided remedying legislation and assured her everlasting popularity among male voters. To pass the Colorado law against abuses by loan sharks, she contended against the most formidable of all lobbyists.

Smith earned such a strong reputation in the House that she was elected to the state Senate in 1944, becoming the third woman to serve there and the *only* woman in the Senate for twenty-five years. As a freshman senator in 1944, she introduced one of the hardest-fought bills ever passed in the Colorado Senate: the one to allow women to sit on juries. The influential League of Women Voters, the Business and Professional Women's Club, and the State Federation of Women's Clubs had written and lobbied for the bill, which was an amendment to the original Women's Suffrage Clause of the state constitution. Several times before, it had come up and gone down to defeat. Now thousands of Colorado women centered their energy upon this one issue. On the day of the debate, the League of Women Voters placed brochures on every lawmaker's desk. Members of the Business and Professional Women's Club buttonholed uncommitted senators. An hour before the debate, women marched to the Capitol to fill all available seats on the floor and most of the balcony.

Eudochia had planned a quiet, reasoning opening. That approach lasted three minutes. She was stunned at the furious response to her bill, which looked like it would be defeated by thirty-three male votes. "Women are too emotional to sit on a jury!" shouted a Western Slope senator. "It must be defeated." A lawyer legislator jumped up and shook his finger: "You and your kind are responsible for juvenile delinquency. A housewife should be in the home all the time. ... Don't encourage any more bread-winner women. ... Keep the home and those within it safe. Defeat this measure!"[4] The farmers block protested: Who wants to build ladies' restrooms in wartime? Extra sleeping quarters for women jurors would cost money, manpower, lumber. Women jurors have no place in wartime.

Meanwhile, Senator Smith was receiving terse, supporting notes from the women's quarter. She must not let them down. Before an audience of angry, red-faced male legislators, Eudochia stepped to the microphone to close her arguments. She looked up to the balcony, at the women from the League of Women Voters, the Business and Professional Women's Club, and the State Federation of Women's Clubs—women who had worked long and hard to pass this bill.

"You gentlemen of the Colorado Assembly," Eudochia began in her soft Southern accent. She continued, reading a statement from a trial lawyer saying he preferred women on the jury because women always took time to review the evidence before they decided on the verdict. She reminded the male senators that when they asked women's clubs to endorse their candidacy, many of them pledged to support their bill for women on juries. She said she had their files, and she riffled through folders of ordinary correspondence papers. She asked them if they intended to alienate the most powerful women's blocs in the state and pointed out that this was the only bill the women were asking for. She further noted that the legislature did not decide the question, it merely voted to place it on the ballot for the voters to decide. The Colorado Assembly passed the bill by the narrowest margin. But at the next general election, voters passed the amendment by a landslide.

After serving two terms in the House of Representatives plus a Senate term, Smith was weary of the demands of campaigning for office, of being on constant call as a speaker, not to mention solving public health problems and answering the assorted needs of aged, handicapped, jobless, and unjustly treated children of her district. Only the stout of body can stand up to such a grueling marathon, she had decided. She called her Democratic county chairman to announce her decision not to run for another Senate term. Instead of murmuring the usual sympathetic regrets, he shouted, "You stay in there and pitch. What's the matter with you? Health programs, war needs of men and women, people suffering. ... Don't you ever let me hear any such talk from you again."[5]

Eudochia Smith was reinvigorated to hear that her party needed her and considered her essential to the welfare of her state. She agreed to stand for a second term in the Senate. This gracious, feminine woman, the only woman in the Colorado Senate for twenty-five years, had gained the highest regard of her colleagues. Her hard work assured the passage of 75 percent of her bills into law. Eudochia Smith succeeded in a field governed by men; yet she never looked like a hard-bitten politician. Eudochia Smith, fifty-nine when she left the legislature for a federal appointment, wrote *They Ask Me Why,* a handbook urging women to enter politics.

In February 1946, President Harry Truman appointed her as registrar of the U.S. District Land Office at Denver. Her office took in more than $3 million a year in oil, grazing, homestead, and other fees. She kept the position until 1961. She served on the Colorado Board of Industries of the Blind and headed St. Vincent's Orphanage for several years. She died in Denver at the age of ninety, and was buried at Mt. Olivet Cemetery.

Hazel Marguerite Schmoll
Born August 23, 1890, in MacAllister, Kansas
Died January 31, 1990, in Boulder, Colorado

Hazel Schmoll grew up riding the high peaks and valleys of the Continental Divide amid the native wild flowers she knew and loved. Later, as Colorado state botanist, she conducted the first systematic study of plant life in southwestern Colorado. Her research led to the discovery of a rare loco weed variety that was renamed for her.

Hazel's storybook girlhood resembles the happy tale of Heidi, a girl of the Swiss Alps. The only child of William and Amelia Schmoll, she was born in a sod shanty on their mining claim three miles north of MacAllister, Kansas. When she was two, they moved to Caribou, a Colorado silver camp 9,800 feet above sea level. Situated on an iron dike, the camp attracted summer lightning storms and was buried deep in snow nine months of the year. The Schmolls soon moved a few miles north to Ward, at that time a town of 5,000 residents and a commercial center for 52 mines in the vicinity. It always delighted Hazel to hear 52 mine whistles blow three times a day and to watch miners walking up the mountainsides to work. After working in a mine for a month, her father opened a livery stable, from which he rented horses and worked as a professional guide.

From the time she was able to ride her own burro—and later an Indian pony named Dimple—Hazel would follow her father up the alpine slopes surrounding Ward. Under his tutelage, she learned to identify most Rocky Mountain wildflowers. With her mother, Amelia, she went "walking after berries" for days at a time. In the 1890s, they could find a profusion of raspberries and scrub blueberries on the burned-over mountainsides, and strawberries and gooseberries in hidden, moist places. When Hazel was a little older, her mother would pack a lunch and Hazel would set out on horseback with friends or her dog to fish, collect flowers, or pick berries. Lacking popular wildflower books, she always pestered visitors who might know some botany.

Through eighth grade, Hazel attended Ward's three-room school. Years later, she told a *Denver Post* reporter, "We didn't have classes in art and music ... and we may have missed some social amenities, but we had a college graduate for teacher and we knew our basics."[1] She also learned about politics during the twenty years when her father was mayor of Ward and her mother served on the school board.

Ward provided lively entertainment for teenagers with its frequent rock-drilling contests, band concerts, and weekly dances. Hazel could take part in these activities after her chores were done. Beginning when she was a little girl, the Schmolls owned a milk cow and Hazel had the job of delivering milk in small buckets to customers, both morning and evening. Her vigorous outdoor life always kept her in splendid health.

Situated in the mountains northwest of Boulder, Ward was big enough to support two newspapers, five hotels, three restaurants, and five saloons. In 1897, a mine railroad was built to climb 4,100 feet up the Switzerland Trail to haul passengers and ore for the mining district. Tragedy struck on January 24, 1900, when a fire started in an ash can. Whipped by the wind, it burned down the business section and most of the town, including the Schmolls' home and livery. Townspeople managed to save the schoolhouse, the Congregational Church, and a stone building.

In 1904, Ward was the country's largest mining camp. But when the treatment of the ores became uneconomical, mines began to close down and mining families started to move away. Will Schmoll, however, saw a future in the alpine beauty and tourist attractions, so he built a new livery and was in great demand as a guide and mountaineer.

In 1904, Hazel started boarding in Boulder while she attended the State Preparatory School, a high school; she continued at the University of Colorado to get her bachelor's degree in botany and a teaching degree in 1913. Through an aunt and uncle, Hazel learned about an opening in the Biology Department of Vassar College in Poughkeepsie, New York. In the fall of 1913, she became the first University of Colorado graduate to land a Vassar faculty position. She began as assistant and half-time graduate student in the Biology Department and advanced the next year to a full-time assistant in the Botany Department.

Hazel gained notoriety at Vassar because, as a Coloradan, she had voted in the first state that granted women suffrage. With other faculty members, she promoted the Suffrage Amendment on campus, although women in New York state did not get to vote until 1917. Her social life flowered at Vassar. The girl from Colorado was soon meeting and working with great men and women in art, music, drama, literature, social work, politics, education, and religion. She met the American poet Edna St. Vincent Millay and heard readings by John Masefield, England's Laureate, and poet Rupert Brooks; she attended stage performances by Ethel Barrymore, John Drew, and Otis Skinner; and heard concerts performed by Paderewski and Fritz Kreisler. On two occasions, John Burroughs escorted her on a nature trip through his woods and acreage on the Hudson River. Hazel also met Dr. P. A. Rydberg, a Swedish botanist and author of the comprehensive *Flora of Colorado.*

Finding in 1917 that she needed an advanced degree to continue teaching at Vassar, she enrolled at the University of Chicago. There, she did her major work with Dr. Henry C. Cowles, founder of ecology (the study of plants in the outdoors). For her project, she surveyed the forests in winter around Glencoe, Illinois, and received her master's degree in 1919. She attended summer school at the University of Chicago in 1916 and again in 1919, for a botany class studying plants at Tolland, Ward, and Rocky Mountain National Park.

While she was in Ward, a director of the Colorado Historical and Natural History Society at the State Museum asked her to do some botanical work for the museum. She expected to be there a month but stayed five years. Her primary assignment was to mount and identify the famous botanical collections of Ellsworth Bethel and Alice East-wood. Her work resulted in a herbarium of 10,000 mounted plants, still considered one of the finest in Colorado. While running the department in the director's absence, she cooperated with Denver's major organizations to conserve the state's natural resources.

Hazel's most visible achievement came when she was a board member of the Colorado Mountain Club. She was appointed chief lobbyist to pass a bill for the protection of the Colorado state flower, the lavender Columbine. The legislation protects the delicate flower by levying a fine of up to $50 on anyone who pulls up a plant or picks more than twenty-five blossoms in one day.

During the 1920s, opportunities and honors poured in for Hazel Schmoll. She unexpectedly came across her name in *American Men of Science*. For the museum, she collected plants in Colorado's Chimney Rock area. She was assembling the first systematic plant collection of Mesa Verde National Park when she and her young assistant found a white milk vetch growing in a pine forest. It was renamed *Astragalus schmolliae* in her honor. She was clerk and assistant curator in the State Bureau of Mines from 1920 to 1921.

In December 1925, she went to Europe with her aunt and uncle to study German and visit Europe's great botanists at botanical gardens in Paris, Florence, Munich, Nymphenburg, Berlin, Zurich, and London. Returning to the University of Chicago for her Ph.D. in ecological botany, she earned her way by peddling papers and cleaning houses. Her thesis, based on work she had done around Chimney Rock, Colorado, was completed in 1932. She was the first woman to earn a Ph.D. in botany at the university. While in Chicago, she rewrote a high school biology textbook, worked in the Botany Department of the Field Museum of Natural History, and was substitute botany professor at a junior college at Mt. Carroll, Illinois.

Dr. Schmoll's life took a sharp turn in 1938 when she learned her father was in poor health. She chose to go home to be with her parents and to share her knowledge of the outdoors with others. To this end, she built Rangeview Ranch, a lodge on 205 acres adjoining Rocky Mountain National Park in the Indian Peaks region, with a stunning view of the high peaks of the Continental Divide. She took in summer guests and served as a nature guide, pointing out wildlife and wild-flowers throughout the high country. Hazel served on the school board, town board, and volunteer fire department of the town of Ward. During World War II, she taught elementary school, then served on a committee to reorganize and consolidate the school districts.

A reporter who visited her in May 1967 described her as "a gentle, cheerful woman who has reached the age when most persons long for a mild climate and soft life, but who tramps the hillsides for glimpses of columbines."[2] Hazel Schmoll died January 31, 1990. She was 99. The Boulder County Historical Society received as a bequest the contents of her home in Ward along with some of the Schmoll property. Her finest gift to Coloradans may have been saving their state flower, the Columbine.

Helen Marie Black

Born June 2, 1896, in Washington, D.C.
Died January 31, 1988, in Denver, Colorado

Helen Marie Black embarked upon a lifetime of wide-ranging careers as a sixteen-year-old society reporter for the *Rocky Mountain News*. In journalism, she discovered her most valuable asset: an instinctive sense of showmanship. From that first newspaper job, Helen Black's unique genius steered her toward a career promoting individuals, business, and ultimately, Denver's symphony orchestras.

Helen's father, Henry Mortimer Black, was a mining engineer; the family moved with him from Washington to Chicago to Salt Lake City, where Black lost his money in a wax mine. Her mother, Palma Lanier Black, held a medical degree but preferred a career as a mother. Palma Black, who was related to the Southern poet Henry Lanier, instilled in Helen a strong affinity for the arts, particularly music and literature.

Clara Brown, Pioneer

Elizabeth Hickok Robbins Stone, Pioneer

Owl Woman, Indian Negotiator

Martha Ann Dartt Maxwell, Taxidermist

Helen Fiske Hunt Jackson, Author

Isabella Bird, Author

Augusta Louise Pierce Tabor, Philanthropist

Caroline ("Kate") Nichols Churchill, Publisher

Mary Rippon, Educator

Frances Wisebart Jacobs, Founder of Charities

Chipeta, Indian Negotiator

Elizabeth Nellis McCourt Doe Tabor ("Baby Doe"),
Folk Heroine

Mary Hauck Elitch Long, Co-creator of Elitch Gardens

Sarah Sophia Chase Platt-Decker,
Women's Club Leader

Mary Florence Lathrop, Lawyer

Margaret ("Molly") Tobin Brown,
Titanic Heroine and Humanitarian

Emily Griffith, Educator

Justina Ford, Physician

Above: Edwina Hume Fallis, Teacher

Left: Florence Rena Sabin, World Renowned Scientist

Helen Bonfils, Publisher and Philanthropist

May Bonfils Stanton, Philanthropist

Josephine Aspenwall Roche, Labor Advocate

Eudochia Bell Smith, State Legislator

Hazel Marguerite Schmoll, Botanist

Helen Marie Black, Civil/Cultural Leader

Left: Mamie Doud Eisenhower, Humanitarian

Bottom left: Golda Mabovitch Meir,
Israeli Prime Minister

Bottom right: Margaret Taylor Curry,
First Woman Parole Officer

Frances Mary McConnell-Mills,
Forensic Medicine Pioneer

Caroline Bancroft, Author/Historian

Antonia Brico, Conductor

Mary Coyle Chase, Playwright

Jane Silverstein Ries, Landscape Architect

Genevieve D'Amato Fiore, Peace Activist

Oleta Lawanda Crain,
U.S. Government Official

Jean Jolliffe Yancey, Entrepreneur

Hannah Marie Wormington Volk, Anthropologist/Author

Helen Louise White Peterson, Indian Advocate

Miriam Goldberg, Newspaper Publisher

Ruth Small Stockton, Colorado Lawmaker

Rachel Bassette Noel, Civil Rights Pioneer

Elise Biorn-Hansen Boulding, Nobel Prize Nominee

Lena Lovato Archuleta, Educator

Mildred Pitts Walter, Author of Children's Books

Hendrika Bestebreurtje Cantwell, Pediatrician

Joan Packard Birkland, Champion Athlete

Anne Flick Steinbeck, National Women's Leader

Dana Hudkins Crawford, Historic Preservationist

LaRae Orullian, Bank President

Elnora ("Ellie") Clausing Gilfoyle,
Occupational Therapy Educator

Dorothy Louise Vennard Lamm, Feminist/Author

Marilyn Van Derbur Atler,
National Speaker for Children's Rights

Sumiko Tanaka Hennessy, Social Worker

Patricia Scott Schroeder, Congresswoman

Lenore E. Auerbach Walker, Psychologist

Wilma J. Webb, Politician

Cleo Parker Robinson,
Colorado's Living Legend of Dance

Terri Helman Finkel, Medical Researcher

Palma Black and the children moved to Denver around 1910. Helen chose to enter Manual High School on the strength of an outstanding art teacher; she also attended North High, graduating when she was sixteen. She promptly approached the managing editor of the *Rocky Mountain News,* to ask his advice regarding the best college education for a newspaper career. He advised her to work on a newspaper instead and hired her on the spot.

Helen began at the *News* as assistant to the society editor at $5 a week (she and the society editor were the only females in the newsroom). She attended social functions in beautiful mansions and performances at the Broadway, Orpheum, and other leading Denver theaters. Her assignment was to write about who attended these events and what they wore. Helen soon had enough of that, and she told the editor that writing about society was not her idea of news—she wanted to write news stories. He moved her to the city desk, where she could occasionally cover crimes. One of her early assignments was the sensational gold bullion robbery from the Denver Mint in 1920. The day after the robbery, Helen interviewed Mrs. Orville Harrington, wife of a mint refinery worker. Police, meanwhile, discovered that Mr. Harrington was stashing gold bars in his hollow artificial leg, walking out with the loot, and burying it in his basement and backyard.

In 1921, Helen was assigned to cover the Denver appearance of Aimee Semple McPherson, a young evangelist known for having healing powers. Helen's first story about McPherson produced a sensation. In order to prolong the interest, everyday she brazenly proposed publicity stunts to the pretty evangelist. First, she invited hospitals to bring patients to church for Aimee McPherson to heal—more than one hundred were carried in. Aimee McPherson later claimed that "practically all" were cured. Next, Aimee and Helen toured Denver's Chinatown to heal the sick and handicapped. Then Helen suggested that McPherson preach on Lookout Mountain west of Denver; a large crowd assembled to hear her highly publicized Sermon on the Mount.

The *News* promoted Helen to features writer. She interviewed luminaries Charles Lindbergh, Helen Keller, Harry Houdini, the wife of Warren G. Harding, and Queen Maria of Rumania. She covered the

1924 Democratic Convention at Madison Square Garden. At the same time, she was the paper's music and drama editor and critic and on the side was doing publicity *pro bono* for Denver's struggling Civic Symphony Orchestra. Editors opened many doors for Helen.

Around 1926, Helen Black was hospitalized—reportedly with tuberculosis—and resigned from the *News*. After recovering, she joined the Denver Dry Goods Company as fashion coordinator "to gain business experience." She did publicity and staged fashion shows and events. Daniels & Fisher department stores offered her a position as full-time publicity assistant. While working there, she interested Anne Evans and other civic-minded women in restoring the historic Opera House at Central City and in jump-starting the Central City Opera Association; at the same time, she was doing volunteer publicity for the summer opera festival, which drew national fame. For a time, Helen ran her own advertising agency at the Brown Palace Hotel, where her accounts included the Red Cross, the YWCA and YMCA, Goodwill Industries, and Christmas Seals.

But a love for classical music was drawing her into Denver's concert scene. In 1933, the Denver Civic Symphony was using both professional and amateur musicians. With the onset of the depression, the Civic Symphony limped through the 1930s with concerts on Friday evenings for a dime admission and Sunday matinees for a quarter. Musicians were paid $5 per concert. Helen, who had been volunteering as the orchestra publicist, banded with two other symphony patrons: Jean Cranmer and Lucille Wilkin. Jean Cranmer had organized the Civic Symphony Society in 1922 and Lucille Wilkin, a Julliard musician, had come to create opportunities for musicians in Denver. The trio's goal was to gather all music professionals into one orchestra, present three concerts a season, and pay musicians union wages. They established the Denver Symphony Orchestra (DSO) in 1934 and the next year organized the Denver Symphony Guild as an auxiliary to oversee orchestra projects and fundraising campaigns. Among their projects, Helen Black and the orchestra cooperated with Denver Public Schools to form the junior symphony that trained young artists for later service in the orchestra. Other innovations included a ballet program, a choral work, and children's concert series in 1941–1942.

Conductor Horace Tureman brought the first stability and artistic distinction to the orchestra. He and Black finagled an annual stipend out of the city although meeting the orchestra's annual budget still required gargantuan effort. Tureman retired for health reasons in 1944 and Helen Black was reduced to canvassing the city for the following year's funds. She found Denverites were reluctant to pay union wages to musicians. Finally, she decided to take a gamble. She would hire a conductor first and then raise the money. She auditioned six nationally acclaimed conductors before signing Saul Caston, who had been associate conductor of the Philadelphia Symphony under Leopold Stokowski.

When Maestro Caston raised his baton in 1945, the orchestra entered a new era. It was a new era for Helen, too. For twelve years, she had "done the symphony out of her purse" as a volunteer, while working a daytime job. Now, she was full-time with the orchestra and became the first female *salaried* business manager of a large professional symphony—and, until 1951, was the *only* woman business manager. As always, she singlehandedly ran the symphony office.

Because the DSO was the only major orchestra in the region, it organized orchestra tours to outlying Colorado towns and into Wyoming in 1946. In July 1947, Helen Black was instrumental in initiating summer concerts at Red Rocks, which spread DSO's reputation nationwide. Red Rocks also opened avenues for Helen Black's most dramatic publicity stunts. Lily Pons, the coloratura who sang like a bird, was coming to sing at Red Rocks, where native birds could join in. Helen had an idea. She called *Life* magazine to send a photographer and then rented a crate of pigeons. When Lily Pons hit high C, Helen released the flock of pigeons around the diva's head. The event was reported nationally. During a 1957 production of *Die Walkure* at Red Rocks, she sent the Valkyries in on horseback. She attracted national coverage for a concert by Wagnerian singers Helen Traubel and Lauritz Melchoir.

Conductor Caston had received international acclaim. But local criticism of his competence began to emerge in 1957. Starting with a group of musicians who complained they just played notes, not music, the revolt spread among critics and concert goers. A dissident group, the Better Music Associates led by Dr. Peter Hoch, agreed to raise funds for the orchestra if Caston and Black would exit after the 1961–1962 season. Black hotly defended Caston, saying "such criticism was predictable … an occupational disease … because of the unstable nature of orchestra musicians."[1] Dr. Hoch debated the issue with Symphony Society President Allan Phipps. At last, a deeply wounded Saul Caston resigned on January 29, 1963. A few weeks later, after thirty years of service to the orchestra, Helen Black followed suit.

She continued to live in her Capitol Hill apartment, a single working woman of ordinary means. Famous for her big, brown eyes and lady like elegance, she went on supporting music, the arts, community organizations, and anyone who needed her. She did free publicity for numerous civic organizations and projects. Having helped promote careers of promising artists like pianist Van Cliburn and violinist Eugene Fodor, she furthered this interest through the Denver Lyric Opera Guild. She also was active in the Denver Woman's Press Club.

Recognition and awards, too many to list completely, poured in during her later years, including: Woman of the Year by the Business and Professional Women's Club, Advertising Woman of the Year, Beautiful Activist of Colorado by Altrusa Clubs of Colorado, and an honorary degree in Humane letters awarded by Metropolitan State College on May 20, 1984.

The Denver Woman's Press Club and the *Rocky Mountain News* honored Helen Marie Black on September 26, 1983, at a black tie dinner emceed by Gene Amole in the Grand Ballroom of the Brown Palace Hotel. Black's longtime friend, distinguished violinist Isaac Stern, toasted her on the program. Highlighting the evening was the announcement of the Helen Marie Black Arts and Letters Award presented by the Denver Woman's Press Club (which she had served as president in 1932) and the *Rocky Mountain News.* The award is given annually to an individual who has accomplished excellence in the field of arts and letters within the Colorado community or has contributed leadership in the field.

Helen Black died on January 31, 1988, at St. Luke's Hospital in Denver. She was ninety-one. E. Atwill Gilman, a DSO board member, said she had been "a leader way ahead of her time. To me she was always a perfect lady. I think she had a hand in everything cultural in Denver."[2]

A *Denver Post* editorial described Helen Marie Black as "a precedent-setter for women in the esoteric and formidable world of symphony music. She molded the Denver Symphony from the Denver Civic Symphony in the early 1930s and managed the orchestra for more than thirty years at nominal salary."[3]

Mamie Doud Eisenhower

Born November 14, 1896, in Boone, Iowa
Died November 1, 1979, in Gettysburg, Pennsylvania

Mamie Doud Eisenhower awoke early on January 20, 1953, and opened the draperies. With relief, she looked out at Washington's wintry landscape—brisk, sunny, invigorating. Perfect Eisenhower weather.

By two that afternoon, Mamie was seated in the temporary bleachers on Constitution Avenue, gazing at the throngs who had gathered to see the presidential inauguration. She wore a new, gray Hattie Carnegie suit and a matching hat that covered her trademark bangs. Her mink coat shielded her slender shoulders from the biting winter wind gusting up the street. At last, the color guard appeared, the Marine Band struck up "Hail to the Chief," and President Harry Truman strode up the aisle with Mamie's husband. The time had come. Chief Justice Fred M. Vinson gave the oath of office to the new president, Dwight D. Eisenhower. All went according to tradition. Almost.

The import of the moment, her pride in her husband, awe for her country, and the long road that led to this podium overcame her composure. As Mamie sank to her seat, President Eisenhower stepped over, put his hands on her shoulders, and quickly kissed her. Revived by his surprise gesture, Mamie sailed through the longest inaugural parade in history, a buffet supper back at the White House, and the grand Inaugural Ball.

Mamie Geneva Doud was born with a rheumatic heart. Her older sister, Eleanor, had asthma. Hoping that the girls' health would improve in Colorado's dry, clear air, the John Sheldon Douds moved from Iowa to Pueblo, then to Colorado Springs, finally settling in Denver in 1905. Eleanor died seven years later but Mamie and her younger sisters, Eda ("Buster") and Frances ("Mike"), thrived in the mile-high climate. The Douds lived for half a century in their two-story, eleven-room house—a "Denver Square" at 750 Lafayette Street. Mamie's parents were not strict, but insisted upon their many family traditions. "Tall and Stately Jack," the butler-chauffeur, added elegance to the household. On Sunday afternoons, the family went driving in their Pierce-Arrow touring car or their Stanley Steamer. Mamie and her sisters attended nearby Corona School (later renamed Dora Moore School) and the Miss Wolcott School for girls and went to Sunday School at Corona Presbyterian Church. The Doud girls played croquet with neighborhood children. (Neighbors later recalled their beautiful manners and soft voices, especially around older people.)

Mamie was an unusually pretty and vivacious girl, whose best features were her deep blue eyes and translucent skin. When she was older, she took to wearing her dark hair in bangs to cover her high forehead. The bangs became her trademark. She liked people and radiated a warmth that made everyone feel welcome and happy. With her friends, Mamie attended stage plays at the Broadway Theater and Elitch Gardens Stock Theater. She took piano lessons, went to dancing school, and graduated from the Miss Wolcott school.

In October 1915, Doud took the family to winter in San Antonio, Texas, to bolster the health of a sister with heart trouble. It was there that Mamie met Second Lieutenant Dwight D. Eisenhower, who was stationed at Fort Sam Houston. He started courting her as soon as there was an opening in her crowded engagement book. The young officer, whom everyone called Ike, had an engaging smile but a very strong jaw. The Douds learned that Ike had worked since he was seven and that he had grown up in a simple Abiline, Kansas, farmhouse. Looking for a college he could attend free, Ike was awarded an appointment to West Point. After graduation, he was ordered to the 19th Infantry Regiment at Galveston, where he met Mamie. The Douds' two homes probably were the most impressive houses he'd ever visited, but it was plain that Ike enjoyed being with Mamie and her family.

The couple announced their engagement on Valentine's Day, 1916. Mamie's father had serious concerns about his nineteen-year-old daughter marrying an obscure second lieutenant who made less than $150 a month. Her friends said Mamie could have had her pick of the Denver boys. Nonetheless, they were married in the Douds' front parlor in Denver on July 1, 1916.

Mamie and Ike had their first—and worst—quarrel on their honeymoon. They were visiting Ike's parents in Kansas when he went to play poker and stayed out late. After a royal row, Ike told Mamie, "My country comes first and always will. You come second." Then he announced he was going on army maneuvers for a month. It was obvious that Mamie would have to make adjustments for the marriage to work. She prepared to embark upon the nomadic life of a military wife.

Their first small apartment, furnished in Army Old Ugly, was at Fort Sam Houston, Texas. Mamie made it homey, cheery, and welcoming, and it became the first in a succession of "Club Eisenhowers" known for the many festive parties the Eisenhowers threw for their military friends. Fort Sam was followed during World War I by Fort Oglethorpe and Fort Leavenworth. At Camp Colt and Gettysburg, Eisenhower was made commander of the heavy tank brigade. Mamie and Ike moved thirty-four times, seven times in a single year. For her, the most familiar visitor was the moving van.

Their first child, Dwight Doud Eisenhower, whom Mamie dubbed "Icky," was born at an army post in 1917. At Christmas 1920, three-year-old Icky came down with scarlet fever and was hospitalized. Mamie also was so sick that Icky's doctor quarantined her at home. It was up to Ike to hold their son when he died on January 2, 1921. Mamie's grief was so intense that her despondency severely strained their marriage. But eighteen months later, Mamie returned to Denver from their post in Panama to give birth to their second son, John Sheldon, and their marriage slowly returned to normal. John not only survived but, like his father, would become a West Point cadet.

After the Japanese assault on Pearl Harbor, Ike was promoted on

March 27, 1942, to the rank of major general. Chief-of-Staff General George Marshall called him to Washington to discuss strategy with President Franklin Roosevelt and Prime Minister Winston Churchill. Mamie moved to Washington, where worried, lonely, and restless, she suffered from endless insomnia and fragile health. Ike's visit to Mamie's Washington apartment on June 24, 1942, was one of the last times they were together during World War II. From the time he became supreme commander of the Allied Expeditionary Forces in Europe, Ike lived at various Allied headquarters in Europe and Africa. His movements and activities were kept secret even from Mamie.

It was on her radio, not through Ike, that Mamie learned of the D-Day invasion of Utah and Normandy Beaches. It was one of the most difficult days of her life. And, for the next three years, she kept her ear to the radio hoping for news of the war—and her husband. She had withdrawn from public view, fearful that any word of hers might endanger Ike and their son, John, by then an infantry officer. General Eisenhower, meanwhile, was engulfed in the myriad responsibilities and burdens of coordinating the Allied invasion of Germany.

Mamie must have become aware that through the long years while she waited at home, Ike's young and attractive English chauffeur, Kay Summersby, was at his side. Summersby's interesting (but temptingly evasive) book *Eisenhower Was My Boss* detailed their day-to-day military activities at Allied headquarters. She discussed personnel, leisure-time bridge games, and VIP parties. As Ike's aide and personal driver, she met such awesome personalities as President Roosevelt, Prime Minister Churchill, and General Marshall. The book follows General Eisenhower through D-Day and the landings at Utah and Omaha Beaches and through moves of headquarters from England to Africa, France, and into Germany.

While Mamie worried at home, Summersby was an observer at the Nazi surrender in the red schoolhouse at Reims. She rode with General Eisenhower through cheering crowds as Allied forces advanced through France. On every page, she spoke of Ike in admiring, almost adoring terms. She mentioned John Eisenhower in connection with his infrequent meetings with his father. But never did she mention the name of Mamie Eisenhower. Mamie heard rumors of a romance with Summersby and even that her husband had considered divorcing his wife to marry his attractive chauffeur. When Ike returned at last after the war, Mamie asked him bluntly if the rumors were true. Ike vehemently denied them. Years later (in a preface to a book of letters from Ike to Mamie), John Eisenhower called the allegation "an egregious falsehood. ... There is no evidence that divorce ever seriously crossed Dad's mind, even in the loneliest moments across the Atlantic."[1]

Before the Eisenhowers could return to a normal life, Americans began clamoring for him to enter the next presidential election. In 1952, with the slogan "I Like Ike," he ran on the Republican ticket against Democrat Adlai Stevenson. Mamie took an active role in the campaign. Her heart-shaped face, framed by short dark hair and her trademark curly bangs, became familiar to every American. Mamie was a great campaigner, winning folks over by just being herself. Ike won the election in a landslide and in January 1953, he became the thirty-fourth president of the United States. As a popular first lady, Mamie was considered to be "a fair organist, first-rate Scrabble player, and always an elegant dresser known for her hats."[2] Her army years had taught her to be efficient, and she ran the White House with competence as well as flair. She was an incomparable hostess. But the Eisenhowers disappointed the Washington press corps when they turned out to be unabashed homebodies. At day's end, Ike would change into comfortable shoes and old clothes. The couple spent most evenings in their second-floor apartment watching television and movies, catching up on reading, or playing bridge and canasta with old friends.

President and Mamie Eisenhower continued to spend summer vacations in Denver, where they stayed alternately at the Doud home, the Brown Palace Hotel, or Lowry Air Force Base. They were in Denver at the Lafayette Street home in September 1955 when the president suffered a heart attack. He was moved to a Brown Palace Hotel suite, which became known as the summer White House because he carried on his official duties from there.

As first lady, Mamie gave her support to many important causes and made the position productive and meaningful. One of her later appearances, on July 8, 1963, was to dedicate the Mamie Eisenhower Library in Broomfield, Colorado, and present it with 337 volumes from her father's personal library.

After Ike completed two four-year terms as president, the couple retired to a farm in Gettysburg, Pennsylvania, at the edge of the historic Civil War battlefield. When Ike died in 1969, they had been married nearly fifty-three years. Mamie continued living alone at the Gettysburg farm until she was eighty-two. She suffered a stroke there on September 25, 1979, and died in her sleep at Walter Reed Army Hospital on November 1. Her small, simple funeral was attended by forty friends and family members. She was buried beside President Eisenhower and their first son, the toddler "Icky," in the small limestone chapel on the grounds of the Eisenhower Library in Abilene, Kansas.

For Mamie, it had been a long road to the White House, but her life as an army wife had prepared her to handle each new role with wisdom and grace. After all the army camps and stations, the Washington apartment, the White House, and the Gettysburg farm, if there was one place Mamie actually called home it was Denver. The historic significance of her Lafayette Street home is marked by a plaque installed on the front porch by the Daughters of the American Revolution.

Golda Mabovitch Meir

Born May 3, 1898, in Kiev, Russia
Died December 8, 1978, in Jerusalem, Israel

In 1913, an ordinary brick duplex stood at 1606–08 Julian Street in Denver. Its humble appearance today gives no hint of the significant political discussions and revolutionary debates that raged within its walls between 1913 and 1915. But the influence of those discussions would extend to a far and future country undreamed of at that time. The conversations that took place in those years left an indelible impression on the mind and passion of the young Golda Mabovitch.

A child of Jewish parentage and tradition, Golda was born in Kiev and lived in Pinsk, Belorussia, until she was eight. Her father, Moshe Mabovitch, a mild-natured carpenter, was born in the Ukraine. Golda's mother, Blume, was a fiery, energetic woman with copper-colored hair and inflexible determination. With their daughters Sheyna, Golda, and Zipke, Moshe and Blume subsisted in a Jewish community in Pinsk.

When Golda was seven, Moshe Mabovitch—convinced they could not survive much longer in Russia—left for America to make a new home for his family. After his departure, life grew intolerable for Blume and the girls, who were left behind to endure poverty and the terror of Cossacks who continually galloped through town with their sabers slashing at the townspeople.

In 1906, Blume Mabovitch made elaborate plans to emigrate with her three daughters. They memorized new identities and traveled secretly on a roundabout route. Crossing the border into Galicia, they hid for two days waiting to catch a train to a seaport. They traveled to Vienna and then Antwerp, where they boarded a ship jammed with Jewish-Russian refugees for a miserable fourteen-day voyage to America. Eventually, the bedraggled immigrants reached Milwaukee and were met by Mabovitch, who had secured a tiny flat and was making a meager income. Golda rode in her first automobile, saw her first skyscraper, and enrolled in an American school.

Sheyna had fallen in love with Shamai Korngold in Russia, and they married shortly after he managed to join her in the United States. Of all the family members, Sheyna had suffered most from their near-starvation diet. By the time of her marriage, she had contracted tuberculosis. The young couple moved to Denver so she could get treatment at Denver's famous Jewish Hospital for Consumptives (later named National Jewish Hospital).

When Golda was a teenager, her mother opened a small grocery store in Milwaukee and insisted that Golda tend the store during the day. Golda was just as determined to pursue her high school studies instead and to earn a diploma. When they reached an impasse and Golda's arguments with her mother became unbearable, Golda started writing secretly to her older sister. In the fall of 1912, Golda defiantly enrolled in a Milwaukee high school. This escalated arguments with her mother, who was convinced that girls with a high school education became spinster teachers because teachers were discouraged from marrying. The last straw for Golda was when Blume engaged a matchmaker and arranged for her to marry an older man.

In answer to Golda's desperate letters, the Korngolds replied on November 12, 1912, inviting her to slip away from home and come live with them in Denver. They sent her a train ticket. When she arrived, they said, she could attend North Denver High School and work part-time to help eke out the added expense. To arrange her departure, fifteen-year-old Golda enlisted the help of her chum Regina. The night before she was to leave, Golda made a small bundle of her clothes and lowered it from her window to Regina waiting below. Regina then delivered it to the railway station. The next morning, Golda left the house—ostensibly for school—but then headed to the railroad station. She was on the train before her absence was discovered. She spent the next two years in Denver, where "my real life began and I started growing up," as Golda recalled in her autobiography. "In the evenings, after supper, Sheyna badgered me to go on with my schoolwork but I was fascinated by the people who used to drop into their home and sit around talking until late at night," she wrote.[1]

Sheyna's West Denver duplex unit (consisting of two small rooms, a kitchen, and bathroom) had become a center for Jewish immigrants from Russia, the intelligentsia who had come West for treatment at Denver's Jewish Hospital for Consumptives. Some were anarchists, some socialists, some Socialist Zionists. Many were infected with tuberculosis. Golda served tea and disinfected their cups while she listened avidly to arguments and quarrels that swirled around worldwide controversies such as the role of women and the future of the Jewish people. Golda hung on their words as though they would change her life. To the young girl, the Socialist Zionists made the most sense. She was enthralled with their dream of a national home for Jews—"one place on earth where Jews could be free and independent ... where no one would be hungry or live in fear of other men."[2]

Golda's carefully planned high school education was somewhat neglected as she found herself far more concerned with thoughts of a Jewish national home in Palestine than with her classes at North Denver High School. Nevertheless, she finished tenth and eleventh grades. Her report cards show As in all subjects but one B in algebra and Cs in mechanical drawing.

Her Denver sojourn brought yet another development. One of the less outspoken young visitors was a Lithuanian immigrant, Morris Meyerson. Unlike the fervent Zionists, he was self-educated and thoroughly versed in poetry, music, and art. Golda and Morris were drawn to one another. They talked for hours about his many interests. He took her to lectures and free concerts in the park (probably the popular band concerts in the pavilion beside City Park Lake). Golda fell in love with Morris "for his encyclopedic knowledge, his gentleness, his wonderful sense of humor ... and his steadiness. ... To this day I associate certain pieces of music with the clear, dry, mountain air of Denver and the wonderful parks in which Morris and I walked every Sunday in the spring and summer of 1913," Golda recalled in her autobiography.[3]

When Golda was sixteen, she quarreled with Sheyna and walked out of the duplex. She was taken in by two of Sheyna's girlfriends and got a job taking measurements for women's skirt linings. During this period, Golda's father wrote, saying they needed her desperately at home. She returned to Milwaukee and found that her parents had mellowed toward her and younger teenage sister, Zipke.

Golda and Morris finally set a date for their marriage. They planned to slip away to Milwaukee City Hall for a civil ceremony, but as usual Blume prevailed. They would be shaming the family if they didn't have a religious ceremony, she protested. On December 24, 1917, they were married in a wedding at home with a few friends. A well-known rabbi officiated.

Golda became increasingly involved in Zionist politics until, on May 23, 1921, she and Morris sailed for Palestine—along with Golda's Milwaukee chum Regina and Golda's sister Sheyna and her two children. Sheyna's husband, Shamai Korngold, stayed behind to work and send them money. They settled first in the twelve-year-old city Tel Aviv and adapted themselves to life in the struggling new Jewish homeland. The

Meyersons had a son, Menachem, and a daughter, Sarah. From that time, Golda increasingly belonged to Israel.

She was moving up the political ladder, which required longer and longer absences from home as she played a major role in the formation of the state of Israel. When she was asked to be secretary of the Women's Labor Council, which involved extensive travel, she realized her marriage, as such, must end. The Meyersons separated in 1928, even though they remained legally married and loved each other until Morris died in Golda's apartment in 1951. The children remained with Golda and maintained their close ties to their father.

In 1948, Golda helped write the Israeli Declaration of Independence. Later, from 1956 to 1966 she served as Israel's foreign minister to Moscow, at which point she took on the Hebraized name Meir ("to burn brightly"). And finally, in 1968, when Golda was seventy, she became the fourth prime minister of Israel, serving from 1969 to 1974.

Golda Meir died in Jerusalem of lymphoma on December 8, 1978. All of Israel and dignitaries from around the world came to pay their last respects. Walking with his parents in a line of 100,000 mourners, a seven-year-old boy asked his mother, "Who will be Golda now?"

Back in Denver, the duplex that played such a germinal role in Golda Meir's future was leading a precarious existence. Heavily vandalized on Julian Street, it was moved to Habitat Park on South Santa Fe Drive, then slated to be razed for tennis courts in 1980. In 1981, a newspaper reported it was scheduled for demolition. Reading the item, Esther Cohen Strauss got a Denver judge to cancel the order. Almost burned down by arsonists in 1984, the duplex was moved once again to Louisiana Avenue and Lipan Street. A tornado that passed within fifty feet, and deterioration, neglect and bureaucracy further endangered its survival. In 1987, Esther Strauss returned to court to save the house from the executioner. The Auraria Foundation spearheaded a last-ditch drive to move it on September 15, 1988, to 1146 Ninth Street in the historic Auraria Campus District, to its permanent home next door to St. Cajetan's Church.

The brick exterior of the house was restored in 1990, followed by work on its 600-square-foot interior. Miraculously, some evidence of

Golda's life in the home was found, including a bank check signed by Shamai Korngold and a tzedaka box (for charitable contributions to the poor) still nailed by the kitchen door. On Colorado Day 1997, Governor Roy Romer dedicated the new Golda Meir House Museum and Political Leadership Center in the duplex. "This modest house will allow us to explore the imperfect art of leadership," said Norman Provizer, chairman of the Political Science Department at Metropolitan State College of Denver, during the museum dedication.[4]

The tiny house was *the* gathering place of Zionist activists in Denver. Some say it was the birthplace of Israel in the United States.

Margaret Taylor Curry

Born July 16, 1898, in Meeker, Colorado
Died February 14, 1986, in Englewood, Colorado

Imagine a Christmas party at which the fifteen women guests arrive in buses escorted by armed deputy sheriffs from the Denver County jail. Margaret Taylor Curry, who was Colorado's first woman parole officer, believed in keeping up morale for "her girls," and she used every possible resource to get them back on their feet, both physically and financially.

For the holiday season, she had established a tradition of filling a Christmas stocking for every woman prisoner at the State Correctional Institution at Canon City. She shopped for bargains and solicited service organizations for cosmetics, soap, shampoo, jewelry, hose, candy—anything to make "her girls" feel special at Christmas. When Margaret Curry decided to extend her Christmas list to include women prisoners at the Denver County Jail, she was told that city regulations did not permit gifts inside the jail. And so, she managed to get permission for the women prisoners to attend a Christmas party at her daughter's home.

On the day of the party, neighbors must have been surprised to see uniformed guards standing outside and inside the house. For the occasion, the women were allowed to dress in their own clothing. Parole Department employees catered the dinner. Even the guards seemed to enjoy the evening but couldn't hide their dismay that Curry had managed to pull it off. In fact, Margaret's Christmas dinner was such a success and her guests' thank you notes so touching that she threw a similar party the next Christmas.

Margaret Taylor Curry, who was born on a ranch outside Meeker, often said that living in rural Colorado during the Dust Bowl and the depression helped her understand the feelings of women who were going through hard times. She was valedictorian of her class and got her bachelor's degree in music at Colorado State College of Education in Greeley. Her first job was teaching music in the Fort Morgan schools. She met Arthur D. Curry, a Ford dealer in the town of Ault, where they moved after they were married. Then came the depression. When their car business screeched to a halt, Curry lost his dealership. Soon the Currys were traveling with their two children from town to town looking for work. Wherever they went, Margaret got jobs as a welfare worker. Finally, the Currys bought a "cottage camp" (now a motel) and grocery store on South Santa Fe Drive in Denver.

In 1941, when she was 43, Margaret Curry enrolled in classes toward a master's degree in social studies at the University of Denver. At the same time, she was working as a medical social worker at Fitzsimons Hospital, raising their children, and assisting in the family motel. She studied late at night and whenever she could find a few extra minutes. On the day that Margaret graduated with her master's degree, her daughter, Rosalie Lay, was celebrating her second wedding anniversary.

The next rung on Margaret Curry's career ladder was to take the Civil Service examination for Colorado's new Parole Department. She achieved the highest grade on the test but was relegated to eleventh position, behind veterans receiving job preference. She emerged on July 1, 1952, as Colorado's first woman parole officer at a beginning salary of $305 a month. To launch her new career, she paid a visit to the women's facility at the Canon City Penitentiary. The first thing she noticed was that there were no rehabilitation or training programs for the female inmates. Their only activity was to wash and iron the clothes for the male prisoners. Curry ordered sewing machines and fabrics, typewriters, even hair dryers and then recruited volunteer instructors to teach the women how to use the equipment. She established an education program so the women could earn a GED (equivalent to a high school diploma), and she arranged for a modeling agency to hold classes in self-improvement.

Another inequity at the prison was that the Pre-parole Center was available only to male inmates. Margaret Curry lobbied to gain access for women prisoners about to be paroled, so they could go to a separate setting, apart from the main prison, to practice dressing in civilian street clothes, eating with a knife and fork (only spoons were allowed in the prison cafeteria), and selecting appropriate associates. As parole officer, Margaret Curry helped women obtain suitable civilian clothing, find a place to stay on the outside, and fit back into society. Most important (and most difficult) was to help them find employment. Among her other achievements, Margaret Curry was instrumental in building Colorado's new Women's Correctional Institution.

Her office was in lower downtown Denver, but she frequently got calls at home in the middle of the night. A parolee might be down on Larimer Street, drunk and scared. Margaret Curry would drive down, pick her up, take her home, and sober her up. Next morning, she'd get the parolee straightened up and start her out again. Male parole officers rarely went to this extent to rescue their charges. She carried an average caseload of forty-two women from Canon City and the Colorado State Reformatory for Women. Her clients ranged from fifteen to sixty-five years of age and came from all ethnic groups. They were incarcerated for crimes that ran the gamut from embezzlement to murder. Most were single parents who had become so desperate for food and money to feed their children that they resorted to forging checks.

One of her parolees, an elderly woman, had served a long prison term for murder. When she was released, she had nowhere to stay, so Curry rented her the basement apartment in her own home. Curry's daughter, Rosalie Lay, recalled that the woman, a loner, barely spoke. When she reached her late seventies, she passed away quietly in her rocking chair.

Margaret Curry retired in 1970 at age 71. At last, she had time for her music and hobbies, among them attending rodeos and riding on the back of a motorcycle. Just before Arthur Curry's death in 1958, the Currys had sold their motel and moved to their dream home in Englewood. Margaret Taylor Curry, who had enjoyed a lifetime of splendid health, remained in that home for the rest of her life, caring for her house and yard. When she was 87, she slipped on the ice and broke her wrist. She never recovered from the complications of the injury and died on February 14, 1986.

For eighteen years, Margaret Taylor Curry had been Colorado's only woman parole officer for adults. Often, she was the only link between women prisoners and the outside world and was the only friend a prisoner had. Because of her efforts, women prisoners and parolees today receive improved rehabilitation, training, and job opportunities.

Frances Mary McConnell-Mills

Born July 9, 1900, in Monument, Colorado
Died December 28, 1975, in Denver, Colorado

In the 1920s, it was unusual to see a pretty young woman peering through a microscope at bloody rags, human hair, and the stomach contents of murder victims. Even more remarkable was her ability to make such scant clues reveal the age, size, and identity of crime victims as well as their murderers. At twenty-five, Dr. Frances McConnell was named Denver's first city toxicologist. As the first woman toxicologist in the Rocky Mountain region and probably America's first woman forensic pathologist, she was instrumental in solving many of the region's most puzzling crimes from 1925 to 1950 and often testified as a key witness.

Frances Mary McConnell, daughter of a country doctor, was born at the McConnell home on Second Street in Monument, Colorado. The doctor had his medical office next door, above the McConnell Drug Store. A pharmacist, he also ran the drug store and pharmacy. Frances's sisters, Margaret and Helen, were born in 1903 and 1909. In response to young "Francy's" interest in his patients, Dr. McConnell took her on house calls to ranches scattered across the Monument Divide. During the long buggy rides, he drilled her on arithmetic and discussed his treatments of basic illnesses.

Plagued with frequent respiratory infections, Francy did not start school until she was eight. She entered the third grade at Monument School, where the first eight grades were taught in three rooms. When she was twelve, her Aunt Lydia and her English grandfather, John Pring, invited her to board with them in Colorado Springs so she could attend Colorado Springs High School. But first, she had to pass lengthy entrance tests. In September 1913, she began commuting by train to Colorado Springs, where she would spend the week, returning to Monument for weekends.

Pring set up a strict study regimen for his granddaughter. Every evening as he and a friend played cribbage, he insisted she do her homework beside them at the table. She learned Latin, history, algebra, and science to the tune of 15-2, 15-4—cribbage scoring terms. She graduated in May 1916, when she was fifteen. As Principal Roscoe C. Hill gave out diplomas, he introduced Frances as the "baby senior" and awarded her a full scholarship to the University of Denver.

After the United States entered World War I in 1917, Dr. McConnell enlisted as a captain in the army Medical Corps, then sold his medical practice and drugstore in Monument. The family moved to Denver so the girls could attend Denver schools. At the university, Frances took courses in English, Latin, French, Greek, scientific German, physics, quantitative analysis, organic chemistry, and astronomy. She joined the Denver University Glee Club and sang in concerts at schools, churches, and military bases. Despite all these commitments, Frances still found time to help make fudge for sick soldiers billeted in the college infirmary during the 1917–1918 influenza epidemic. One day, she handed her fudge to "a very tall, blond, thin private in charge of a tent."[1] David Mills thanked her so graciously that for once she forgot to blush.

After acquiring her bachelor's degree in May 1918, she continued for her master's. As usual, she spent most of her time in Science Hall and wrote a master's thesis investigating the detection of morphine poisoning. While researching her thesis she became absorbed in toxicology, the science of poisons.

Frances was blossoming into a slender, petite woman with curly black hair, brown eyes, and a warm smile. She began dating men she had shyly avoided. Dave Mills, the former army private, turned up in her zoology class and again on the No. 8 streetcar, working as a student conductor to pay his way through law school.

Frances received her master of arts in chemistry when she was nineteen. At graduation exercises, the dean announced that she was the youngest student ever to receive a master's degree from the University of Denver. Frances started teaching at Englewood High School in September 1919. The superintendent overloaded his rookie instructor with classes in general science, biology, chemistry, plane geometry, trigonometry, and physics. Her classroom was a vast lecture hall and some of her students were taller and older than she. She enjoyed teaching every subject but physics, which she had to study late every night to keep up with her advanced students. Then came frigid months with heavy snow. In February 1920, she came down with a cold, tonsillitis, and infected ears that confined her to bed with a high fever. Although critically ill, she was forced to return to school in two weeks.

At the close of the May term, she inquired about entrance to the University of Colorado Medical School. The dean approved her application and said the medical profession would be fortunate to have a member of her caliber. But going to medical school proved far more demanding than Frances had expected. Her father, who during his lifetime advanced money to put seventeen young men through medical school, unexpectedly refused to help pay his own daughter's tuition, saying, "Medicine is too hard a life for a woman." So Frances and her sister Margaret got a job playing piano and violin duets between films at the Lux Theater in Denver. To pay her medical school bills, Frances also sang and played the piano in local night clubs, tutored, and worked as a lab assistant.

While studying infectious diseases, she and her classmates practiced using their stethoscopes. They were startled to hear a murmur in Frances's heart valve and she realized she had contracted rheumatic fever during her year at Englewood High School. Despite her heart problems, she received her medical degree on June 15, 1925, and was accepted into the prestigious Denver General Hospital internship program, becoming the second woman to intern there. Other interns helped her through the long days in surgery by swapping surgery rotations for medicine and pathology.

Frances unexpectedly ran into the former soldier–streetcar conductor, Dave Mills, who was tutoring a fellow law student, Frank Mobley, who was her cousin. They began dating seriously and were married on November 14, 1925, at her home in University Park. Dave joined a Denver law partnership, while Frances spent long hours completing her internship in the hospital wards, laboratories, and morgue. Three months later, her breathlessness and atrial fibrillation intensified. Her father knew why—she was pregnant—and he insisted she spend the rest of her pregnancy in a wheelchair. Frances's daughter, who was born prematurely, was so tiny they carried her around on a pillow.

After her internship, Dr. McConnell continued at Denver General Hospital as a toxicologist in the coroner's officer, headed by the deputy coroner George Bostwick and city pathologist Dr. W. S. Dennis. In 1926, she was appointed city toxicologist and, in 1927, assistant pathologist. Most of her criminal work involved poison analysis. She became expert at finding clues among mundane objects like pocket dust, hairs, stains, bone splinters, and clothing scraps. But she tended to ignore toxicology's perils. In her first major court case, the young toxicologist testified as an expert witness for a pharmaceutical company being sued by a farmer who said he lost his voice after taking its cough syrup. During the trial, the plaintiff's attorney challenged Dr. McConnell to swallow the offending medicine. She felt obliged to demonstrate the medicine's safety. But when the lawyer handed her the bottle, questions raced through her mind. Had the contents been switched? Would she lose her voice? Her hands shook as she poured the liquid into the spoon. She closed her eyes, swallowed the medicine, and—with inward relief—continued her testimony. The farmer lost his case.

In her next investigation, Dr. McConnell tested the stomach contents of Archie Fennell, whose body had been found beside his wrecked car. During the autopsy, Doctors Dennis and McConnell determined that Fennell had committed suicide. In the process, they almost followed him to the grave. Both physicians fell violently ill—overcome by arsenic fumes that had formed in the deceased man's stomach.

One of her most famous cases began the morning of October 15, 1930, when ten-year-old Leona O'Loughlin disappeared from her Denver home. Learning Leona hadn't shown up for school, her father, a police detective, combed the neighborhood and then launched an intensive police search. Days later, police pulled little Leona's body from Berkeley Park Lake. Dr. McConnell conducted the autopsy. Finding no poison in little Leona's stomach, she ran other tests and came across ground glass. When she submitted her report, police arrested the child's stepmother, pretty, red-haired Pearl O'Loughlin. Next, they brought in a stained tire iron from the O'Loughlins' family car. Dr. McConnell identified the red stain as human blood.

Before the trial, scheduled for November 24, *Rocky Mountain News* headlines disclosed: "Hovering Stork Menaces State in O'Loughlin Trial." In fact, the district attorney's office was growing anxious that "Dr. Stork" might seriously handicap the prosecution's case by eliminating Dr. McConnell's scientific testimony in what had become Denver's most famous and controversial murder case. Unperturbed, Dr. McConnell appeared in court on schedule to testify without interruption and see the stepmother sentenced to a life term in the State Penitentiary at Canon City for feeding Leona ground glass, then bludgeoning and drowning her. "Dr. Stork" meanwhile, waited until January 6, 1931, to deliver the Millses' son.

In 1935, Dr. McConnell was called to Raton, New Mexico, as chief witness in the trial of a rancher accused of killing his neighbor with an axe.

The *Raton Ranger* reported during the trial that "the attractive 35-year-old woman has gained a national reputation ... in her blood analysis work, especially in connection with criminal cases." The writer went on to describe her as "a charming, gracious and attractive woman."[3]

After her marriage, Frances McConnell continued using her maiden name professionally to keep her children out of the limelight. She avoided the public eye as much as possible and granted only one interview during her long career. But she was involved in several dramatic and highly publicized cases, including one in Pueblo in which two young girls were brutally beaten in their bed. Although police captured Joseph Arridy, who had escaped from the State Mental Hospital in Grand Junction, they had no witnesses to the crime and lacked strong evidence to convict him. In unraveling the puzzle, Dr. McConnell analyzed minute fingernail and bedspread fragments found at the crime scene and on the victims and suspect.

At Arridy's trial, Dr. McConnell exhibited before the jury the cerise bedspread on which the crime had been committed, showed scrapings from Arridy's fingernails that contained cerise fibers from the bedspread and blonde hairs identical to those of one of the victims. Darkening the courtroom, she projected onto a screen the highly magnified fibers and hairs. Arridy became noticeably agitated during her testimony. He conferred with his attorney and within minutes, he changed his plea to guilty. Arridy was convicted of the murder and later executed in the Canon City gas chamber.

Frances McConnell once said, "Of all murder methods, poisoning is the most sophisticated. It's premeditated. You need to plan. Carry it out. Be patient."[4] Of the poisoners, none was more sophisticated than the Lucretia Borgia of Cincinnati, Anna Marie Hahn, a comely blonde nurse, who cared for a procession of elderly, well-to-do men in her home. One by one, her patients died, leaving Hahn with bequests and insurance amounting to $70,000. Even with autopsies, police could not link the deaths to Hahn. In 1936, Hahn brought George Obendorfer, a middle-aged shoemaker, to Colorado Springs where neighbors reported sex orgies and strange goings-on. When he died, Dr. McConnell did the autopsy and found traces of arsenic and croton oil. Had they been used as a body preservative or as a poison? She went on to test the urine and bile and discovered the lethal arsenic dose—revealing Hahn's scheme of delivering her victims to undertakers who still used arsenic as embalming fluid, which would disguise the arsenic used as the poison. On the strength of her evidence, Cincinnati police exhumed Hahn's previous victims. Sure enough, Hahn had poisoned a dozen other men with the same method. Dr. McConnell testified in Cincinnati and saw Hahn sentenced to die in the electric chair.

In addition to her high-profile work in toxicology, Dr. McConnell had begun research in 1934 on passive immunity, or convalescent serums. After a scarlet fever epidemic hit her daughter's school, Frances injected her with a convalescent serum she had developed. The serum protected her daughter, who unknowingly passed scarlet fever on to her brother. In 1938, Dr. McConnell developed an early polio serum and in the 1940s, she produced shots for head colds and acne to use on family members. During this time period, Dr. McConnell was working in the private laboratory of Dr. Harry Baum, a Denver ear, nose, and throat specialist. While there, she developed safe hair rinses and invented one of the first successful rinses, which Dr. Baum named "Noreen"—a popular hair product for decades. Noreen was still being produced in 1994.

Dr. McConnell returned to hospital laboratory work in April 1941 when the Colorado State Board of Health named her director of the laboratory division of the State Board of Health. During World War II, when the state laboratory's staff and funding were drastically reduced, Dr. McConnell and her eighteen technicians turned out a record 900 lab tests a day. To alleviate the personnel shortage and enhance opportunities for women, she founded and directed the School for Medical Technologists at Denver General Hospital.

Frances McConnell took a month's leave of absence from the State Board of Health in 1941 to undergo advanced training in serology (a science dealing with blood serums) at the University of Michigan. Two years later, she went to Chicago's Cook County Hospital for specialized postgraduate work in surgical pathology. She left the State Board of Health in June 1943 to become full-time pathologist and laboratory director at St. Luke's, a private Denver hospital. Although working full-time at the hospital, she continued to assist in murder investigations. Her last murder case was the murder-rape of University of Colorado coed Theresa Foster in November 1948. After a wide manhunt, Boulder police arrested Joe Sam Walker, whose wife turned him in. During the trial, Dr. McConnell was interviewed by mystery writer Erle Stanley Gardner.

Frances McConnell's career was interrupted in April 1944 by an emergency appendectomy. Her rheumatic heart apparently withstood the anesthesia but a blood clot lodged in the artery supplying blood to her legs. Surgeons were obliged to amputate her right leg above the knee. After four surgeries and a six-month hospital stay, Frances finally came home in September. She experimented with a procession of artificial legs, an exhausting process for her weak heart. She finally chose a light-weight, experimental prosthesis. With characteristic humor, she named her new leg Matilda. In January 1945, less than a year after her illness, she was reappointed director of laboratories at Denver General Hospital. In response to her family's disapproval, she repeated, "It's criminal to waste a good education." She no longer could drive, so Dave delivered her every day to the hospital and an ambulance brought her home.

During this period, Dr. McConnell consulted in her field of pathology with the distinguished Dr. Florence Sabin, who was drawing up Colorado's new public health laws. The two physicians drew up an examination for the State Board of Basic Sciences to test and approve applicants for licenses to practice health science in Colorado. In 1956, Governor Edwin C. Johnson appointed Dr. McConnell to the State Board of Basic Sciences. The only woman on the board, she represented the medical profession and served with dedication until two weeks before her death. On December 23, 1974, she received an award as a fifty-year graduate of the University of Colorado School of Medicine and for being one of two women who practiced medicine in Colorado for fifty years.

After her husband, David L. Mills, died on September 13, 1967, Frances lived alone. Although confined to a wheelchair, she conducted a small allergy practice, pursued many volunteer activities, consulted for the Denver Poison Center, and encouraged other women in medicine. Her family would produce three more physicians and another chemist. Frances McConnell-Mills died at St. Luke's Hospital on December 28, 1975. She was seventy-five.

Caroline Bancroft

Born September 11, 1900, in Denver, Colorado
Died October 8, 1985, in Denver, Colorado

Colorado history should be told as it was—"alive and kicking"—said Caroline Bancroft, who called herself a social historian because she enjoyed people. Because of her forthright tongue, Bancroft became famous for her feuds. She had a knack for making enemies, whom she enjoyed as much as her friends.

Caroline was larger than life. Backing up her imposing personal presence was her six-foot, 190-pound physique. With her auburn-dyed coronet of braids surmounted by a spray of silk flowers, she did not go unnoticed. A third-generation Coloradan and granddaughter of Dr. Frederick J. Bancroft, a founder of the Colorado Historical Society, she was born into Colorado history—and into Colorado's "upper-crust" society, which eventually would open many doors for her.

When a child, she wrote to *St. Nicholas,* a popular children's magazine, beginning her lifelong habit of corresponding with publishers and famous personages. She also loved to ride the family's horses, stabled at the Wentworth Livery on Corona Street. On weekends and summers, she caught the Barnum streetcar out to her father's Clover Knoll Farm or visited the family summer home in Bear Creek Canyon, where she covered the Bancrofts' 2,500 acres on horseback. Caroline and her younger sister, Peggy, graduated from Corona School and

North Denver High School. In the afternoons, Caroline gave dancing lessons at her parents' dancing studio at 220 Broadway.

When she was seventeen, she ran away to New York City and was hired as an understudy at the Ziegfield Night Follies. "I was vivacious and good-looking and a maverick," she recalled.[1] But her mother, Ethel Norton Bancroft, heard about Caroline's escapade and soon a "batch of relatives" arrived to dispatch her back to Denver.

Ethel Bancroft was determined that Caroline have a proper education, even though her father, George Jarvis Bancroft, Jr., "had blown half a million on wine, women, and mining," as Caroline later told it. Ethel somehow got her daughter into Smith College in Massachusetts. After graduating, Caroline taught at a country day school in Connecticut, gave dancing lessons, and exercised horses.

Summers were best. She chaperoned student tours on a cruise ship to finance her extended forays through Europe and the Far East. She collected celebrities and then wangled a traveling assignment with the *New York Evening Post* to publish her interviews with John Galsworthy, George Bernard Shaw, G. K. Chesterton, Somerset Maugham, Andre Maurois, and Rabindranath Tagore.

Portraits of Caroline from the period show a good-looking young woman with large, expressive eyes. The lifestyle, alas, took its toll on her health and pocketbook. In 1928, she returned to Denver, where she talked "F. G."—Frederick G. Bonfils of the *Denver Post,* an old neighborhood acquaintance—to take her on as book editor. In those days, the *Post* was considered a scandal sheet and no place for a daughter of the gentry. That didn't stop Caroline. As literary editor, she enlarged her celebrity correspondence to include Carl Sandburg, Eve Curie, Louis Untermeyer, Dorothy Thompson, Libbie Block, and Lucius Beebe.

Bancroft's next move unexpectedly changed her life. To appease *Post* Managing Editor William Shepherd, who was not sold on the book editor idea, she began writing old-timer stories. To bolster her knowledge of the subject, she took a history course at the University of Denver—a course that turned into a master's degree. Her grandfather's pedigree, her own 1923 society debut in Troy, New York, and the family's many prominent friends gave her access to every big name in the state. As a charter member of Denver's Junior League, she also wrote frequent articles for its magazine and in the 1940s taught history at Randall, a private school. Without realizing it, she was becoming addicted to Colorado history.

In 1927, a trip with her father, a mining engineer, took her to the Matchless Mine above Leadville to meet Baby Doe Tabor. At the time, Caroline was unimpressed by the second Mrs. Tabor, who threatened to run them off with her "rifle"—a broomstick carved and painted to resemble a gun. "She was old and didn't like women anyway," Caroline wrote later.[2] In 1938, Caroline had a chance to write a five-part biography about Baby Doe for *True Story* magazine. She became so obsessed with Baby Doe's story that she didn't stop researching it until long after the story came out.

After World War II, Easterners who had been going abroad began coming to Colorado. Caroline noted the shortage of "readable" accounts of Colorado history. The Central City Opera Association asked her to write a booklet. She was thinking in terms of "something that was light—light on the pocketbook and light in the suitcase." Using her master's thesis on Central City, she put out her first booklet, "A Guide to Central City," in 1946. It sold for 50 cents.

This first booklet led to others. *Silver Queen: The Fabulous Story of Baby Doe Tabor*, was probably Bancroft's best-selling booklet. Bancroft paid $500 for printing 5,000 copies, marketed them at 50 cents each, and netted $800. A later edition in 1950 sold out in four months at $1 and the price rose to $1.50 for the eleventh edition. Just to be fair, she added *Augusta Tabor: Her Side of the Scandal.* She went on to write *Denver's Lively Past, Famous Aspen, Glenwood's Early Glamour, Six Racy Madames, Tabor's Matchless Mine and Lusty Leadville,* and *The Unsinkable Mrs. Brown.* The booklets, which caught on as fun to read and easy introductions to Colorado history, became Bancroft's greatest contribution to Colorado. Johnson Books of Boulder continues to publish Bancroft's booklets.

Her interest in Leadville and the Tabor stories spurred her to set up a Baby Doe Museum at the Matchless Mine. She also was a founding member of the Central City Opera House Association and Historic Denver. In 1957, when vandals broke into the Matchless Mine and inflicted severe damage, she wrote a blistering letter to the Leadville *Herald Democrat* on July 9, accusing townspeople and local police of being "stuck back in shabby Depression and Prohibition periods" with "morals of hillbilly illiterates." She noted that they were afraid of strangers because they were "ignorant, rude, and surly." Angry Leadvillites responded, calling Bancroft a "self-styled Leadville historian ... and [inquiring] who asked her to do anything."[3] There was talk of hanging her in effigy, but the feud apparently died down.

Caroline was known among her contemporaries for her high-handedness and eccentricities. A dispute with her former history cohort, Fred Mazzulla, hit the newspapers and continued for years. She also had many close friends, including Mary Coyle Chase, the Denver playwright, with whom she maintained a lifelong correspondence. Patricia Wilcox, well-known Lakewood newspaper woman and later a Bancroft chum, recalls inviting the historian to dinner at her home. "She was escorted by 'Uncle Bob' Lupo, who worked as bartender at Caroline's famous cocktail parties," Wilcox said. "Caroline arrived wrapped in a shower curtain, to protect her from the dog hairs in Lupo's car. (Caroline, herself, raised Persian cats.) Everyone at the party was so entertaining, they stayed until 4 A.M."[4]

Caroline continued to live at the Bancroft home at 1081 Downing Street until she moved to the Waldman Apartments, 1515 East Ninth Avenue. She divided her time during the last fifteen years between Denver, Hawaii, and Jamaica, seeking relief from her health problems. She had tuberculosis three times, cancer four times, and once was blind for almost a year. Afflicted with tinnitus, she later walked with a peculiar gait. "There's nothing golden in old age," she would say. "It's only brass."[5]

Before Caroline died, she planned her own funeral services to be conducted at St. John's Episcopal Cathedral. She arranged to be buried at Fairmount Cemetery across from her favorite madame, Jenny Rogers (who is interred under the pseudonym of Leah J. Wood).

Antonia Brico

Born June 26, 1902, in Rotterdam, Holland
Died August 3, 1989, in Denver, Colorado

During a lifetime of standing ovations and dashed hopes, Antonia Brico carved out a spectacular career as an orchestra conductor and pianist. Her lifelong dream was to be the full-time music director of a major professional orchestra. But the music world labeled her with the catchword "woman conductor" and too often portrayed her as a novelty.

The popular folk singer Judy Collins, Dr. Brico's most famous and devoted vocal student, wrote and directed an award-winning documentary film titled "Antonia: A Portrait of the Woman" to dramatize the conductor's struggle to make her way in a male profession. The film premiered in 1973 at the Telluride Festival. It was then shown at the New Filmmakers Series at the Whitney Museum in New York and was nominated for an Oscar as the best documentary of 1974.[1]

In *There Was Light*, edited by Irving Stone, Antonia Brico revealed her early history in a cameo autobiography. Her mother—the daughter of a "respectable" Amsterdam family—fell in love with a nightclub piano player. When she became pregnant, the piano player rejected her and she returned home in disgrace. To save face, the family sent her to Rotterdam to work as a domestic until the baby was born. Antonia's mother took her infant to a convent and then advertised for foster parents. A Mrs. Wolthuis answered the ad and for a sum she took the baby as a foster child; she called her Wilhemina Wolthuis although she never adopted her. Mrs. Wolthuis beat Wilhemina and degraded her as an illegitimate child who never would amount to anything. When Wilhemina was five they moved to Oakland, California.

Wilhemina first touched a piano when she was ten and instantly was smitten with a passion for music. After attending her first concert, she commented, "I liked the piece in the key of G." She then saw a band concert at Lakeland Park, and as she later recalled, "I was fascinated by what a small stick could do."[2] The Wolthuises gave her piano lessons in hopes of getting her into a vaudeville troupe. When they learned that vaudeville did not use classical pianists, the lessons stopped. Wilhemina continued studying on her own, and when she graduated from high school she sneaked out to register at the University of California. When she told her foster parents where she had been, they threw her out.

Now fully on her own, she started calling herself Antonia Brico—most likely her original name. Supported by scholarships, a full-time job at Woolworth's, and waiting tables, she studied piano with Paul Steindorff. The campus was her home and faculty members were her parents—although no one could compensate for the absence of her own mother.

By the time she was nineteen she had become a concert pianist. But she had her sights on conducting a major symphony orchestra. In preparation, she learned to play every instrument and to speak many languages. In 1923, she acquired her bachelor of arts in music from the University of California. She was admitted to the prestigious Berlin State Academy of Music Master School of Conducting—the first American conductor, man or woman, accepted there. She studied under several great maestros including Dr. Carl Muck, who termed her "a very great talent."

In 1930, Antonia sponsored her own world conducting debut with the Berlin Philharmonic Orchestra, a triumph that led to an engagement directing the Warsaw Philharmonic. In her American debut later that year, she conducted a concert at the Hollywood Bowl in Los Angeles. In 1931, she performed before the Belgian Queen Elizabeth in Brussels.

During the Depression, conducting invitations dried up and Antonia sank into deepest despair and poverty. For six months, she stayed with poor friends in Vienna until help came unexpectedly from a Jewish friend in Riga, Latvia. Mrs. Ernest Feigenberg, a soprano whom Antonia once had coached in operatic roles, invited her to conduct a series of summer concerts. Buoyed by their success, Brico became guest conductor for twenty concerts in Latvia and Poland. Returning to Berlin in January 1932, she accompanied six opera singers as they performed at cabarets in Baltic seaport towns. When the Nazis began moving in, the troupe had to go underground in Dusseldorf. Antonia managed to borrow some money there and the singers sneaked her aboard a train to Holland. From there, she sailed to New York, where she again found herself broke and out of work.

Despite the setbacks, Antonia kept climbing toward her goal. Mrs. Sydney Prince and Mrs. Olin Downes, wife of the *New York Times* music critic, asked her to conduct a symphony concert at the Metropolitan Opera House. Mrs. Prince made her a concert dress, fed her at her own table, and the two women sold $1,000 worth of tickets. The success of this concert led Antonia to conducting engagements with the Detroit Symphony, some operas in Manhattan, and then to direct the Works Progress Administration Symphony.

She was playing chamber music with nine women in New York in 1934, when she realized that if nine women could give a concert, then ninety women could do it too. She founded the New York Women's Symphony Orchestra (later Brico Symphony Orchestra to include male musicians). Under her baton, the group presented Verdi's *Requiem* at Carnegie Hall with full orchestra, four soloists, and a 285-voice chorus. New York music critics gave the performance rave notices.

Four years later, Mills College in Oakland, California, awarded her an honorary doctor of music degree for outstanding contribution to the progress of music. While at Mills in the summer of 1940, she taught classes in conducting. Her career advanced when she conducted the New London Symphony and appeared at Lincoln Center in New York and Kennedy Center in Washington. She stopped in Denver in 1945 to guest-conduct the Denver Civic Orchestra, directed the annual *Denver Post* opera, and gave a course on Wagner operas at Colorado College. She still dreamed of becoming a permanent musical director and saw an opening in 1945. The Denver Civic Symphony Orchestra (forerunner of today's Colorado Symphony Orchestra) intended to become a full professional orchestra and was interviewing for the position of director.

Dr. Brico moved to Denver with the understanding that the position would be hers. But conducting orchestras was still an all-male profes-

sion and women were not welcomed into its pristine ranks. The orchestra board denied that it had made her a firm offer or that it had invited her to join the list of male conductors auditioning for music director, despite her imposing credentials. It was a heartbreaking defeat
for Dr. Brico. But she liked Denver. She opened the exclusive Brico Studio at 959 South Pennsylvania Street and soon seventy students were
enrolled. Joanna Palacas, a classical piano teacher from Washington,
D.C., brought her ten-year-old daughter, Helen, for lessons. Dr. Brico
said her time was filled; she could not audition Helen until she had a
cancellation. If accepted, however, Helen might start with lessons on a
cancellation basis.

"Dr. Brico had a very strong, intelligent face and a stern manner,"
Palacas recalled. "Mothers were required to attend each lesson and take
notes for their children's practice. ... Antonia was the most systematic
and consistent teacher I ever observed. Although I had studied piano
pedagogy in college, I really learned to teach from her methodical system. I became her assistant, taking borderline students until they were
ready for Brico."[3]

The Brico Studio was impressive with two Steinway grand pianos
that filled the room. The walls were lined, floor to ceiling, with photographs of such musical giants as Bruno Walter, Artur Rubinstein,
Finnish composer Jean Sibelius, and humanitarian Albert Schweitzer.
Dr. Brico spoke of having befriended Schweitzer in Aspen and visiting
him in 1958 at his jungle hospital in French Equatorial Africa. On five
occasions she went to study Bach with Schweitzer, who was an organ
builder, musician, writer, philosopher, theologian, and renowned authority on Bach and Goethe. Dr. Brico also recounted her two visits to
Jean Sibelius's home in Helsinki, where she studied his music with
him. In 1946, Sibelius announced that Brico was the greatest interpreter of his work and chose her to conduct the Helsinki Symphony in
an all-Sibelius concert. After the concert, she was decorated by the
Finnish government.

In Denver, Dr. Brico served as music director at Trinity Methodist
Church for five years. In 1947, the newly organized Denver Business-
men's Orchestra asked her to be permanent conductor and music

director of its amateur musicians. Although it was difficult for Brico, the perfectionist, to pull perfect sounds from unpaid musicians, the orchestra had many shining moments. For Verdi's *Requiem,* she directed the orchestra along with soloists and four choruses—again to rave reviews. The orchestra's many fans maintained it was far superior, in its heyday, to the Denver Symphony and later renamed it the Brico Orchestra in her honor.

"When you joined the Brico Studio you became fully involved," Palacas noted. "Spring Spectaculars in the 1960s and '70s were very exciting. Antonia (wearing her same black dress), would be leading the orchestra, children's chorus, and her many students who also participated."[4] Dr. Brico insisted that her most promising students learn two instruments so they could play with the orchestra. Young Helen Palacas took up the violin along with the piano and it paid off. When she was fifteen, Helen was playing with the Brico Orchestra and became a top young pianist in Colorado.

Betty Frandsen, a Jefferson County soprano who was coached by Dr. Brico for eight years, often appeared as a soloist with the Brico Orchestra. Frandsen considered Dr. Brico an inspiring teacher who had the gift of perfect pitch. She recalls the Rachmaninoff Steinway Grand in Brico's living room and her devoted secretary, Elizabeth Jans, who looked after Antonia and kept up the apartment.

The Denver Symphony was interviewing conductors again in 1963 and once more bypassed Dr. Brico. Denver audiences by then were familiar with her brilliant work with the Denver Businessmen's Orchestra. *Rocky Mountain News* writer Marjorie Barrett wrote a column urging the Denver Symphony Society to offer the post to Dr. Brico. *Rocky Mountain News* music critic Allen Young feared privately that the opportunity came too late, with Brico perhaps past her prime. In the end, the symphony selected the aging Vladimir Golschmann, a conductor with European charm and heavy commitments abroad.

As years passed, Antonia became increasingly eccentric. She would say that Americans were more into the emotion of music than the technique. Her mind closed to musical progress in the United States; her music grew more rigid and Germanic. In 1985, the Brico Orchestra accepted her retirement after thirty-nine years. Guest conducting invitations were dropping off, too, and some of her students went elsewhere. Her loyal secretary, Elizabeth, continued to care for Antonia, while a small corps of students and mothers drove her to do weekly shopping and errands with the reward of lunch afterward. On January 30, 1988, Antonia was leaving a Judy Collins concert when she slipped on ice and broke her shoulder and hip. Her health declined rapidly after the accident and she died in a nursing home on August 3, 1989.

She came so close so often to the dream of having her own major symphony orchestra, but was defeated first by gender prejudice and later by the limits of her personality. Some say her greatest triumphs came from her inspired teaching, both instrumental and vocal. Her most famous students, James Winn and Cameron Grant, continued to perform in concerts at home and abroad as two-piano virtuosos.

Antonia Brico once said that music was her life and soul and that it transcended language differences. She constantly listened to music when she ate, when she awoke, and when she went to sleep. Music was her family—along with a treasured little dog, which she nurtured like a child. She had succeeded repeatedly as the "first woman who was an orchestra conductor,"[5] blazing a path for later generations of woman impresarios. How ironic that the same Denver symphony orchestra that denied Dr. Brico an audition later hired a woman conductor—Marin Alsop.

Mary Coyle Chase
Born February 25, 1906, in Denver, Colorado
Died October 20, 1981, in Denver, Colorado

Colorado's first Pulitzer Prize–winning playwright was a true Irish lass reared on legends of banshees and leprechauns. Mary Coyle Chase grew up in the Catholic household of Frank Coyle, a flour salesman, who raised his four children in a wee house in west Denver. Mary's mother, Mary McDonough Coyle, an immigrant from Ulster, North Ireland, was a spinner of tales and fantasies from the old country. The four McDonough uncles from County Tyrone regaled the Coyle children with stories of sprites and wee folk. It was said that one of Mary's brothers did a stint as a circus clown; the other, Colin, became a priest. Such early Celtic ties reinforced Mary's emotional and whimsical nature and later supplied imaginary characters for her plays.

Mary was eleven when she saw the Denham Theatre Stock Company presentation of *Macbeth*. The experience turned her into a lifelong drama devotee who read plays and attended performances whenever she could get a ticket. Mary graduated from West High School at age fifteen and enrolled at the University of Colorado.

When she was seventeen, she got a job as reporter with the *Rocky Mountain News* and began her daredevil days at the paper. *News* historian Frances Melrose later wrote that Mary didn't seek the job for its glamour or pay but as a forum for studying people and their reactions to life for later use in her plays. In the style of Helen Black, an earlier *News* reporter who rode on the back of a motorcycle, Mary often was seen flying around town beside *News* photographer Harry Rhoads in a Model-T Ford. Mary Coyle was a ravishing beauty who often dressed in lace bodices and black velvet hats. Newsmen called her the most beautiful newspaper reporter in Denver and admired her clear blue eyes, flawless skin, dark hair, and elegant taste in clothes. She covered everything from three-alarm fires to Reddy Gallagher's prizefights at the Denver Athletic Club.

Competition between newspapers was fierce at that time—the height of Denver's yellow journalism era. When the *News* needed a photo of a prominent husband in a racy divorce scandal, Mary remembered his portrait was at the Denver Country Club. She caught a bus to the club and snatched the portrait off the wall. Running out just ahead of the club's manager, she stopped a truck for a ride back to the *News*. Rhoads copied the picture and Mary got the original back to the angry club manager. While a reporter, Mary met many celebrities, among them Dorothy Parker who later described Mary as "the greatest unacclaimed wit in America."[1]

Mary's journalism days instilled in her priceless qualities: a sense of fairness, objectivity, and a human touch to her writing. But her best asset was fellow reporter Robert Lamont Chase, whom she married on June 7, 1928. Chase, later city editor and then associate editor, was the solid, steadying influence in her life—and the father of their three sons, Michael, Colin, and Jerry.

Mary worked at the *News* for seven years—until she was fired for one of her notorious telephone pranks. The *News* was co-sponsoring the Christmas Good Fellow Club's food basket distribution to the poor. As the holidays rapidly approached, one editor, known for his short temper, was working feverishly to meet a deadline. Mary—a gifted mimic—phoned the editor and flew into a tirade, accusing him of handing out wormy apples to poor children in the name of charity—and not a shred of turkey, she added. She even asked him if he had kept all the good apples. The editor began to apologize and explain but she interrupted: Did he want her kids to get worms? "Mrs. Beatrice Lillian Gwendolyn O'Hanrahan" carried on until the poor editor screamed that he'd have someone check her basket and hung up. Admiring the gag, other reporters tried their own versions until the editor learned Mrs. O'Hanrahan's real identity and fired Mary.

She later got her job back but then quit to work briefly for United Press and International News Service. But with a husband and three boys to see to, there was plenty to do at home. Besides, she was ready to start writing her long-delayed plays. She set up an ancient typewriter on the dining table of their house at 1376 St. Paul Street and wrote at night after the boys were asleep. Her first play, *Now You've Done It,* flopped on Broadway in 1937. Her second play never was produced. Then she wrote *Sorority House* based on her brief college life, which was bought for a few thousand dollars and made into a moderately successful movie.

A leprechaun must have been sitting on the curb one bleak morning in 1942 as Mary walked her boys to school. They passed a working woman trudging to the bus stop. Mary had heard about the poor widow, who worked for years to put her only son through college. He was called into the military during World War II and was killed in action in the Pacific. Trapped in her empty days, the widow just kept going to work. Mary became obsessed with the idea of writing something so funny it would make even that poor mother laugh again. For months, she waited for inspiration. Then she remembered her mother's tales of the pookah, a fairy in the shape of an animal that could be seen only by an owner who believed in pookahs. For two years, she wrote and rewrote the play.

In the first draft, the owner was a woman and the pookah was a six-foot canary. Gradually, the owner evolved into an easygoing lush named Elwood P. Dowd and the canary became a six-foot white rabbit named Harvey. She polished the manuscript and read it to neighborhood children, her cleaning lady, and her friend Caroline Bancroft. Then she took a deep breath and sent if off to New York producer Brock Pemberton.

Pemberton soon called to say he was putting *Harvey* into production and she must come to New York at once to oversee rehearsals and rewriting. As Mary Chase later recalled, that one phone call shut the door to her past life and opened another. Comedian Frank Fay, the first of many Elwood Dowds, was followed by Joe E. Brown, Gig Young, and Jimmy Stewart. *Harvey* played in several cities before opening on Broadway in November 1944. Mary had to borrow money to follow the openings from city to city. In her purse, she carried a note from her husband: "Don't be unhappy if the play doesn't succeed. You still have your husband and your three boys and they all love you."

After opening night on Broadway, Frank Fay called Mary to announce she had a hit on her hands. *Harvey* ran on Broadway four and one-half years and toured Europe, Australia, and the United States repeatedly. Movie rights were sold for more than $1 million, the highest price paid for a film script until that time. The movie starred Jimmy Stewart, and in 1945 *Harvey* won the Pulitzer Prize. Mary never met the poor working widow, but the play became famous.

Returning to their little house on St. Paul Street, where dust had gathered and weeds had grown up, Mary tried to work. But the phone and doorbell rang constantly. She had trouble sorting out friends and well-wishers from hangers-on, salesmen, social climbers, and interviewers. Funny, outgoing Mary changed into a quiet, guarded, disillusioned rich woman. It took years to regain her peace of mind.

In 1945, the Chase family moved to a gracious mansion on Denver's palatial Circle Drive because Mary's father, eighty-five and in failing health, needed a first-floor bedroom. She went though a period of buying furniture and antiques and shopping for designer clothes and spectacular hats (always a comforting pastime). Mary, who had many friends and loved a good party, took a long time getting back to those pleasures. She struggled with alcoholism and later founded the House of Hope, a home for women alcoholics. She resumed her education at the University of Denver, and in 1947, the university presented her with an Honorary Doctor of Fine Arts Degree.

Despite the failure of one of her earlier plays, *The Next Half Hour,* which had opened on Broadway and closed in a week, she got out her typewriter and started a new one. It sprang from her memory of a woman who had changed from a loving mother into a whining harridan. A comedy intended for children, it took five years to complete and was titled *Mrs. McThing.* As before, Mary tested her script on the neighborhood children and then polished, and rewrote. She sent *Mrs. McThing* to her New York agent with orders that it was for amateurs only and not to be performed on Broadway. But a year later, a director talked her into a two-week Broadway production of the play. At the same time, her hit comedy, *Bernadine,* was playing at the Playhouse Theater on Broadway. *Mrs. McThing* opened at the theatre next door and starred Helen Hayes with Ernest Borgnine, Irwin Corey, and Fred Gwynne. It was so successful that Helen Hayes starred in a week-long performance at Central City.

Mary Chase told Mark Barron in a *News* interview on October 26, 1952, that playwriting is a complicated craft that takes a long time to learn. She used a four-foot portable model theater to plot out how the stage would look as each line was spoken. "An important ingredient in a good play is craftsmanship. ... A play is like a building. One false line and the structure collapses. ... You can go so far [with] workmanship and technique, but from there playwriting is a hunch. ... It's good or bad but you can't quite tell why."[2]

Despite her success in New York, she worked closely with those in the Denver theatre scene. In 1951, she commended Helen Bonfils and the Civic Theater for their fine work and for always giving a beginning playwright an opportunity. Donald Seawell—former New York producer and lawyer who took over the Bonfils Foundation and Denver Center for the Performing Arts—praised Mary as "a friend and valued board member of Bonfils Theater and the Denver Center, because she was a professional."[3]

Mary Coyle Chase died October 20, 1981, a few hours after suffering a heart attack at home. Newspapers eulogized her for her literary accomplishments and her unique personal qualities. Helen Hayes said she was "a wise woman, an Irish mystic. There was no arrogance in Mary at all, [just] such charming humility and modesty."[4] Mary Chase, an honorary member of Denver Woman's Press Club, was posthumously inducted into the Colorado Women's Hall of Fame.

She wrote fifteen plays, most of them with at least one imaginary character, and always kept one thing in mind: "When you begin to think you're good, you're through."[5]

Jane Silverstein Ries

Born March 10, 1909, in Denver, Colorado

Jane Silverstein Ries was Denver's first woman landscape architect. A pioneer in her field, she was a leader in seeking creative solutions to problems created by Colorado's changing lifestyle and environment. A tiny sprite of a woman with snapping dark eyes, a shock of white hair, and an air of crisp authority, she still ran her large practice in landscape architecture until well into her eighties. (She liked to introduce herself as an "octo-geranium.")

Jane Silverstein was born in Denver of German parentage. Her father was a Latin professor at the University of Colorado. Although she was not the most brilliant student at East High School, she decided early that she wanted to enter a profession but she was not sure which one. A family friend who had gone into landscape architecture spoke of the enjoyment in planning and developing gardens and recommended it as a fine career for a woman. When Jane expressed interest, the friend gave her a brochure from the Lowthorpe School of Landscape Architecture for Women in Groton, Massachusetts, which was founded in 1901 and now is part of Harvard College. Jane possessed a natural sense of artistic balance, scale, proportion—and a willingness to work. At Lowthorpe, she learned about land construction, surveying, drafting, and Eastern plant material. The years 1928 to 1932, when Jane was at Groton, were the era of America's great estates. Her professors took students on tours of America's palatial houses along the North Shore. She particularly recalled the Crane Estate (of the plumbing fixture Cranes), with its thirty-five gardeners but she fell in love with Boston's small Beacon Hill city gardens—and city gardens became her specialty.

After graduating in 1932, Jane Silverstein came home to Denver, where just three landscape architecture firms were practicing at the time. She worked for one of the firms for a year and learned to adjust her training, which was geared to the East, to Colorado's alkaline soil and arid conditions. The Denver landscape at the time consisted of wide, open lawns and a very limited palette. Her first efforts focused on expanding that palette by searching out new plant materials in a variety of colors. She rarely used red in gardens—she hated Salvia—but brought in boxwood, Nandina ("heavenly bamboo"), the American cranberry bush, hawthorns, and Lantana.

After Jane left the firm, she set up her office above the garage of her parents' home at 725 Franklin Street, where she had lived since she was twelve years old. The surrounding property became her experimental work area and she created a stunning walled city garden. (In 1992, Jane's home was listed as a Denver Historic Landmark in recognition of her exquisite garden.) Jane's first jobs came through family connections. For her parents' friends, she charged $5 to design a garden. Her reputation soon spread like wild daisies. She did mostly residential landscaping—"city gardens, where people can relax." She refused to call them yards. "Yards are where you hang the laundry or dump your trash," she would say.[1]

An important aspect of landscape architecture is landscape preservation. In 1932, Jane worked under a famous New York architect who redesigned the historic landscape surrounding Senator Lawrence Phipps's lovely old Georgian house. Jane learned much from the project. When the University of Denver acquired the property and subdivided part of the land, she presented her landscape plans to the Denver Public Library Western History Department. Jane Silverstein was chosen as the landscape architect for General Electric's all-electric house on Denver's posh Circle Drive in the 1930s. This work did more for her reputation than any other single commission.

In 1941, she interrupted her landscaping career to work for the Federal Housing Authority. In 1943, she enrolled at the U.S. Coast Guard Academy to become a SPAR (a woman member of the U.S. Coast Guard). Because of her drafting training, she was assigned to the Civil Engineers at the Port Authority Director's Office in New York. Among her assignments was a property survey of Coast Guard lighthouses. In that capacity, she went to the New York City Library to select and purchase exquisite original drawings and paintings of old lighthouses, which she then appraised.

After leaving the Coast Guard, Jane Silverstein worked for two years as a landscape architect with Skidmore, Owings and Merrill in New York. When she resumed her private practice in Denver, her first commission was to landscape a racetrack. She drew up a design that called for planting in a small space at the center of the track, brought in hardy evergreens and Russian olives, and put in a garden with thousands of red roses.

Jane's friends remember her as a proper woman for her age, small and vivacious in a gentle way, interested and enthusiastic. She would joke about how she liked to force one hundred forsythia branches by bringing them indoors in containers. "They occupy a lot of window sills and it takes a long time to get them all watered. I have an indoor sick bay, too, where I nurse ailing plants," she said. She also loved to play tennis and owned a succession of dogs.

When she was forty-five, the dog she owned at the time brought an unexpected dimension into her life. One day, after a public speaking class, she was untying the dog when a classmate stopped to talk to the dog and introduced himself as Henry Ries. They struck up a conversation. Ries was a forty-nine-year-old insurance actuary who worked for the state, auditing the books of companies that sold insurance in Colorado. His work took him on the road half the year. Jane and Henry soon married and their unusual occupations meshed surprisingly well. Right after the wedding, she joined him for nine months in Connecticut where he was working. When she was alone at home, she concentrated on her business. They called their marriage "the original commuter marriage." At one point Henry created a small silver vase for Jane that attached to her lapel with a pin. She regularly carried small shears to snip a flower or ivy sprig to slip into the vase, which became her trademark and later was copyrighted.

She had an unusual commission in the 1960s, after the Boettcher family presented its mansion at 400 East Eighth Avenue to the state for use as the Governor's Mansion. The grounds needed plantings that would be practical around such a large house open to the public. She installed stepstones about the yard and screened out distracting neighborhood scenery.

Julia Andrews-Jones, who worked with Jane during her later years, described her unique style and strengths. She recalled her bringing evergreens down from the mountains and instead of blue grass, using native grasses (buffalo grass and gramma) and ground covers. Finding them became a challenge but she liked creating low-maintenance gardens. "Jane's specialty was the romantic city garden, from tiny plots to large estates. Her style has been described as simple, classic, with wide walks and big trees; clean, peaceful, and not decorated," Andrews-Jones recalled. "She always insisted upon providing privacy in her gardens. Without privacy, people won't use them."[2]

By the 1980s, the Silversteins' older friends were moving from large houses into smaller homes; they wanted smaller gardens. These clients presented new challenges: Some wanted privacy, which required creative screening, and some lived in high-rise buildings, whose balconies were prone to high winds that tore at rooftop plants. "Jane was the consummate designer," Andrews-Jones said. "She was very intuitive, could sense what the client wanted. She used walls, fountains, good sculptures ... and was known for her garden steps, patio balustrades, and comfortable seating in both sun and shade. She designed to conform to clients' wishes."[3] Jane Ries often remarked that "a garden should be lived in, loved, and used. There are constant surprises, new things to learn everyday. Plants do things you don't expect. You see things happen."[4]

Jane's landscaping practice grew. She was eventually handling twenty-five commissions at a time. She landscaped more and more public buildings: hospitals, churches, schools, city halls, and museums. She even designed a parking lot for Moore Mortuary. For the Denver Botanic Gardens, she created, *pro bono*, the Herb Garden and the Scripture Garden. She did a delightful minipark at Larimer Square, the plantings at the entrance of the Denver Country Club, and a small mountain garden adjoining the Central City Opera House. When she landscaped the roof of the Colorado Historical Museum, she had to figure in the planters' weights and the wind velocity. In later years, Jane Ries's chief interests centered around plants, animals, birds, and population control. During a long career, Jane Silverstein designed more than 1,500 private residences, from tiny city gardens to great estates.

"Denver does not have a good land use plan," she said in a videotaped interview in 1989. "The city could learn from work being done in other states. Landscapers need to move into the political arena [and] lobby the legislature to consider the landscape ecology. Traffic should be planned to save neighborhoods, rather than letting big, new buildings force them out."[5] To support her beliefs, she served on scores of public committees, including the citizen advisory committee and Urban Environment subcommittee of the Denver Planning Board; the State Board of Examiners of Landscape Architects (of which she was chairman); the Mayor's Citizen Advisory Board for City Parks; Park People, Art in the City, the Platte River Development Committee, the Ninth Street Park Committee, the Colorado Nature Conservancy, and the Horticulture Committee for the Denver Botanic Gardens.

Although Jane Ries was the first woman in an all-male field in Colorado, she said she had no trouble working with men in a man's profession. "They were gentlemen and I tried to be a lady. I didn't need to be aggressive. I let them know they had great ideas and I worked with them." She advised women entering landscape architecture to be persistent and consistent. "Any part of the land belongs to the profession. We landscape architects must adjust human behavior to this land and work in civic needs and politics."[6]

Jane Silverstein Ries was named Woman of the Year in 1982 by the Colorado Garden and Home Show; she is listed in *Who's Who in America* and was the first president of Rocky Mountain Chapter of the American Society of Landscape Architects (ASLA). The Jane Silverstein Ries Award was established in 1983 by the Colorado Chapter of the ASLA to recognize her contributions to the profession, the Colorado community, and the environment. The award annually recognizes a person, group, or organization demonstrating a pioneering sense of awareness and stewardship of land use values in the Rocky Mountain region.

When Jane Silverstein Ries had practiced almost sixty years, she fell while playing tennis and broke her leg. The fracture healed, but thereafter she walked with a limp. Her mind, once as full as the *Farmer's Almanac,* finds it harder to recognize old friends. She still lives in her Franklin Street home and her long-time associates Cathe Mitchell and Gail Barry continue Jane's practice under the name Land Mark Design. Gardens, like people, change and sometimes wither with time, but many of Jane Silverstein Ries's unique landscapes continue to brighten the Rocky Mountain region.

Genevieve D'Amato Fiore

Born January 20, 1912, in Sunrise, Wyoming

Genevieve Fiore was a board member at Steele Community Center in north Denver when she learned the first regional UNESCO conference would be in Denver in May 1947. An enthusiastic advocate for world peace, Fiore borrowed the center director's registration to attend one of the first UNESCO conferences as an official observer.

At the next Steele Center board meeting, a woman who had also attended the conference threw her packet of UNESCO pamphlets on the floor and exclaimed, "Who wants this junk? None of this will work!" Genevieve gathered up the discarded literature to start her United Nations library, which ultimately contained several thousand volumes plus films, posters, slides, and videos.

The conference inspired Genevieve Fiore to establish the Steele Center UNESCO (United Nations Educational, Scientific, and Cultural Organization) Group. She convened three exploratory meetings to consider a six-month UNESCO discussion and action group. Only seven people attended her first meeting but they voted to call a public meeting the next month. The four who showed up for the second meeting preferred a current affairs or civic affairs group instead, but Genevieve begged them to give UNESCO a six-month trial.

At the first regular meeting on December 3, 1947, Fiore became the UNESCO group's first chairman when the other fourteen declined the honor. She continued to call UNESCO meetings, which featured potluck suppers, folk dancing, and speakers. She also gave speeches around town. Her first talk was before an unlikely group of unwed mothers, but it gave her public speaking experience. Every time the group faltered, Fiore revived it with talks. World peace mattered to her.

"I never planned my life at all; things just happened," Genevieve recalled.[1] In 1908, her parents, Lorenzo and Anna D'Amato, left their native Petina, Italy, to settle in Sunrise, Wyoming. Genevieve was born there on January 20, 1912—the second of six children. Her father worked in the iron mine and then trained himself to be a mining blacksmith. She loved watching him fashion things for her at the forge. The family moved to a ten-acre farm in Welby, north of Denver, in 1919 and struggled through the Depression with everyone working on the farm. Her dad made wine and sausage and helped her mother bake bread. They were strict parents, but treated their sons and daughters equally—no one was allowed to date, not even in high school.

Books and newspapers were hard to come by for young Genevieve, who loved to read. After rescuing a copy of *The Complete Works of Shakespeare*, which had been dumped alongside Clear Creek, she studied every play and sonnet in the old volume and began writing poetry. Her first poem was published in 1924. Always active in the Catholic Church, the D'Amatos sent their children to parochial school. When Genevieve learned the school was not accredited, she approached the Adams County School Board and convinced the board to pay half the tuition for her and a brother Dominic so they could attend Union High School No. 1, which was not in their district. As two of the school's first Italians, they were ostracized and ridiculed. A group of girls asked Genevieve why she didn't smell like an Italian. Dominic threw his lunch at boys who called him "dago" and "wop."

Genevieve decided to show her classmates what an Italian-American girl could do. She became president of the senior class and class salutatorian, graduating with honors. At graduation, she was awarded a Waiver of Fees Scholarship by the University of Colorado. To her disappointment, she could not attend CU despite the scholarship because her parents couldn't afford room and board.

The war years brought tragedy to the family. Genevieve never forgot the day a black-bordered letter came for her father during World War I, notifying him that his nineteen-year-old brother had been killed in Italy. "That was the first time I saw my father cry," she said.[2] She also wept later when two of her brothers were inducted into the service during World War II. One came down with malaria and heat exhaustion. Both brothers were decorated for bravery. Despite the D'Amato family's wartime contributions, some people continued to insult them with ethnic names and slurs. Genevieve was outraged. But her experiences spurred her to work the rest of her life for world peace and tolerance.

Genevieve lived at home until she married John R. Fiore, a printer, on June 25, 1933. The Fiores bought a house in North Denver in 1956, where they raised a daughter, Roxanna, and sons David and Philip Dominic.

When Fiore founded the UNESCO group in 1947, she had intended to organize the office and then turn it over to a paid director. But everyone urged her to stay on. For fourteen years, she was volunteer executive director with only a small monthly stipend. As the only employee, she worked a seventy-hour week assisted by volunteers. The office furniture consisted of several boxes in the Fiore basement. Donations provided the group's only income and much of that went to UNESCO headquarters. With strong support from her husband and children, Fiore continued her work for UNESCO, even when it meant spaghetti for dinner four nights in a row—and a dozen or more strangers from foreign countries at their table several times a week. No matter how many visitors or how often they came, Roxanna Fiore always did the dishes. She was rewarded when some Venezuelan guests arranged for her to travel to their country.

Through the years, Fiore presented more than 4,000 programs for UNESCO on television, radio, at schools, and for countless organizations, often speaking on behalf of UNESCO relief programs for children of developing countries. The UNESCO group had become so extensive by 1959 that the office outgrew the Fiores' basement. Genevieve moved the headquarters, along with the International Hospitality Center and the UN Speaker Service, to Denver International House and for fourteen years, she worked full-time as executive director. She also served as president and board member of People-to-People Corporation of Denver.

In addition to her UNESCO work, in 1953, Fiore helped organize Il Circolo Italiano for Italian-Americans and as a board member worked to establish free Italian classes in Denver. In December 1975, the Italian government rewarded her with the title of Cavaliere and presented her with its Star of Italian Solidarity for promoting friendship and understanding among nations.

Genevieve's work with peace-related organizations brought unexpected personal rewards. In 1954, the National Federation of Settlements and Neighborhood Centers awarded her a fellowship to a UN seminar in New York City in recognition of her UNESCO program at the Steele Center. At seminar sessions, she met Kurt Waldheim, conversed with UN officials and delegates, heard Henry Cabot Lodge address the Security Council, and saw U Thant elected secretary general. In 1958, the American Labor Education Service awarded her a scholarship to a World Affairs Residence School on the UN and human rights in New York. Fiore was one of thirty delegates invited to luncheon at Eleanor Roosevelt's cottage, situated on 825 acres at Val Kill near Hyde Park in New York.

Genevieve Fiore's several trips to Italy were enriched by her ability to speak Italian. As a Catholic, she attended the General International Meeting of Experiment in International Living in Siena, Italy, in 1962. She took a train to Rome, where she was invited to a special mass conducted by Pope John XXIII. Genevieve and John Fiore were in Rome again in 1972 when they received an invitation to attend an audience with Pope Paul VI in the new Audience Hall.

Her most inspiring experience took place at the International Women's Tribunal in Mexico City in 1975. She happened to enter a large auditorium where Mother Teresa was speaking of love and compassion. Genevieve took note of the small and frail woman with a face like shoe leather. She was struck by this humble person, who was not a fiery speaker, but who—in a good, strong voice—inspired listeners with her message. As the audience was leaving, Fiore waited next to the stage with another woman. Mother Teresa walked to them, grasped their hands and wrists, and spoke to them. Genevieve met Mother Teresa again at the Habitat forum in British Columbia the next year. After her speeches, Mother Teresa was almost mobbed and Genevieve could say only hello, but seeing her was a tremendous thrill.

The United States withdrew its UNESCO membership in January 1983, citing UNESCO's mismanagement, excessive spending, and anti-Western bias. Fiore defended UNESCO, reminding the public that Denver's independent UNESCO chapter always had been supported by donations—not by government funds. Her support of the UN is continued by the Genevieve Fiore Educational Trust Fund, which was established in 1979 to provide awards for winners of an annual national high school essay contest on the UN.

To create a permanent monument to her tireless crusade for worldwide peace and understanding, Genevieve Fiore became involved in the Peace Pole Project of the World Peace Prayer Society in Japan. The project, which began in 1955, aims to inspire humankind toward harmony instead of conflict by erecting hand-crafted obelisks bearing the message "May Peace Prevail on Earth," written in English, Swahili, Hopi, and Spanish. By 1997, more than 100,000 poles had been planted in 160 countries. Fiore headed a group that commissioned a Peace Pole of Colorado rose granite, seven feet high by six inches square, to be erected at the Denver Civic Center. She also gave Peace Poles to Radio Station KUVO and the Five Points Media Center in Denver.

Genevieve Fiore has received many awards and accolades for her life's work. Among them are the National Award from *Reader's Digest* and the Institute of International Education to the outstanding individual in the nation for promoting international understanding through exchange programs and the George Washington Medal from the Freedom Foundation at Valley Forge. She was honored by the UNESCO Association of Colorado at its fiftieth anniversary and was presented with a gold-framed clock for fifty years of dedicated service; she also received the Medaille Officielli de UNESCO in Paris. She is listed in *World's Who's Who of Women* and was inducted into the Colorado Women's Hall of Fame in 1991.

Genevieve had to slow down after suffering a nasty fall in her home on New Year's Eve 1993 and a series of accidents. The Fiores moved to the St. Elizabeth Center in north Denver and now, using a cane and wheelchair, she concentrates on activities closer to her home. In January 1994, she began airing "Focus International," a weekly radio show on KUVO FM, 89.3. She continues to host, write, and produce the program, which focuses on international news.

Now in her late eighties, Genevieve Fiore continues to present her weekly radio show and leads poetry and Great Books groups at the St. Elizabeth Center. The fruit of her labor—Denver's UNESCO group, the third oldest in the world—still exists. Genevieve Fiore's work of a lifetime is spelled out on every Peace Pole: "Peace begins in the heart and mind of each individual. Let it begin with me."

Oleta Lawanda Crain

Born September 8, 1913, in Earlsboro, Oklahoma

During the early months of World War II, Oleta Crain decided to join the army so she could play in a military band and help win the war. She was already proficient at playing the cornet, the French horn, and the saxophone. She quit her job at the Remington Arms Plant in Lakewood and relinquished her chance for a master's degree from Iliff School of Theology in Denver. On September 21, 1942, she enlisted in the Women's Army Auxiliary Corps (WAAC).

But when she reported for duty, the army told Private Crain she couldn't play in the band because she'd be "the only colored in a white woman's band."[1] Oleta was part Cherokee and always considered herself as American as anyone. Her grandmother, a Seminole, had come over the Andrew Jackson Trail of Tears in Oklahoma Territory, where the government had given land to her and her children. Her mother, "Miss Polly," who had received a good education in the Indian School, insisted on proper behavior and table manners and encouraged her daughter to get into the mainstream. Oleta attended the Black School and was valedictorian of her class at Douglas High School. She attended Langston University in Oklahoma and obtained her bachelor of arts in history and physical education at Lincoln University in Jefferson City, Missouri.

In the six Rocky Mountain states, Oleta Crain was the first woman of color to enlist in the WAAC. Her class of 175 women comprised the first enlisted black WAACs; all but three held college degrees. On November 15, the army sent her to Fort Des Moines in Iowa for basic training.

Until World War II, organized women's units were rare in the armed forces and the military was not set up to accommodate them. On many bases, highly trained women were assigned as clerks, placed in menial positions, even used as babysitters. In particular, the army didn't seem to know what to do with the first black WAACs. When Crain's unit arrived at Fort Des Moines, some women GIs met them at the train and drove them to the base in a truck. Early the first morning, a whistle blew and Crain rushed to the washroom only to find a long line of WAACs waiting to use the lone sink. She looked around and saw a better sink with no one waiting and started to wash up. The room fell silent. She looked up and saw the women pointing to a sign that read "This Sink Is for Officers Only." In addition, there were no WAAC uniforms. The army issued the women heavy overcoats instead to provide warmth and hide their civilian clothing until regular uniforms arrived. The first WAAC uniforms, cut to men's measurements, were uncomfortable and unsightly on women's figures. Eventually uniforms arrived for Oleta's unit.

When the sergeant asked for volunteers, Private Crain volunteered for the Military Police—until she found that meant picking up cigarette butts. She volunteered, instead, to be mail clerk so she could get her mail on time. Private Crain met occasionally with the "charcoal burners"—about forty WAACs—who got together to discuss events of the day. They noticed the army didn't have many plans for black WAACs, so they asked a lawyer in Des Moines to help them. Soon after the commandant heard about it, all those WAACs disappeared. Oleta heard later they had been sent to the Mojave Desert.

She was promoted to corporal in December 1942 and to leader (sergeant) on February 20, 1943. As leader, she was in charge of physical education for black women. Her job was to lead her troop to the swimming pool every Tuesday. White WAACs swam on Mondays. When Oleta's troop reached the pool, they usually were told the schedule had been changed. If they did swim, the pool was cleaned the next day.

Another of Sergeant Crain's duties was to drill her troop during a review. But Oleta, who had never drilled, didn't know when to call out the orders, so at the review, her command marched in all directions in total disarray. To remedy the situation, the army sent in drill sergeants from Fort Riley, Kansas, who arrived in their fancy boots, trousers, and whips. When they learned they were to teach women to drill, they were angry, figuring their careers were ruined. They complained that the women's steps were too short for marching and their voices were too high to give commands. Every evening, Oleta's troop practiced marching in long steps, and Oleta barked out commands in a deep voice, until her drill unit became the best in the WAAC.

Sergeant Crain was discharged from the Women's Army Auxiliary Corps in 1943, so she could be admitted to the regular Women's Army Corps (WAC) as an Air Force second lieutenant on September 1, 1943. Of three hundred women entering officers' training, she was one of three black women.

But the swimming problem hadn't gone away. She went to see the captain in charge. "He really read me out, so I reported to the commandant and laid my soul to rest," she said. The commandant asked her, "Do you think you represent the colored race?" "Yessir." She saluted, then asked to speak. "I remember the day you came here. Sir. How pleased we were. We thought you would stop the segregation. Where I come from in Oklahoma, we had nice homes and schools. Segregation was no problem. Now you're scheduling Basics No. 2 and Service Club No. 2 for the black WACs." After that conversation, the captain discontinued segregation in the swimming pool.[2]

In April 1945, Lieutenant Crain was sent to Lincoln Air Force Base in Nebraska, the last stop for 20,000 male troops going overseas. As the commander of a company of black WACs, she faced several disturbing situations. Some people intimated the black WACs were lesbians and prostitutes. When the colonel asked her to investigate this charge, she learned the black soldiers often entered the women's quarters uninvited at night. In addition, she reported that black soldiers tried to take advantage of the women, who then refused to date them. When the same women dated white officers, the situation nearly resulted in race riots. Lieutenant Crain called in the military police to quiet things down.

When Lincoln Air Force Base closed in December 1945, she was transferred to Amarillo Air Force Base in Texas and then to Lockbourne Air Force Base in Columbus, Ohio, where she commanded the WAC squadron at the request of Ben O. Davis, who became the first black air force general. First Lieutenant Crain was the only black woman retained in the military after the war. In 1947, President Truman integrated the armed forces and the Pentagon asked Crain to stay because she got along so well with the troops. She was promoted to captain in May 1948, and in 1949 went to Westover Air Force Base, Massachusetts, to work in intelligence.

But racial and political slurs continued to hound her. Shortly after *Sepia* magazine ran a two-page spread about Captain Crain and her troops, Oleta's superior officer, who was heard to say that she didn't want to work with "any damned n————," told her superior she thought Captain Crain was a Communist because "she appeared in *Sepia,* [allegedly] a Commie magazine."[3] The military decided Captain Crain should be investigated in case the allegation might be true. The investigation took months and went into every aspect of her life. When she came out clean, she was given a top-secret security clearance.

In 1951, she spent eleven months as personnel director at Elmendorf Air Force Base, Alaska, where she was one of nine women at the base. WACs were never allowed to wear slacks—even in Alaska. Although she bundled up in everything she had, the few inches of exposed legs between her boot tops and skirt nearly became frostbitten. She was the last woman to leave the Alaska base.

Her next assignment was at Ruislip, England, as test control officer. While in England, she became a major and once again faced some serious challenges. The area around the U.S. base near Hyde Park was overrun with Communist sympathizers who hated "Yanks" and routinely beat up U.S. soldiers. One night two sentries on duty were shot. Major Crain studied the situation and then requisitioned Jeeps for all U.S. soldiers so they would not be vulnerable on the streets. In town one day, she was grabbed by some English soldiers, who were about to hustle her away when the English police intervened. She had a more pleasant experience in England while attending a Cambridge University course in world powers and international affairs.

She stayed in a bedroom once occupied by King Henry the Eighth. On another occasion, she was invited as photography officer to Queen Elizabeth's lawn party at Buckingham Palace honoring King Haile Selassie of Ethiopia. She treasures a photo she took of the three English queens. The combination of her race and her military status often attracted attention. At Lindsey Air Force Station in Wiesbaden, Germany, Crain was window shopping downtown one day when she realized she was surrounded by people who never had seen a black woman in uniform.

Major Oleta Crain retired from active duty while at Lindsey Air Force Station on June 1, 1963. She had risen from a private to the rank of major and was one of the last black WACs from World War II still in the service. The Women's Army Corps was dismantled in 1978 when women were integrated into the regular military.

Crain joined the Department of Labor on September 24, 1964, in Washington, D.C., and rose through the ranks just as she had in the WACs. She earned her master's degree and taught for five years at Northeastern University's graduate night school while working as associate regional administrator with the Office of Job Service for the New England states. She transferred to Denver on June 1, 1984, as regional administrator for the U.S. Department of Labor Women's Bureau, representing working women in six states. Few women of any race have risen as high in the Labor department as Crain has. Established by Congress on June 5, 1920, the Women's Bureau promotes the welfare of wage-earning women and children by alerting them to their rights in the workplace, proposing beneficial policies and legislation, and compiling and publishing statistics affecting working women. Crain oversaw conferences on child care, health benefits, job training, working conditions, and earnings ratios. She retired from her post on December 31, 1998.

During her long and varied career, Oleta Crain has received countless awards. She was commissioned a Kentucky Colonel by Kentucky Governor Edward Breathitt. She holds a U.S. Air Force Longevity Award with four Bronze Oak Leaf Clusters, a U.S. Department of Labor Award for Distinguished Career Service, a Martin Luther King, Jr., Humanitarian Award; she was inducted into the Colorado Women's Hall of Fame.

Oleta Crain, who joined the WAACs to play in a military band, never dreamt that she would serve her country far beyond her first ambitions. She spent her adult years as an advocate for black women. Before retiring as an air force major, she did much to desegregate the armed forces. In the Women's Bureau, she continued to research and upgrade conditions for working women and children. After fifty-six years of public service, she was honored in Denver on December 14, 1998, at a retirement luncheon and reception. Attending were officials of the Department of Labor, the Women's Bureau, Denver city officials, and her many friends and associates.

Jean Jolliffe Yancey
Born August 18, 1914, in Clarksburg, West Virginia

In May 1997, Jean Jolliffe Yancey was interviewed in her high-rise building, where she could gaze across the city to the mountains. At eighty-two, she moved about her apartment in a wheelchair with apparent ease, her oxygen tank hooked onto the back. Nothing seemed to affect that familiar, loving voice, keen mind, and those blazing blue eyes. Eighty-two years was quite a vantage point for looking back at a long and constantly moving lifetime that took her from a high school fashion show to a successful business career.

"I was born into a middle-class Protestant family and when I was eight we moved to 1270 Clayton Street in Denver," she began as she leafed through a bulging scrapbook.[1] Jean's father, Edward, a floor wax salesman, was on the road most of the year. The rest of the family— Jean, her mom, Nell, and brother, William—had fun and excitement on their own. When Jean arrived in Denver as a third grader, she spoke with a Southern mountain twang but before long she was a confirmed westerner. Jean was just fourteen when her mother died. Her father later remarried, but no one could replace her mom.

"Here's a picture of my best friend, Jane Smith. I met her on the first day of third grade and we've been friends ever since," she reminisced.[2] At East High School, Jean, Jane, and a group of chums dubbed themselves "Jean & Jane & their High School Mannequins." The girls talked the president of Denver Dry Goods Co. (affectionately called Denver

Dry or just The Denver) into allowing them to present the nation's first fashion show for high school girls. At that time—1929, the word "teenager" hadn't been coined and high school girls had to wear clothes designed for younger girls or for college women.

Five thousand girls and their mothers turned out and the style show was such a success, it was extended to three days. *Seventeen* magazine wrote an article about it years later, praising The Denver for putting on the first high school fashion show in the United States.

After high school, Jean went to the University of Denver for three years where she majored in theatre. But she left college and went to New York City to pursue an acting career. Once there, Jane befriended some actors, who invited her to parties. When she realized many of these hopefuls were getting high on cocaine, Jean quickly lost interest in becoming an actress.

Her fashion show background helped her get a job at B. Altman & Company, a New York department store. She soon was in charge of Altman's telephone shopping service. In her next job, she produced beauty-supply trade shows, for which she planned and presented programs for as many as 2,500 beauty-shop owners.

Friendship with a neighbor, Lenard Yancey, who was living in the apartment below hers, blossomed into romance and they were married in Scarsdale, New York, in April 1937. During World War II, Lenard became an army air corps gunner instructor at MacDill Field, so Jean moved to Tampa, Florida, and got a job as manager of a retail store.

After the war, they moved to Denver and their first son, William "Buzz" Yancey, was born. Next, the Yanceys were off to Des Moines, Iowa, for fifteen years. Two more sons, Alan and Andrew, came along, making Jean a full-time mom, but she kept intellectually stimulated by working as area coordinator for the Great Books program until the Yanceys moved back to Denver in 1959.

Jean began managing the bridal department at the Denver Dry in 1960. Two years later, she was ready to take on a partner and start her own business. She and Lorraine Hutchinson opened the Bridal Loft at the Cherry Creek Shopping Center. "This shop was unique—and absolutely oozing with customer service," Jean said. No effort was too great for their customers and the shop won national attention. Yancey bought out her partner in 1964.

Jean and her friend Dorothey Goldstone would never forget a night in 1969. After having dinner together, they stopped by the Bridal Loft and saw smoke pouring from the building. Jean ran to the staircase, which was full of black smoke. Dorothey yelled to a bystander to call the fire department. Jean started up the stairs, determined to get into the shop. Dorothey was equally intent on stopping her. They found themselves in a wrestling match until Jean wound up on the floor. When Lenard came, they took Jean to the hospital and Dorothey had to call the brides that night and tell them their dresses had burned up.

But Jean and Dorothey were back the next day, setting up a sewing room in space provided by another shop owner. All her competitors came to the rescue. Miraculously, every bride had the right wedding gown; some were even borrowed from brides who had worn the same gown a few months earlier. Yancey sold the Bridal Loft in 1970. She continued to manage it, but soon realized the time had come to move on.

For the first time in her life, Jean Yancey wasn't sure what to do next. "I investigated possibilities for the next two years," she confessed in an interview.[3] She took the opportunity to travel and visited the Acropolis and the Parthenon in Greece, fulfilling a lifelong dream. She took trips to fashion houses in Italy, and went to Africa, the Orient, and around the world.

Finally, she forced herself to decide the next step in her career. "I listed twenty things I could do. I couldn't make a living doing one thing, so I went for five," she recalled. As Jean Yancey & Associates, she decided to combine business and career counseling, lecturing, teaching, and writing. When Jean became a business consultant, she knew what she was doing. She, too, had been an entrepreneur. Wherever she was, she had used her ingenuity to get a job or start a business—and had worked hard to succeed. Just as important, she had the foresight and courage to shut down when she needed to move on and start over again.

When Jean Yancey set out on the lecture circuit, she focused on change and the future. "Someone would call me to speak at a national convention of the insurance industry or operating-room nurses, whatever. I did research on that industry and then built change and the future into my talk," she explained.[4] Within six months, she had enough consulting clients and lecture dates to keep her very busy. She became a leading keynote speaker at national conventions. Later, when she ceased traveling on business, she continued to speak on aspects of gerontology to students headed for doctorate degrees in the University of Denver psychology department. She advised her audiences: "Today's woman should make sure her life has movement. Winds of change are so strong that if she stands still she could be passed by."

As if her work weren't rewarding enough, Jean has enjoyed other tangible rewards. In May 1982, she received an invitation to a ceremony at the White House Rose Garden, where President Ronald Reagan presented her with the award for national Advocate of the Year to Women in Small Businesses. It recognized her work promoting women in the business community. Jean Yancey also was inducted into the Colorado Women's Hall of Fame and received the Community Recognition Award on October 25, 1996, from KRMA-TV, Channel 6.

On August 18, 1995, Jean's many friends and associates celebrated her eightieth birthday with a colossal party at Cherry Creek State Park in Aurora. A park bench was dedicated in her name "in celebration of the life and energy generated by this remarkable woman." Her friends also presented her with a scrapbook of letters, memories, and congratulations. Proceeds accepted on her behalf will continue her legacy through a fund to assist women in need. During the program, a representative of Denver Public Library formally accepted Jean Yancey's papers, awards, and mementos into the Western History Collection.

Mrs. Yancey continues to mentor women contemplating career and business changes—at her new assisted-living home and "office" in Harvard Square, in southeast Denver. An army of her friends and colleagues threw an extravaganza birthday celebration on August 18, 1999, to help the plucky business entrepreneur, consultant, and lecturer celebrate her eighty-fifth birthday.

Hannah Marie Wormington Volk

Born September 5, 1914, in Denver, Colorado
Died May 31, 1994, in Denver, Colorado

Hannah Marie Wormington was known to prefer older men—men at least 10,000 years old. As a young woman, she became enthralled with Folsom Man and early North American cultures dating back 25,000 years. During her distinguished career, she became a highly respected authority on the Paleo-Indian cultures of North, Central, and South America from 9000 to 6000 B.C.E.

Her father had moved to Denver in 1863. He married Adrienne Roucolle, daughter of French immigrants and a former *Denver Post* reporter. The Wormingtons later divorced and Marie (as she was called) was raised by her mother, who taught her to read and speak fluent French as well as English.

An only child, Marie grew up in Denver—first in a big house on Broadway, and then at Twelfth and Gaylord Streets. Marie was a personality of unusual interests and surprising contrasts. She loathed millers, those unpleasant moths that invade the house every spring, but she was fascinated by snakes. After graduating from East High School in 1931, she enrolled at the University of Denver to major in zoology, partly to pursue her interest in reptiles. She was filling out her sophomore class schedule when she happened to sign up for an archaeology class. From the first day, Marie was hooked on studying prehistoric relics of ancient mankind. During her senior year, she went to the Dordogne area of France to help excavate paleolithic sites. She graduated in 1935.

Against the advice of friends and family, who warned that openings were rare for women archaeologists, she went to England and France to continue her study under European experts. When she returned, she managed to get a position at the Denver Museum of Natural History as staff archaeologist. Two years later, she moved up to curator and taught archaeology at Denver University for two years.

When Marie Wormington was twenty-six, she published her bestseller, *Ancient Man in North America*. Written in language the nonprofessional can comprehend and enjoy, her book enabled the public to understand Stone Age Man. Used for years by university archaeology students, *Ancient Man* has been revised and expanded through four editions. Wormington went on to publish six more books about prehistoric Indians of the Southwest.

In 1954, she went to Radcliffe College (at Harvard) for her master's and doctorate degrees. She was the second woman admitted to study in the Harvard anthropology department and the first woman to obtain a doctorate degree in anthropology. Her specific field of study was the earliest North American hunting cultures that lived 10,000 to 25,000 years ago. She came across an early report on obscure sites in southeast Utah, which led her to reappraise the Fremont culture and enabled her to expand her research on North America's earliest human population.

As a member of anthropology delegations and to further her research, Dr. Wormington visited twenty-nine foreign countries. She was one of the first professional exchange archaeologists to enter the former Soviet Union and to visit the Republic of China. While in the USSR, she was the first American scientist to be flown into southern Siberia—a trip that fulfilled her dream of reaching the Siberian side of the Bering Strait, where primitive man made his first crossing into the New World many thousands of years ago. She saw ancient stone tools, weapons, and implements that indicated the first emigration across the Bering Strait had been a two-way trip. She concluded that some early migrants may have returned to Siberia, taking with them new techniques of making stone tools.

Scholars of the day believed that the first humans in the Americas migrated across the thousand-mile-wide Bering Strait during the last Ice Age. Dr. Wormington dated campsites of roving North American hunters as early as 12,000 B.C.E. But her hunch was that they crossed the strait 20,000 years before the common era.

Exciting as were her travels, it was the southwestern summer, with its extended digging expeditions, that became her favorite season and the Southwest her favorite workplace. She once described the onset of her fieldwork: Someone (usually an amateur) would find a pottery shard or possibly an old weapon that might indicate a buried civilization. Then the archaeologists would come in to dig, taking care not to disturb or break old bones, fire remnants, refuse, or any sign of Paleo-Indians (from a past geologic period) who might have lived near the site before the advent of agriculture and pottery. She once said, "The qualifications for an archaeologist are a strong back and a strong mind. … The archaeologist who dies rich either married money or inherited it."[1] From 1936 to 1952, Dr. Wormington led excavations at the Folsom site near LaPorte, Colorado, as well as at rock shelters in Mesa and Montrose Counties and at a Fremont village site in Utah. Her rare gift was integrating scattered discoveries into a broad view of Paleo-Indian archaeology.

Marie Wormington made an important change in her personal life on September 6, 1940, when she married George D. "Pete" Volk, a petroleum engineer who shared her interest in archaeology. They took many archaeological trips during the 1960s. Her husband joined her on a three-week trip to Mexico to acquire Aztec pottery and figurines for the Denver Natural History Museum. From there, they proceeded to an International Congress for Prehistoric Sciences in Rome and then visited Etruscan tombs in Florence and the island of Sardinia. Back in Denver, they displayed their masks from the Easter Islands, artifacts, and art collection in their large home at 4600 East Seventeenth Avenue.

In 1967, Dr. Wormington's friends were shocked to read in the *Denver Post* that "personal friction" had caused a rift between her and Museum of Natural History director, Alfred M. Bailey. She said she had been dismissed. Bailey termed it an "informal resignation." Dr. Wormington already had been granted a year's leave of absence to teach at Arizona State University. Bailey's letter stated that because she had accepted a "much more lucrative position … it has become necessary to review our financial affairs. … I advise you no funds will be available in our museum budget for archaeological studies at the conclusion of your academic year at Tempe in 1969."

No records reveal Dr. Wormington's reaction to her "dismissal," but her former student and close friend Sally Lewis Rodeck said that she never went back to work at the museum. After teaching at Arizona State, Wormington became a visiting professor at Colorado College for a year and then taught at the Universities of Minnesota and Wyoming. For many years, Dr. Wormington was a research associate in Paleo-Indian studies at the University of Colorado Museum in Boulder.

In April 1970, she was awarded a Guggenheim Foundation research fellowship to write *Ancient Man in the Americas*, a book dealing with the sequence of prehistoric Paleo-Indian cultures in North, Central, and South America between 9,000 and 6,000 B.C.E. She was the first archaeologist in the world and first woman to receive a Guggenheim Foundation fellowship. By 1977, Dr. Wormington had participated in fourteen excavations as director or consultant. During her career, she attended archaeological congresses, conferences, and symposiums in twenty-nine foreign countries. Her scores of honors are equally imposing. She was awarded an honorary Doctor of Humane Letters by Colorado State University in 1977. Alpha Gamma Delta Sorority named her its Distinguished Citizen of Colorado in 1981. And the Society for American Archaeology presented her with its Distinguished Service Award in 1983.

After her husband's death, Dr. Wormington continued to live in their Park Hill home. "Marie always was a dignified and dominant woman," Sally Rodeck recalled. "Then she fell and broke her hip, and steadily went downhill. She had to stop giving her many cocktail and garden parties. But she still went to the beauty shop to have her hair and nails done and maintained her well-turned-out appearance."[2]

During her last years, Marie Wormington's friends grew concerned that she was drinking too much. She employed Russ, a young man, who kept up her home, drove her about in her Mercedes, and looked after her. Russ finally got Marie to quit drinking but she never gave up smoking.

Early on May 31, 1994, firemen were called to put out a blaze at the Wormington home. They found the world-famed archaeologist in her bedroom holding her cat. Both were dead—overcome by smoke. Firemen said the possible cause of the fire was a smoldering cigarette that set the sofa ablaze. According to her wishes, her ashes were placed in a copy of a prehistoric bowl and interred at Fairmount Cemetery.

Many of her ancient masks, pottery pieces, and other treasures were destroyed in the fire. The Denver Museum of Natural History dedicated a scholarship in her name and presented a program in her memory. Friends and associates came from all over the country to reminisce about Marie Wormington, their internationally known and respected colleague.

"Archaeology is more than old arrowheads, carved bones, and broken pottery," she told a newspaper reporter on July 28, 1964. "It's the study of people and how they managed to get along in the world; how they solved their problems of food, shelter, clothing, culture, entertainment and survival."[3] As an archaeologist, Dr. Marie Wormington made substantial strides in acquainting the public with prehistoric North American peoples.

Helen Louise White Peterson
Born on August 3, 1915, on the Pine Ridge Reservation in South Dakota

"Helen White Peterson is the 'Deborah' of the American Indian people—she is truly a great warrior woman, an important leader," declared Vine Deloria, Sr., a former Episcopal archdeacon, in 1982.[1]

Helen Louise White was born on the Pine Ridge Reservation in South Dakota in a log house miles from the nearest town. Part Cheyenne, part Lakota Sioux, she had an Indian name, Wachi, meaning "one to trust, depend upon." She grew up in nearby Chadron, Nebraska, in the household of her Cheyenne grandmother, Lucille Mae White—niece of the great peace chief, Black Kettle. Grandmother White told this first grandchild Indian stories and taught her ancient tribal lore, constantly coaching the precocious little Helen to "read, write, and talk good so you can work among Indians and help them."

The countryside around northwestern Nebraska and South Dakota, homeland of her Oglala Sioux and Cheyenne ancestors, still bears many familiar American Indian names. During her girlhood, the Episcopal Church and her priest, Vine Deloria, Sr., provided the community's social life and gave Helen a sense of security, belonging, and protection.

After Helen White graduated from Hay Springs High School in 1932, she began taking classes at Chadron State Teachers College toward a business education degree. She married a man named Peterson and worked to pay her tuition and help him through graduate school. Helen always was employed—at first at low-level jobs such as babysitter and theater cashier. In college, she gave piano lessons while working as a student assistant and then was a clerk-stenographer for the U.S. Land Use Resettlement Administration.

Helen was pregnant when Peterson entered the military during World War II. When they were divorced, she had to raise their son, R. Max Peterson, with her mother's help. The two women and the boy moved to Denver in 1942, where Helen accepted a position as executive director of the Rocky Mountain Council of Inter-American Affairs under Dr. Ben Cherington at the University of Denver. The agency was created by the State Department during the war because of concern that Nazis were moving from Daka, Africa, to Brazil where they had gained a foothold.

Surprisingly, her career in minority relations began not with American Indians but with Hispanics. After the war, a national Mexican-American labor program imported sugar beet and other farm workers into Colorado. But the program was resented by some old-line Spanish-American families, who for generations had owned land and were prominent in their communities. They felt threatened by Mexican nationals working in Colorado beet fields.

A thirty-five-year-old liberal Democrat, James Quigg Newton, became mayor of Denver in 1947. Newton planned to end Denver's segregation that extended even to public facilities like swimming pools. But the change would require revising the city charter. He persuaded several civic groups, headed by the Anti-Defamation League and

Reverend Dean Paul Roberts of St. John's (Episcopal) Cathedral, to conduct a study that resulted in the Mayor's Committee on Human Relations.

In 1948, the mayor's office brought in Helen Peterson to work under Bernie Valdez through the Chicano Rights Movement of the Commission on Community Relations and the city's Department of Health and Welfare. With her staff of one part-time employee, she focused on getting minority people to work together to pass state laws for fair employment and fair housing. Helen Peterson immediately set out to register minority voters by affidavit. Carrying a stack of affidavit blanks, she went door-to-door in minority neighborhoods and made the rounds of bars, restaurants, and other public gathering places in a district covering twenty-seven precincts. Everywhere she went, she doubled the existing number of registered voters. "I count the registration of those people, particularly minorities, with bringing them into full participation, full recognition, full enjoyment of all the rights of citizenship," she said later.[2] Helen Peterson always saw herself as a community organizer getting people to work together to end racial discrimination.

Peterson's work produced a climate in which minorities started running for political office. She helped Mayor Newton recruit minority employees, who brought in other minorities. Many stayed on the job until retirement. Another result was that Denver passed one of the nation's first fair housing laws. Peterson's office developed cultural programs, lecture and concert series, and visits with civic leaders. When federal funding for her job ran out, the University of Colorado paid her until 1948. At that time, she became director of Denver's Commission on Community Relations. During this period, she was invited to attend the Second Inter-American Indian Conference in Peru as an adviser to the U.S. delegation.

Helen's long-time associate in Denver, Lucille Echohawk, described her as an articulate, forceful, and thoughtful woman. "She was a forerunner in efforts to organize Denver's Agency for Human Rights and Community Relations, which is now fifty years old," said Echohawk. "Helen is a big-picture person, very forward minded. Where most people bog down in the issue at hand, she always worked on issues relative to the overall picture in our country. In that regard, she was a pioneer in her day. Now, government agency employees no longer work in a vacuum—we have to deal constantly with other agencies." Reinforced by her years of experience, Helen Peterson had developed a forceful and commanding presence, yet always was available and giving of her time. In Echohawk's words, "She certainly was no shrinking violet but a strong mentor, respectful of everyone."[3]

In 1953, Helen Peterson had an opportunity to take up her Cheyenne grandmother's agenda to "work among Indians and help them." In response to pressure from Native American leaders, she was named executive director of the National Congress of American Indians (NCAI), which had been founded by tribal representatives meeting in Denver in November 1944. She moved to Washington, D.C., to become the first American Indian woman director of the NCAI.

When she arrived, she found the NCAI shriveled to its lowest point, with only three tribes as paid members, and nearly bankrupt. President Dwight Eisenhower had signed a bill to terminate the organization. American Indians appeared powerless to save their NCAI. She knew this would be devastating for tribes and individual Indians. Helen Peterson orchestrated an unheard-of gathering of American Indian tribes in Washington, D.C. In February 1955, "a massing of American Indians" turned out—tribes that no one had heard of, tribes that had never heard of the NCAI. As a result of the spectacular demonstration, the NCAI termination faded and halted altogether in 1960. Next, Peterson had a new NCAI constitution written that would place the Congress under the control of elected tribal governments. Ever since member tribes adopted the constitution, the organization has been on a permanent, solid footing.

Flathead Indian scholar D'Arcy McNickle joined with Helen Peterson to develop and promote a summer workshop series for American Indian students at Colorado College from 1956 through 1970. Their workshops became a model for all ethnic studies programs in the United States. Many who took the workshops became Indian leaders. Peterson also started a training program at NCAI headquarters that

prepared some of her bright young women trainees to enter professions in Indian communities.

Helen Peterson spent nine years at NCAI, becoming its longest serving executive director. She placed the organization firmly on its feet
with a membership of a hundred member tribes and fostered cooper-
ation among the tribes. Now fifty years old, NCAI is the American Indians' only national advocacy organization, equal to the National Association for the Advancement of Colored People for African
Americans. Her work for the Congress of American Indians stands as
her most significant contribution to her Native American people. After
leaving Washington, she organized her papers and documents relating
to NCAI and presented them to the Smithsonian Institution. Soon
after, the Smithsonian placed them on exhibit.

Peterson returned to Denver in 1962 as executive director of the
city's Commission on Community Relations. She saw positive changes
in Denver, such as the fading of neighborhood boundaries that once
separated minorities from the rest of the population. Congress had
passed the Relocation Act to encourage American Indians to leave
reservations, where job opportunities were meager, and relocate in one
of eight cities, including Denver. There, they would be given job training and employment. Many came to Denver and at one time an esti-
mated 20,000 Native Americans, of many tribes but predominantly
Sioux, were living in the metro area. Unfortunately, Congress did not
appropriate enough money to provide the promised services.

In 1970, Peterson moved to the Bureau of Indian Affairs (BIA) as
field liaison officer and coordinator in the Denver U.S. Customs Office.
At this time, she also chaired the Interagency Indian Committee's Federal Regional Council for the area. She was involved in ensuring that
the government and tribes dealt fairly with tribal members. She served
as a consultant provided by the BIA to assist tribal governments as well
as its own bureaus and trained and assisted Indian peoples to manage
their tribal governments.

In 1971, she returned to Washington in the position of assistant to
the Commissioner of Indian Affairs, the highest position held by a
woman in the Bureau. Among her special assignments for the com-

missioner, she oversaw creation of international forums and Native American exhibits. BIA transferred Helen Peterson once more—in 1978—to its Portland Area Office as tribal government services officer. Her mission was to develop cooperating links among federal departments, the tribes, local and state governments, churches, and local leaders. She kept bishops in ten western states informed on Indian issues and urged them to publicly support Indian health, treaty issues, and alcoholism treatment programs.

Almost as a footnote to her cultural responsibilities, Helen Peterson has edited five publications, among them White Buffalo Council of American Indians publications and *Pan-American News.* Her countless and ongoing awards include the Wonder Woman Award from Wonder Woman Foundation, New York; induction into the Colorado Women's Hall of Fame; an honorary doctorate degree in 1973 from University of Colorado; Distinguished Service Award from Columbia University in 1974; and Outstanding American Indian Citizen in 1955 from the Oklahoma Anadark Exposition.

Since retiring in Portland in 1985, Helen Peterson has served on numerous national boards and commissions, including the National Committee on Indian Work of the Episcopal Church, the Girl Scouts' national board, the National Indian Lutheran Board, the American Indian Civil Liberties Trust, Colorado Common Cause, and the National Council of Churches Commission on Race and Religion.

At home, Helen cared for her mother until she was in her nineties. Her son, R. Max Peterson, is a veterinarian practicing outside Portland. Helen, now in her eighties, is suffering from Parkinson's disease and has moved into an assisted-living home.

Dr. Owanah Anderson, her longtime friend and associate in the Indian Ministry of the Episcopal Church, wrote about Helen's inspired leadership. "She has been a supportive friend with a remarkable ability to meet people, remember their names, and engage strangers in conversation."[4] In a long career crowded with service to minorities, Helen White Peterson more than fulfilled her grandmother's mandate to work for her own Indian people.

Miriam Goldberg

Born May 18, 1916, in Chicago, Illinois

Whenever the post office fails to deliver the *Intermountain Jewish News* on a Friday, the phone at the newspaper office rings off the hook. "Where's our paper?" demand irate subscribers. "How do you expect us to get through the weekend without it?" As often as not, editor and publisher Miriam Goldberg delivers the copies herself.

Miriam Goldberg is the heart and soul of the *Intermountain Jewish News* (IJN). She refers to her staff as her family, and, in fact, many of them are. In return, the people who work for her obviously regard her as a benevolent and beloved matriarch.

A near-native of Colorado, Miriam Harris Goldberg has long-standing ties to the state. Her great grandparents were living in Denver by the end of the century. Her father's family made its way from Ohio to Trinidad and later moved to Cripple Creek, where her grandfather owned a clothing store. Miriam's parents later spent summers in Manitou Springs and winters traveling. The family was living in Denver when it was time for Miriam to be born, but her mother went to Chicago so the best doctors could deliver her baby. Six weeks later, she returned to Denver with her new daughter.

Miriam attended Denver schools: Teller Elementary, Aaron Gove Junior High, and East High School. Her father sent her to Lindenwood, a women's college in St. Charles, Missouri, because it stressed the graces of living, manners and propriety, top scholarship, and training in English. She later attended the University of Colorado/Denver.

During the 1930s, she recalled, it was customary for young men to crash weddings. She was a wedding guest at Denver's old BMH Synagogue when Max Goldberg was one of the gate crashers. Meeting at a wedding—what could be more conducive to romance? The Goldbergs' wedding took place on February 12, 1936.

A man of many interests, Max Goldberg acquired a struggling, thirty-year-old Jewish weekly newspaper in 1943. At the time, he was writing "Side Street," a financial column for the *Denver Post* and during the 1950s, organized a group that founded television station KBTV (later Channel 9). He also had a "day job"—his own business—the Max Goldberg Advertising Agency, along with running the newspaper. In 1965, he and Miriam decided to work full-time at their weekly newspaper, the *Intermountain Jewish News.*

Miriam, who was by this time a mother of four children, worked with Max at the newspaper for seven years until his death in October 1972. Rabbi Hillel Goldberg, her son and now executive editor, praises her heroism in taking over the paper without missing an issue. "From the first, the paper's advertising and total size began to grow under her direction. She originated the concept of special editions with an education section and a very important women's section now called Focus on People," said Rabbi Goldberg.[1]

Miriam Goldberg immediately undertook the planning of each edition along with copy editing, selling ads, setting up schedules, overseeing press runs, and meeting deadlines. The hardest area for her to step into was labor relations, in which she had neither schooling nor experience. Before long, the union printers who did their typesetting called a strike. It was up to Miriam to negotiate the settlement.

One of her greatest thrills through the years was the modernization of the IJN's production department. Originally set with hot type, the newspaper later switched to cold type and today is printed entirely by computer. The computer modem receives national and international news.

Now in her eighties, Goldberg is a tiny whirlwind of a woman with snowy white hair and a ready smile. She continues to be involved in every aspect of the *Intermountain Jewish News.* Her life is so closely interwoven with the fabric of this regional Jewish publication that it is next to impossible to visualize one without the other. At the office, she keeps her hand in the paper's daily business operations and management, supervises the layout, and edits the business section. In personnel, she oversees the hiring of employees and sets vacations. Her presence is felt in staff loyalty—both the associate and assistant editors have been on board twenty-two years and the office manager for fifteen years.

Miriam Goldberg's greatest satisfaction comes in starting each week with a blank page and seeing a paper well done at week's end. She reaches her office at 1275 Sherman Street, Denver, by 8 or 9 A.M. unless she has an earlier meeting. Her quitting time? "That's open-ended," she says with a laugh. "Usually around 7 P.M."[2] The layout is completed on the computer by Monday. Tuesdays are more intense as editorial members gather and write the hard news. By Wednesdays, editorial policy has been set for that issue and the newspaper goes to press Wednesday night. On Thursday morning, she plans special editions, works on layout pages for the coming week, anticipates the advertising, and starts work on early deadlines for that week. The office closes Saturday for the Jewish Sabbath but is often open for work on Sunday. When Goldberg presides at a staff meeting, her manner is quiet but she persistently brings issues into perspective. She supplies information and creative ideas. Most of all, she is loved for her gentle humor that defuses explosive situations and pressures.

The IJN puts out fifty-two issues a year plus two slick-paper, full-color magazines and many special editions that focus on subjects of interest to Jewish readers—from Jewish holidays to Kosher Living and Focus on People.

Miriam Goldberg's family is well represented on the newspaper. Her son, executive editor Hillel Goldberg, is a rabbi and holder of a Ph.D. from Brandeis University. He was IJN's Israel correspondent for eleven years and has received fifteen Rockower Awards for Excellence in Jewish journalism. Hillel's wife, Elaine, writes features. Their five children include daughter Temima "Mimi" Goldberg Shulman (she has a master's in journalism from Columbia University), who provided first-hand coverage on life in Israel during the Gulf War and then became East Coast correspondent from New Jersey; Mattis Goldberg, who has been IJN's correspondent in Jerusalem; and Shana Goldberg, who served as a summer intern during her years at Brandeis University. In addition to IJN's twelve staff members are Carl Alpert, the Israel correspondent, author Joanne Greenberg, and Robert Rothstein.

Intermountain Jewish News celebrated its eighty-fifth birthday with a 152-page special edition in June 1998. Under Miriam Goldberg's leadership, IJN has become more than a community newspaper. It is a vital force in regional Jewish journalism and a paper willing to take controversial stands. In 1982, for example, the IJN predicted Israel would invade Lebanon and called upon readers to take action to prevent it. Miriam Goldberg's editorial policy is to present all sides of an issue to Jewish readers, who range from the traditional to the more liberal. The influence of IJN is evident from the endless awards covering its walls and its weekly readership of 50,000.

In addition to her induction into the Colorado Women's Hall of Fame, Miriam was named Colorado Press Women's Woman of the Year in 1987, runner-up for the National Federation of Press Women's Woman of Achievement award, and winner of the Award of Excellence from the Colorado Press Association in 1979. As an editor and publisher, Miriam Goldberg plays a strong leadership role in the Jewish community. She represents the IJN with her friendly charm and graciousness at important community events and volunteers in many Jewish organizations.

She is proudest of her family. In addition to her son, Hillel, Miriam Goldberg has a daughter, Dorothy Scott; and two other sons: Judge Charles Goldberg and Richard Goldberg, a lawyer. Her family, in turn, marvels at Miriam's enormous energy and ability to remain relaxed while being constantly busy.

Anyone who makes the mistake of asking Miriam Goldberg when she plans to retire will get a hot response: "Why should I retire? I'm right here with everything I love—the paper, the people, and all that I love doing."[3]

Ruth Small Stockton

Born June 6, 1916, in Ridgefield Park, New Jersey
Died October 21, 1990, in Lakewood, Colorado

Ruth Stockton once acknowledged that being a woman handicapped her legislative career, yet allowed her to be a peacemaker and to make compromises. During her tenure in the House and Senate, she was one of Colorado's most powerful legislators. Unlike so many male lawmakers, Ruth Stockton was never a "mike grabber." She did her work in the Colorado General Assembly quietly and effectively. When she did go to the microphone, people listened.

Politics and her family always were Ruth's first interests. She was born in New Jersey, the eldest in the Smalls' family of seven children. She attended Vassar College until the Depression when she dropped out and got a job at Macy's; later, she took classes at Columbia University.

Both her parents were active in politics. Her father, Arthur Small, was a writer for the Republican National Committee and a member of President Theodore Roosevelt's "kitchen cabinet." For Ruth's twentieth birthday, he took her to the 1936 Republican National Convention in Cleveland; the experience affected the rest of her life. Ruth was put to work as a page, delivering election materials. When she stopped at the Colorado booth, she met Truman Stockton, president of the Young Republicans and a delegate in the Colorado delegation that included Gordon Allott (later a U.S. Senator) and business tycoon Claude Boettcher.

Stockton, a transportation lawyer practicing in Denver, promptly invited the young, hazel-eyed page to go out to dinner. Even though her mother accompanied them, Truman continued to date Ruth and then proposed to her after only seven dates. Her family was unable to attend her wedding eighteen months later. Ruth rode the train alone to Denver for her wedding on November 1, 1937. Soon afterward, Ruth's father disappeared, leaving his wife with five children still at home. In 1942, her mother moved to Colorado with the children; four of Ruth's sisters stayed in the state and eventually raised their families in Colorado.

The Stocktons' daughter, Alexe—always called Boots—was born in 1942. The family moved to Wheat Ridge in 1943 and in 1945 bought their permanent home in Lakewood's picturesque Glen Creighton subdivision. Ruth became active in the PTA and was involved in consolidating Jefferson County R-1 schools. As president of Metropolitan United Way, she came to know people all over Denver. She continued her education with classes at the University of Colorado Extension Division and the Emily Griffith Opportunity School, where she learned to type. (Ruth was so impressed with the Opportunity School, she instigated a drive in 1974 to have Miss Griffith's portrait recreated in stained glass and hung in the Colorado Senate chambers.)

Ruth maintained her interest in politics. As a bride, she joined Colorado Young Republicans and started earning her laurels: first, as precinct committee woman, then as a delegate to county and state assemblies, and as life member of Jefferson County Republican Women's Club. In May 1942, the Colorado Young Republicans unanimously supported her election as co-chairman of the Young Republicans' national convention, which was held in June 1947 in Milwaukee. In February 1954, she became Colorado's National Republican committeewoman.

Ruth waited until Boots entered Colorado College in 1960 to announce her candidacy for the Colorado House of Representatives. Door-to-door campaigning was considered compulsory. Ruth enjoyed meeting voters; Boots helped, although she hated knocking on doors. Truman, a successful transportation lawyer, avoided the political arena. "I'll handle the business, you handle the politics," he would tell her.[1] (Truman's passion was his antique automobile collection. At its peak, the collection totaled seventeen cars, including a huge Lincoln Continental convertible. Sometimes dressed in period costumes, the Stocktons rode in local parades—especially during election campaigns—and waved from the front seat of Ruth's parade car, a spiffy 1932 Cord Phaeton convertible.)

At the Republican County Assembly, Ruth always went for top designation on the ballot. She never had a primary opponent but only in 1980 did she run unopposed in the general election. She took office in the State House of Representatives for the first time in January 1961 and served until 1965. She ran for her second term the year that Barry Goldwater ran for president and was the only Republican elected in Jefferson County. After that, she moved up to the State Senate.

Ruth's assistant in the legislature was her daughter, who answered all the phone calls and often called constituents with answers to their questions. Lobbyists came to Boots with questions because she had a direct line to Senator Stockton. "For all her friendly nature, nobody scared Ruth Stockton. Nobody," Boots recalled. "She was so poised, never offensive, always confident she could handle any person or situation. The ultimate politician, she could say no with her trademark smile and you wouldn't mind."[2] Her skill was demonstrated in an incident involving the late Alan Berg, the talk show host. Senator Stockton was on the Senate floor supporting a bill that would allow grocery stores to remain open on Sundays. Boots was at home when her "Aunt" Sally Kerzic called, incensed that Berg, in his radio broadcast on the issue, said, "Sending Ruthie Baby to handle a group of angry women was like sending a fox to guard the hen house. ... I bet Ruthie Baby won't even call me back," he sneered. Boots scurried down to the Senate floor and signaled her mother. At noon, Senator Stockton marched over to the radio station and stormed into Berg's office unannounced. His secretary, alarmed, said: "This is Senator S-t-o-c-k-t-o-n." Berg paled. "Er—Give me a minute." He went into his office and shut the door. After composing himself, a contrite Alan Berg sent for Ruth. When she came out, they were speaking together cordially."[3]

Ruth Stockton considered herself a moderate Republican. Senator Tilman Bishop, Republican from Grand Junction, sat next to her in the Senate and became her close friend and admirer. "She was one of few in the GOP who promoted legislation for children's health and education," he recalled. "Some people would call her bills social programs. She championed the low income and less fortunate people."[4] Senator Stockton supported the Equal Rights Amendment and abortion rights for women. Her cohort pushing the legislation in the House was young Democrat Dick Lamm, who later became governor.

In gratitude for her helping hand to Cenikor, a drug rehabilitation center in her neighborhood, Senator Stockton became an honorary fire chief and acquired a fireman's badge. At the time, the Lakewood Fire Department was buying a large building at 1533 Glen Ayr Drive for the fire station. Too late, the firemen found that Glen Ayr Drive was so narrow they couldn't get their big fire trucks around the corner and in and out of the garage. Ruth Stockton arranged to sell the building to Cenikor. In appreciation, the firemen made her honorary fire chief.

Ruth's friends and constituents remember her ready smile, a smile so broad it covered her face until her eyes seemed to disappear. But she could be very stern when she had to be. Senator Bishop recalled how valuable she was in the state's budget process. With her thorough knowledge of state government and budgets, she became an astute member of the Joint Budget Committee and later was elected the first woman chairman of that committee. "She'd let the men get away with their politicking, posturing, horseplay, and tantrums. But when she was ready to firm up, she let us know it," Senator Bishop said. "Although she represented greater Denver, she appreciated problems in outlying areas. When things needed to be done in western Colorado, she always saw that money was in the budget for them."[5]

Among Stockton's successes was the Jefferson County Law Enforcement Authority, which created an affordable means of increasing police protection in the unincorporated county. She crossed party lines many times for her people-oriented legislation. For example, she carried the bill to allow hearing ear dogs in restaurants and on buses; advocated rehabilitation of alcohol and drug abusers; and worked for mental health programs, transportation improvements, and highway safety. In her twenty-three years in the Colorado General Assembly, Ruth Stockton served from 1979 to 1981 as the first woman president pro tem of the Senate. Her key positions and ten years as chairman of the Senate's Health, Environment, Welfare, and Institutions Committee marked her as Colorado's most significant woman legislator of her era.

Senator Stockton won every battle she took on—except one. A heavy smoker, she quit many times but always took it up again. In the summer of 1980, she underwent gallbladder surgery. The operation went well but doctors nearly lost their patient trying to clear the anesthetic from her lungs. Ruth Stockton's health continued to decline and in 1984 she retired from the Senate.

In December 1986, Colorado lawmakers dedicated a stained-glass window in the Senate chambers to Senator Stockton for her twenty-three years in the legislature. During ceremonies honoring her contributions to countless humanitarian causes, then State Treasurer Roy Romer said, "She was gentle, she was wise, she was firm, but most of all she was gracious."[6] (Ironically, to hang her portrait, they had to move Emily Griffith's window to the old Supreme Court chambers.)

Ruth Stockton believed you couldn't get anywhere in the legislature without party discipline and teamwork. "The other ninety legislators don't see my way all the time but I'm ready to sit down and work it out. When the going gets rough, they know I'm not the weak sister," she often said.[7]

Ruth Stockton died at her home on October 21, 1990. She was seventy-four.

Rachel Bassette Noel

Born January 15, 1918, in Hampton, Virginia

Rachel Noel, who shares her birthday, January 15, with Dr. Martin Luther King, visited with him in Denver. Their talk inspired and encouraged her in her work for equal opportunity for all children. Noel firmly believes in the importance of education and in racial equality, although she grew up in a segregated society in the South. In her family, education was a priority. Both parents had college degrees. Her father, A.W.E. Bassette, Jr., was a lawyer who represented people in their small Virginia town.

Lawyer Bassette, as he was called, continually urged blacks to vote and helped them register. He instructed them in how to mark the ballot and sometimes even paid their poll taxes. At the time, Virginia law allowed only Caucasians to vote in primary elections, but one of his clients filed suit to vote in the Democratic primary. The case went all the way to the Supreme Court, which ruled in his favor.

As a young girl, Rachel came face to face with racial discrimination. One day, her mother sent her to a nearby department store to buy a spool of thread. Although Rachel was first in line at the counter, the clerk waited on all the white customers first and then spoke gruffly to Rachel. The little girl wondered what she had done wrong.

In 1938, Rachel got her bachelor's degree in education, finishing first in her class at Hampton Institute (now Hampton University); then she completed her master's in sociology at Fisk University in Nashville. Her graduate work strengthened her convictions about educational equality and opportunity for all children. In her first job after graduating from Fisk, she worked at Southeast House, a settlement house in Washington, D.C. As part of her work, she became a Girl Scout troop leader. When she learned that the girls had no money for uniforms, she enlisted the parents to help raise funds to buy fabric and then persuaded a friend to help her make the uniforms.

During World War II, she married Edmond F. Noel, a physician. The day he graduated from medical school, he was commissioned in the army. After serving two years in the states, he was sent to the South Pacific. During his absence, she was employed by the Rosenwald Fund as a staff member of the *Monthly Summary of Events and Trends in Race Relations,* a journal of information about minorities.

On November 30, 1949, the couple moved to Denver with their three-year-old son, Buddy. In January, Dr. Noel opened his medical office at Twenty-sixth and Welton Streets above Radio Drugstore, a well-known pharmacy in the Five Points community. "My husband did surgery and also delivered many babies," Noel recalled in 1997. "I hardly go anywhere today without seeing one or more of his patients, who always sing his praises."[1]

When the Noels' son, Edmond, Jr. (Buddy), and their daughter, Angela, who was born in 1950, were growing up, Mrs. Noel maintained a busy schedule serving many volunteer groups including the PTA, the Girl Scouts, and the Colorado child welfare board. In 1964, the Denver

School Board appointed her to an advisory committee to help plan a proposed junior high school in northeast Denver. It soon became apparent that it would be just another all-black school. Spurred by her work on the committee, she boldly announced her candidacy in 1965 for a six-year term on the Denver School Board. With strong support from her family and the black community, she became the first black woman elected to public office in Colorado and the first black person elected to the seven-member board. Motivated by her own experiences of discrimination as a black person, she seized the opportunity while she was on the school board to work toward desegregating Denver's public schools.

On April 4, 1968, Dr. Martin Luther King was assassinated in Memphis, Tennessee. During a memorial service on the steps of Denver City Hall, one of the speakers urged those who were in a position of power to use their power *now* to make a better world. Rachel Noel was further inspired to bring about equal educational opportunity for all. She wrote what became known as the Noel Resolution, which directed School Superintendent Dr. Robert Gilberts to devise and present to the Denver School Board by September 30, 1968, a plan to integrate the Denver Public Schools. Her resolution called for the plan to be acted upon by the school board no later than December 31, 1968.

As she presented her resolution to the board on April 25, 1968, she was not aware that the discussion would become angry and heated along racial lines. "I was calmer than I have ever been," Noel recalled. "I felt this was so important that the opportunity should not be missed. I knew I had support from my community and from many whites, too. All those years, so little had been done. In those times, there was a feeling of high morality across the country, about consideration of black people and all the wrongs against our schools and our children—our future adults."[2]

Finally, on May 16, the school board approved an expanded version of her resolution by a vote of five to two. Public opposition to the resolution was immediate and emphatic. Letters poured in to the school board, many against the resolution. Noel was hounded by hate mail and angry phone calls. In May 1969, a new school board overturned the desegregation measures that had been passed by the previous school board. But a diverse group of parents filed suit against the board, claiming the rescinding was illegal. U.S. District Court Judge William E. Doyle reinstated and broadened the original school desegregation implementation measures. Several years later, the U.S. Supreme Court upheld his decision.

In February 1970, thirty-eight buses were dynamited at the Denver Public School Service Center in violent opposition to the busing-for-integration policy. "Everyone associates me with busing. I never spoke about busing. It's a mode of transportation, that's all," Noel maintains. "My stand was for equal education opportunity for all children, not for minorities to be in a segregated, afterthought status but to have all the rights and privileges. If it took a bus to do it, then so be it."[3]

Simply giving segregated schools more money will not solve the problem, Rachel Noel insists. She believes that when people of different races know each other, go to school and work together, they can develop open minds about each other. She adds that when school personnel reach out to parents and work with them on an equal basis, they see them as people who want the best for their children. She thinks the Denver Public Schools integration plan would have been more successful if it had started at the elementary rather than junior high school level.

Judge Doyle's order included a Community Education Council and he appointed a citizens' committee to monitor progress of the schools' integration. Noel was one of the committee members. They visited schools, wrote reports, and presented their conclusions at meetings. Judge Richard Matsch, who succeeded Judge Doyle, eventually abolished the committee. Noel surmised he may have thought committee members were just doing paper work, but she disagreed with his move. "I felt ... we were a serious citizen group overseeing compliance of a court order," she said.[4]

Rachel Noel continued her volunteer work for civil rights on numerous boards, including the Metro Denver Urban Coalition, the Colorado Advisory Committee, the U.S. Civil Rights Commission, and later, the Denver Housing Authority. In 1969, she became an assistant professor of sociology at Metropolitan State College in Denver and chairman of the new Afro-American Studies Department at the college. (The department was abolished after she retired in 1980 suffering from a back ailment. Later, it was reinstated and the Rachel B. Noel Distinguished Professorship was established.)

While at Metro State College, she served as chairman of a committee to investigate student charges that the University of Colorado Law School had not sought to hire minority and women faculty members. Her committee's controversial report criticized the law school for having no full-time women or minority faculty. A few months later, on September 27, 1976, Governor Dick Lamm named Rachel Noel to fill the final two years of a CU Regent's six-year term and she became CU's first black Regent. She later ran for a full term at large and served six more years, one as chair. Noel was concerned that CU, a tax-supported institution, did not have more black students, faculty, and administrators.

In keeping with their family's belief in education, both Noel children attended East High School. Buddy graduated from Dartmouth College, got his law degree at Harvard, and practices law in Denver. The Noels' daughter, Angela, graduated from Smith College in Massachusetts. Now a widow, Rachel has five grandchildren. Walls and shelves of her elegant East Denver apartment bear testimony to her contributions to Denver. In 1963, the Denver Classroom Teachers' Association presented her with the Eddy Award for dedicated service to education. The Malcolm Glenn Wyer Award honored her for outstanding service to education in 1972. In 1990, she received the Martin Luther King, Jr., Humanitarian Award. In 1993, the University of Colorado awarded her an honorary doctorate of public service degree, and Shorter A.M.E. Church dedicated a stained-glass window honoring her in 1998.

After serving out her term as Regent, Noel returned to volunteering in city and church activities. For Shorter A.M.E. Church, she co-chairs the education and scholarship committee. She also is a member of the Denver Public Schools' Black Education Advisory Committee and a 1996 inductee of Colorado Women's Hall of Fame.

Now in her eighties, she walks with a cane but maintains her gracious, dignified manner. Her trademark charm still shines through in a warm smile and that soft Southern voice.

Elise Biorn-Hansen Boulding

Born July 6, 1920, in Oslo, Norway

The year Elise Biorn-Hansen was born in Oslo, Norway, her country was undergoing a severe depression. When she was three, her family migrated to the United States, which was known throughout Europe as the land of opportunity. The Biorn-Hansens eventually arrived in Orange, New Jersey, and rented an apartment. Spurred by hearing the children on the street speaking what she thought was jibberish, Elise rapidly learned to speak English. Her mother, however, was so homesick the family spoke only Norwegian at home and Elise did her lessons after school in Norwegian as well as English so she could be bilingual. Her mother often told stories of Norway, which Elise pictured as safe and wonderful.

Elise's family soon moved to Hillside, New Jersey. When Elise saw American movies and news features of terrifying war scenes, she decided if war broke out in America she would go to Norway where she could be safe. Then Hitler's armies invaded Norway, her "safe place" and Elise was deeply shaken. She realized that if ever there would be safe places, people, together, must make them. From that experience, she committed her life to the cause of peace.

Elise attended Douglass College (later New Jersey College for Women and now part of Rutgers) to get her bachelor's degree in English literature, French, and German in 1940. She loved playing cello with string quartets and in orchestras. At that time, she began attending meetings of the Society of Friends in the basement of the college chapel.

After graduation, Elise worked a year for a New York City publisher. She soon realized big-city life was not for her and moved to Syracuse, where her family was living. She continued attending Quaker meetings and applied for membership in the Society of Friends. At that time, she met Kenneth Boulding, a brilliant economist ten years her senior. They were married in 1941 after a whirlwind Quaker courtship.

Kenneth was working for the economic and financial sector of the League of Nations, which was housed at Princeton. During the war years, he and Elise drafted a letter urging fellow Americans to refuse to serve in the war in Europe. But the League of Nations staff were not allowed to express personal views on public issues, so he had to resign from the League and leave Princeton. Shortly after, Kenneth was called for a physical examination for the draft. He explained his religious objections to military service to an examining psychiatrist, who then asked, "Do you hear the voice of God?" Boulding answered, "That depends upon what you mean by the voice of God." With that, the doctor wrote down "mentally unstable" and classified him as 4-F.[1]

Dr. Boulding got a teaching post at Fisk, a black college in Nashville, Tennessee. They both enjoyed Fisk's warm and welcoming community. Bolstering her interest in doing peace work, Elise discovered non-governmental organizations (NGOs) such as churches, the YMCA, Rotary, and the Scouts—all local branches of international people's organizations working worldwide for human betterment.

Kenneth Boulding, meanwhile, was gaining an international reputation as an economist that brought him frequent university assignments. His next post, at Iowa State University in Ames, offered excellent facilities where he could expand both his research and teaching. Elise, hoping to start a family, began work on a master's degree in sociology. Her course work and faculty seminars with other faculty wives provided a stimulating environment. Six years later, when Kenneth was a visiting professor at McGill University in Montreal, Elise finally became pregnant, but was ordered to stay off her feet, which provided time for thinking and reading. Their son John was born in 1947.

From Canada, they returned to Iowa State. Along with her new duties as a mother, she completed her master's in sociology in 1949 with a study of the effect on Iowa farm wives of husbands being drafted into the military. She was impressed by how inventive women were in managing farms without husbands in those difficult years.

Once started, there was no stopping the babies. Mark joined the family in 1949 and Christine in 1951. Elise continued course work on her Ph.D. until Phillip Daniel was born in 1953. By then, life was so complicated she decided that Phillip D. would be her Ph.D. When William was born in 1955, the Boulding family numbered four sons and one daughter.

From Iowa State, they moved to the University of Michigan where Dr. Boulding could divide his time equally between teaching and research. While at Michigan, Kenneth Boulding founded the first Conflict Resolution Center in the United States. Elise worked as a volunteer taking notes at seminars and answering letters of inquiry from around the world. She saw the benefits of putting the inquirers in these new fields of conflict resolution and peace research in touch with one another, so she began what became the International Peace Research newsletter. Out of the newsletter was born the International Peace Research Association. Elise and Kenneth were considered the association's mother and father.

In the 1950s, during the Bouldings' year-long stay in Palo Alto at the Institute for Advanced Study in the Behavioral Sciences, Elise met the Dutch sociologist and futurist Fred Polak. While her children were in school, she found time to translate his masterpiece, *Image of the Future,* from Dutch into English. When the translation finally was published in 1961, it was considered an important and inspiring work and Elise became known as a "futurist."

Elise had been active in the Women's International League of Peace and Freedom (WILPF) and in 1962 was chosen as one of twelve women to meet with a delegation of Russian women to strengthen peace processes and disarmament possibilities. By then, she was editing the International Peace Research Association newsletter and a newsletter for a new group, Women's Strike for Peace.

In 1963–1964, the Bouldings went to Japan where he was a visiting professor. Already involved in Women's Strike for Peace, Elise was fascinated to find Japanese women, normally so quiet and shy, doing "this unseemly thing of demonstrating in the streets."[2] Elise had written an article about the WILPF and saw an opportunity for a counterpart in Japan. With the help of a Japanese graduate student fluent in English, she interviewed hundreds of women working in Tokyo. She applied for grants in order to be able to pay her assistant, but always was notified that grants were given only to Ph.D.s and not to researchers with master's degrees. The Japanese project introduced her to the little-known but courageous activism of Japanese women. She described their work in an article titled "Japanese Women Looked at Society."

The years between 1947 and 1965 were crowded with family activities and projects. Their home was always filled with neighborhood children taking part in their activities. Elise learned more sociology from listening to lively children's conversations than from any college course. The Bouldings' youngest child was in fifth grade by the time the family returned to the University of Michigan. Elise felt ready to start teaching and was offered an instructorship in family sociology. But at the last minute, she was told they had found a candidate who had a Ph.D. No longer could she ignore the doctorate degree that would enable her to choose what she wanted to do. With her family's full support, she started work on a Ph.D. at the University of Michigan in January 1965, while still raising five active children. She was writing her dissertation when they moved to the University of Colorado at Boulder in 1967. Since her studies focused on peace as well as women and development, it seemed timely to help found the Consortium on Peace Research, Education, and Development as the North American branch of the International Peace Research Association. Within the community, Elise Boulding was a driving force behind the Boulder Parenting Center, where parents congregated to learn child-rearing and family-building skills. She regarded this kind of local arena as a major step in humankind's drive to achieve and maintain global peace.

She received her long-sought doctorate in 1969—twenty years after her master's. At the University of Colorado, *Dr.* Elise Boulding became an assistant, then an associate, professor of sociology. She was known in three new fields: peace studies, women's studies, and future studies; and she initiated the Conflict and Peace Studies program at CU. Elise found herself in demand everywhere—traveling, writing, teaching— but continued to spend precious time with her family.

As work piled up, she underwent mastoid surgery, which affected her sense of balance and for several months she was unable to walk. She found herself in a profound spiritual crisis. The time had come for her to take a year's leave from the university. The next year, with her youngest in college and her husband's blessing, Elise built a secluded retreat on forty acres of the Bouldings' land in the mountains above Boulder. There she lived in solitude, reading, meditating, praying, and writing, in wordless communion with nature. At the end of her year's seclusion, she felt renewed and ready to return to teaching at the University of Colorado. The retreat property later was deeded to the Sisters of Loretto.

Back at CU, Elise developed unique workshops and continued to shape the university's peace studies programs. She consulted for twenty years on peace research for UNESCO and other UN agencies. She was on the congressional commission that proposed the National Academy of Peace and Conflict Resolution, which became the U.S. Institute of Peace. In 1978, she became interested in teaching in a smaller college when Dartmouth invited Kenneth and Elise as Montgomery House fellows. She was offered a full professorship and soon became head of Dartmouth's sociology department.

Although forced to retire from CU at age seventy, Kenneth did not want to move permanently from Colorado. He accepted various visiting professorships and Elise commuted to and from her assignments until 1985, when she retired so they could enjoy a few years of uninterrupted togetherness.

The American Friends Service Committee nominated Elise Boulding for the 1990 Nobel Peace Prize. The AFSC, a Quaker organization that won the Nobel Prize in 1947, described her as a leader in the international peace research movement, who promoted women's and children's human rights. In nominating her, Asia Bennett, the committee executive secretary, wrote: "She believes that women have an indispensable role not only in nurturing in the home but in peacemaking and peace building in the public arena."[3] Irwin Abrams, author of *The Nobel Peace Prize and the Laureates,* supported Elise Boulding for the award: "She is qualified in every way and is the best woman candidate in the world."[4] Elise Boulding did not win the Nobel Prize, but dozens of other distinguished awards have poured in to honor the woman peace scholar and activist: the National Women's Forum "Woman Who Made a Difference Award," Peace Studies Association Award, Rutgers Hall of Distinguished Alumni, Global Citizens Award from Boston Research Center for the Twenty-First Century—to mention only a few.

Kenneth Boulding died in March 1993. Although working always in their separate fields, the couple had been partners in a lifelong crusade for peace. Her greatest reward has been their fifty years together, raising five children, who produced sixteen grandchildren. From this experience, she advocates peace building on three levels: personal and family, community, and global. Commuting from her Boulder home, she circled the globe to speak, write, and expand her vision of a peaceful world.

After living in Colorado thirty years, Dr. Elise Boulding moved in November 1996 to Wayland, Massachusetts, outside Boston, into an apartment that her daughter and son-in-law built behind their home. The new location is also closer to the United Nations.

Retirement is still in the future. She has been writing her twenty-first book, *The Culture of Peace;* making new connections in Boston; and extending her work for peace and social justice. She went to Sweden in the fall of 1997 to speak about how non-governmental organizations can work with governments and the UN's need to reduce reliance on military defense and increase the use of diplomacy, including what is called "second-track diplomacy."

To all who know her, Elise Boulding is a motherly woman who exemplifies wisdom and understanding. In her lifelong work to bring about permanent world peace, she has more than kept her pledge to the Quaker faith.

Lena Lovato Archuleta

Born July 25, 1920, in Clapham, New Mexico

A light, airy apartment in Denver's Cheesman Park neighborhood is Lena Archuleta's operations center, where she conducts her network of activities in the American Association of Retired Persons (AARP) and assists her Colorado Latino community. During a long and energetic lifetime, she has built two outstanding careers: first, as a wise and intuitive classroom teacher and second, as a full-time volunteer.

Born on a farm in Clapham, a small town outside Clayton, New Mexico, Lena clearly recalls the Union County dust bowl in the 1930s that brought poverty and hardship to her grandparents' family. As a World War I veteran, her father, Eusebio Lovato, received training in shoe repair in Pueblo. In 1922, he moved his wife and two daughters to Raton, New Mexico, where he worked as a mail carrier and at other jobs until he could open his shoe repair shop.

The Lovato's daughter, Lena, graduated from Raton High School as valedictorian and then enrolled at the University of Denver to major in Spanish with a minor in Latin and education. As a graduating senior, she was tapped for Mortar Board and Phi Beta Kappa.

Beginning in 1942, Lena taught school in El Rito, New Mexico, and in 1943 married Juan Archuleta. They moved to Denver in 1951, where she joined the Denver Public Schools (DPS) as a classroom teacher and school librarian at Westwood Elementary and Kepner Junior High Schools. Juan Archuleta went to work for the school district, maintaining power and water systems.

In 1961, Lena Archuleta took a year's leave to serve as acting executive secretary and then president for the Denver Classroom Teachers Association. For the ensuing fifteen years, she worked in administrative assignments for the DPS in the Department of Library Services and the Office of Community Relations, and on federal projects in bilingual education. During this period, she obtained her administrative certificate from the University of Denver Graduate School of Education.

As administrator of the Denver Public School's bilingual program, Archuleta stressed the importance of making Spanish available to non-English speaking children for the first few years so they can catch up to their English-speaking classmates as quickly as possible. At the same time, children should be learning English language skills early, she insists, because it is impossible to live in this country without knowing English and all its nuances. Latino immigrants, especially those from Mexico, tend to cling to Spanish because they often go back and forth to Mexico and think about moving back there someday. Asians, however, come to the United States knowing they are not going to return to their native country. The Archuletas' experience as mentors to a young Mexican boy reinforced their belief that family support is important. Although the boy spoke English fairly well, he had to travel a long distance to his high school. Unfortunately, he did not have support from his family, who continually returned to Mexico. Eventually he dropped out of school and married.

Archuleta's management certificate and her earlier assignments led to a challenging and rewarding opportunity in 1976 when she became the first Latino woman to be named a Denver school principal. It wasn't an easy job. Archuleta's school, Fairview Elementary at 2715 West Eleventh Avenue, was a school for kindergarten through grade three. Then it was paired with upper middle-class Traylor Elementary; the new combination mixed Fairview's 100 pupils with poor children from housing projects, plus more than 100 Vietnamese, 100 Latinos, and 100 Anglo pupils. Her first task was to integrate the school's many socioeconomic levels and deal with the wide disparity in classroom knowledge. At first, the kids reacted to the differences and had some scraps. Overall, they adjusted better than their parents did. She concluded that school pairing works best if children come from the same economic level.

"It was particularly difficult because today's poor children watch so much television [that shows] them the many material things they can't have. TV brings home to them just how poor they are," Archuleta said. "Parents who use television as a babysitter make it so much harder for teachers. My favorite job involved working with kids and their parents. I had gained credibility with people, and I didn't have much trouble with overt discrimination. I could have taken every waking moment to knock on kids' doors."[1]

Lena Archuleta received the Regis University Civis Princeps Award on April 19, 1973, for supervising bilingual education in the Denver Public Schools. The award recognized her as First Citizen in humanitarianism for activities in numerous civic and educational organizations, for service to the Hispanic community, and as a DPS employee since 1951.

Lena and her husband, who had become a school services area administrator, both retired in 1979. She continued until 1982 as a part-time consultant for the Department of Elementary Schools. She was also president of the Colorado Library Association and has been active in both the Colorado and National Education Associations. In the 1970s, she joined a twelve-member group that performed Spanish dances with castanets and Mexican folk dances.

Lena Archuleta is a petite woman—five-foot-one, lively, sharp, perky—and businesslike, especially at directors' meetings and presiding at conferences. She has always been interested in volunteer organizations. With Bernie Valdez and Charles Tafoya, Lena Archuleta was a founding member of the Latin American Research and Service Agency (LARASA) in 1964. A nucleus of Latino volunteers joined them to raise the quality of life for Colorado Latinos. Thirty years later, LARASA celebrated its birthday with a luncheon and presentation of awards and scholarships.

In 1988, she joined the board of Brothers' Redevelopment, a nonprofit group that provides housing and home repairs, including modifying residences, for low-income and disabled clients. Brothers' volunteers teach seniors how to make their homes fit their needs and show them in what areas a house is not compatible with their health and age. They suggest adjustments such as ramps, grab bars, and appropriate faucet handles. Clients pay only for materials. As a Brothers' board member, Archuleta helps formulate policy, raise funds, and manage HUD apartments for low-income elderly and disabled clients.

Lena Archuleta recently rejoined the board of Rude Park Community Nursery near Fairview School on Thirteenth and Decatur Streets. Built by the Lions Club and managed by Mile High Child Care, the nursery cares for seventy children including babies. Other boards and commissions she served in the 1980s include the Denver Public Library Commission (when it was preparing to open the new Central Library), Mi Casa Resource Center for Women as founder and board member, the Denver Landmark Preservation Commission, the Denver Planning Board, and the Denver Catholic Archdiocese finance committee. In 1986, she was inducted into the Colorado Women's Hall of Fame.

In the 1990s, Lena Archuleta has concentrated her efforts on the American Association of Retired Persons because she applauds AARP's belief that seniors should be independent, contributing members of society. "Seniors should be in charge of their own health, money, and safety—or they're vulnerable," she adds.[2] Since taking speakers' training, she has presented free public forums for seniors to explain all options and services of available forms of health care. She teaches them about preventive health and nursing home issues. She was also a speaker and moderator in a forum exposing fraud, a leading crime against the elderly.

Archuleta is president of Greater Denver Rainbow Chapter, an AARP organization that connects nursing home elders with young volunteers, and she meets with an AARP Rainbow Chapter in her apartment building. In May 1995, she represented Colorado at the White House Conference on Aging.

As spokeswoman for the National Association of Retired Federal Employees, she supported the Colorado Health Care Reform Project at a rally conducted at the Capitol for public support of universal health insurance coverage. During her six-year term as vice chairman of the AARP board of directors, she often traveled to Washington, D.C., for meetings. She wrote frequent letters to the editor of Denver newspapers to publicize AARP's views on such issues as proposed Medicare cuts.

The Hispanic community bestowed upon her the Bernie Valdez Community Service Award and Hispanic Annual Salute Award. In 1997, she received Rainbow Bridge's Golden Rainbow Award and a Trailblazer Award from the Denver Branch of the American Association of University Women.

Of all her accomplishments, Lena is most proud of being married to the same man for fifty-six years. Her longtime activism in organizations would have been impossible without understanding support from her husband Juan, whom she describes as her best friend and confidante. They have no children, but are close to many nieces, nephews, and cousins in Colorado and New Mexico. Since undergoing a total knee replacement in 1997, she is anticipating having more time to play her piano and finish making a quilt that has been languishing in the closet.

Mildred Pitts Walter

Born September 9, 1922, in Sweetville, Louisiana

Vivid African paintings, carvings, and sculptures enliven the rooms of Mildred Pitts Walter's home in northeast Denver. These images inspire her writing and are reflected in her books about African American children.

Mildred's childhood goes back to De Ridder, a small Louisiana town where she grew up—the youngest of seven children of Paul Pitts, a log cutter, and his wife, Mary, a midwife and beautician. Her life was further enriched by their active church and school that formed a congenial black community where everybody knew everyone. Her parents and teachers exerted a strong influence by reinforcing her sense of being a beautiful and worthwhile person.

During the 1930s Depression, local timber-cutting jobs dried up, forcing her father and a brother to seek work in Houston, Texas. During that period of deepening poverty, her parents instilled in her the value of work. Racial segregation was pronounced in rural Louisiana and particularly in their community. They came in contact with whites only in stores, when police ventured into their neighborhood, or when whites drove by. Often, they would see signs forbidding them to use "white" restrooms or to patronize "white" restaurants.

As a black child in the South, Mildred was not allowed to enter a public library, but books always were important to her. When she finally gained access to books, she read all the African American writers and much of Virginia Woolfe's and Doris Lessing's works. Her high school teachers were young women students from Southern University, a black college outside of Baton Rouge. Mildred was so impressed by them, she resolved to attend the college and become a teacher. Starting in 1940, she worked two or three jobs at a time during vacations to pay her tuition and become the first in her family to go to college. At Southern University, Mildred was chosen to escort Lillian Smith, author of *Strange Fruit*, around campus. "[It] was my first [contact with a] real, live author, but she was not highly acclaimed in the South.

From her, I learned it's much more important to have stature than status. She had so much courage and so much going for her."[1]

After graduating, Mildred moved to Los Angeles in 1944 to find work. She had only $10 when she arrived. Her plan to stay at the YWCA fizzled when she learned that the YWCA refused to rent rooms to black women. She got a sales job and started attending a black church. In Sunday School, she met Earl Walter, a racial activist who believed in nonviolent protest. They were married in 1947.

Walter joined the Congress of Racial Equality (CORE), in which he eventually became a national vice chairman. Through him, Mildred met James Farmer, Martin Luther King, Jr., and Adam Clayton Powell. She also met James Baldwin when he came to Los Angeles to address CORE. After the *Los Angeles Times* printed a scathing review of his book *The Fire Next Time,* she wrote a letter to the editor rebutting the review. She later became a book reviewer for the *Times.*

Mildred attended California State College from 1950 to 1952 to earn a teaching certificate and then taught in the Los Angeles School District until 1970. In looking for stories to read to her pupils she was frustrated by the lack of books written by African Americans about African American children. When she asked an employee of Ward Ritchie, a publishing company, to publish books for her black pupils, he retorted, "Write some." At first she thought he was passing the buck, but he encouraged her to submit a manuscript. So she wrote her first book, *Lillie of Watts: A Birthday Discovery,* in 1969 and followed it in 1971 with *Lillie of Watts Takes a Giant Step.* Her first two books were well received but her next efforts resulted in a pile of rejection slips. She joined the Watts Writers Group and through self-criticism and trial and error, she honed her craft.

Meanwhile, the Walters both worked with CORE to desegregate housing and motels in Los Angeles. Then she underwent the most difficult experience of her life, the final three-month illness and death of her husband. "After that, other things—like not having shoes—became insignificant," she recalled.[2] In 1970, Walter and her younger son, wishing for a quieter city, moved to Denver.

After a five-year gap in her writing career, she secured an assignment for a Scholastic Sprint editor to write a book for children who were reading at low levels but had great interest. The result was *Liquid Trap,* set in the Louisiana bayou country. It was followed by several action books for adolescents—*The Girl on the Outside* and *Trouble's Child.* Her *Justin and the Best Biscuits in the World* received the Coretta Scott King Award for Literature in 1987. Walter had agreed to participate in a peace walk from Leningrad to Moscow on the day later set for the award presentation. After much soul-searching, she reluctantly passed up the award ceremony to go on the march. Two of her other books— *Brother to the Wind* and *My Mama Needs Me*—also received recognition. Her nineteenth book, *Second Daughter,* is a story of a young woman whose sister, Elizabeth Freeman, is well known in American history.

Unlike many successful authors who follow a writing regimen, Walter does not write a specific number of hours each day. "I write when I have something definite to get down. I don't go to the computer unless I have something to say. I do other things to empty myself; when I'm full, I write."[3] Although her books are about African American children and are written from an African American perspective, she writes for all children. She sets her works in the African American culture but not in Africa.

Except for historical novels, she does not specify a location, so all the children can imagine the story takes place in their home town. "I try to give young readers a sense of who they are by writing out of their language and [of their] culture. I describe [the] foods they eat, [the] people they know. Then children can identify with these characters and say, 'They are like me; even in our differences we share a common thread in our humanity.' I want children to discover things outside themselves, too."[4] She believes children's literature is valuable because it gives children the opportunity to discover that life is a series of choices and that they must have the courage to stand by their choices.

Walter brings her years of teaching experience into creating characters and story lines. "Writing children's books resembles teaching," she says in her quiet voice and soft Louisiana accent. "The teacher provides a lot of good experiences and then lets children create. In writing, I create the characters. The characters then set the stage for the story and bring the material for the writer to work with. But I must know where I want the story to go. Then I have to be still and listen. I have to deal with these characters so they will give me what I want and yet don't run away from me. If I control too much, the characters do nothing. They won't be spontaneous and creative. Just as a teacher should not try to shape children the way she is—because they will rebel—if I [am] still and listen, [the characters] will unfold.

"The real test of creativity is an ability to limit and direct the characters [to make] a good story. I find that challenging. I sometimes get to the end [of a story] and find it has changed [from what I had planned] because the characters have led me to the best conclusion. Characters do write the book but it won't be a good story without control."[5] Walter does not directly retell her life story or her family's activities, but draws her books out of a different and deeper place. This approach is less limiting. Rewriting is important but she finds it tedious—it's her least favorite aspect of the process.

She travels to schools around the country to talk to children about her writing and her books. She continues to receive letters from children who have read and enjoyed her books. Walter has received many honors and awards, such as the 1993 Christopher Award for best books. The children of New York chose her book *Ty's One-Man Band* as one of the hundred best books of the century. Some of her earlier books are still selling and appear as excerpts in textbooks.

She has also extended her energy to helping women in her community who need special attention. In 1979, she teamed up with Hazel Whitsett and Shirley Sims to found the Northeast Women's Center, which offers GED tests and gives classes in computer science and parenting. It trains and places women in jobs and encourages them to enhance their lives with careers. She still volunteers at the center and makes financial contributions to it. As a grandmother of two, her life continues to center around her family and her writing.

Hendrika Bestebreurtje Cantwell
Born May 3, 1925, in Berlin, Germany

A citizen of the Netherlands, Hendrika Bestebreurtje was born in Berlin, Germany, grew up in Zurich, Switzerland, and migrated to New York City when she was fifteen. By the time she reached Colorado, Hendrika already had lived an exciting life. She went on to become a pioneering champion for Colorado's abused and neglected children.

Hendrika was the youngest of four children of the Dutch Bestebreurtje family. Her father's company had transferred him to Berlin, where Hendrika was born. By the time she was six, Germany was sinking into a severe depression, with factions of communists, socialists, republicans, and royalists fighting in the streets. To escape Germany's violence and upheaval, the Bestebreurtje family moved to Zurich.

Hitler came to power in 1933 and war began in Europe in 1939. Hendrika's older sister, Annie, was studying medicine in Holland in 1940, when the Nazis bombed Rotterdam and occupied Holland. For six months, Annie pestered Nazi officials for a visa so she could rejoin her family in Zurich. In November, Annie reached Zurich and the seven Bestebreurtjes—two parents, three daughters, a son and his wife—embarked upon a dangerous migration to the United States.

They had to pass through Nazi sympathizer countries, all the while fearing the Nazis might arrest Hendrika's brother, a Hollander of military age. But Hendrika's father convinced authorities that he couldn't possibly travel as the only man with five women and the authorities let the young man proceed. The family finally reached the neutral port of Lisbon and took passage on the only available vessel, a Portuguese ship built to carry 300 people. It left with 1,000 aboard. They later heard the Germans sank that ship on its next voyage. The Bestebreurtjes reached New York City on April 25, 1941. Hendrika became a naturalized citizen in 1947.

When Hendrika was nineteen, she graduated from Barnard College in New York. Influenced by Annie, she wanted to become a pediatrician and enrolled at the University of Rochester Medical School. Midway through medical school, Hendrika married William Cantwell, a law student. While she completed her internship at Buffalo Children's Hospital, he practiced law in Buffalo, New York. A business and vacation trip to Iowa and then to Denver and Glenwood Springs convinced them to move West after Hendrika finished her internship. They considered five cities and in 1952 settled on Denver because of the nearby ski slopes. Their son Peter was born in September, followed by a daughter, Rebecca, in 1953, and another son, Chris, in 1956.

In 1954, Dr. Cantwell began working part-time in school immunization and well-baby clinics. Dr. Ruth Raatama had organized Denver's exemplary Neighborhood Health Program, which enables parents to walk with their children to well-baby clinics for immunizations and physicals. In 1967, at Dr. Raatama's urging, Dr. Cantwell accepted a full-time post, serving both a Neighborhood Health Station situated in the Children's Hospital outpatient clinic and the Stapleton Clinic. She also taught in a new pediatric nurse practitioner program and instructed nursing and medical school students and pediatric residents. In recognition of her ongoing lecturing, writing, and teaching, the University of Colorado Health Sciences Center appointed her a clinical professor of pediatrics.

Dr. Cantwell served on a committee called by Mayor Bill McNichols in 1973 to investigate the highly publicized death of a child. In a newspaper series about the case, *Denver Post* writer Fred Gilles quoted Dr. C. Henry Kempe, founder of the Kempe National Center for Prevention and Treatment of Child Abuse and Neglect, as charging that the Denver Department of Social Services (DDSS) had caused the child's death by mishandling its cases. When Gilles called Dr. Cantwell the night before publishing these allegations, she told him, "There was a lot more to the case than you were aware of. ... DDSS cannot divulge information because it is confidential. ... The child's death was not 'caused' by DDSS."[1]

One recommendation of the Mayor's committee was that Denver Social Services hire a doctor who could see children promptly in questions of abuse. The only doctor who applied eventually declined after the interview saying the job would be too depressing. Finally, in February 1975, Dr. Cantwell agreed to take the post. (She arguably was the first physician anywhere to serve with a child protection agency.) Her appointment increased public awareness of child abuse, causing the DDSS patient caseload to soar.

Dr. Cantwell helped Social Services establish a Family Crisis Center in its own building, to which police could bring child victims of suspected abuse. Dr. Cantwell and social workers could then interview the children in the center's friendly, natural setting instead of at the site where the abuse had occurred. When parents came to visit, she could observe and report on the interaction. DDSS could either release children to their families or keep them at the center, depending upon Social Services' findings and the home situation. If children were not allowed to return home, the medical report was entered as evidence for a Juvenile Court hearing to be held within 48 hours to determine where they should be sent. In the safe Family Crisis Center, as many as 40 percent of the girls questioned voluntarily revealed experiences of sexual abuse. In 98 percent of abuse cases, children under seven had been abused by family and friends. Social Services became involved in family-perpetrated cases. Schools and police began educational programs for preventing sexual abuse by strangers.

Dr. Cantwell found family-perpetrated sexual abuses the most difficult to deal with. "Parents ... are supposed to love, nurture, and protect children," she said. "If the father (statistically the largest number) betrays this trust by promoting the child to be his whore (and often calls her that), one is at a loss how to treat such a betrayal."[2] A child's testimony might put the perpetrator in jail, which is usually a terrible burden for the child to carry. A girl summed up the situation best to Dr. Cantwell: "I want to go home. Just tell Daddy not to do that anymore. He promised he wouldn't." Dr. Cantwell noted, "We teach parents to realize that children are not bad but what they did may have been wrong. It's the same thing with children: They love Daddy but they want him to stop [behaving in a] sexual [manner with them]. After parents have abused them and their trust, children enter the world mistrusting other people. Attention and love may be equated with sexual stimulation. The results are tragic."[3] She witnessed the tragic results often, seeing as many as fifteen sexually abused children a day. Too often she felt she could not undo the immense damage they had suffered and was unable to set their lives on a healthier course.

A conversation with a fourteen-year-old mother whose infant child had been placed at the Family Crisis Center particularly shocked Dr. Cantwell. The young mother, who had been raped by her father when she was eight, said she would rather be with her family than with a "nice" foster care family—she was "used to" being raped! The interview caused Dr. Cantwell to reexamine her work: Was sexual abuse less significant than they had thought? Apparently, it was the only form of "affection" these children knew.

Starting in 1975, court cases increased dramatically. Many parents were diagnosed as being unsuited for treatment because of their own miserable childhoods, serious alcohol or drug addiction, retardation, and homelessness. Social workers soon asked Dr. Cantwell to give child development classes. In dealing with the pain of neglected and abused children, she herself had perceived the damage was so massive that greater efforts should be directed toward prevention and parenting education. "That means a ... change in basic attitudes, by which women and children will not be seen as possessions to be taken advantage of because of their smaller size," she said.[4]

In an effort to reach abusive and negligent parents, Dr. Cantwell started the first parenting classes for court-ordered cases in 1975. They met weekly at the Emily Griffith Opportunity School for the next ten years and were copied throughout Denver. She saw some pitiful parents—mentally ill, homeless, too ill to function as parents. She encouraged them to talk about their problems and learned how child abuse is passed down from one generation to the next. Instead of accusing and punishing the parents, she patiently helped them understand why they were mistreating their children and how to correct their behavior.

"It led me to feel great sorrow for parents and their abused children," she recalled. "No one had listened to these parents. Most had been abused. ... They felt singled out by drunken fathers. It's normal to take our perception of child-rearing from our parents. It was amazing that they didn't realize how mistreated they were. Instead, they blamed themselves for being rotten kids. Schools had punished them for inattention, fighting, failing to do their work. But no one asked *why* they did poorly. Most painful was their recurring question, 'Where were you when I needed protection?'"[5] Parenting classes continued in Denver under auspices of the courts and DDSS. The Emily Griffith Opportunity School supplied teachers and Dr. Cantwell published the curriculum in a book that still is being used. The Association of Retarded Citizens also conducts a parenting class for retarded parents who need help.

Dr. Hendrika Cantwell has been involved with 30,000 cases reported by hospitals and doctors to Denver Social Services. Many of these required her court testimony. "Court appearances are not a happy experience," she declared. "Lawyers try to confuse the witnesses, making them feel incompetent or like liars. Much information affecting cases' outcomes is ruled inadmissible in motions hearings."[6] Nonetheless, Dr. Cantwell's publicized court testimony has brought her widespread public recognition.

When the Cantwells' second grandchild was born in 1989, Hendrika realized that the emotional burden of her work was blocking her ability to enjoy her own grandchildren. In August 1989, she resigned from Denver Social Services and Denver General Hospital and turned to consulting part-time for the Colorado State Department of Social Services in child abuse and neglect. She also taught at the nursing school, did training programs for Volunteer Court-Appointed Special Child Advocates (CASA) at the Kempe Center and Colorado State University. In her capacity as consultant and clinical professor of pediatrics, she trained students and case workers. Instead of appearing in court, she taught case workers to testify.

Dr. Cantwell also traveled throughout Colorado giving workshops, consultations, and lectures. She trained and spoke to social workers, school employees, police officers, attorneys, doctors, public health and clinic nurses, judges, county officials, foster parents, and the general public. In addition, she published a large body of her work in national and international journals, teaching manuals, and as book chapters.

Her honors and awards, which are numerous, include "Dr. Hendrika Cantwell Day" designated by the governor in 1983 and by the mayor of Denver in 1989 and the Colorado Bar Association's Hendrika B. Cantwell Annual Award (established in 1983). She was inducted into the Colorado Women's Hall of Fame in 1990 and received the Henry C. Kempe Award in 1991. She retired in 1996 and moved with her husband to Driggs, Idaho, near the Wyoming border, where they can look out at the Tetons and ski.

Hendrika Cantwell, one of the first American pediatricians to work on a large scale with neglected and abused children, has shared what she learned with others concerned about children's welfare. Outside of Colorado, she is known for her work in defining and describing problems of child neglect and how it damages children. Donald Bross, a children's health lawyer with the C. Henry Kempe National Center, paid this tribute to her: "It is rare to see a single human being who could so energetically pursue the care of her own children and marriage, be so active in the field of medicine, as well as be an articulate advocate for neglected and abused children."[7]

Joan Packard Birkland

Born November 17, 1928, in Denver, Colorado

With all of City Park as her front yard, Joanie Packard grew up as Denver's number one tomboy. She was a born athlete and every sport came easy to her.

Joan, one of three daughters of Dr. George Packard, a prominent Denver surgeon, was a product of the Denver schools: Park Hill, Smiley, and East High. The family home was at Eighteenth and York, across the street from City Park, where Joanie spent her youth playing tackle football and baseball, shooting baskets with the boys, or picking up games on the tennis courts. Surprisingly, the first blue ribbon she ever won was at the National Western Stock Show as best 10-and-under rider. At the Denver Country Club, she took tennis lessons from Jack Cella, a top local pro and player. By the time she was fifteen, Joanie Packard had won the state tennis championships for her age group. After that, she quit tennis because she couldn't find enough competition.

Joan's blue eyes spark with amusement as she reminisces about her sports activities in high school and college. Because Denver high schools did not provide girls' inter-school sports, she had to settle for after-school sports such as basketball, soccer, and field hockey. It was the same story at the University of Colorado: No women's intercollegiate sports. Women's teams could not compete with those of other colleges. CU did sponsor club sports, so Joan played on the basketball and field hockey teams. "Four ... colleges, such as Wyoming and CSU, would come on play day. We could play a quarter [or fifteen minutes] with ... every other team," she recalled. "Then they served cider and doughnuts. No one mentioned who had won. Colorado lagged far behind other states in girls' athletics."[1]

However, the Amateur Athletic Union (AAU) was open to women and for ten years she played on a Denver Metro women's AAU basketball team, the Denver Viner Chevrolets. Among her teammates were All-Americans Phyllis Lockwood, the captain, and Peg Gibson, center. Joan was a runner-up All-American. Gibson remembers her as being "very team oriented; she wanted to win but that was not the only thing. She wanted to win as a team, not just as a star."[2] The Viner Chevrolets competed in eleven National AAU Tournaments and finished in third place in 1953. After Lockwood retired, Joan was elected team captain.

Joan credits her basketball teammate Phyllis Lockwood with getting her back into tennis. After she ran into Lockwood on a tennis court, they paired up and soon were winning doubles trophies. She often played mixed doubles with Lockwood, Ann Rose Dyde, and her former instructor, Jack Cella. Lockwood, who was Colorado tennis champion and one of the best woman players, routinely defeated Joan in singles. One of Joan's great satisfactions in tennis came when she was finally able to beat Phyllis. Joan's most exciting match took place when the noted black player Althea Gibson came to compete in the Colorado state tournament immediately after she had won the U.S. National Tennis Open. Joan played against her in the first round and was ahead 5-3 in the first set. After that, Miss Gibson dug in and won 8-6, 6-4. "That was still the most fun I ever had," Joan said.[3]

While Joan was at CU, her life took a new turn. Her close friends Ruth and Bill Wierman introduced her to Ormand ("Orm") Birkland. The meeting turned into a romance and they were married in 1948. Orm loved to play golf and for Christmas in 1952, he gave her a set of clubs. To please him, she took lessons from Denver Country Club Pro Noble Chalfant. Before she was aware of it, golf had become all she thought about. "I'd lose six or seven pounds in the summer being just scared and not eating, worrying about who I was going to play that afternoon," she told a *Club Ties* magazine writer. "I often played a golf match in the morning and a tennis tournament in the afternoon."[4]

In the 1960s, Joan Birkland achieved two rare feats and her greatest thrill in sports. Her fellow players persuaded her to try winning the state championships in both tennis and golf in one summer. "It was hard mentally," she said. "The tournaments were back to back. I'd play golf in the morning and tennis after that." Not only did she succeed in winning championships in two sports in one summer—she actually did it twice. "This would be impossible today," she said. "You're made to concentrate on one sport; you can't do more and win. People spend five hours a day working at [one sport] and parents are [very involved in] it now."[5] In 1962, after winning both golf and tennis state championships in one summer, she received the Robert Russell Award as the best amateur athlete in Colorado. She also skied and bowled on Denver Country Club teams.

More honors poured in. In 1996, Birkland was inducted into the Colorado Women's Hall of Fame—the only athlete so honored. She was named to the Colorado Golf Hall of Fame in 1977. The Colorado Sports Hall of Fame inducted her in 1981—only the fourth woman accepted, following the great Babe Didrikson Zaharias, ice skater Peggy Fleming, and Joan's friend Phyllis Lockwood. She since has served actively on both boards of directors.

A proof of Joan's golf prowess was the Denver Country Club's "Beat

Joanie Day." At the end of every season, other members could challenge her. The event was held annually for six years because she was the perennial women's champion. She retired from club competition after she'd won the title thirty consecutive years. She has continued competing at city and state levels and likes to play against the men at Denver Tennis Club. (She was president of that club in 1991–1992.) After undergoing two shoulder surgeries for a torn rotator cuff, her high 5.0 ranking dropped to 4.5 and she no longer plays in tournaments.

Joan is still serving—but serving less on the tennis court and serving more on sports boards of directors and teaching disabled children. She has taught swimming to Wallace School children, was a golf instructor in the Children's Hospital amputee program, taught basketball to asthmatic children, and bowling to children with cerebral palsy. Her many board positions have included the Pioneer Sportswomen at Denver University, Boys and Girls Clubs of Metro Denver, Hospice of Metro Denver, the Institute of Health Education board, Colorado National Bank Boulevard board of directors, and the Colorado Xplosion (women's) Basketball team's advisory board. As a board member of Girls in Golf, she helps run a rec center program that buses girls to the Harvard Gulch Golf Course for instruction and play. Several girls in the program are getting good enough to play college golf.

In sports, you have to do it to know how to run it. Recently reelected for her second consecutive term as chairman of the USGA Women's Committee, Birkland headed the committee of twenty-four women from throughout the United States who run the seven women's USGA championships each year. "This committee runs the entire women's end of golf, focusing on the championships," she explained. "We are in charge of the Curtis Cup Match when it is played in the United States. It pits America's eight best women golfers against the best eight women of Great Britain and Ireland."[6]

A typical Joan Birkland month would run the legs off ordinary people. In July 1997, for example, she spent ten days in charge of the U.S. Women's Open. The following week she helped with the Colorado Women's Open, arriving at 6 A.M. to talk to the volunteers and make sure the course was marked correctly for the tournament. The next week, she traveled to Minneapolis to set up another tournament course; and then went on to Boston for ten days to oversee the Women's Amateur tournament. In between, she gave a rules seminar for the Denver Country Club women's championship event. Twice she attended Rules School—an intensive, four-day session that ends with a test, to qualify for officiating at the Women's Open. (The Women's Committee also does the officiating.) Despite the hours and responsibility involved, she donates her time and energy to innumerable organizations.

She is executive director of Sportswomen of Colorado, which receives about a hundred nominations for sports awards annually; a committee of nine media representatives selects winners, who are recognized at a big dinner in the spring. Sportswomen of Colorado also sponsors a quarterly television show with help from El Pomar foundation.

Birkland still likes to play golf and tennis—she considers herself a better tennis player than golfer—but hasn't had time to compete in tournaments lately. Of course, she'd love to play golf twice a week and add a couple hours of tennis on the weekend, but not even Joan Birkland can do everything. She is a healthy-looking woman with a strong, lean frame about five-feet-seven in height, with short gray-peppered hair, and has a cordial, relaxed, down-to-earth manner.

Joan Packard Birkland has had it all. Born into a prominent Denver family, she grew up in a happy household. With City Park—Denver's largest—at her doorstep, she developed her natural athletic talent to become a champion in three sports: basketball, tennis, and golf. Many consider her one of the greatest all-round athletes, man or woman, that Colorado has produced. How easy it would have been to retire after earning top trophies in every sport in which she chose to compete. But instead of resting on these laurels, she spends her time, energy, and wide experience promoting a spectrum of women's sports at both local and national levels.

Anne Flick Steinbeck

Born October 20, 1929, in Gunnison, Colorado

Anne Flick Steinbeck keeps the wheels spinning in Gunnison, a college town on the Western Slope. Once a waitress, teacher, newspaper accountant, and choir soprano, she became director of the combined Gunnison-Hinsdale Counties' Departments of Social Services. But her contributions to Gunnison County are only part of her record. At the state level, she has headed the Board of Trustees for State Colleges and testified before Colorado legislative committees. In 1985, she was the first Colorado woman elected national president of the Business and Professional Women's Clubs (BPW).

As Anne Steinbeck powers through life, every new interest or experience has become her occupation. Her kaleidoscope of occupations is dizzying. In addition to all her professional roles, she adds those of homemaker and champion pie maker.

Family influences date back to Anne's grandfather John M. Flick, who homesteaded a ranch in 1879 on Quartz Creek near Ohio City, Colorado. Her father, Raleigh E. Flick, was born and raised on the ranch. When he was grown, he married a young teacher from Nebraska. They settled in the Quartz Creek Valley. Margaret Ritner Flick, Anne's mother, raised five children while teaching, editing a rural newspaper, and being a ranch wife.

Anne attended Western State College in Gunnison while working part-time waiting tables and doing accounting at night for the Gunnison newspaper. She graduated in 1951, with an English major and minors in accounting, speech and drama.

Anne's brother introduced her to his friend Archie Steinbeck, an assayer at Whitepine for Callihan Lead & Zinc Mines. A month after Anne's graduation, she and Archie were married. They settled in a three-room house that she could scrub in an hour. She put her extra hours to use teaching grades five through eight in the country school. It was "a tremendous experience. I felt I learned more than the pupils did."[1] The Steinbecks moved to California, where both were employed at Douglas Aircraft Corporation. But after five months, they had not adapted to life in Los Angeles, so they returned to Gunnison. Archie went into business in propane sales and services and they had a daughter, Lois Anne.

The newspaper soon asked Anne to resume her accountant position. Before long, she was writing news stories and editorials, editing copy, selling ads, and covering a beat. She even managed the business when the owners were out of town. "What you learn on a newspaper stays with you," she said. "I gained a sense of public service and what is needed in the community."[2]

In 1962, Anne Steinbeck was appointed director of the Gunnison Department of Social Services—a position she trained for through in-service seminars at Colorado State University and University of Wisconsin. In 1965, Hinsdale, a smaller county, started contracting its department's services from Gunnison County.

"Problems of the elderly comprised much of our early social work. It was sad having to move the area's elderly from the community for needed care and I began advocating for a nursing-home facility in the community," she said.[3] Steinbeck helped organize a core group for a drive to fund and build a county nursing home and to form a corporation to put it in place. She served on the board from the start. After twenty years, Gunnison County bought the entity to provide financial stability. "The nursing home gives me a lot of pride in community investment," she added.[4] She went on to work on a project for a child care center.

Anne's skills in public speaking, developed when she was a member of her college speech and debate team, serve her well at commencements and as a distinguished lecturer at several colleges. As an adjunct instructor at Western State College, she has taught courses in social work. She was named to the Board of Trustees for State Colleges for eight years and chaired the board for two terms. In this capacity, she attended monthly meetings and task forces that required her to drive or fly across the state in all kinds of weather. She is noted for never missing a meeting. In 1985, Western State College honored Anne Flick Steinbeck as a Distinguished Alumna.

In 1963, she joined the Gunnison local organization of Business and Professional Women's Clubs, the nation's oldest and largest organization of working women. As Colorado Federation president, she headed award-winning programs such as Keep America Beautiful in Colorado and was a founder of Colorado's BPW Foundation for scholarships and fellowship funds. She worked up through national offices to become the first Colorado woman to serve as national president of BPW/USA and simultaneously was a leader in the National Women's Organization Council. In 1985–1986, she addressed delegates of BPW's 3,500 organizations as president and presided at the national convention.

As BPW president and a member of the National Blue Ribbon Committee for restoring civil rights for all citizens—disabled, minorities, women—she spoke at a press conference on the east steps of the nation's Capitol and discussed family issues on national television and in testimony before congressional committees. Steinbeck also presided at a Task Force on Women in the Work Place. One of its goals, seeking quality dependent care, was the topic of a two-day national seminar that she chaired. The Task Force captured the attention of Congress and the public on the need to address the issue. Since then, federal, state, and county monies have become available to help provide quality care for all ages.

She continued her work on behalf of women when she spoke, along with U.S. Senator Barbara Boxer, during a major airline strike, to argue against severe cuts in pay and in favor of equitable wages for women flight attendants.

During her BPW/USA presidency, Steinbeck urged the organization to renovate its Washington, D.C., national library and foundation home, which as a historic building is pointed out on tours of the city. She was instrumental in raising funds for the restoration. A magnificent showplace once again, the building is available to other organizations as a meeting place. Its Marguerite Rawalt Resource Center contains the most extensive library on women in the workplace. Washington-area college students are among hundreds of persons who do research at the resource center.

Since her presidency, she has worked for BPW's international organization and as regional coordinator for North America and the non-Spanish-speaking countries of the Caribbean. In January 1989, she represented North American countries at a ten-day international conference in Ghana to help overcome starvation and malnutrition in African Sub-Saharan countries.

Cognizant of Steinbeck's unique talents, four Colorado governors have appointed her to state commissions and boards. As part of her work with the elderly, she represented Colorado at the White House Conference on Aging. She was a board member of Rocky Mountain Arthritis Foundation. For twenty years she has been chairman of the Gunnison Salvation Army unit, and for ten years, she served the Gunnison County Republican Party as vice chairman.

In recognition of her leadership, Colorado Common Cause and Colorado BPW named her Woman of the Year. She considers her induction into the Colorado Women's Hall of Fame in 1985 as her most significant honor.

As one might imagine, Anne Steinbeck maintains a crammed work schedule and puts in a minimum of 45 hours a week. She is a director for Western Colorado Housing Development. She also chairs a regional committee to establish One-Stop Career Centers to facilitate job finding, upgrade training and vocational rehabilitation, and help employers connect with employees. Her contributions to her community are ongoing. For the Community Church of Gunnison, Steinbeck taught Sunday school for thirty years and a young adult class for a decade. In tune with her love of music and her fine soprano voice, she still sings for special occasions. She continues to be powered by good health, enormous energy, and an endless supply of interests. The high point of her life is being a grandmother, mother, wife, and daughter. At home, she likes to cook and bake (she's famous for her doughnuts and pies). She enjoys history, folklore, and giving historical programs, public speaking, playing bridge, reading, hiking, and collecting antiques.

Dana Hudkins Crawford

Born July 22, 1931, in Salina, Kansas

"Dana Hudkins Crawford believes Denver's past should figure more prominently in its present."[1] Crawford promoted her philosophy that business and historic preservation should work closely in restoring the city's rundown but historic neighborhoods. She was a relative newcomer in the 1960s when she ran up against the city's practice of tearing down its historic old buildings to make way for new development and parking lots. Denver appeared to be suffering from an identity crisis. Its skyline presented a hodgepodge of concrete and glass skyscrapers that dwarfed the historic, but decaying wood and brick buildings awaiting demolition.

Dana Hudkins grew up in Salina, Kansas—a community rooted in tradition. She was the only child in a family that maintained a strong interest in history and family heritage; her grandparents lived in an important and beautiful home on the Ohio River. She graduated from Monticello, a women's college founded in 1835 by a man who had twelve daughters and who believed that if you educate a woman you educate a family. Monticello was set on a lovely campus that sparked Dana's interest in architecture and landscaping. She went on to attend the University of Kansas and the Business Management Program at Harvard-Radcliffe.

Dana moved to Denver in 1954 to enter the public relations field and soon found herself loving the city "for being so liveable. If you grew up in a town like Salina, you've experienced heat and bugs. You could never have big patios there and enjoy eating outside. Beyond that, Colorado people are divine and Denver was beginning to feel like home."[2] Her life in Denver was enhanced when she married John W. R. Crawford III on October 12, 1955. A geologist, he worked for the Argo Oil Company and later in independent oil exploration. The couple raised four sons: Jack, Tom, Peter, and Duke.

As Dana explored Denver's older downtown neighborhoods, she was reminded of historic buildings she had admired in Massachusetts when she attended Radcliffe College. She couldn't help but wonder why Denverites were so unconcerned about losing their early landmarks. Denver's preservation movement began when a group of volunteers formed in 1970 to save the Molly Brown House at 1340 Pennsylvania Street from demolition. Dana Crawford was a founder of the resulting organization and she suggested the name Historic Denver, Inc. The group also worked to save Ninth Steet, a block of charming middle-class houses built in the 1870s and 1880s, which is now part of the Auraria Campus and is officially the Ninth Street Historic District.

Historic Denver and the Denver Urban Renewal Authority (DURA) emerged as bitter antagonists. In the 1970s, DURA was planning to tear down twenty-six lower downtown blocks including Larimer Street. Saving the remaining important districts became an ongoing battle that attracted Dana. Inspired by a *Time* magazine article about the Gaslight Square development in St. Louis, she began to formulate her plan for Denver. She discussed the idea with her husband and they agreed she should go East to study urban restorations. She visited several major cities, hoping to learn what to do about Denver. Her first stop was St. Louis, where she quickly learned what *not* to do.

She had her eye on Denver's Larimer Street district between Fourteenth and Fifteenth Streets with its surviving business and commercial buildings. The rows of small buildings with their warm, local brick and ornate facades had acquired a quaint charm. Even more important is Larimer Street's history. Denver was "born" on November 16, 1858, when William Larimer's ox wagons pulled up to where Cherry Creek flows into the South Platte River. Standing in the vicinity of present Larimer Street, Larimer lay claim to 2,200 surrounding acres for the Denver City Town Company.

Larimer Street quickly became a main thoroughfare in Denver's original downtown. After the great fire of April 19, 1863, wiped out the business section, the town passed a law requiring all new buildings to be constructed of fireproof material such as brick. From 1870 to 1890, seventeen commercial buildings were erected in what is now the Larimer Street Historic District in architectural styles typical of the period. After the 1893 silver crash, downtown business moved eastward, causing Larimer Street to decline; eventually its neglected structures were used as flophouses, pawnshops, or saloons or were simply abandoned.

Dana became obsessed with saving and renovating the historic blocks. In 1965, she and John formed a partnership—the Larimer Square Associates—and got twelve friends to help them put up $400,000. After the Crawfords realized multiple ownerships were not the best arrangement, Dana quietly started buying up buildings on the block until she had exhausted their funds. Then they publicly announced the Larimer Square project and put together an ownership group—an aspect of the business that was new to Dana. She received excellent professional advice from accountants, attorneys, and the late Central Bank loan officer "Ozzie" Asborno. She also received support from Central Bank Chairman Elwood Brooks, which was a turning point.

Dana's Radcliffe training had given her a strong business background but she still had a lot to learn. As a woman, she lacked a track record with a male banking establishment, which she soon realized was key to funding her development. When it came to getting funding for major developments and working with the construction industry, she found there were many who objected to taking orders from a woman. "It always was very hard [to work] with the banks," she recalled. "Women have made significant progress ... but they still find enormous prejudice out there—getting loans, for instance."[3] After a decade of patchwork financing, they arranged long-term banking with the New York Life Insurance Company. One of Crawford's most significant achievements as a developer has been raising money for major projects without the requisite track record.

They chose architect Langdon Morris to design Larimer Square "as an early and classic example of preservation through adaptive reuse, the process of renovating—rather than restoring—old structures into economically viable contemporary uses."[4] Each building (or block, as buildings once were called) presents a different facade with its own decorative trim and brick color. An open space in the square forms the Court of the Bull and Bear and features a stone bull and bear from the demolished Mining Exchange Building. The Larimer Square Historic District was Denver's first area to receive historic district designation.

Dana Crawford still had a lot to learn. Her next step was to apprentice herself to the manager of the Belcaro Shopping Square in Denver, whom she followed around to learn how to operate a shopping center. She also drew upon the Urban Land Institute, a treasure house of information. Larimer Square became a catalyst for a Lower Downtown ("Lodo") revival and a model for urban preservation in other cities. Another happy result came during the 1980s when DURA began cooperating to preserve historic and renovation values along with removing urban blight. Dana the developer did not escape mishaps and missteps, one being her downtown public market. It seemed logical to create a market that sold groceries for people working in the neighborhood. She did not foresee that people preferred to stop for groceries on their way home from work. The public market lasted five months.

In 1980, Dana Crawford joined with Charles Callaway to acquire the Oxford Hotel at 1600 Seventeenth Street. Designed by Frank Edbrooke and built in 1889, the eighty-one-room, European-style hotel had faded although the Cruise Room retained its original appearance. Dana and her partner undertook renovation of the hotel and an adjacent office building and built a parking garage. After the venture emerged successfully from Chapter 11 bankruptcy in 1992, she added the Aveda Spa and Salon next door. Situated near Denver's Union Station, the Oxford has become one of Denver's finest small hotels.

The mid-1980s brought an unexpected and sorrowful event. John Crawford—her husband and partner—died suddenly in October 1985. Dana sold Larimer Square in 1986 for $13.5 million. It was time to move on to new ventures. She realized that her most successful projects were started when times were bad. "In good times, people with better skills at borrowing money follow me around to get the properties I have to pass up," she said with a wry smile. In 1989, commercial property was going for $8–$15 a building square foot and she kept saying Denver's downtown was going to explode. (And it did. By 1997, properties were being sold for $80 a foot unrenovated.) In 1986, after selling Larimer Square, she turned her attention toward Union Station and Beatrice Foods's long-abandoned cold storage building at 1801 Wynkoop Street. Under Crawford's wand, the square building, with its decorative brick exterior, turned into the Design Center at the Ice House, a stylish center for interior designers. She also believed Denver's downtown needed more housing, so in 1988, she converted her company Urban Neighborhoods, and set it up as a real estate office between the Oxford and Union Station. With an eye to providing housing, Crawford bought the Hungarian Flour Mill beside the railroad tracks at 2100 Twentieth Street in 1997. Built by J. K. Mullen, its grain silos date back to 1906. The building has seen use as a flour mill, metals shop, construction office, and finally a free flophouse for the homeless, who called it The Birdcage and The Silos. An $18 million project in 1998, the Flour Mill was transformed into Flour Mill Lofts—seventeen dwellings priced from $300,000 to $1,000,000. Other Crawford projects include the Market Center, an office complex at Market and Seventeenth Streets composed of five connected buildings that offer office and restaurant space; the Edbrooke Lofts (1450 Wynkoop Street), a warehouse built in 1880, which she converted to the first condominium loft in Denver, with forty-four units; and the Acme Lofts (1333 Wazee Street), thirty loft-style condominiums in the 1909 Brecht Candy Company factory and former Acme Upholstery Supply Company building.

Crawford finds it has become harder to get projects approved by the city. "Bids come in higher than for other [kinds of] building, so I have to rake a razor blade to every item. Preservation development is tougher, too, because of the many environmental requirements and the American Disabilities Act," she said.[5]

In the late 1980s, Dana Crawford served on the design committee for Coors Field, home of the Colorado Rockies baseball team. As she sat among the sports experts on the committee, she stubbornly insisted that the stadium structure should blend with its environment by following the architecture of the surrounding old warehouses. "Coors Field is Denver's landmark of the twentieth century and should reflect the architecture and landmarks of the nineteenth century," she told the committee.[6] She hired a photographer to take pictures of Union Station and other structures of the period and presented them to the architects. She was thrilled when they got her message. Dana Crawford's stubbornness paid off. Coors Field is pure Denver. For years, Denver's lower downtown warehouse neighborhood was visited only by trucks and delivery vans. Now new restaurants throb with music and activity for younger Denverites, who have taken it to their hearts.

Generously sharing her experience and energy, Crawford sits on the Colorado Historical Society board and has served on the boards of the Denver Art Museum, the Denver Performing Arts Complex, the Downtown Denver Partnership, and the National Trust for Historic Preservation. In appreciation of her work, a coalition of historic preservation groups established the annual Dana Crawford Award for Outstanding Achievement in Historic Preservation.

Perhaps most distinguished among her procession of awards is the Louise du Pont Crowninshield Award, the nation's highest in historic preservation. The National Trust for Historic Preservation recognized Dana Crawford as the 1995 recipient for "pioneering efforts in recognizing aesthetic and economic potential in historic commercial buildings of ... Denver [and] more than three decades of creative commitment to historic preservation at the local level and to the preservation movement nationally." Crawford has developed more than 800,000 square feet of historic properties valued at $50 million. First among her accomplishments, Larimer Square showed the way for urban preservation; other cities refer to it as a seminal project. Teamed with Coors Field and the Colorado Rockies baseball team, it is considered the spark for the Lower Downtown resurrection.

Dana Crawford loves cities, especially down-and-out cities, because they're the ones with fabulous buildings. To accomplish her goals, she used extraordinary toughness, shrewdness, energy, and an ability to tolerate high risks. Through her achievements, she has demonstrated remarkable competence, patience, and vision.

LaRae Orullian

Born May 15, 1933, in Salt Lake City, Utah

LaRae Orullian, the oldest of four children, grew up in a town outside Salt Lake City. Her mother, a traditional mom, taught her to cook, sew, mend, and iron. LaRae remembers their lovely home and vegetable gardens and "a happy childhood in a warm and cohesive family." She also remembers saying, "When I get old enough, I'll never iron again."[1]

LaRae was in high school when she got a summer job as a bank messenger girl. Within two weeks she was promoted to coin wrapper, then to file clerk, next to loan processor, and on up the ladder until she headed the Federal Housing Administration's Title One Department. Wishing to continue that success, she decided to venture to Wall Street to become a businesswoman. On her way to New York, she stopped in the first city of significant size.

"Denver just fit me," she said. "I found some excellent opportunities and immediately put down roots." She began as a secretary and soon was promoted to executive secretary to four senior officers at Union Bank on South Broadway. When one of her bosses was leaving to join the new Guaranty Bank, he talked her into going along as his executive secretary. As secretary of the board at Guaranty, she still had to make the coffee. LaRae began planning her move from executive secretary to bank officer—a position held primarily by men. To do so she would have to attend banking school, where banks traditionally sent men—not women. LaRae spent fourteen years in night school until she graduated with three certificates from the American Bankers Association's (ABA) American Institute of Banking.

She made her next breakthrough in 1969, when the National Association of Bank Women awarded her its first scholarship to the graduate banking school at Ohio State University. She used her vacations to spend two weeks a year on campus and did the rest by correspondence and graduated in the top 5 percent of her class with a degree in real estate finance.

Returning to Guaranty Bank, she set up a succession of presidents.

Orullian would train each new president and often clean up the mess when he left. She discussed the situation with the board chairman and asked, "Why don't you consider me for president? After all, I'm running the bank." "Well, LaRae, there are two reason," he said. "The first is, you don't have gray hair; and second, Denver isn't ready for a woman bank president."[2] The next week, she had her hair frosted. During her twenty years at Guaranty Bank, Orullian worked up through the ranks to executive vice president. As the only woman among twenty-five men on the board of directors, she still had to make the coffee.

In 1976, several women interested in forming the Women's Bank asked her to join their founding group. Serving would have been a conflict of interest with her duties at Guaranty Bank, but she agreed to advise them. Mary Roebling was named chairman of the board of Women's Bank. As the first woman president of a large city bank, Roebling was considered one of the most astute businesswomen in the world. She became Orullian's inspiration and mentor.

When Women's Bank received its preliminary charter, the founding group offered Orullian the position of president and chief executive officer. She understood what a heavy burden Women's Bank would carry. What would happen if it should fail? It might set women back to the dark ages. On the other hand, gender discrimination was illegal, but it was difficult to prove. Women still had trouble getting bank loans and a primary purpose of Women's Bank was to give women an equal opportunity to obtain loans and credit. After soul searching, she recognized Women's Bank as the opportunity she had been waiting for. She decided to take on the risk of building a new bank.

LaRae Orullian experienced the most memorable moment of her life on the morning Women's Bank opened. As she walked out in front for the ribbon cutting, she saw people lined up and down Seventeenth Street, waiting with checks in hand to open accounts at the bank. She was so excited and nervous, her own hands shook as she cut the ribbon. She needn't have worried. Women's Bank entered $1 million in deposits each *week* for its first twelve weeks. The stock was selling at $20 a share. The financial success was only part of the story. Bank customers would say they "belonged to" Women's Bank—not just that they banked there. A full-fledged bank, it was a friend of women and small businesses as well as male investors.

"We have very strong women in our community," Orullian said. "They participate on an equal basis with men and are represented in the city's business, political, and academic leadership. In traveling a lot across the country, I see how Denver stands above other cities in providing women's opportunities."[3] The Women's Bank has been a catalyst in opening up business to women. By proving that women can succeed, the bank advanced the status of all women and became the most successful women's bank in the country. Of the original eight women's banks started in the early 1980s, the other seven have changed their names, been absorbed, sold, or merged. Denver Women's Bank took over four troubled banks: Market National, Chancery, Union Bank on West Colfax, and Littleton Bank.

In 1980, Women's Bank formed Equitable Bankshares of Colorado as its holding company, with LaRae Orullian as chairman of the board of directors. In 1984, the company added Equitable Bank of Littleton. In 1993, an independent investment group bought Equitable Bankshares of Colorado for $17,470,000 and purchased shareholders' stock (originally $20 a share) for $166.44 a share.

After seventeen years of running Women's Bank, LaRae Orullian conducted a search for several months for her own replacement. In June 1995, she handed over the management to Virginia Berkeley, a native Denverite with twenty years' banking experience. Now named Colorado Business Bank and still locally managed, it is focused as a business bank that also serves women and small businesses. LaRae Orullian continued as board chairman under a management contract until December 1997. She expressed mixed emotions about the sale but believes that change was on the horizon. "The owners felt the time had come and I'm trying to make the transition as smooth as possible," she explained. "Women's Bank has consistently been among the banking industry's strongest performers in capital ratio and return on assets and equity," she added. "We opened a lot of doors for women and put all women forward a great deal. As a result, other bankers decided that women working in their banks would save women's business, because women take care of women."[4]

When Orullian was approached by Guaranty Bank & Trust Co. to take the position of vice chairman of the board of directors, she accepted the position. She smiled as she noted that she had made a complete circle and was now back to the bank she had served for twenty years, with the intervening twenty years at Women's Bank. In her current position, she strives to bring women into the mainstream of the banking business and serves on corporate boards of directors.

She continues to give time to her favorite causes. She was co-chair of the Foundation of the National Association of Bank Women, an educational foundation that solicited funds so women could get the necessary basic education to advance to higher banking positions. It developed a seminar program to help women understand how the corporate structure works, how to work with a team, to get along with people without being threatening, and how to be efficient and bring in new ideas in order to move ahead. "We gave seminars all over the country to help women in banking understand how to get ahead. Banking was founded by men for men. We don't want to become men or be like men, but we must understand how the structure works," she said.[5]

Orullian is chairman of the board for three major corporations: Frontier Airlines, Colorado Blue Cross/Blue Shield, and Rocky Mountain Administrative Services Corporation headquartered in Denver. For a number of other companies, she serves on the board of directors, including Pat Lange Golf Company of Lakewood (which manufactures custom golf clubs and supplies 150 outlets across the country), Rocky Mountain Life Insurance Company, and Pro Card.

Nearest to her heart is the Girl Scouts, which approached her in 1978 to help raise money to build a new program center for the Mile-Hi Council. After she raised $1.5 million, they asked her to serve as national treasurer. Then she was nominated to serve two terms as national president. From there she was elected to the world board; and now she is on the world board of directors for Girl Guides and Girl Scouts headquartered in London, where meetings are conducted once a year. "You just can't say no to the Girl Scouts," she said. "There are up to ten million Girl Scouts in the world with the largest number in the United States—we have 3.5 million Girl Scouts. But Girl Scouts are facing tremendous problems worldwide. In some countries [families] can't afford even the $50 dues and too many governments don't care about girls."[6]

And then there's women's basketball. Years ago, LaRae played guard and forward on the Viner Chevrolets, a Denver AAU basketball team. Among her teammates were Joanie Birkland, Peg Gibson, Dorothy Major, and Phyllis Lockwood. LaRae was on the advisory board of the women's professional basketball team, the Colorado Xplosion. Although the team won the American Basketball League's Western Division, the franchise was not a financial success and recently disbanded.

Along the way, Orullian has met other "challenges"—her term for setbacks. A bicycle accident put her in the hospital and then into a wheelchair. But she soon learned to get the wheelchair into her office. She also has recovered from back surgery.

In the course of her forty-eight-year career, LaRae Orullian has been recognized in countless ways. The Women's Forum, an organization Orullian helped found, presented her with its Ellie Guggenheim Award in 1986. She was featured in the *Los Angeles Times,* the *New York Times,* and *Cosmopolitan, Working Woman, Ms,* and *Money* magazines. Two first ladies, Barbara Bush and Hillary Rodham Clinton, entertained her at the White House. Orullian has received awards for her achievements from more than sixteen major organizations and she has been inducted into the Colorado Women's Hall of Fame. Perhaps most significant, as chairman of the Board of Colorado Business Bank, she attained the highest rank of any American woman in banking.

She is looking forward to her retirement, to spend more time gardening, playing golf, traveling, reading, and writing a couple of books. Nowhere does she mention ironing or making coffee.

Elnora ("Ellie") Clausing Gilfoyle

Born May 19, 1934, in Ottumwa, Iowa

"Ellie" Gilfoyle was the youngest of the Clausing family's four children, but certainly not the smallest. Because she was tall and mature for her age, everyone expected more of her and she tried to live up to their expectations.

Born into a poor family in Ottumwa, Iowa, Ellie thought her family was rich because children always came to their house to play. She cannot recall specific rules in her home, but her parents were strong role models who instilled in their children firm values and ethics, personal pride, and respect for others. Her early experiences as a Brownie and Girl Scout impressed her with the importance of rendering service to the community.

After graduating from high school in Ottumwa, she enrolled at Iowa State University to major in science, interior decorating, or social service. As a sophomore, she transferred to the University of Iowa, where a friend suggested she could combine her interests in art, science, and social services into a career in occupational therapy. On a visit to the children's hospital at the University of Iowa, she watched therapists working in the clinic and was excited to observe how children learn. She always had been fascinated with how the body functions and wanted to enable handicapped children to have a good life. She liked the idea that occupational therapy (OT) is based on a patient's abilities rather than disabilities. Although occupational therapy is a fairly young profession, there were specialists who worked to rehabilitate soldiers during World War I. The mission of occupational therapists is to help people retain human dignity by enabling those with health problems and handicapping conditions to become as independent as possible. Getting patients active in their environment is a way of promoting their self-sufficiency. "I realized OT was what I wanted to do. I had been given good health and a strong family, and wanted others to experience what I had," she said.[1] She got her bachelor's degree in OT in 1956 and an advanced certificate in professional OT in 1958.

Ellie, who came to Colorado as a graduate student intern, was met by her sister Lyda at the train in Denver. That day, Ellie's life took a sharp detour. They drove directly to Boulder to a "tall persons party" hosted by the Timberline Club, which pleased Ellie. As a woman 6'3" tall, she was overjoyed to get together with men over 6'2". At the party, she met Gene Gilfoyle, one of the members, who was enchanted by her warm smile and friendly personality. Ellie and Gene were married in 1958 and their son, Sean, was born November 7, 1966. Gene has been a strong and valuable supporter of Ellie's career.

Ellie Gilfoyle got a job at Denver General Hospital as an occupational therapy clinician. Later, she joined Craig Rehabilitation Hospital in Denver as a clinical supervisor in the Occupational Therapy Department, working primarily with people who had spinal cord injuries or brain damage. At Craig, she helped develop orthotics and taught patients to use them. In the 1960s, she became director of the Children's Hospital OT department, working with children with various kinds of health problems.

During the Kennedy administration, grants were made available for research and services for children with developmental disabilities. After Gilfoyle helped establish the John F. Kennedy Child Development Center at University of Colorado Health Sciences Center, she spent much of her time consulting with other health care professionals and families. Her work at the Sciences Center gave her the opportunity to collaborate with the City and County of Denver in a grant-funded project for children with developmental dysfunction and children who were battered and abused. Observing the importance of family care for children, Ellie developed OT programs that involved families as part of the rehabilitation team.

In the 1970s, parents of children with handicaps were campaigning to make public school education accessible to their youngsters. Gilfoyle was asked to work with the American Occupational Therapy Association in drafting the law that ultimately gave all children the right to get an education. She also developed an extensive curriculum to prepare OTs who were trained to work in health care to be part of the educational team. Her curriculum, for OTs working in schools, is the foundation for OT education in more than two hundred community college and baccalaureate programs.

Ellie's career followed different directions in the 1980s. In 1981, her fascination with discovering how children learn to function led her to write *Children Adapt* with co-authors A. Grady and J. Moore. The book continues to be used by those who establish occupational therapy programs for children with handicaps secondary to brain damage. Colorado State University (CSU) in Fort Collins awarded Ellie Gilfoyle an Honorary Doctor of Science Degree in 1981 for her "outstanding record in research and scholarly contributions in advancing occupational therapy." In 1984, Dr. Gilfoyle received the Eleanor Clarke Slagle Lectureship Award, the American Occupational Therapy Association's highest scholastic award.

While Dr. Gilfoyle was waiting for a research grant to come through, she took a temporary job at CSU as a special OT lecturer. She found she enjoyed being at the university so much, she gave up the grant to become an associate professor in the OT department. Two years later, in 1983, she was promoted to full professor and became head of the department of OT. In quick succession, Dr. Gilfoyle became associate dean at the College of Applied Human Science, 1988; dean of the College of Applied Human Sciences, 1989; and in 1991, she was named interim provost/academic vice-president.

Colorado State University offered Dr. Gilfoyle the post of provost/ academic vice president in 1992, which meant she was second in command at the university. In announcing her appointment, CSU President Albert C. Yates said she would "be responsible for leadership of the academic programs in the university's eight colleges, Graduate School, and divisions of Continuing Education and Armed Forces Services. She would oversee University Libraries, Honors Program, and offices of Instructional Services, Equal Opportunity, and International Education. She also would be actively involved with faculty governance."[2]

With this promotion, Ellie Gilfoyle, who had established her reputation as an occupational therapist doing research and working with children, would increasingly work in the realm of academic leadership and curriculum development. Despite her ability to do this job, she faced some hurdles. When Dr. Gilfoyle became provost, she lacked traditional academic credentials that take instructors to higher positions. Some faculty members felt she "had not *earned* her Ph.D." In response, she forged ahead and let her performance speak for her. "That's the way all society should be, not so hung up on having a string of titles after your name. Credentials are important, but a person earns credibility because of her performance," she reasoned.[3]

As provost, she saw her job as getting everyone moving in the same direction. She spent hours in meetings—mostly listening and learning. At that time, universities were being asked to emphasize undergraduate programs as much as graduate education and research. President Yates asked her to chair a committee to streamline a core curriculum that would give undergraduates a base on which to build their education and career. Her committee identified a profile of CSU students, researched undergraduate programs elsewhere, and shared results with the university's departments. As a result, CSU adjusted its baccalaureate program to stress such areas as liberal arts and sciences, problem solving, multicultural issues, scientific methods, math, world civilizations, history, literature, and communication. In addition, the university set a goal to develop new ways of delivering the curriculum and making education—and professors—accessible and exciting to all students.

During her years of working in OT, Ellie had not encountered gender discrimination. But as a university dean and provost, she learned of and experienced severe gender discrimination that faculty and staff women face regularly. In talking with these women, it became clear to her that the university did not value women; the campus was not a psychologically safe and welcoming place for them. This attitude is not entirely surprising at a land grant institution with specialties in traditionally male-dominated fields—agriculture, business, engineering, and veterinary medicine. "But it was time for the university to move forward, to accept that women and men have different cultures and both genders have much to offer," she said.[4]

In 1995, she asked CSU President Yates to let her retire from her position as provost/academic vice president so she could develop a new program focusing on women and leadership. He gave his enthusiastic support to the venture. She began by assembling a committee to identify issues and work out solutions. "Women and men need to learn about each other's cultures and how they influence communication and relationships. ... The renaissance of the feminist movement in the 1960s helped women get ahead. Now women should maintain a positive attitude and avoid male bashing because that doesn't work. Angry women won't help the women's cause, nor will their anger advance women now. Instead, we should continue to be proud of our female culture. We need to learn how to gain respect. We have special qualities and we need to establish that what we have is unique and valuable," she said.[5]

The Institute for Women and Leadership at CSU is northern Colorado's only program that provides research, education, and outreach on women's leadership and gender cultures. The institute addresses barriers women face by providing mentoring circles, leadership seminars, and workshops. It offers internships with regional leaders, community partnerships, a library of leadership resources, and a program in women's studies. Dr. Gilfoyle foresees women and men as equal leadership partners in a very strong society.

Despite hard work and long hours in meetings, Ellie Gilfoyle does have a private life. Her half-time, transitional faculty appointment allows a few hours for aerobics, walking, and reading. Most important is having social time with her husband, Gene, a financial systems project coordinator at Storage Technology Corporation.

Ellie Gilfoyle continues as head of the CSU Occupational Therapy Department. She misses research and teaching but still meets with students and gives guest lectures. Her goal is to see the Institute for Women and Leadership established as a vital and permanent institution of the CSU campus. Who knows what women can become, once they are free to be themselves? Dr. Ellie Gilfoyle is a fine example.

Dorothy Louise Vennard Lamm

Born May 23, 1937, in New York City

Dottie Lamm has called herself a second banana. Others see her as a superwoman: Colorado's first lady, mother of two, cancer survivor, Democratic candidate for the U.S. Senate, and a standard bearer for many issues that are important to Colorado women. Political observers have noted that the maturing of Dottie Vennard Lamm from a liberal to a seasoned, moderate Democrat—still a feminist, a crusader, and now a writer and lecturer with the courage to speak out on critical issues.

Dottie's childhood lay a foundation for her upbeat, reasoned outlook as an adult. She was the first child of John and Dorothy Vennard; her sister, Jane, was born three years later. Their father, a professor of civil engineering, taught at New York University. When Dottie was nine, he joined the Stanford University faculty and they moved to Palo Alto, where he could ride his bicycle to work. The Vennards were a close, traditional family who hiked, skied, and attended the Congregational Church together. Dottie was a popular cheerleader and student council member. Her grades were "good enough," while Jane was the serious student. Dottie and Jane had the usual sisterly rivalries but presented a united front to outsiders.

John Vennard believed that "women should be highly educated in order to be the best possible wives and mothers."[1] Accordingly, Dottie attended Occidental College in California. Always curious about the human mind and how it works, she majored in psychology. She was inducted into Mortar Board and graduated in 1959. At that time, after graduation, women either got married or went to graduate school. To delay the decision, she trained to become a United Airline stewardess. With her dynamic, outgoing personality, classy five-foot-seven-inch figure, bright blue eyes, and auburn hair, she was a natural for the job. United assigned her to its Denver base.

On Christmas 1961, Dottie and her roommate decided to celebrate by throwing a party at their apartment. One of the guests called ahead to ask if she might bring "two guys from Wisconsin." The hostesses were reluctant—they already had too many guests—but the friend begged until they agreed. One of the "guys" was a lawyer named Richard D. Lamm.

Soon after the party, Dick Lamm called Dottie to ask her out. She had to confess she couldn't remember him. Anyway, she was too tired to go out. He asked if he could call back in a week. To her amusement, he called precisely one week later. She agreed to a date and they would see how it went. Later, they laughed about Dottie not remembering him. "But Dick always liked a challenge," she said.[2] And Dottie, raised as a moderate Republican, soon was fascinated by Dick's liberal ideas. They were married on May 11, 1963, at the First Unitarian Church.

After working eighteen months at the Denver Department of Welfare, Dottie enrolled at the University of Denver for her master's degree in psychiatric social work—a step that would shape her feminist leanings and influence her future career. In 1967, Dottie received the university's Social Work Sinnock Award as the outstanding graduate in her class. She went to work at the venerable Florence Crittenden Home and, from 1967 to 1970, at University of Colorado Health Sciences Day Care facility for emotionally disturbed children. In her work, Dottie often assisted minority people. Having noted that women's rights were the last to be considered, she was particularly incensed by a remark made by a liberal male social worker in her office. He told her and a coworker (a widow struggling to raise two children), that women did not need equal pay for their work—their husbands probably earned larger salaries, anyway. "He just didn't get it," Dottie said with disgust.[3] Social work developed Dottie's "third ear," which helps her understand what is going on under the surface. It has been invaluable in politics, and an asset in writing her newspaper columns. Her interest in social work and women's rights soon expanded. In March 1965, Dottie and Dick decided to march in Martin Luther King's demonstration in Selma, Alabama, to support federal voting rights. Although Dick had to cancel because of a trial, Dottie joined the march on her own.

Dick Lamm ran for his first major political office in 1966 and was elected state representative. Their first child, Scott Hunter, was born December 19, 1967. During Dick's first term, Dottie found that political life could be hard on a young mother. For the next election, she had to force herself to ring doorbells (with her baby on her back) but soon realized she enjoyed meeting fellow voters. During the campaign, she started writing the personal journal that made her aware of her own political voice and fulfilled a need that would continue as a primary force in her life. After Heather was born on November, 17, 1970, Dottie decided it was time to be with her children all day. She made the hard decision to quit her job.

When Dick began his first campaign for Colorado governor in 1973, Dottie hired a part-time, live-in baby sitter and went on the campaign trail. She was invigorated by the process. Their first gubernatorial campaign was a crusade to resolve Colorado's environmental issues. When Dick won the election, she realized their work was just beginning. Dottie Lamm had suddenly acquired several careers. Laughingly, she called herself the "second banana." Combining her public life with her life as a mother of two small children was not easy. At home, she wiped noses and cooked dinner with her left hand while her right hand held the phone to her ear, took messages, and resolved crises for Dick, the husband-governor-lawyer-father. Dick began helping Dottie out at home, too, "doing more of that house and children stuff," she said. "Dick and I were raised in traditional families where women did it all. Women have to give up the power of doing everything at home themselves; and there's still the conception that the man's career takes precedence, especially if his salary is higher."[4]

As Dottie settled into the Governor's Mansion in January 1975, she found that although Colorado is very tolerant of its first family, problems arose for the "first children." Scott was camera shy and avoided the press but Heather got caught up in some political brouhahas. Her room, the Gladys Cheesman-Evans bedroom upstairs, was in poor condition when the family moved in. The Lamms redid the bedroom and made part of it into their family room. The $4,000 cost of replacing the worn-out carpet was turned into a scandal by the press. That issue was followed several years later by another complaint against Heather and Scott who occasionally helped out during public functions at the mansion to earn a little pin money. This time it was the labor unions that objected, saying the children were taking jobs from union members.

Nevertheless, Dottie felt privileged to be Colorado's first lady. The position provided an ideal platform for her to raise issues she cared about—women's rights, both reproductive and in the work force, and the right to equal pay for equal work. In 1976–1977, Dottie Lamm headed the Governor's Task Force on Children and was a member of the Colorado Commission on Women.

Her career as a writer received a boost when a woman's magazine published much of the journal that she began during Dick's first campaign. Next, she approached the *Denver Post* about writing a weekly column. Readers had an opportunity to learn about Dottie's life and her roles as a mother, wife, and friend, and her attitudes on such issues as balancing feminism with partnerships and relationships with men. The columns were an immediate success, and she enjoyed developing her journalistic skills.

In 1983, Dottie Lamm experienced what would be a calamity for any woman. Her regular breast self-examination revealed a lump that proved to be cancerous. On August 31, she underwent a mastectomy. "Dick wanted to keep it secret at first but I said, 'Have you lost your mind?' We had no choice about going public," she recalled. "My greatest reward came from that experience: to help women get mammograms and demonstrate that they can still live their professional and personal lives after a mastectomy. I was buoyed by letters from supporters throughout Colorado. That brush with death made me appreciate each day to the fullest. Now, after sixteen years, I'm cancer free."[5]

The experience caused Dottie to reinforce her spiritual dimension and her Unitarian religion helps her remain centered. An important aspect of her role as first lady was to keep the governor calm and protect him from outside strains. The role was akin to being "second banana,"—a term she used as the title of her book of columns and poetry published in 1983. Another book, *Dottie Lamm's Choice Concerns, 1980–1986,* and a reprinting of sixteen years of her *Denver Post* columns later were published by Johnson Books.

After serving two terms as governor, the "first banana"—Dick Lamm—took a teaching post at Dartmouth and the Lamms moved to

New Hampshire in 1987. When they returned to Denver, he started teaching courses at the University of Denver in medical ethics and liberal and conservative politics.

In reality, Dottie Lamm never was a second banana. In 1997, she gave presentations about the necessity for world population stabilization because overpopulation engenders world poverty and endangers the environment. She was inducted into the Colorado Women's Hall of Fame and served on the National Women's Political Caucus, and Peace Links—Women Against Nuclear War. She strongly supports the movement, which started in India in 1991, under which women form cooperatives, get bank loans for small-business assets (such as looms), and repay the loan later. The movement gives women in third world countries and in poor areas of the United States means of supporting themselves and their families.

Another primary concern of hers is entitlement reform. She is deeply concerned about the need to rewrite U.S. Social Security and Medicare laws. "The laws were written when the elderly were our poorest group. They are living longer now and are more comfortably fixed, while children comprise the poorest segment."[6] Dottie Lamm still considers herself a feminist but her definition of feminism has evolved into a philosophy that supports partnerships with men in families and in the workplace. "We have emphasized women's rights and not partnerships. Both are important," she said.[7]

In the summer of 1997, writing seemed to dominate Dottie Lamm's activities. She still kept a journal and wrote opinion pieces for the *Rocky Mountain News.* But she was ready for a new venture. The evening news, on July 12, revealed that she was considering a run for the U.S. Senate on the Democratic ticket. Soon after, Democratic Congressman David Skaggs dropped out of the Senate race. *Denver Post* columnist Chuck Green wrote on July 13, 1997: "Dottie Lamm, former airline stewardess ... [has] matured into a thoughtful and popular state's first lady, crafted a successful career as a writer and political analyst, and triumphed as a courageous cancer survivor."[8]

As a first-time political candidate, Dottie Lamm faced State Representative Gil Romero from Pueblo for her party's designation. After winning the primary, she began a grueling uphill campaign against incumbent Republican Ben Nighthorse Campbell. She campaigned with dignity and integrity on an agenda to build a vision of a better fiscal, educational, and environmental world for Colorado's children and grandchildren. Although she raised a sizable war chest, Senator Campbell raised triple the amount and broadcast his message throughout the state. On November 3, 1998, she lost her first run for political office.

Dottie Lamm is glad she took on the contest. She still believes in her platform. In the future, she plans to work on the state or local level as more of a doer than a commentator, which will entail volunteering at the Denver Department of Social Services. Beyond that, she is considering several options, always bearing in mind her goal of helping to make the world a better place for our children and grandchildren.

Marilyn Van Derbur Atler

Born June 6, 1937, in Denver, Colorado

Marilyn Van Derbur smiled across the television screens of America as she walked the victory runway, the Miss America tiara glittering on her head. The year was 1957. She was twenty years young, happy, and wholesome, the All-American Girl. For Marilyn, the Miss America crown was *the* victory in a long succession of successes.

Those who knew her would agree she started at the top and went up from there. Of the four daughters of wealthy and socially prominent Francis and Gwendolyn "Boots" Van Derbur, Marilyn was the youngest. Her maternal grandfather founded Olinger Mortuaries in Denver; later Van Derbur took over as president.

From the Van Derburs' six-bedroom house in east Denver, Marilyn went to East High School, where she excelled in every undertaking. A straight-A student, she was swimming champion, golfer, skier, and equestrian. She was elected a representative to National Girls' State. *Seventeen* magazine chose her Miss Young American in Denver. In

Marilyn's sophomore year, a handsome senior named Larry Atler caught her attention. She immediately set her cap for him. Soon they were dating and by summer, they were madly in love.

At the University of Colorado, she pledged Pi Beta Phi, a sorority known for producing beauty queens. Marilyn later recalled that she didn't fit in with sorority life and avoided the parties and football games. One afternoon, she left a chapter meeting for a lengthy phone call. When she returned, most of the members had dispersed but she was told that she had been elected the sorority's candidate for the Miss CU's beauty contest. "I decline," Marilyn retorted. But the meeting was over and her name was turned in. For Marilyn, who was painfully shy, the idea of appearing in a swimsuit before judges was terrifying. She didn't think she had the figure for the swimsuit segment. And what could she do for the talent portion of the contest, she wondered. "You'll think of something," her sorority sisters replied.

She decided that competing for Miss CU wouldn't be too bad. But when she won that title, she automatically qualified to run for Miss Colorado. With each contest, she endured absolute terror. Soon, Marilyn was intensively preparing for the Miss America pageant. For her program, she chose two popular numbers—"Tea for Two" and "Tenderly"—which she practiced constantly on the family organ until she could play them as automatically as she could walk. As the day of the pageant approached, she became so desperate that she asked her friends not to attend. Marilyn just wanted to get through the ordeal. In her room in Atlantic City, she had a panic attack before each event. She suffered most through the swimsuit segment. Her only hope was of being able to finish without falling off the ramp.

At last the competition was concluded and the emcee announced—to her disbelief—"The new Miss America is ... *Miss Colorado, Marilyn Van Derbur!*" Somehow she got through her acceptance speech. When she could slip away, she went to her room and sobbed convulsively as if she were going to die. (Later, Marilyn wrote the pageant directors, advising them to discontinue the swimsuit portion. She saw a great contradiction, on the one hand, of awarding women college scholarships to pursue professions and, on the other hand, of including a swimsuit competition, which emphasized physical attributes. The contestants often resorted to extreme diets—some even became anorexic—to compete in this segment. Despite her protest, the swimsuit competition is still used.)

She was crowned on Saturday night and the next day she sped with the pageant director to New York to address the National Mayors' Conference in New York. Her grueling year-long reign as Miss America had begun. During that time, Marilyn had to keep up with the demands made of her. On-the-job public speaking training, she called it. On one occasion, on a flight to an important speaking engagement in Winston-Salem, North Carolina, she suffered from severe stomach cramps and thought she wouldn't be able to get off the plane. Then Marilyn understood that she was secondary to the Miss America image. "I have to be the best Miss America because I represent the pageant," she told herself and took it more seriously than anyone ever had.[1] During her reign, she made speeches throughout the United States and six foreign countries. Among her countless Miss American assignments, she was official hostess for Colorado's Rush to the Rockies celebration in 1959. On one day in Denver, she made twenty-two appearances.

When her year as Miss America finally ended, Marilyn returned to CU. She joined the ski team and graduated Phi Beta Kappa. She married well-known CU football player Gary Nady, who took a coaching job in Iowa after graduation. After three months, they separated and later they divorced. Marilyn moved to New York to be spokeswoman for Bell Telephone Hour commercials. She was also the television hostess for the Miss America Pageant, the World's Fair opening, and other television programs.

When she was twenty-four and in Los Angeles to do some filming, she arranged to meet with D. D. Harvey, her former youth minister, who had moved to California. Harvey long suspected that despite Marilyn's bright smile she was suffering from a secret inner trauma. Why, he wondered, did she set such impossibly high standards for herself? He kept pressing her gently until suddenly the dam broke. Between her wrenching sobs, Harvey pulled out Marilyn's terrible secret: She had been sexually violated by her own father from the time she was five until she was eighteen. The trauma was so intense she "split" her mind into a day child and a night child to survive. The day child was happy and laughing but always pushing herself to the limit. Gradually, Marilyn learned that her need to excel was an attempt to create another side to the tragic, guilty night child that her father was violating. From the happy day child, she turned into a shameful night child who curled up in bed, unable to sleep without sleeping pills and ever alert for footsteps coming down the hall. Her panic attacks before public appearances came from her terror that the secret might be exposed. Marilyn begged Harvey not to tell anyone.

She admitted to him that she particularly didn't want to tell Larry Atler. For nine years, she had loved Larry with all her heart. He thought of her as the ideal woman who succeeded at everything, but she kept breaking off their relationship—terrified that he would learn her dreadful secret and discover who she really was. That night at Harvey's urging, Marilyn took her first big step. She called Larry and asked him to come to California. He hesitated, having been rejected so often before by Marilyn. But he flew to Los Angeles the next day. "Telling Larry was agonizing," Marilyn recalled. "When he understood, he held me in his arms a long time, then said quietly, 'Today is the happiest day of my life. I understand everything now.'"[2] They were married two years later. Since then, Larry has been her mainstay, her love and support.

Marilyn's feverish pace accelerated. She became a motivational speaker and formed the Marilyn Van Derbur Motivational Institute in Denver, which had an extensive library of motivational films. She was in great demand to speak at national conventions for bankers, executives, and business associations. For sixteen years she was General Motors' only woman guest lecturer.

Eight years after the Atlers were married, Marilyn became pregnant with their daughter, Jennifer. She devoted herself to raising a healthy, happy daughter. But when Jennifer was five, the age Marilyn was when Van Derbur had started molesting her, Marilyn's health problems intensified. Still, she continued her motivational programs. The National Speakers Association, after tallying 30,000 questionnaires, chose Marilyn Van Derbur as Outstanding Woman Speaker in America. Returning one day from a major presentation, she lay down and then found she couldn't get up. Her arms and legs were paralyzed. Although the doctors could find no physical cause, she suffered recurring attacks of paralysis and often sobbed and cried out at night. When Jennifer entered puberty, pain and memories overwhelmed Marilyn.

Finally, in desperation, Larry called Marilyn's oldest sister, Gwen, who flew to Denver. The sisters talked for days. Gwen revealed that she, too, had been abused and beaten. But she was able to spend time with her grandfather and always had hope of confiding in him. The sisters' reunion was a breakthrough for Marilyn but she still suffered critical emotional and related physical problems.

Facing her next challenge, Marilyn worked up courage to meet with her father at his home. Just as she started to confront him, he excused himself and went upstairs. When he returned, she told him of her recollections of the years of sexual violation and the effect it had had on her life. Revealing the gun he had brought downstairs, he said that if he had known what grief it would cause her, he wouldn't have done it. He said nothing more. Marilyn clearly understood that if she exposed him during his lifetime he would kill them both. So she kept her silence. Later that year, her father died of a heart attack.

Her emotional distress continued to deepen. Shortly after, she was admitted to the Cedars-Sinai Hospital psychiatric ward in Los Angeles. Larry feared she never would be able to come home, but Marilyn worked extensively with several psychiatrists and learned she could exorcise her night demons and her guilt if she went back in her mind to relive her terrible childhood experiences as a six-year-old. "I was a happy day child because I could block out the night terrors," she recalled. "But those memories were stored in my body. Years later, the only way I could recover was to relive the memories—not as a woman but by becoming that night child again—[it was] a long, painful ordeal."[3]

Marilyn did come home eventually, but more hurdles loomed. One day, after a painful phone conversation, Jennifer entered the room to find her crying. When Jennifer asked, "Mommy, what's wrong?" the Atlers realized it was time to tell Jennifer the secret. Sitting beside her precious thirteen-year-old daughter on the porch steps, Marilyn searched for words. As she sobbed out her story, Jennifer started to cry. Marilyn took her in her arms. But it was Jennifer who rocked her mother. At length she said, "Mom, you have changed so many people's lives with your speeches. Think how many more lives you could change if they knew this about you." Her daughter's acceptance of the humiliating secret and the fact that she was not ashamed of her was a major breakthrough in Marilyn Van Derbur's long convalescence.

The next year, when she was forty-eight, Marilyn went to her mother with her terrible secret. Boots Van Derbur indignantly accused Marilyn of making the story up. She was concerned only with holding the family together and was unable to comfort Marilyn or to reach out to her. Happily, fate had given Marilyn the mother she always longed for—her mother-in-law, Dorothy Atler, who always accepted, loved, and cherished her.

Marilyn did not convert to Judaism, Larry's religion, although they raised Jennifer in the Jewish tradition and observed the holidays. In 1989, her spiritual side began to emerge. Feeling a strong religious relationship, she prayed for guidance: "Here's the deal. I'll do whatever you want—just give me a job." Immediately, she was given two "jobs."

After working two years with the Kempe National Center for the Prevention and Treatment of Child Abuse and Neglect, Marilyn Van Derbur addressed a meeting sponsored by the Center on May 8, 1991. It was then she went public and revealed the terrible secret at a press conference before an audience of thirty-five psychologists and survivors. Backed by her husband and her mother-in-law, she related her grim childhood as an incest victim and her slow, painful recovery. In conclusion, she announced the formation of the Adult Incest Survivors Program (later named Survivors United Network—SUN) at the Kempe Center, to which the Van Derbur family was donating $240,000. Her youth minister, D. D. Harvey, came out of retirement to manage SUN.

Marilyn's second spiritual challenge was even more grueling. In the media hubbub that followed her revelation, Congresswoman Patricia Schroeder asked her to speak at a congressional hearing on family violence in Washington. Marilyn expected to see three people; instead, she was ushered before 900 people at a child advocacy hearing to testify on child abuse. Marilyn's shining moment occurred when 1,100 incest survivors met with her at Montview Presbyterian Church to hear what incest had done to her life. Many in the audience lined up afterward to say a few words to Marilyn. To her, this was the most dramatic and fulfilling moment in her life. From that night on, Marilyn was free of her guilt. No longer need she live in terror that her secret would come out. She could speak before groups of any size or distinction without fear or nervousness. Although Marilyn's night child never left her, it gradually merged with the happy day child. For two and a half years, SUN saw 500 incest survivors a week and arranged for them to meet in thirty-five different support groups at no charge. SUN continued to operate until May 1993. "During that time, the floodgates opened," she said. "We had thousands of men and women who had never spoken out before."[4]

Marilyn Atler believes that becoming Miss America was a keystone in her life's plan. Because of the title and the national attention, she was able to take her personal message nationwide. She will continue to lead this crusade every day for the rest of her life. Marilyn—the perfect Miss America—is even more stunning in her sixties than she was as a young beauty queen. Her vivid blue eyes fill with a galaxy of emotions and recollections as she speaks of her extraordinary life. Marilyn Atler sends this message to incest victims: "You can survive. You can come through it serene, calm, peaceful—my message is HOPE."[5] Hearing her words, other victims think, "If she can do it, maybe I can, too."

Sumiko Tanaka Hennessy

Born November 8, 1937, in Yokohama, Japan

Sumiko Tanaka Hennessy, an immigrant from Japan, is building a bridge to help other Asian immigrants adapt to life in the United States. A tiny, dynamic woman with a keen sense of humor, she is well qualified to direct the bustling Asian Pacific Development Center in Denver. Under her leadership, the Center offers a wide spectrum of services for Asian-Americans in all age groups. Many immigrants go to the center to become more fluent in English and to learn to adjust to American culture. They also may receive individual and family mental health therapy.

Sumiko was born in the seaport city of Yokohama, Japan, the first-born grandchild of influential maternal and paternal grandparents. Because her family had been expecting a boy, her father wrote a poem in her honor, starting, "Sumiko, Sumiko, why were you not a boy?" Little Sumiko (pronounced Soo'miko and nicknamed Sumi) forgot the rest of the poem but remembered she was supposed to be a boy. With that image of herself, she grew up to be strong and assertive—unusual traits, indeed, for a Japanese girl. As the oldest of her fourteen cousins and siblings, she found herself looked up to and regarded as a leader. This experience helped forge her personality. For as long as she can remember, she has strongly advocated equal opportunities for women.

When Sumi was five, another daughter was born into the family. Under her mother's influence, Sumi's sister became a traditional Japanese woman skilled in cooking and Japanese ancient dance. But Sumi, always her own person, attended the Alliance Française to learn French after school because she had her sights set on a diplomatic career. She chose to attend Tokyo University of Foreign Studies, from which many graduates went on to become diplomats. As she prepared to take a test to enter into a Foreign Service career, she was told that as a woman in Japan, she could be promoted only to a certain grade level and never would become an ambassador. Sumiko decided then to switch to her second choice, social work.

While at college, she was active in the Yokohama Catholic Students Association that did charity work. The association's counselor, a Belgian priest, helped Sumi get a scholarship to a Belgian school of social work. After receiving her B.A. in French, she entered the Belgian school as a second-year student in 1960. A professor there strongly urged Sumi to work toward her master's degree in the United States.

Sumi reached New York in the summer of 1961 and was granted a graduate scholarship to Fordham University's Graduate School of Social Service. There, she met and later married classmate Richard Hennessy. After graduation in 1963, Sumi practiced social work at the Henry Street Settlement in New York's Lower East Side, at Bird S. Coler Hospital for the chronically ill, and at Maimonides Medical Center in Brooklyn. From 1969 to 1974, she was an assistant professor at New York University's Graduate School of Social Work. Richard Hennessy began teaching social work at Long Island University.

In 1974, the Hennessys decided to get their doctorates so they could continue in the field of social work education. They chose the University of Denver partly because of the proximity of the Vail ski area. Richard began work on his doctorate while Sumi became chief social worker in the Division for Developmental Disabilities of Colorado's Department of Institutions. She received a fellowship to start her doctoral studies while working for the state half-time. When the Hennessys received their Ph.D.s in social work in August 1978, it was announced that they were the only couple at the University of Denver to get simultaneous doctorates.

Sumi took on a challenge in 1980 as assistant superintendent in charge of education and therapy at Wheat Ridge Regional Center (also known as Ridge Home for the Developmentally Disabled). For four years, she supervised education programs for institutionalized residents, managed a $15 million budget, supervised a staff of 150, and coordinated residential and education programs. During the period, Ridge Home began to close down its institution portion and to relocate residents throughout the community in group homes, each of which houses eight. Hennessy believes this change is proving to be beneficial to the residents.

Hennessy embarked upon a project close to her heart in October 1980 when she helped establish the Asian Pacific Development Center—a place where Asian-Pacific immigrants can seek help in dealing with trials of life in America. In her role as chairman of the board, she helped the center buy a spacious old house facing City Park. She served on the board until December 1983. When the center suffered a personnel crisis, Sumiko Hennessy was asked to help out. In October 1984 she became executive director with a mandate to strengthen programming, personnel, and financial management.

In order to overcome the Asian discomfort with mental health assistance, she added practical services such as classes in English as a second language, job counseling and placement, and a youth program. She continues to oversee programs for three main age groups. For at-risk children and youth, the center offers after-school programs and leadership and peer counselor training. Eligible teens are placed in summer internships with corporations. For adults and seniors, the center provides psychological and psychiatric evaluation, medication therapy, individual and family therapy, day treatment, counseling for domestic abuse perpetrators, and alcohol-abuse education and therapy. To help Asians acquire and hold jobs, the center schools them in job-related English and pre-work training. The staff arranges internships with local companies and finally, job placement.

She has plans for the Asian Pacific Development Center to work with Asians who do not speak English and help them develop skills to succeed in this country. The center counsels clients in twenty-one languages and has interpreters who can expand their repertoire to thirty-five languages. (Dr. Hennessy speaks fluent Japanese, English, and French; she reads and writes Chinese.) The center supplies interpreters for courts, hospitals, and businesses by training and matching them to requests. By 1998, the Asian Pacific Development Center's 73 staff members were serving 2,500 clients in Metro Denver's community of some 89,000 Asians. Sumiko, herself—now in her sixties—puts in an eighty-hour week.

Through her years at the center, Sumiko had heard the questions of other Asians: Who are we? How are we different from other Americans? How are we similar? As she thought and read about these issues, she identified significant factors. She noted, for example, that first-generation Asian immigrants tend to go into small businesses, but the second generation is encouraged to become professionals. In addition, Asian-American families face intergenerational conflicts. Expecting their children to succeed in school, Asian parents urge them to absorb everything the school system offers but remain obedient to their parents. In traditional Asian families, children do not contradict their elders or act against their parents' wishes. But in the United States, young people are encouraged to ask questions and think for themselves. Asian children who become more independent and assertive are bound to be in conflict with their elders. Similar conflicts occur in marriages. Asian men do not always understand their wives' new independence; likewise, Asian women who gain economic independence threaten their husbands' sense of superiority. Such differences between generations and genders are a central theme of the center's mental health program.

Even in the choice of her successor, Hennessy faced intergenerational issues. In Asia, a business leader who is thinking about retiring brings up a successor and stays on for a couple of years as adviser. Sumiko Hennessy had thought about stepping down to be a program director and giving her position to the next in line. But new board members, who are third-generation Asian-Americans, prefer to conduct a national search for the next executive director. Dr. Hennessy therefore, has set her retirement date as January 31, 2000.

Because so few funds are available for the medically indigent population, Dr. Hennessy raises money herself by giving lectures and offering courses for area businesses and the public. These programs (which include courses in understanding Asian cultures, stress management Asian-style, and doing business in Asia) are marketed to large corporations by Adrienne Hynes Associates.

In 1985, Dr. Hennessy became incensed over the plight of mail-order brides. Her investigation revealed that a mail-order company was photographing girls and women in Asian Pacific countries, usually the Philippines, in revealing and alluring poses. The women were then marketed, catalog-style, in male-oriented American magazines. The girls did not understand that the advertisements suggested something akin to prostitution. Many American men saw the ads, selected a woman, and sent for her. Often they were expecting a quiet, submissive Asian girl who would obey them and wait on them without question. The "brides" arrived with hopes that their "husbands" would be kinder than Asian men. But some of the men were batterers and often isolated their wives so they could not extricate themselves from their marriages. Many men were not even interested in marriage. At this point the Asian Pacific Development Center would intervene, offering the wives support groups, counseling, and referrals to battered women shelters.

Sumiko takes a broad view of racial discrimination. "I grew up as a member of the predominant race in Japan, so I'm not too sensitive to racial discrimination against myself. My husband tries to protect me from racial discrimination. But I feel more discriminated against because I am a woman. My hot button is sexism more than racism!"[1]

In June 1998, the Robert Wood Johnson Foundation presented Sumiko Hennessy with its Community Health Leadership award of $100,000 and designated her as one of "ten outstanding individuals changing the shape of health care in America." The award will help the center move to a building large enough to accommodate its expanding personnel and outreach into a new community. Numerous other awards to Sumiko Hennessy include the Silk Wings Award from the National Network of Asian and Pacific Women (for leadership and achievement among Asian women), 1988; the Women at Work Award from the Council on Working Women, 1986; and the Asian Human Services Association Outstanding Leadership Award, 1984.

Sumiko Hennessy described her vision: "What I wish and work for—I want to help all Asians who come to the United States to learn to be valuable to their community. I want to see Asian women become assertive—to be their own person rather than what their husbands say they should be. In Asia, women always are second-class citizens. I take pride in our female staff members, who are blossoming into assertive, confident, and professional women."[2]

Patricia Scott Schroeder

Born July 30, 1940, in Portland, Oregon

Patricia Schroeder faced a crowd of excited constituents gathered at Denver's Civic Center on September 28, 1987. They had come to hear the congresswoman from Denver announce her candidacy for president. Overwhelmed with conflicting emotions, Congresswoman Schroeder looked out at those familiar faces. Could she, indeed, become the first American woman president?

Since June 5, Pat Schroeder had been taking her political temperature. When she made public her interest in the office, the media latched onto the prospect of the first woman to enter the ring and reporters grilled her on every possible issue. In the past eight days, she had flown to Hartford, Washington, Minneapolis, New York City, Washington again, Davenport, Los Angeles, San Jose, and San Francisco, and then back to Washington and Des Moines. She had slept in endless hotels, lived on airline food, and ridden in strangers' cars. Could she survive through an entire campaign? The hectic schedule of this trip did not allow Schroeder the time and privacy to consider the many tough choices of her candidacy. Among the less serious issues raised, she had been told to do something about her "flaky" appearance. "You don't look presidential," well-wishers said. "That's right," she quipped, "They're still trying to figure out what a woman president looks like."[1]

Daunting blockades stood between her and the White House. She was entering the race late. Would she be able to make up the lost time? She needed a nationwide campaign organization—not yet organized. A successful presidential campaign requires a considerable war chest. Could she raise so much money in so short a time? She needed solid party backing, but not one colleague had come to her support. Thoughts galloped through her head as she stood before her supporters at noon in Denver's Civic Center.

Schroeder began her speech by thanking her family and supporters for their work and their faith in her. When she announced her decision not to run, she heard a long groan in the audience. People started

258

chanting, "Run, Pat, run." She knew how hard they had worked and how they counted on her. To her horror, she started to cry. Through tears, she finished her speech and left the platform.

The media reacted instantly. It was not so much her decision, but the fact that she had cried that made the evening news. She was lambasted by some who said crying was unpresidential and would set back all women in the political arena. Others defended her, saying her tears showed she was human. At least, she had the courage to try.

For a political career that began so simply, Pat Schroeder's life had been fraught with towering challenges and withering setbacks. She was born into the active, widely traveled family of Lee and Bernice Scott. Her grandfather had homesteaded a Nebraska farm in the 1860s. In the Populist movement of the 1880s, he was elected to the Nebraska legislature and served with William Jennings Bryan, the famous orator and three-time presidential candidate. During the Depression, the Scotts lost most of their money but managed to support themselves on the farm. Bernice Scott was a teacher and Lee Scott sold aviation insurance—a business that necessitated family moves to seven states during Pat's school days. Whenever the moving van pulled up at a new home, Pat would set out her toys to attract attention from kids on the block.

"We were a flying family," she explained in her autobiography *Champion of the Great American Family: A Personal and Political Book.* "My father jokes that [my brother] Mike and I were born and raised in an airplane. Some people called me a tomboy because I was adventurous and pretty fearless."[2] Pat could pilot a plane by the time she was fifteen. Her sympathetic parents helped young Patricia Scott through a difficult childhood. She woke one morning when she was very young to find that her eyes had become crossed. Her doctor called it ambliopia, a condition in which a "lazy" eye weakens from lack of use. At the age of eighteen months, she started wearing glasses, which her parents had to strap to her head so she couldn't knock them off. Later, she had to wear an eye patch. Classmates would ask if she was a pirate or if she had a glass eye. Poor depth perception kept her from participating in sports. It was difficult always being the new girl at school—tall, gangly, and wearing thick glasses. But Pat, who loved people, collected a supply of stock answers that helped develop her famous sense of humor. The skill came to her rescue years later when, as a politician, she faced regular quizzes by the press. In addition, her eye problem helped her to understand others with handicaps far worse than hers—the loneliness, fear, and isolation they feel. To compensate for her social difficulties, she concentrated on schoolwork—possibly not realizing how tough it can be for a child so much smarter than the others.

In 1961, she graduated magna cum laude from the University of Minnesota. Three years later, she completed work for a law degree at Harvard. She had learned to defend her position in debates and acquired the best possible legal training for a future writing legislation in Congress. Another plus was meeting a fellow law student, James White Schroeder. Soon after, she stopped by Harvard's job placement office to inquire about applying at a law firm, and the counselor advised that she was not likely to be hired because firms would think a woman like her would probably get pregnant. (No one told Jim he wouldn't be hired because he someday might be a father, she noted wryly.)

Pat and Jim were married on August 18, 1962. He said he hoped their marriage wouldn't be boring. She said she didn't want to be stuck in the suburbs. Denver seemed to fill the bill so they settled there. Jim joined a law firm and Pat became a field attorney with the National Labor Relations Board. She opened a private practice in 1966, taught at the University of Colorado–Denver, the Community College of Denver, and Regis College; she also did volunteer legal work for Planned Parenthood.

Pat and Jim, meanwhile, were trying to start a family but every pregnancy ended in loss. Finally, their son, Scott, was born. The next pregnancy, however, was misdiagnosed and they lost twin babies. Pat then sailed through the pregnancy and birth of her daughter, Jamie Christine, but nearly bled to death in the aftermath. She was left with chronic anemia and doctors warned her against further pregnancies.

She returned to her work part-time and Jim ran for the legislature in 1970. He lost by 42 votes but stayed on as a Democratic precinct captain. About a year later, Jim was meeting with a committee to find a candidate to run in Colorado's First Congressional District primary for Congress against Democrat Arch Decker. The nomination was considered a suicide mission because Colorado traditionally elected a Republican. The incumbent—popular Republican and former District Attorney Mike McKevitt—would be running again.

After calling several Democrats, who turned them down, a young man on the committee turned to Jim. "We need someone different. How about your wife?" Jim answered, "How about *your* wife?" By the end of the meeting, they had settled on Pat! The nomination was a total surprise to Pat, who was putting the kids to bed at home. But her motto was: Make the most of opportunities as they come up. Besides, Jim agreed to be her campaign manager. Always a bleeding-heart liberal, she considered it a chance to field some issues. She decided to run on an anti-Vietnam War platform plus issues concerning children, the elderly, housing, and environment.

The Democratic National Committee denied her request for funds. Pat and Jim opened a campaign office in their basement and made clever posters, while celebrities Shirley McLaine and Gloria Steinem gave impressive help at fund raisers. Pat canvassed her district to meet individual voters and win their votes. When the 1972 general election returns came in, the Schroeders were surprised to find that Pat had won 52 percent of the vote. The family plunged headlong into a new life. They had two months to find a house in Washington, move, and settle their children, ages two and six.

At age thirty-two, Congresswoman Pat Schroeder was the only member of Congress ever to arrive with small children. She made her grand entrance into the House of Representatives with diapers in her purse. Jim, who had given up his Denver law practice, was available for trips to the grocery store and pediatrician. He even filled in as unpaid press secretary until the regular secretary arrived. At last, he found a job that didn't interfere with Pat's position. Only then could they hire help for housework, laundry, cooking, and chauffeuring.

When Schroeder entered Congress in 1973, the women's movement was erupting with demands for an Equal Rights Amendment, federal assistance for child care, an end to gender discrimination at work, and freedom of choice in relation to abortion. Her interest in the Vietnam

War spurred her to fight for a position on the Armed Services Committee, an impenetrable male stronghold. Chairman F. Edward Hebert, Democrat, was not happy to have her on his committee; he said she was unworthy of the seat because she had never served in the armed forces. She looked up the committeemen's records—few male members had been in the military. Schroeder secured a seat on the committee but was forced to physically share a chair with freshman Representative Ron Dellums, a black Democrat from California.

Pat had come up against the exclusive Old Boys (Only) Club, which she said keeps a tight rein on legislation and snubs and trivializes female members. "Congress is a reflection of society. You can get things done but you're never in the club," she said.[3] Years later, she was delighted when Congress passed a ruling that committee chairmen must be selected by vote of the full committee rather than by seniority.

In her book *Women on the Hill,* Clara Bingham wrote that Schroeder often failed to get male support because she refused to compromise on any issue. Schroeder did not "trade" votes with other representatives. When she voted against a bill introduced by her Post Office Committee and the Education and Labor Committee, her family leave bill withered. The Democratic leadership could not depend on her vote for issues like perks and franked mail. Thus, she alienated party leaders by not voting with them and became known as a loner in the House. Schroeder argued that refusing to compromise was the only way she got anything done. When she introduced the Family Medical Leave Bill in 1982, many legislators feared it would anger business interests. They didn't want to upset the status quo and preferred just to pass a resolution honoring working mothers—which was no help to women facing issues like the tax code. When she first got family leave passed in Congress, President George Bush vetoed it. (The Family Medical Leave Bill allows employees eighteen weeks of unpaid, job-protected time off to care for a newly born, just adopted, or seriously ill child. It finally became law in spring of 1988.)

When Schroeder came to Congress in 1973, she met informally at lunch with women legislators to discuss ways of getting their bills through. They considered women's issues, gathered information, and met with the Cabinet staff to explain their agenda. The group evolved into the Congresswomen's Caucus in 1977 and, in 1981, reorganized into the formal Congressional Caucus for Women's Issues, an important and powerful arm that unified women in the House and Senate.

Pat Schroeder's first bill was the Child Abuse and Protection Act, which she sponsored in the House and Walter Mondale carried in the Senate. Using the Kempe National Center for the Prevention and Treatment of Child Abuse and Neglect in Denver, she researched the problem extensively. The bill passed overwhelmingly in 1973. Fifteen years later, Congress passed the Child Abuse Prevention, Adoption, and Family Services Act establishing the National Clearinghouse for Child Abuse and Neglect.

By 1992, hailed as the Year of the Woman, Congresswoman Schroeder stood at the threshold. Described by Clara Bingham in *Women on the Hill* as "the fifty-two-year-old 'dean' of congresswomen," Schroeder is a tall, big-boned woman with a handsome face and high cheekbones.[4] For years, she wore her salt-and-pepper hair in a pageboy and nearly every photograph showed her laughing or smiling. After twenty years in Congress, Schroeder had become known as a spokeswoman for feminists across the country. That year—1992—with forty-eight women in the House and six in the Senate, they could act as a voting bloc. It was now or never for Schroeder's legislation benefiting women and families. Jobs, education, and health care were her major issues. She fought to expand women's combat roles in the military; worked to allow acknowledged gays and lesbians to serve in the military; and made a concerted effort to follow up on deadbeat parents. She strove to cut defense spending and led a march of women representatives against perpetrators of the Navy tailhook scandal.

With Schroeder as co-chair, the Women's Caucus, boasting twenty-four freshwomen, announced it was solidly pro-choice and supported the Family Medical Leave Act, which she had introduced in 1985. For the twelve years that Schroeder co-chaired the Congressional Caucus for Women's Issues, much was accomplished. Schroeder's success list includes the Economic Equity Package bills to guarantee equal pay for equal work and the support of scientific studies (performed on women by women scientists) on ovarian cancer, breast cancer, AIDS in Women, domestic violence, osteoporosis, menopause, and heart disease. In 1992, more family and child-related legislation was passed than ever before. "It took long, hard work with [many] people mad at me," she said.[5] Newt Gingrich was named Speaker of the House in 1994 and soon halted funding for congressional caucuses. A critical casualty was the Women's Caucus. Pat Schroeder's main accomplishment for her district was the cleanup of the Rocky Mountain Arsenal and its establishment as a wildlife refuge. In addition, she helped push through a rule change requiring members of Congress to abide by the same rules and requirements as the American public.

During her tenure, Congresswoman Schroeder chaired the Select Committee on Children, Youth, and Families from 1991 to 1994; she was the third ranking Democrat on the House Armed Services Committee, the second ranking Democrat on the House Judiciary Committee, chairman of the Civil Service Committee, and was the longest serving woman in Congress.

Asked who became her best ally in Congress, Schroeder replied, "The Press." Always in demand for witty, quotable quotes and sharp criticism of opposing views, she could count on the media to bring out important issues that were hushed up in Congress. It was Pat Schroeder who called Ronald Reagan "The Teflon president" because problems would just rub off him. Unfortunately, the press often capitalized on her glibness rather than her intelligence. Her lowest point in Congress came as she watched the debate on her bills turning personal. "Debate should be a factual give and take. But the men worked personal attack into an art form. In the last few years, the tone in Congress got lower and lower," she said.[6] Republicans regarded Schroeder as the ultimate liberal feminist, which they abhorred. Later Congresses tried to kill some of her bills supporting women and family. But as Eleanor Clift wrote in *Working Woman,* Schroeder "was the first modern woman in the House"—and that in the face of the worst-possible gender discrimination.[7]

Among countless honors and awards, she was inducted into the Colorado Women's Hall of Fame and in October 1995, she entered the National Women's Hall of Fame in Seneca Falls, New York, as one of the most influential women in American history.

One morning in 1995, Pat Schroeder realized that she was fifty-five and her job on the Hill had become more like trench warfare than public service. "Unless I wanted to stay in Congress for life, it was time to go while I was on top of the game. I didn't want them to have to help me out," she said.[8] She wanted to try her hand at other things. While serving on the Judiciary Committee, she had become interested in intellectual property issues, which led to her present position as president and CEO of the Association of American Publishers in New York.

When she stepped down from Congress in January 1966, she left an unprecedented legacy of rights and benefits for women and the family. She believed her greatest accomplishment was "getting out with my reputation, family, and marriage intact. It's hard to live in that pressurized environment."[9] And she still was the same bleeding-heart liberal. Ted Sorenson once summed up Patricia Schroeder when he introduced her as "a politician who could draft a bill, stir a crowd, fly a plane, bake a cake, pass a law, coin a phrase—and run for president."[10]

Lenore E. Auerbach Walker
Born October 3, 1942, in The Bronx, New York

"Lenore Walker, mother of the movement to protect battered women's rights, is now O.J. Simpson's defender," proclaimed the *Denver Post* in a front-page story on January 29, 1995. Lenore Walker's name was blazoned in national headlines during the sensational trial of Simpson, a professional football player accused of murdering his wife, Nicole, and her friend Ronald Goldman. The announcement by Simpson lawyer Johnnie Cochran that Dr. Walker had agreed to testify for Simpson's defense team sent a shock wave through the psychology community.

"Walker, a Denver-based psychologist with a national reputation, appears to have abandoned her cause after decades of testifying for abused women. ... Her work has come to be commonly accepted by therapists and courts," the *Post* article added. The public wondered how Walker came to be the "mother of battered women" and why she was testifying for a man accused of killing his wife.

The study of human behavior had fascinated Lenore Elizabeth Auerbach from childhood. She was born into a middle-class Jewish family in New York and grew up in the Bronx. In high school, she was encouraged to become a teacher. Lenore attended Hunter College at City University of New York. Because the college did not offer an education major, she turned to psychology with an eye to becoming a school psychologist. She received her B.A. in psychology in 1962 and continued her studies over the next decade, earning her M.S. degree in clinical psychology from City College, New York, in 1967 and a Doctor of Education at Rutgers, the State University of New Jersey, in 1972. She was also trained in community psychology at Harvard University.

While attending City College, she taught emotionally disturbed elementary school children. She then worked as a staff psychologist in a mental health clinic in New Brunswick, New Jersey. As a part-time mental health specialist in Coney Island from 1967 to 1969, she taught parents how to tutor their children. She noted that parents and children became closer through the learning process, which raised self-esteem and academic achievement for both children and adults.

Her work with abused women began when she was a psychologist at Rutgers Medical School in 1975. She had observed how the blame for child abuse fell consistently upon the mother. Some women clients, in turn, began telling her that they were physically and psychologically abused by the men in their lives. "I was very curious," she said. "I knew that wife abuse was not masochism (which some psychologists claimed). But to really understand it I had to do research rather than rely on feminist shouting."[1] No other psychologists were studying abused women as victims in early 1975 when she started collecting data. Women patients felt at ease with Dr. Walker, a feminist psychologist, and colleagues began referring women patients to her. The pain these women expressed when telling their stories indicated that none of them ever felt a psychological need to be battered.

In her private life, Lenore had married in 1962 and had two children, Michael and Karen. Later divorced, she moved to Denver in the summer of 1975 to marry Dr. Morton Flax, also a psychologist. That same year, she joined the faculty of Colorado Women's College as chair of the psychology department. She taught, established the Battered Women's Research Center, and served as psychologist for an abused women's shelter. In 1978, she also opened her private practice, Walker & Associates of Denver, which she describes as "a very general but small practice."[2]

Lenore Walker's husband, Morton Flax, who was executive director of a community mental health center, died in 1978. After his death, Dr. Walker threw herself into her work and returned to the case studies of abused women that she had brought from New York. To expand her research base, she spoke on radio shows, gave interviews for newspaper articles and television programs, and made personal contacts. Soon, she was inundated by women wanting to tell their stories.

When she had 120 interviews and pieces of another 300 stories, she began to pull her material together. She defined and named a battered woman as one who is "repeatedly subjected to any forceful physical or psychological behavior by a man in order to coerce her to do something he wants her to do without any concern for her rights."[3] Batterers use coercive techniques such as physical, sexual, and economic abuse as well as social battering and family discord. Her research revealed how violent men instill "learned helplessness" in their wives and how they abuse them in random and intimate ways. An abused wife gradually loses the ability to judge her capacity for protecting herself and narrows her options for escaping from the relationship. She comes to believe that she will fail to escape no matter which way she turns. She becomes submissive and passive.

Dr. Walker found that male batterers subject their women victims to three distinct battering cycles. In the first cycle, the tension-building phase, the man inflicts minor physical and/or psychological abuse. The wife forgives him because she believes she can pacify him and prevent further abuse. But the episodes continue to escalate until the explosion, or acute battering, incident occurs. In this phase, the man becomes so enraged he has no control over the beatings, rapes and psychological attacks that he wreaks upon his wife. The torture may last two hours or two days and can result in severe injuries. Walker called phase three the honeymoon reconciliation. After the batterer calms down (often during his wife's hospitalization), he brings flowers, candy, promises, apologies—to persuade her to come home. An expert at charm and persuasion, he convinces her that he can't live without her. If she goes back to him, the cycles resume. Surprisingly, a battered woman can be almost *any* woman—and not necessarily a neurotic masochist, said Dr. Walker.

Dr. Walker worked her interviews, research, and conclusions into a book she called *The Battered Woman.* Then she embarked upon a two-year search for a publisher. When it was finally published in 1979, Walker and the publisher were totally unprepared for the book's reception. The first landmark study of battered women, it was awarded the Distinguished Media Award in 1979 by the Association for Women in Psychology and it became the textbook on battered women.

Now a recognized authority in the area of abused women, Dr. Walker was invited to speak on domestic violence at President Reagan's Task Force on Victims of Violence in Denver, and in 1980 she testified before the Senate Subcommittee on Child and Human Resources. She received the Colorado Salute to Women Award for Outstanding Contribution to Women in Human Services in 1980 and the Women Who Care Award from Denver Women's Partnership and Passages in 1984. Later, she was inducted into the Colorado Women's Hall of Fame.

A prolific writer, Walker has published nine books and countless journal articles, book chapters, papers, studies, and handbooks on the battered woman phenomenon. *The Battered Woman Syndrome,* her 1984 work, is based on the results of a three-year research program started in July 1978 and funded by the National Institute of Mental Health. Written for psychology students, it contains the results of Walker's Battered Woman Syndrome Questionnaire, which many interviewers still use for forensic evaluations in battered women cases.

In *Terrifying Love: Why Battered Women Kill and How Society Responds,* published in 1989, Dr. Walker describes the process that led her to become an expert court witness. In 1977, a well-known defense attorney, Charles Moses of Billings, Montana, asked her to appear in court for his client. When she replied that she had no experience as a forensic witness, he offered to school her in courtroom strategies. With his counseling, she learned what to wear on the stand, to avoid technical jargon, to face the jury when answering questions, and ways of getting through tough cross examinations. Walker became an expert witness, who has since appeared in many high-profile trials of abused wives who ultimately killed their abusers in self-defense. She testified in the trial of Donna Yaklich of Pueblo, Colorado. She hired two brothers to kill her policeman husband, who brutally abused her and their three children. Dr. Walker was a consultant for both sides in the Lorena versus John Wayne Bobbitt trial. (The attorneys used her methods to evaluate both the husband and wife in the case.)

Walker had met O. J. Simpson's lawyer Johnnie Cochran at a domestic violence conference in the 1980s, but was surprised to get a call in September 1994, asking her to consult with the Simpson defense team. When, several months later, Cochran announced that Dr. Walker had agreed to testify, many of her critics wondered publicly whether the champion of battered women had sold out. "I assured them I would say the same thing if testifying for either side and still represent women's rights," she answered. "I had a very different vision from other people. I originally thought Simpson's team didn't have access to all the battered women literature because they were blaming Nicole for the abuse. They asked me to figure out if [there] was abuse in the relationship. They were starting to talk about Nicole in very negative ways. I respect the defense team and felt the prosecution was misusing data: not all batterers are necessarily murderers. If Simpson committed the crime, it should be proved in other ways."[4]

Dr. Walker was not asked to testify but the Simpson team hired her to monitor the trial on television and to fax them questions they could be asking witnesses. In this very high tech trial, she watched lawyers instantly presenting her questions, reworded, on the stand. In the end,

Simpson was acquitted. "There was no question that O. J. was a batterer but he was clear in saying he didn't commit the murder. A fascinating case. It taught me so much. I think I did the right thing and, yes, I probably would do it again if facts are the same," she said.[5]

Lenore Walker correlates the battered women syndrome with feminism. "The woman's movement is big in Colorado. Our western culture is an important addition to East Coast feminism. We're fiercely independent here, less rooted in tradition. The Colorado women's movement has a sense of community that is hard to find elsewhere. Our Achilles heel is a tendency to be harsh with each other. We haven't let ourselves celebrate our mentors and it's important to allow our heroines to make mistakes."[6]

Since *The Battered Woman* was published in 1979, the plight of abused women has come out of the shadows and is being dealt with more openly by the media and courts—a result of Lenore Walker's significant contribution to our culture and justice system.

Wilma J. Webb
Born May 17, 1943, in Denver, Colorado

The wife of Denver Mayor Wellington Webb and mother of four children, Wilma Webb forged her own political career in Colorado. "A need to be taken seriously is a cornerstone of Wilma Webb's personality," wrote a *Rocky Mountain News* reporter in 1991. "Her political stamp is: 'How is this decision or legislation going to affect the people?'"[1]

The daughter of Frank and Faye Gerdine, Wilma was born in Denver and grew up at East Twenty-third Avenue and Williams Street. The second child in a family of seven children, she attended schools in northeast Denver. An excellent student, she also studied music and art. Many who knew her suggested she might become a teacher but her ambition was to become a writer and book publisher, possibly publishing her own writing. But fate injected surprising twists in her life.

Who could have guessed that Wilma, an African American Denver girl, someday would be hostess to wives of presidents and prime ministers of the world's leading industrial countries?

Her first clue to the future surfaced during school days. She and Wellington Webb both attended Cole Junior High and Manual High School, but he was several years ahead of her. They had not met but she, of course, knew about Wellington—the all-star athlete, all-star everything. He was aware of Wilma as class president and school leader. In Wellington's senior year, the yearbook came out with his picture but the name beneath it was *Wilma* Webb. Wellington was so appalled, he refused to buy a yearbook.

When Wilma was sixteen and in eleventh grade, she married and had her first child, a son. She spent a lot of time reading and thinking about her future. She didn't want to be like some high school girls who don't become self-sufficient as young mothers and face a bleak future. "I was determined to forge a good future for myself and my family," she said.[2]

Encouraged by her parents, Wilma enrolled at Emily Griffith Opportunity School, where she could progress at her own pace. She left classes for the birth of her son and later returned to Manual to graduate with her class. Wilma also tried to make her marriage work and she and her husband had a daughter. But after eight years of marriage they were divorced.

When her children were fifteen months and three years old, she was hired as a bookkeeper in a doctor's office. She acquired work experience there but no other benefits. In 1963, major corporations were opening up to people of color. Wilma was hired by Mobil Oil Corporation, where she worked fifteen years and was promoted to a position as executive administrative assistant. While at Mobil, she took classes after work at the University of Colorado–Denver until 1978, when she resigned to attend college full-time, majoring in small business management and English.

Wilma was a community volunteer who registered people to vote, helped impoverished families, and encouraged equality in education. At meetings, she kept running into another activist—Wellington Webb—who was in a job placement program. She was pleasantly surprised when he called her one day and asked her to have lunch with him. As they reminisced, they laughed over the yearbook misprint and decided it must have been destiny that printed her name under his picture.

Both had been married previously and they were cautious not to move too fast for the sake of their families. Her son was oldest of the four; his twins and her daughter were the same age. They took all their children with them nearly everywhere they went. After dating two years, Wilma and Wellington were married in 1971. "It was difficult to do, but we both raised each other's children," Wilma Webb recalled. "All four are [unique] individuals. ... We made sure each had his or her interests addressed. It was a financial challenge with three the same age; high school proms, tuxes, graduation expenses came in triplicate. So did college."[3]

The Webbs' children were in elementary school when Rachel Noel presented her initiative to desegregate the Denver Public Schools. Wilma recalled having the most caring, capable teachers and the best school spirit in the schools she had attended, which were predominantly black. She also remembered Manual High School offered only three foreign languages while the other high schools had five; Manual lacked up-to-date textbooks and modern equipment. "I wanted our children's school to be equal and offer equal opportunity. That's why I got involved in desegregation of schools."[4] She became a spokesperson, which launched her on a political career—something she never had envisioned for herself.

Wilma was elected a Democratic committeewoman in 1970 and then a captain. Wellington was elected to the legislature in 1972, 1974, and 1976, while she was twice elected secretary of the Colorado Democratic Party and edited the Democratic State Newsletter. In 1980, the year their three youngest children graduated from East High School, she was appointed to finish State Representative King Trimble's term in Denver District 8, after Trimble was elected to the Denver City Council. Hearing that people thought she stepped into the legislature because her husband paved the way and vacated the seat, she reminded them she was filling Trimble's seat, not Webb's, and pointed to her own political background. Although advised not to expect to get much done in the House of Representatives, Wilma Webb reminded herself she was not constituted to involve herself in idle activities.

She was appointed to serve as the first minority woman on the state's powerful Joint Budget Committee (JBC). During her first year, she introduced a controversial bill to establish a statewide holiday on Martin Luther King Jr.'s birthday. Four times, from 1981 to 1984, she presented her bill and four times Speaker of the House (Republican) Carl "Bev" Bledsoe fought it. The day before the bill was to come up for final consideration on the fourth attempt, Bledsoe put the House in recess for a day so he could lobby to change members' votes. Thirty-three votes were needed for adoption and Representative Webb had fifty votes. On Monday morning, the bill came up for final vote. Webb made some parliamentary maneuvers and it passed. It took effect in 1986.

At the start of the 1985 session, House Minority Leader David Skaggs reappointed Webb to the JBC. But Bledsoe rejected the appointment and named Westminster Democrat JoAnn Groff instead. He said appointing Webb would give Denver too much representation on the committee. She was furious and arrived early to occupy her seat the day the JBC convened. She arrived to find only the exact number of chairs for committee members. It was *not* fate that Representative Webb was occupying her seat when Representative Groff arrived. The controversy dragged on until Representatives Webb and Skaggs took the matter to court and the judge ruled in Wilma's favor. She kept the JBC seat but the next year, none of her bills were considered.

During her tenure, Webb worked closely with Republican Senator Ruth Stockton, who had passed legislation for providing treatment for alcoholism; Webb sponsored and passed the only comprehensive bill to provide for drug addiction treatment. She sponsored legislation enabling frail elderly people to be cared for at home instead of in nursing homes, as well as laws requiring state-chartered Savings and Loans to carry FSLIC insurance, and providing subpoena power for the Civil Rights Division. She also introduced bills for full-day kindergartens throughout Colorado (not adopted), pay increases for election judges, and legislation to keep a viable Colorado Civil Rights Commission.

Wilma Webb served on the JBC during several state budget short-falls when the Democrats were in the minority. The JBC would complete the budget, but if revenue was insufficient, the committee would have to go back and decrease state programs and reappropriate dollars. She considers her finest legislation was done on the JBC, passing the drug treatment law and adopting the Martin Luther King Jr. holiday.

After her appointment to the House in 1980, Webb was reelected six times to become Colorado's senior Democratic woman legislator. Among the committees she served on were the JBC, Business Affairs and Labor, Education, Appropriations, State Affairs, Long-Term Health Care, Federal Budget Task Force, New Federalism, Legislative Priorities, and the Judicial Caseload and Juvenile Sentencing.

In the fall of 1991, Wilma had decided not to run for another House term. Wellington was city auditor when Mayor Federico Peña decided not to run again for mayor. Wellington Webb quickly announced for the position, although polls gave him only a 7 percent approval rating. The Webbs developed a strategy of portraying Wellington as a dedicated "workhorse" against his "flashy racehorse" opponent, Norm Early. The centerpiece of their plan was to stump the city together on foot. During the campaign, they covered 335 miles and stayed in forty-two private homes of people they didn't know. They learned a great deal about Denver's citizens. Mrs. Webb remembers a moment the night Wellington became mayor. A happy constituent ran on stage to give Wellington a bear hug. Wilma was standing behind her husband when the constituent's big hand circled the mayor and cuffed her sharply on the jaw—just before they went live on television.

One of the most exciting events of Wilma Webb's years as Denver's first lady was the 1997 Economic Summit of Eight, when leaders of Russia, Great Britain, Canada, Germany, Italy, Japan, France, and the United States met in Denver to consider world economic and trade matters. For this summit, the leaders' wives accompanied their husbands to Denver. While the men focused on economic issues, their wives could get to know each other. The hostesses for the women's events, Bea Romer, Hillary Rodham Clinton, and Wilma Webb, accompanied their guests on a luxury train ride to Winter Park, to dinners at the Governor's Mansion and the Fort Restaurant, and to other events. In a friendly, informal setting, the wives discussed their countries' issues concerning women, families, and related matters.

The summit was an opportunity for Denver to shine in the international spotlight. "Everyone was in such a cooperative spirit. When the visitors came, the city was glowing with friendship," Mrs. Webb said. "Our city was in full bloom and our guests could appreciate who we were."[5] During the summit, the Webbs also strengthened their friendly ties with President Bill Clinton and Hillary Rodham Clinton.

After several years as first lady, Wilma Webb senses that "a lot of people question the role of first lady, a role the public expects and wants. It needs to be made an official one. I've tried to be appropriate but to make a difference. I don't try to be mayor, but just to be me."[6]

Wilma Webb's political expertise led her to be considered for the post of superintendent of the Denver Mint until the Clinton administration converted the job into a civil career position. In June 1997, Washington sources confirmed that Wilma Webb was being considered for a federal appointment. On October 3, 1998, she was appointed by U.S. Labor Secretary Alexis M. Herman as the secretary's representative for Region VIII, encompassing six Rocky Mountain states. In her position, she works with the administration to improve the quality of the workforce, to help create better jobs, and to ensure a safe workplace.

Wilma Webb presents an elegant appearance, often photographed in a well-cut black outfit that complements her well-coiffed black hair. She has come a long way from the school girl who married at sixteen. "I've had to climb many mountains because of my gender and my race as an African American woman," she said. "I think the way to improve the world is by positive actions coming from love instead of hate or resentment. Being the good person you can be makes the world a better place."[7]

Cleo Parker Robinson

Born July 17, 1948, in Denver, Colorado

The stage, with its music and drama, is her home. Dance is her magic word: It saved her life and now brings her joy and wide celebrity. Cleo Parker Robinson is an exotic beauty in the flower of her life. She radiates electricity and excitement that catch up her dancers and spill over into audiences. Her signature, CLEO, is known throughout the dance community of the world.

Cleo credits her artistry to her family's past. Her mother, Martha, was a white child prodigy, who played French horn as an apprentice with the San Diego Symphony Orchestra at the age of twelve. As a young woman, Martha was traveling through Colorado when she stopped at the University of Denver. She stepped into a music room to listen to a black musician practicing on his trombone. The musician, Jonathan Parker, introduced himself. They discovered many common interests: civil rights, the theater, and above all, music. A chance acquaintance became a romance. Jonathan and Martha were married and their first child, Cleo, was born in Denver. As a baby, she lived in her parents' tiny apartment on the third floor above the Rossonian Lounge in Five Points.

The Parkers were so poor that a dresser drawer served as Cleo's crib. Her lullabies were the jazz and blues soaring upward from the lounge. In those days, the Rossonian was frequented by the finest musicians— George Morrison, leader of an early black jazz band in Denver; famous folk singer Pete Seeger; and legendary bass singer Paul Robeson.

In search of work, the Parkers moved to Dallas. Cleo's black grandparents took them in, but segregation there was so pronounced that a mixed marriage was extremely controversial. As the only white woman in the neighborhood, Martha was at risk just being there. She could sing in an all-black choir only because the congregation protected her. Cleo attended a black Catholic school taught mainly by white nuns— a bizarre arrangement for her. Bewildered by the racial bias, she was afraid to say much. In dance, she found comfort, solace, and a means to communicate, so she used it to keep herself from crying and taught children in her neighborhood to dance.

By age ten, the little dancer, who was suffering with kidney failure and nephritis, suffered a heart attack. After some confusion over whether a black or white hospital would take her, she was finally admitted. Doctors said she never would dance again, but Cleo decided differently. In 1959, the Parkers moved back to Denver to a home at First and Jackson Streets. Still tormented by racism and insecurity, Cleo developed ulcers. She would dance so energetically, she feared she would have another heart attack. Finally, she decided if she were to die, dancing would be the best way to go. Dancing became her medicine.

In contrast to her painful childhood, Cleo's teens were magical. Music, dancing, and theater were staples in the Parker household. Cleo danced at home, danced at the grocery store, danced with her father. Cleo's sister and brothers joined the family troupe and never was there a dull moment at home. Her father, Jonathan, was stage manager at Bonfils Theater and her mother made the costumes. For Cleo, all the excitement was backstage. Jonathan Parker also became the first black actor hired at Elitch's Theater.

When Cleo was fifteen, she was teaching college-level dance classes at University of Colorado in Denver and later was on the staff of CU's Black Studies Department in Boulder. She was sixteen when the Bonfils Theater was casting *Kiss Me Kate*. She longed to dance in the show but was told she was too tall for the male dancers, so she auditioned for a singing role, got in the show, and then convinced the director to let her join the ballet.

Then there was Tom Robinson. Cleo had met Tom, a Regis High School scholar and football player, when she was in seventh grade at Hill Junior High School. He would bring little delicacies all the way from Regis for her to eat. She idolized Tom and continued to see him through her years at Denver's George Washington High School. He graduated from Colorado State University and was planning to play professional football for the San Francisco 49ers. "I had my bags packed by the front door, ready to go with him to San Francisco," Cleo says with a laugh.[1] Instead, she entered Colorado Women's College, which offered an excellent dance program. She studied under Rita Berger, a ballerina from the Metropolitan Opera Company, who introduced her to a new world of dance.

As a college senior, Cleo applied for a job teaching dance at the Model Cities Cultural Center on Twentieth and Welton Streets. She got the job but found that the "studio" she was about to teach in was a tiny office that was crammed with boxes, had no mirror, no dance floor—not even a barre. Cleo and her father drove her little Volkswagen to the lumber yard for building materials. "Our tiny building was too small for practicing leaps. It had poles holding it up. We had to dance around them until it got so we couldn't dance *without* poles. When our studio didn't have heat, we warmed up in our coats until we could dance. My dancers and I survived so many setbacks that setbacks became a part of everything we did, the Yin and Yang of life. In that little Welton Street space and another on Twentieth and Lawrence Streets, we created our company and theater."[2]

Going to New York became her next dream. Tom, who had played basketball in Madison Square Garden, had taken her there in 1969. Dazzled by the city, Cleo knew right away she was a New Yorker. She studied at the Alvin Alley Dance Center and with the Dance Theatre of Harlem. In her dance classes, she heard people speaking foreign languages and noted with shock how well trained the dancers were. She felt she'd been cheated. In New York, it was all there: dance, music, art. "I knew if I ever returned to Denver, I'd have to create a New York there for myself," she said.[3]

After a year, Cleo came home. It was 1970, a year marked by tragedy and accomplishment. Grief entered Cleo's life when her nineteen-year-old brother, a star athlete, died unexpectedly in his sleep of a heart attack. Cleo had expected she'd be the first one to die. It took time for the pain of her brother's tragic death to subside. In that same year, she married Tom Robinson in the chapel of Colorado Women's College. As director of the Model Cities Dance Program, she opened her tiny Welton Street studio. She gave dancing lessons and collaborated with others who offered programs in music, drama, sculpture, film, and pottery. All were free. Then the let-down: No one came to sign up for classes. Dance was not yet accepted in the community. Cleo's poet friend Schyleen Qualls, who had seen the New York spark in Cleo's eyes, collaborated with Jo Bunton Keel, Cleo's first student, to make posters and brainstorm for ways to get the word out. Cleo decided to take her dancing to the people by offering free dance lessons in gym classes at Manual and East High Schools. The kids ignored her classes until, in desperation, she charged each student 25 cents a lesson. Miraculously, they started coming.

She wanted to make dance as vital as acting and began giving workshops and lectures. Gradually, more people wanted to see her dancers perform. Cleo reached out in all directions to gain exposure for her studio and students. In 1970, her landmark year, she established her own performing company, the Cleo Parker Robinson Dance Ensemble (CPRDE), using dancers from the Model Cities Cultural Center. A contemporary company, it specializes in modern dance rooted in the Afro-American experience as well as ballet, jazz, improvisation, and master classes. The dance ensemble was the region's first full-time salaried dance company with a year-round training center.

Her company sought exposure by performing at child-care centers, schools, prisons, army bases, and colleges. Her next dream was to incorporate dance into the public school curriculum. CPRDE introduced its Season of Schools program to Denver and the outlying school districts, where it continues to perform for thousands of school children. Her ongoing Project Self-Discovery presents dance workshops, drama, music, visual arts, and positive choice experiences for at-risk youth.

In 1973, Cleo began to choreograph *Carmina Burana*, a contemporary work set to music by Carl Orff. She was pregnant at the time and while driving to Fort Collins to watch another group perform *Carmina*, she went into labor. She turned around and drove to the hospital for the birth of her son, Malik. In 1974, Denver's new Boettcher Concert Hall opened with *Carmina Burana*, played by the Colorado Symphony and choreographed by Cleo Parker Robinson. She considers *Carmina* her finest artistic accomplishment.

In 1977, CPRDE's predominantly black dance ensemble was invited to perform in Dragos, Nigeria, at a filming of *Americans at Festac.* Two dance companies were invited—Robinson's from Denver, one from New York—to join 70,000 artists from the African diaspora. On the eve of their departure, the Denver community turned out to raise money for the trip—a send-off that helped the ensemble achieve one of its greatest triumphs. That year, Cleo Robinson obtained a Rockefeller Grant to choreograph the Migration Series with Jacob Lawrence; her work dramatizes the blacks' exodus from the South.

By the late 1980s, Cleo's little studio had become hopelessly inadequate for the ensemble of dancers and its wide array of projects. A miraculous remedy lay just blocks away: the aging AME Church at 119 Park Avenue West in Five Points was no longer in use. The City of Denver agreed to lease the building to CPRDE for $1 a year and awarded the company a Community Development grant to renovate and build studios and a theater. After a major remodeling, the 1920s building reopened in 1989 with a 300-seat theater, three dance studios, and four individual classrooms for visual arts, music, drama, and martial arts. Cleo's office is in the belfry, along with those of CPRDE business manager Tom Robinson and the staff.

The center's community programs gained a generous boost from the Metro Scientific Cultural Facilities District, when the ensemble moved up to a Tier II recipient. The company also received generous grants from the National Endowment of the Arts. The budget exceeds $1 million. CPRDE contains four elements: an international company, the year-round dance school, Project Self-Discovery and the theater, which can be rented for community events. The dance school, considered among the most multicultural in the country, involves more than 350 students attending sixty classes a week taught by fourteen instructors. A children's program provides training in basic ballet, tap, and jazz. It takes constant work on the part of the Robinsons to sustain the center.

A major event for CPRDE, "Cleo Parker Robinson Debuts in New York City," was an ensemble performance in the Lincoln Center Out-of-Doors Series in 1994. A *Dance Magazine* critic described the ensemble's "collaboration on many levels, encouraging company members to stretch into new areas, and creating dances around subjects of substance."[4] The reviewer commented on the strength, athleticism, boundless energy, and joy of Robinson's dancers. In another first, the company performed a barefoot, modern version of Igor Stravinsky's *Firebird Suite,* which Cleo choreographed in Polynesian style. The performance, in December 1997 at the Cairo Opera House in Egypt was repeated in collaboration with the Colorado Symphony Orchestra at Boettcher Concert Hall in May 1998.

Robinson has received abundant recognition for her work, including an Honorary Doctorate Degree from the University of Denver and an invitation to be baccalaureate speaker at Colorado College. In November 1997, she was honored by a collaboration of five eastern colleges as one of five Living Legends of Dance, at the New Jersey Performing Arts Center. The tribute to five leading African American women in dance included a Smith College symposium on the influence their art has had on their communities. Cleo spoke about her dance experiences and her ensemble performed. CPRDE was described as a cultural ambassador representing Colorado. In 1998, CPRDE presented "Masterpieces of the Black Tradition" with the Dayton, Ohio, Contemporary Dance Company at the Kennedy Center in Washington, D.C., in May and at the American Dance Festival in Dayton in June.

A lifelong dream came true on July 21, 1999, when Robinson was named to the National Council on the Arts, which designates recipients of national grants to nonprofit arts programs. Of the council's twenty members, she is the only member representing the world of dance.

Having won so many laurels, there's no resting for Cleo Parker Robinson. She still dances but tries to pace herself. She trains with several teachers including famed dancer Katherine Dunham, who is in her nineties. Her best medicine still is dancing, which she serves by teaching, choreographing, and performing. "Every day is a dance, for which we have an opportunity to create our own choreography. We have just the moment. Every moment is a blessing and life is a miracle."[5] This is Cleo Parker Robinson's philosophy of life.

Terri Helman Finkel

Born May 19, 1953, in Minneapolis, Minnesota

Terri Finkel, M.D., Ph.D., gained a national reputation as director of the Center for Childhood Arthritis and Autoimmune Disorders at National Jewish Medical and Research Center. At the world-famous hospital in East Denver, this tiny woman—just an inch shy of five feet tall—directed two research laboratories and oversaw the care of four hundred sick children.

Getting through one of Dr. Finkel's typical work weeks would be like running in a perpetual-motion marathon for seven days. The wife of Denver neurologist Dr. Richard Finkel and mother of two children, she lived two lives—one at her Englewood home, the other at the Denver hospital. She was up by six A.M. to get her daughter, Val, and son, Paul, through breakfast and off to school. By nine, she was at work at the hospital. On the research side, she supervised the twelve scientists who staff her two laboratories. In her office, she wrote papers and articles, read grants, met with colleagues to discuss research and administration matters, and attended one or two conferences a day. She spent two formal days a week seeing patients at National Jewish and Presbyterian/St. Luke's Hospitals, as well as in Colorado Springs. Dr. Finkel usually got home from work around seven, followed in thirty minutes by her husband, who does the family cooking. She also worked at the hospital on Saturday and Sunday afternoons.

"My daughter says my hobby is work," Dr. Finkel said with a laugh. "I'm trying to cut back—I want to spend more time with my family. For twenty years I played classical piano and plan to pick that up again. Meanwhile, I run our two huskies for exercise and ski well enough to get down the mountain."[1] Helping to make this possible is Terri's mother, Edith Helman, a microbiologist who now edits medical textbooks and helps oversee her grandchildren.

"I was going into medicine when I was in the womb," Terri said. "My mother always thought medicine was a very good profession for a woman raising a family." Terri was unusually curious as a child, demanding to know all the gory details about how and why everything happened. That same curiosity helps today with her scientific research. When Terri graduated from high school in Minneapolis, she and a male student tied for designation as valedictorian. Without a word to Terri, school authorities resolved the dilemma by naming him valedictorian and her salutatorian. It was a blow to Terri—and surprisingly the only time she has experienced such blatant gender discrimination.

Terri Helman enrolled in a Medical Scientist Training Program at Stanford, where students are permitted to design their own academic programs. Her plan was to become a researcher with a medical degree. But this major would require her to earn a medical degree *and* a Ph.D. in research at the same time. To accomplish her goal, she had to alternate between a year of studying medicine and a year studying research. Switching in and out of such diverse disciplines presented great challenges. "With research you always spiral in on a problem; with medicine you can't be so narrow, you must consider all possible causes and results," she explained. Every time she switched rotations, she had to spend the first month adjusting to the change, but she learned to "flip" her brain, a skill that became an asset in her present work. "In medical school thinking, horses are preferable to zebras because horses are more common," she said.[2] A doctor looks for common symptoms and diseases most likely to afflict a patient—as common as a horse. But a researcher seeks the unknown cause or treatment, rare as a zebra. Terri came to think of herself as a zebra doctor—something rarely seen.

In her last year of medical school, Terri wanted to go into neurology. She learned the best program was at Harvard but the only way to get an internship was to do her rotation there. When she met her senior resident at Harvard, Dr. Richard Finkel, she fell in love with him on the spot and was crestfallen when she heard him talking to someone about "my kid." She later learned that "my kid" meant "my patient." They dated until Richard went off to Ethiopia to treat refugees. When he came back, she was interning at Boston Children's Hospital and then returned to Stanford to complete her Ph.D. During that period, Richard and Terri decided to get married.

Their search for a good medical practice for Richard and a challenging residency for Terri led them to Denver, where she took six months to write her doctoral thesis about MYXO bacterial cells, highly evolved bacteria that communicate with each other. At last, she culminated her years of study and went before a committee to defend her thesis, which for many grad students is a traumatic experience. But for Dr. Finkel this process gave her an opportunity to talk with some of the greatest minds in chemistry. She noticed they were asking her opinion, not testing her. At the close of the examination, her advisor, Dr. A. Dale Kaiser (recipient of the Lasker Award, the American equivalent of the Nobel Prize), congratulated her. When she thanked him for his help, he said, "Just do good work." Dr. Arthur Kornberg, a Nobel laureate, came up, hugged her, and told her, "You have become a true biochemist."[3]

Dr. Terri Finkel entered the residency program at the University of Colorado Health Sciences Center in Denver. In 1986, her residency rotated through National Jewish, which ranks high in the world of immunology. There, she worked closely with Drs. John Kappler and Philippa Marrack, both recipients of Columbia University Lasker Awards for their research on the body's immune system. She joined the National Jewish staff in 1990, became division head of pediatric rheumatology in 1992, director of the Stobin Laboratory for Pediatric Research in 1993, and an associate professor at the CU Medical School in 1996.

In a rapid-fire career, Dr. Finkel has researched and made significant discoveries in three areas: cell signaling in T-cell development; viral infection as a trigger of autoimmunity; and cell death in AIDS. Her research focuses around T-cells—the body's protective immune cells—and the immune system. Dr. Finkel likes to watch T-cells in the microscope as they assume various shapes and sizes, sometimes resembling starbursts, then fingers pulling apart as in a kaleidoscope.

She has uncovered a novel T-cell signaling mechanism, a framework or skeleton that the T-cell uses to turn cells "on" and "off." The framework acts as the scaffolding on which "on" signals and "off" signals can anchor themselves and talk to each other. Her discovery could enable scientists to turn T-cells "off" when they wreak havoc by being "on" as in juvenile rheumatoid arthritis or cancer. National Jewish has submitted a patent application for her work.

In an autoimmune response, the body fights its own tissues. Some autoimmune diseases are Lupus (in which all organs are susceptible), rheumatoid arthritis (which affects the joints), and vasculitis (an inflammation of the blood vessels). Research by Dr. Finkel has shown that some common bacteria and viral infections can trigger autoimmunity. Later, the body may appear to be rid of the invading virus, but the virus can leave behind pieces of itself to reproduce. Or the body's immune system *thinks* part of the infection is still there and turns against itself. Infections like colds, flu, or childhood diseases can be the triggers. Dr. Finkel discovered that a usually mild childhood illness, fifth disease (a disease with a rash), can turn into deadly systemic necrotizing vasculitis, which damages blood vessels and surrounding tissues.

She was curious about the relation of infections to vasculitis. A little boy, who had started having problems as a two year old, came to her when he was six. When he was a baby, he was unable to fight off a severe illness. He became so anemic he had to be airlifted to Children's Hospital. Suspecting that a childhood disease involved parvovirus B19, a common childhood infection, Dr. Finkel developed a treatment using intravenous gamma globulin that cured the illness. "New information suggests that the parvovirus B19 hides itself in the body," she said.[4] To find it, she gets blood, bone marrow, and muscle pieces to look for parvovirus B19. But parvovirus can set off rheumatoid arthritis. Dr. Finkel has shown that gamma globulin also is effective in treating some juvenile rheumatoid arthritis.

HIV (human immunodeficiency virus) attacks the helper T-cells, the body's first line of defense, and can develop into AIDS (acquired immune deficiency syndrome), the mysterious disease that cripples the body's disease-fighting mechanisms. AIDS then ushers in pneumonia, a strain of cancer, and now a drug-resistant tuberculosis. Dr. Finkel's laboratory was first to describe a mechanism whereby HIV kills innocent bystander T-cells, thereby immobilizing the body's immune defenses. Her research may help doctors develop medications to inhibit or reverse the death of healthy cells not infected with HIV.

She also was first to demonstrate that T-cells may not die during the invasion of the AIDS virus, but instead become virus factories. Dr.

Finkel calls the HIV research her Trojan horse–Achilles heel theory. The virus factory is the Trojan horse and these factories remain even after long and hard treatment with anti-AIDS drugs. Dr. Finkel is close on the heels of the HIV gene that keeps the virus factory alive—its Achilles heel. Her goal is to make the HIV-infected cells, the Trojan horses, commit suicide, thus eliminating the virus and curing the disease.

Dr. Terri Finkel has received numerous honors for her research and her clinical work treating children with autoimmune diseases. In 1995, she was the only Colorado physician selected by her peers as a "Miracle Maker" because of "her skill, extraordinary care, and dedication." In 1996, she was inducted into the Colorado Women's Hall of Fame. She has published her work in sixty-eight publications, is associate editor of the *Journal of Immunology,* and an editor of the international journal *Apoptosis.* She has received a total of $7 million in grants from sources such as the National Institutes of Health and has been invited to speak before more than a hundred scientific groups.

In July 1998, the University of Pennsylvania invited Dr. Terri Finkel to become the first pediatric rheumatologist to fill its Hollander Chair in pediatric rheumatology at the university's Children's Hospital. This distinguished professorship is the country's only chair in pediatric rheumatology. The family left Colorado for Philadelphia early in 1999.

As Dr. Terri Finkel looks toward the twenty-first century, she has three goals: to find a cure for AIDS; to effect legislation for universal health care; and, with her husband, to raise their own happy, healthy, and productive children.

Notes and Bibliographic Sources

Clara Brown

Notes

1. "Clara ... Still Strong, Vigorous," *Council Bluffs Nonpareil*, March 4, 1882, p. 7, cols. 1–2.

2. Letter from A. G. Rhoads, January 19, 1884, Kathleen Bruyn Papers, Western History Department, Denver Public Library.

3. "Clara Brown Died at Her Home," *Denver Republican*, March 7, 1884, p. 5, col. 3.

4. "Clara Clearly Remembered the War," *Denver Tribune-Republican*, June 26, 1885, p. 2, cols. 1–2.

5. Kathleen Bruyn, *"Aunt" Clara: Story of a Black Pioneer* (Boulder, Colo.: Pruett Publishing, 1970), pp. 190–191.

Sources

Bruyn, Kathleen. *"Aunt" Clara Brown: Story of a Black Pioneer*. Boulder, Colo.: Pruett Publishing, 1970.

Bruyn, Kathleen. Papers, including letters and manuscripts. Western History Department, Denver Public Library.

Byers, William N. *Encyclopedia of Biography of Colorado*, Vol. 1. Chicago: Century Publishing and Engraving, 1901.

Frost, Aaron. "History of Clear Creek County." In *History of Clear Creek and Boulder Counties*. Chicago: Baskin, 1880.

Hafen, LeRoy. *Colorado and Its People*, 4 vols. New York: n.p., 1948.

Rhoads, A. G. Letter dated January 19, 1884. Kathleen Bruyn Papers—Manuscript Collection. Western History Department, Denver Public Library.

Elizabeth Hickok Robbins Stone

Sources

Keays, Elizabeth. Journal of her overland journey to Colorado, ca. 1866. Western History Department, Denver Public Library.

Mumey, Nolie. *The Saga of "Auntie" Stone and Her Cabin*. Boulder, Colo.: Johnson Publishing, 1964.

Peterson, Guy. *The Post and the Town.* Fort Collins: Old Army Press, 1972.

Stone, Elizabeth. Nomination letter by Marilyn Van Brunt Chapmann. Colorado Women's Hall of Fame files. Denver.

Swanson, Evadene Burris. *Fort Collins Yesterdays.* Self-published.

Owl Woman

Notes

1. David Lavender, *Bent's Fort* (Lincoln: University of Nebraska Press, 1954), p. 239.

Sources

Bent, George. Letters and MSS to George Hyde. Western History Department, Denver Public Library.

Hyde, George. *Life of George Bent Written from His Letters.* Norman: University of Oklahoma Press, 1968.

Lavender, David. *Bent's Fort.* Lincoln: University of Nebraska Press, 1954.

Martha Ann Dartt Maxwell

Notes

1. Mary Dartt, *On the Plains, and Among the Peaks, Or, How Mrs. Maxwell Made Her Natural History Collection* (Philadelphia: Claxton, Remsen, and Haffelfinger, 1879), pp. 106–107.

2. Dartt, *On the Plains,* p. 43.

3. Hunt's articles can be found in Helen Hunt Jackson, "Mrs. Maxwell's Museum." Reprinted in *Boulder County News,* June 5, 1874, October 2, 1874, October 15, 1875, December 3, 1875, December 24, 1875, and November 17, 1876; no pp. In Martha Maxwell, clipping file and pamphlet file, Norlin Library, University of Colorado, Boulder.

4. Dartt, *On the Plains,* pp. 118–119.

5. Mabel Maxwell Brace, *Thanks to Abigail: A Family Chronicle* (N.p.: privately printed, 1948), p. 101. As quoted in Maxine Benson, *Martha Maxwell: Rocky Mountain Naturalist* (Lincoln: University of Nebraska Press, 1986), p. 183.

6. Spencer Baird to Nathan Meeker, November 16, 1876, Cullen Collection. Family papers. Mrs. E. Geoffrey, St. Louis, Missouri. As quoted in Benson, *Martha Maxwell,* p. 173.

7. Benson, *Martha Maxwell,* p. 172.

8. Benson, *Martha Maxwell,* p, xiv.

Sources

Barker, Jane Valentine, and Sybil Downing. *Martha Maxwell: Pioneer Naturalist.* Boulder, Colo.: Pruett Publishing, 1982.

Benson, Maxine. *Martha Maxwell: Rocky Mountain Naturalist.* Lincoln: University of Nebraska Press, 1986.

Dartt, Mary. *On the Plains, and Among the Peaks, or, How Mrs. Maxwell Made Her Natural History Collection.* Philadelphia: Claxton, Remsen, and Haffelfinger, 1879.

Jackson, Helen Hunt. "Mrs. Maxwell's Museum." Reprinted in *Boulder County News,* June 5, 1874, October 2, 1874, October 15, 1875, December 3, 1875, December 24, 1875, November 17, 1876. In Martha Maxwell, Clipping file and pamphlet file. Norlin Library, University of Colorado, Boulder.

Robertson, Janet. *The Magnificent Mountain Women.* Lincoln: University of Nebraska Press, 1990.

Schooland, John B. "Mrs. Maxwell's Museum." In *Boulder in Perspective.* Boulder, Colo.: Johnson Publishing, 1980.

Helen Fiske Hunt Jackson

Notes

1. Polly Kemp, "Early Author Was a Woman for Her Time," *Denver Post,* December 28, 1985, pp. 1C–4C.

2. As quoted in Marshall Sprague, *Newport in the Rockies* (Denver: Sage Books, 1961), p. 74.

Sources

Bueler, Gladys R. *Colorado's Colorful Characters.* Golden, Colo.: Smoking Stack Press, 1975.

Jackson, Helen Hunt. Papers. MS of Ramona plus 17 boxes of HHJ memorabilia. Colorado Springs Public Library.

Jackson, Helen Hunt. *Ramona.* Boston: Little Brown, 1932.

McClurg, Virginia. "Helen Hunt Jackson" (manuscript, 1891). Helen Hunt Jackson Collection. Starsmore Center, Colorado Springs Pioneers Museum.

Sprague, Marshall. *Newport in the Rockies.* Denver: Sage Books, 1961.

Wilcox, Rhoda. Biographical sketches of Helen Hunt Jackson (1830–1885) and William Sharpless Jackson (1836–1919) (manuscript, September 1965). Helen Hunt Jackson Collection. Starsmore Center, Colorado Springs Pioneers Museum.

Isabella Bird

Notes

1. Isabella Bird, *A Lady's Life in the Rocky Mountains* (Sausalito, Calif.: Comstock Press, 1960), p. 75.
2. Bird, *A Lady's Life,* p. 8 (note 3).
3. Bird, *A Lady's Life,* p. 102.
4. Bird, *A Lady's Life,* p. xviii.
5. Bird, *A Lady's Life,* p. xiv and xviii.

Sources

Bird, Isabella. *A Lady's Life in the Rocky Mountains.* Sausalito, Calif.: Comstock Press, 1980. (Originally published in London by J. Murray, 1899.)
Bird, Isabella. *The Yangtze Valley and Beyond.* Sausalito, Calif.: Comstock Press, 1980. (Originally published in London by J. Murray, 1879.)

Augusta Louise Pierce Tabor

Notes

1. Alice Polk Hill, *Tales of the Colorado Pioneers* (Denver: Pierson & Gardner, 1884), p. 218.
2. Betty Moynihan, *Augusta Tabor: A Pioneering Woman* (Evergreen, Colo.: Cordillera Press, 1988).
3. Hill, *Tales of the Colorado Pioneers,* p. 222.
4. Hill, *Tales of the Colorado Pioneers,* p. 222–223.
5. Caroline Bancroft, *Augusta Tabor: Her Side of the Scandal,* 7th ed. (Boulder, Colo.: Johnson Publishing, 1972), p. 11.

Sources

Bancroft, Caroline. *Augusta Tabor: Her Side of the Scandal,* 7th ed. Boulder, Colo.: Johnson Publishing, 1972.
Hill, Alice Polk. *Tales of the Colorado Pioneers.* Denver: Pierson & Gardner, 1884.
Moynihan, Betty. *Augusta Tabor: A Pioneering Woman.* Evergreen, Colo.: Cordillera Press, 1988.
Perkin, Robert L. *The First Hundred Years.* Garden City, N.Y.: Doubleday, 1959.
Sherr, Lynn, and Jurate Kazickas. *Susan B. Anthony Slept Here: A Guide to American Women's Landmarks.* New York: Random House, 1994.
Smith, Duane A. *Horace Tabor: His Life and the Legend.* Niwot, Colo.: University Press of Colorado, 1989.
Tabor, Augusta. "Cabin Life in Colorado." *Colorado Magazine,* 1927, 1959. Bancroft Library, Berkeley, Calif.

Caroline ("Kate") Nichols Churchill

Notes

1. C. M. Churchill, *Active Footsteps* (Colorado Springs, Colo.: self-published, 1909), p. 80.

2. Churchill, *Active Footsteps*, pp. 82, 84.

3. Churchill, *Active Footsteps*, p. 89.

4. Churchill, *Active Footsteps*, p. 106.

5. Robert Athearn, *The Coloradans* (Albuquerque: University of New Mexico Press, 1976), p. 163.

6. Churchill, *Active Footsteps*, p. 81.

Sources

Athearn, Robert G. *The Coloradans*. Albuquerque: University of New Mexico Press, 1976.

Churchill, C. N. *Active Footsteps*. Colorado Springs, Colo.: self-published, 1909.

Churchill, C. N. Nomination letter by Walter and Elma Stewart. Colorado Women's Hall of Fame files. Denver.

Churchill, Mrs. C. M. Editor and publisher. Complete runs of *Colorado Antelope* and *Queen Bee*. Microfilms. Stephen H. Hart Library, Colorado Historical Society. Denver.

"Churchill, Mrs. C. M., Editor and publisher, *Queen Bee*." In *N. W. Ayer & Sons Newspaper Annual*. Detroit, Mich.: Gale Research, 1880–.

Leonard, Stephen J. "Bristling for Their Rights—Colorado's Women and the Mandate of 1893." *Colorado Heritage*, Spring 1993: 9.

McMurtrie, Douglas C. "*Queen Bee*." In *Early Printing in Colorado*. Denver: Hirschfeld Press, 1935.

Schwartzkopff, Nancy. "A Salute to Women in Colorado's History; Pioneer Publishers Wrote Book on Ambition, Achievement." *Colorado Woman News*, March 1995: 11.

Writers Program, "Colorado Journalism in Denver—Newspaper Personalities." Stephen H. Hart Library, Colorado Historical Society. Denver.

Chipeta

Notes

1. P. David Smith, *Ouray, Chief of the Utes* (Ouray, Colo.: Wayfinder Press, 1986), p. 134, 162–166.

2. Eugene Field, "Chipeta," in Charles Harmon Leckenby, *The Tread of Pioneers* (Steamboat Springs: Pilot Press, 1945), pp. 34–36.

Sources

Byers, William N. *Encyclopedia of Biography of Colorado.* Vol. 1. Chicago: Century Publishing and Engraving, 1901.

"Chipeta, Queen of the Utes." *Utah Historical Quarterly,* vol. 6 (1933): 103.

Daughters of Utah Pioneers. *Heart Throbs of the West.* Vol. 1. Salt Lake City, n.p., 1939.

Field, Eugene. "Chipeta." In Charles Harmon Leckenby, *The Tread of Pioneers.* Steamboat Springs: Pilot Press, 1945.

Jefferson, James, Robert W. Delaney, and Gregory C. Thompson. *The Southern Utes: A Tribal History.* Ignacio, Colo.: Southern Ute Tribe, 1972.

Monaghan, J. Interview of Cato Sells, government Indian commissioner, and others for information about Chipeta's last years in Utah. Stephen H. Hart Library, Colorado Historical Society. Denver.

Pettit, Jan. *Utes: The Mountain People.* Boulder: Johnson Books, 1990.

Smith, P. David. *Ouray, Chief of the Utes.* Ouray, Colo.: Wayfinder Press, 1986.

Stacher, S. F. "Ouray and the Utes." *Colorado Magazine,* vol. 27: 134–140.

Frances Wisebart Jacobs

Notes

1. Ida Uchill, *Pioneers, Peddlers, and Tsadikim* (Denver: Sage Books, 1957), pp. 80, 104.

Sources

"Death of Mrs. Jacobs" and biographical sketch. *The Coloradan,* November 15, 1892: 4–5.

Hornbein, Marjorie. "Frances Jacobs: Denver's Mother of Charities." *Western States Jewish Historical Quarterly,* vol. 15 (January 2, 1983): 16–19.

Jacobs, Abram, obituary. *The Trail,* vol. 5, no. 10 (May 1913): 28.

"Jacobs, Frances." *Webster's Dictionary of American Women.* New York: Smithmark, 1996. Pp. 309–310.

Jacobs, Frances Wisebart. Memoir. F. W. Jacobs Collection. Western History Department, Denver Public Library.

Semple, J. A. "Pioneer of 1863." *Representative Women Biography.* Denver: Alexander Art Publishing, 1911.

Smiley, Jerome. *History of Denver.* Denver: Old Americana Publishing, 1901.

Uchill, Ida. *Pioneers, Peddlers, and Tsadikim.* Denver: Sage Books, 1957.

Mary Rippon

Notes

1. Karen Whitehair, talk given in Boulder, Colo., February 21, 1988.
2. Whitehair, talk.
3. Quoted in Terry Byrne, *Flatirons*, May 1974, p. 33.
4. Silvia Pettem, "A Forbidden Love," *Rocky Mountain News*, October 5, 1997, p. 8F.
5. Pettem, "A Forbidden Love," p. 8F.

Sources

Burger, Leslie. "Boulder's Restless Past: Digging Up the Dirt at Pioneer Cemetery." *Boulder Magazine*, September 1988: 15, 16.

Byrne, Terry. "Two Boulder Women." *Flatirons*, vol. 2, no. 1 (May 1974): 20–26.

McClurg, Kathy "Mary, Mary, Extraordinary." *Summit Magazine*, Winter 1987: 12, 13.

Pettem, Silvia. *Separate Lives: The Story of Mary Rippon*. Longmont: self-published, 1999.

Rippon, Mary. Nomination biography. Colorado Women's Hall of Fame files. Denver.

Rippon, Mary. Papers and letters. Norlin Library, University of Colorado, Boulder.

Smith, Mary Kaye. "The Secret Life of CU's Mary Rippon." *Colorado Daily*, May 16, 1996: 10, 11.

Elizabeth Nellis McCourt Doe Tabor ("Baby Doe")

Notes

1. Birth and death dates from the card catalog of the Western History Department, Denver Public Library, and also the *Denver Post*, March 8, 1935, p. 1. At some point Baby Doe changed her middle name from Nellis to Bonduel.
2. Donald Menzel, letter dated April 25, 1973, to Colorado Historical Society. Baby Doe Tabor file. Stephen H. Hart Library, Colorado Historical Society. Denver

Sources

Bancroft, Caroline. "The Belle of Oshkosh." In *Westerners 1953 Brand Book*. Denver: Westerners Denver Posse, 1954.

Hart, Patrick. Interview by author. 1975.

Leonard, Stephen J., and Thomas Noel. *Denver: Mining Camp to Metropolis*. Niwot, Colo.: University Press of Colorado, 1990.

Parkhill, Forbes. "How Tabor Lost His Millions." In *Westerners 1953 Brand Book.* Denver: Westerners Denver Posse, 1954.

Perkin, Robert L. *The First Hundred Years.* Garden City, N.Y.: Doubleday, 1959.

Smiley, Jerome. *History of Denver.* Denver: Old Americana Publishing, 1901.

Smith, Duane A. *Horace Tabor: His Life and the Legend.* Niwot, Colo.: University Press of Colorado, 1989.

Mary Hauck Elitch Long

Notes

1. Caroline L. Dier, *Lady of the Gardens* (Hollywood: Hollycrofters, 1932), pp. 45–46.

Sources

Dier, Caroline Laurence. *Lady of the Gardens.* Hollywood: Hollycrofters, 1932.

Dorsett, Lyle W. *The Queen City: A History of Denver.* Boulder, Colo.: Pruett Publishing, 1977.

Hunt, Corinne, and Jack Gurtler. *The Elitch Garden Story: Memories of Jack Gurtler.* Boulder, Colo.: Rocky Mountain Writers Production, 1982.

Long, Mary Elitch. "Memories of Elitch's Gardens Music," *The Echo,* May 1926. Fine Arts Department, Denver Public Library.

Long, Mary Elitch. Nomination letter. Colorado Women's Hall of Fame files. Denver.

Sarah Sophia Chase Platt-Decker

Notes

1. "Mrs. Decker Is Dead. End Comes Suddenly and Quietly … ," *Rocky Mountain News,* July 7, 1912, p. 1.

2. Ellis Meredith, "Mrs. Decker One Woman Who Could Enjoy Joke Turned on Herself," *Rocky Mountain News,* July 8, 1912, p. 3.

3. "Tribute to Memory of Mrs. Decker," *Rocky Mountain News,* July 8, 1912, p. 3.

4. "Tribute to Memory."

5. "Mrs. Decker One Woman," p. 3.

Sources

Conine, Martha A. Bushnell. Scrapbook, ca. 1896–1910. Western History Department, Denver Public Library.

Mary Florence Lathrop

Notes

1. Elinor Bluemel, "Mary Lathrop: Lawyer," in *One Hundred Years of Colorado Women* (Denver: self-published, 1973), p. 42.

Sources

Bluemel, Elinor. *One Hundred Years of Colorado Women*. Denver: self-published, 1973.

Melrose, Frances. "Mary Lathrop Thrived as a Woman of Firsts." In *Rocky Mountain Memories*. Denver: Denver Publishing, 1986.

Pohle, Linda. "That Damn Woman: Mary Florence Lathrop." In *The Denver Woman's Press Club: The Women Who Made the Headlines*. Lakewood: Western Guideways, 1998.

Margaret ("Molly") Tobin Brown

Notes

1. "Society at the Opera and Slaves' Ball," *Denver Times*, December 9, 1900, p. 8.

2. "Catholic Fair Promises to Be a Great Event," *Denver Times*, November 4, 1900, p. 8; "Society at the Opera," *Denver Times*, November 4, 1900, p. 2.

3. "All the World Visited the Catholic Fair," *Denver Times*, November 25, 1900, p. 8.

4. "On Ismay, Speedmad, Rests Blame for *Titanic* Horror," *Denver Times*, April 30, 1912, p. 1.

5. "*Titanic* Heroine at Last Breaks into the 'Sacred 36,'" *Denver Times*, May 1, 1912, p. 1.

Sources

Bancroft, Caroline. *The Unsinkable Mrs. Brown*, 8th ed. Boulder, Colo.: Johnson Publishing, 1963.

Brown, Lawrence. Family papers and correspondence (Box C, files 1, 14, 34). Stephen H. Hart Library, Colorado Historical Society. Denver.

Forbes, Malcolm. *Women Who Made a Difference*. New York: Simon & Schuster, 1990.

Goodstein, Phil. *Denver's Capitol Hill*. Denver: Stuart McPhail, 1988.

Grinstead, Leigh. Director, Molly Brown House Museum. Interview by author. August 1998. Denver.

Hafen, LeRoy. *Colorado: The Story of a Western Commonwealth.* Denver: Peerless Publishing, 1933.

Halaas, David F. "The Many Facets of Molly Brown." *Colorado History Now* (Colorado Historical Society Newsletter), January 1998: 3, 8.

Iversen, Kristen. *Molly Brown: Unraveling the Myth.* Boulder: Johnson Books, 1999.

Melrose, Frances. "Molly Brown Found Field Quite Unsinkable." In *Rocky Mountain Memories.* Denver: Denver Publishing, 1986.

Morris, Langdon. *Denver Landmarks.* Denver: Charles W. Cleworth, 1979.

Shafroth, Morrison. Papers (Boxes 18, 33-8). Western History Department, Denver Public Library.

Smiley, Jerome. *History of Denver.* Denver: Old Americana Publishing, 1901.

Stout, Mark. "The Unsinkable Lady of Capitol Hill," *Life on Capitol Hill.* Part 1, October 1994: 11; Part 2, November 1994: 13, 16. Denver Woman's Press Club archives.

Whitacre, Christine. *Molly Brown: Denver's Unsinkable Lady.* Denver: Historic Denver, 1984.

Emily Griffith

Sources

Bluemel, Elinor. "Emily Griffith and the Emily Griffith Opportunity School." *In One Hundred Years of Colorado Women.* Denver: self-published, 1973.

Griffith, Emily. Clippings and chronological biography ("Emily Griffith and the Opportunity School"). Western History Department, Denver Public Library.

Huffman, Yale. "Prairie Pluck: The Mission of Emily Griffith." Sunday *World Herald Magazine of the Midlands,* February 21, 1988, pp. 38–39.

Justina Ford

Notes

1. Mark Harris, "The Forty Years of Justina Ford," *Negro Digest,* March 1950, pp. 43–45.

2. Matthew Soergel, "Group Honors Black Pioneer," *Rocky Mountain News,* June 13, 1989, p. 10.

3. Victoria Cooper, "The Baby Doctor: Legendary Five Points Obstetrician Brought 7,000 Youngsters into the World," *Rocky Mountain News,* February 22, 1988, p. 67.

4. "Dr. Justina Ford Honored as First Black Female Physician in Colorado," *Colorado Medicine* 15 (February 1989): 60.

5. Harris, "Forty Years," p. 45.

6. Magdalena Gallegos, "Dr. Justina Ford: A Medical Legacy Continues," *Urban Spectrum*, September 1988: 5.

7. Diana Griego, "Home to Honor Black Heritage," *Denver Post*, November 24, 1987, p. B1.

Sources

"Dr. Justina Ford Honored as First Black Female Physician in Colorado." *Colorado Medicine* 15 (February 1989): 60.

Gallegos, Magdalena. "Dr. Justina Ford: A Medical Legacy Continues." *Urban Spectrum*, September 1988: 4–5.

Harris, Mark. "The Forty Years of Justina Ford." *Negro Digest*, March 1950: 43–45.

Smith, Jessie Carney, ed. "Justina L. Ford, Physician, Humanitarian." In *Notable Black American Women*, Book 2. Detroit: Gale Research, 1996.

Florence Rena Sabin

Notes

1. "Acceptance of the Statue of Dr. Florence Rena Sabin." Presented by the State of Colorado to 85th Congress of the United States in 1959. Senate Document No. 132. (Washington, D.C.: Government Printing Office, 1959), p. 16.

2. "Teacher, Physician Dies at 81," *Denver Post*, October 4, 1953, pp. 1A, 2A.

Sources

"Acceptance of the Statue of Dr. Florence Rena Sabin." Presented by the State of Colorado to 85th Congress of the United States. Senate Document No. 132. Washington, D.C.: Government Printing Office, 1959. Western History Department, Denver Public Library.

Bluemel, Elinor. "Dr. Florence Rena Sabin: Woman with Two Careers." In *One Hundred Years of Colorado Women*. Denver: self-published, 1973.

Downing, Sybil, and Jane Barker. *Florence Rena Sabin: Pioneer Scientist*. Boulder, Colo.: Pruett Publishing, 1981.

Monnett, John H., and Michael McCarthy. *Colorado Profiles*. Evergreen, Colo.: Cordillera Press, 1987.

Perkin, Robert L. *The First Hundred Years*. Garden City, N.Y.: Doubleday, 1959.

Sabin, Florence Rena. Files and documents. Stephen H. Hart Library, Colorado Historical Society. Denver.

Sabin, Florence Rena. Nomination letter and files. Colorado Women's Hall of Fame files. Denver.

Sherr, Lynn, and Jurate Kazickas. *Susan B. Anthony Slept Here: A Guide to American Women's Landmarks*. New York: Random House, 1994.

Edwina Hume Fallis

Notes

1. Edwina Hume Fallis, *When Denver and I Were Young* (Denver: Big Mountain Press, 1956), pp. 87–88.

Sources

"Edwina Fallis." *Colorado Genealogist,* vol. 9, no. 3.

Fallis, Edwina. Biography. Denver Woman's Press Club archives. Undated.

Fallis, Edwina. "Tell Me a Story." *Page* (newsletter of the Denver Woman's Press Club), June 1941. Denver Woman's Press Club archives.

Fallis, Edwina. "Write It Down." *Page* (newsletter of the Denver Woman's Press Club), June 1941. Denver Woman's Press Club archives.

Fallis, Edwina Hume. *When Denver and I Were Young.* Denver: Big Mountain Press, 1956.

The Bonfils Sisters

Notes

1. Patricia Wilcox, "The Last of the Victorians," in *Seventy-Six Stories of Lakewood* (Lakewood, Colo.: Lakewood Centennial-Bicentennial Commission, 1976), p. 82.

May Bonfils Stanton

Sources

Barnes, Maxine. "May Bonfils Berryman Stanton." Unpublished manuscript. April 8, 1988. Lakewood's Historical Belmar Village.

Noel, Thomas, and Barbara S. Norgren. "The May Stanton House." In *Denver: The City Beautiful.* Denver: Historic Denver, 1987.

Ondrusek, Betty Stouffer. Interview by author. Telephone. Fall 1997.

Stanton, May Bonfils. Collection and clippings. Stephen H. Hart Library, Colorado Historical Society. Denver.

Wilcox, Patricia. "The Last of the Victorians." In *Seventy-six Stories of Lakewood.* Lakewood, Colo.: Lakewood Centennial-Bicentennial Commission, 1976. Also, author's interview with Mrs. Wilcox for recollections of Belmar.

Helen Bonfils

Notes

1. Betty Stouffer Ondrusek, telephone interview by author, Fall 1997.
2. Ondrusek, interview.
3. Cleo Parker Robinson, interview by author, Denver, October 6, 1997.
4. Hornby, Bill. "New owners acquire colorful heritage ..." editorial, *Denver Post*, December 1, 1987.
5. Lester Ward, telephone interview by author, 1997.

Sources

Dorsett, Lyle W. *The Queen City: A History of Denver.* Boulder, Colo.: Pruett Publishing, 1977.

Goodstein, Phil. *Denver's Capitol Hill.* Denver: Stuart McPhail, 1988.

Goodstein, Phil. *Ghosts of Denver.* Denver: New Social Publications, 1996.

Leonard, Stephen J., and Thomas Noel. *Denver: Mining Camp to Metropolis.* Niwot, Colo.: University Press of Colorado, 1990.

Ondrusek, Betty Stouffer. Interview by author. Telephone. Fall 1997.

Perkin, Robert L. *The First Hundred Years.* Garden City, N.Y.: Doubleday, 1959.

Unsatisfied Man (Denver Colorado Media Project; quarterly), June 1972 (vol. 2, no. 10): 7, 8.

Ward, Lester. Interview by author. Telephone. 1997.

Josephine Aspenwall Roche

Notes

1. Marjorie Barrett, "She Fuels an Historic Era ... ," *Rocky Mountain News,* April 20, 1975, p. 15.

Sources

Bluemel, Elinor. "Josephine Roche." In *One Hundred Years of Colorado Women.* Denver: self-published, 1973.

Dorsett, Lyle W. *The Queen City: A History of Denver.* Boulder, Colo.: Pruett Publishing, 1977.

Halaas, David F. "Josephine Roche, 1886–1976: Social Reformer." *Colorado Heritage News,* March 1985.

Monnett, John H., and Michael McCarthy. "Josephine Roche." In *Colorado Profiles.* Evergreen, Colo.: Cordillera Press, 1987.

Perkin, Robert L. *The First Hundred Years.* Garden City, N.Y.: Doubleday, 1959.

Roche, Josephine Aspenwall. Biography. Colorado Women's Hall of Fame files. Denver.

"Rocky Mountain Fuel Company." Typescript. Morrison Shafroth Collection, Box 33. Western History Department, Denver Public Library.

Smith, Phyllis. "She could stop a row or riot." *Colorado Daily*, February 16, 1983, pp. 11, 12.

Eudochia Bell Smith

Notes

*Senator Smith's first name is sometimes spelled *Eudocia*. Her obituary said she was born in 1887; LeRoy Hafen in *Colorado and Its People* states 1889; and she submitted the year 1891 to the Colorado Historical Society. All agree on September 9. Perhaps, like Emily Griffith, she shaved her age two years at a time.

1. "Woman Became Legislator in Seeking Aid," *Denver Catholic Register,* October 15, 1942, pp. 1, 6.

2. Eudochia Bell Smith, *They Ask Me Why* (Denver: World Press, 1945), p. 8.

3. Smith, *They Ask Me Why,* p. 20.

4. Smith, *They Ask Me Why,* p. 20, 21.

5. Smith, *They Ask Me Why,* pp. 34, 35.

Sources

Hafen, Le Roy, "Eudochia Bell Smith" and "Joseph Emerson Smith." In *Colorado and Its People: A Narrative and Topical History of the Centennial State,* Personal and Family History. New York: Lewis Historical Publishing, 1948, vol. 3: 12–13; vol. 4: 673.

Smith, Eudochia. Biographical clippings. Stephen H. Hart Library, Colorado Historical Society. Denver.

Smith, Eudochia B. *They Ask Me Why.* Denver: World Press, 1945. (A copy of this book is in the Stephen H. Hart Library, Colorado Historical Society, Denver.)

Hazel Marguerite Schmoll

Notes

1. Jane Cracraft, "At Home in the High Country," *Denver Post*, May 14, 1967, p. 6.

2. Cracraft, "At Home," p. 7.

Sources

Robertson, Janet. *The Magnificent Mountain Women.* Lincoln: University of Nebraska Press, 1990.

Schmoll, Hazel. Autobiography. Colorado Women's Hall of Fame files. Denver.

Schmoll, Hazel. Papers and typescript.The Boulder Historical Collection of the Carnegie Branch Library for Local History. Boulder.

Wolle, Muriel Sibell. "Caribou" and "Ward." In *Stampede to Timberline*. Boulder: n.p., 1949.

Helen Marie Black

Notes

1. James Bailey, "Notes of Turmoil: Sixty Years of Denver's Symphony Orchestras," *Colorado Heritage,* Autumn 1992: 45.

2. Bill Husted, "Helen Black Set Tone of Elegance," *Rocky Mountain News Sunday Magazine,* February 14, 1988: n.p.

3. Editorial, *Denver Post,* February 2, 1988, p. 4B.

Sources

Bailey, James Michael. "Notes of Turmoil: Sixty Years of Denver's Symphony Orchestras," *Colorado Heritage,* Autumn 1992: 33–47.

Black, Helen Marie. Clipping files and collection. Stephen H. Hart Library, Colorado Historical Society. Denver.

Black, Helen Marie. Denver Woman's Press Club archives.

Black, Helen Marie. Papers and taped interviews. Rare Books and Special Collections, University of Wyoming. Laramie.

Black, Helen Marie. History of the Denver Symphony Orchestra. Typescript, 7 pp. Denver Woman's Press Club archives.

Brown, Edith. "A Tribute to the Music Lady." *Senior Edition,* October 1983: 22, 28.

Melrose, Frances. "Mint Robber Tripped on Hollow Leg Scheme." In *Rocky Mountain Memories.* Denver: Denver Publishing, 1986.

Parce, Gladys. "Everyone Asks Helen Black for Advice … ," *Colorado Editor,* June 1948: 6.

Parce, Gladys. Rough outline of Helen Black's biography. Typescript, 12 pp. Denver Woman's Press Club archives.

Quigley, Pat. "An Interview with Helen Marie Black, 'I Thought I Could.'" Typescript, 11 pp. Denver Woman's Press Club archives.

Mamie Doud Eisenhower

Notes

1. "Ike's Widow Dies in Sleep," *Denver Post,* November 1, 1979, p. 1.

2. "First Lady's First Term," *Newsweek,* May 28, 1956, p. 31.

Sources

Brandon, Dorothy. *Mamie Doud Eisenhower: A Portrait of a First Lady.* New York: Charles Scribner's Sons, 1954.

Eisenhower, Mamie Doud. B file. Stephen H. Hart Library, Colorado Historical Society. Denver.

Eisenhower, Mamie Doud. Clipping file. Stephen H. Hart Library, Colorado Historical Society. Denver.

Goodstein, Phil. *Denver's Capitol Hill.* Denver: Stuart McPhail, 1988.

Goodstein, Phil. *Ghosts of Denver.* Denver: New Social Publications, 1996.

Hatch, Alden. *Red Carpet for Mamie.* New York: Henry Holt, 1954.

Summersby, Kay. *Eisenhower Was My Boss.* New York: Prentice Hall, 1948.

Tully, Andrew. "Ike and Mamie at Home." *Collier's,* June 20, 1953, p. 15.

Golda Mabovitch Meir

Notes

1. Golda Meir, *My Life* (New York: Dell, 1975), p. 42.

2. Meir, *My Life,* p. 43.

3. Meir, *My Life,* pp. 45, 66.

4. Mike Patty, "Golda Meir Museum Dedicated," *Rocky Mountain News,* July 28, 1998.

Sources

Meir, Golda. *My Life.* New York: Dell, 1975.

Strauss, Esther Cohen. Interview by author. September 25, 1998. Denver.

Margaret Taylor Curry

Sources

Curry, Margaret Taylor. Nomination letter by Rosalie J. Lay. Colorado Women's Hall of Fame files. Denver.

Lay, Rosalie J. Interview by author. No date. Lakewood, Colo.

Frances Mary McConnell-Mills

Notes

1. Frances McConnell-Mills, unpublished memoirs, author's collection.

2. McConnell-Mills, memoirs.

3. Undated clipping, Frances McConnell-Mills's scrapbook, author's collection.

4. Personal communication.

Sources

Collier, Helen McConnell. Interview by author. Denver, 1994.

Cummings, J. Hoyt. "Solving Colorado's Triangle of Death." *Real Detective,* Fall 1945: 34–37, 64–67.

Humphreys, Ray. "The Pearl O'Loughlin Case." In *Denver Murders,* edited by Lee Casey. New York: Duell, Sloan and Pearce, 1946.

Lowall, Gene. "The Spider Man." In *Denver Murders,* edited by Lee Casey. New York: Duell, Sloan and Pearce, 1946.

McConnell-Mills, David. Interview by author. Lubbock, Texas, 1995.

McConnell-Mills, Frances. Listings in *International Who's Who in World Medicine.* New York: American Universities Research Publications, 1947; *Who's Who in the West.* Chicago: Marquis Who's Who, 1949–; and *Who's Who in Colorado,* edited by Daniel T. Valdes. Denver: 1958.

McConnell-Mills, Frances. Obituary. *Rocky Mountain Medical Journal,* March–April 1976: 113.

McConnell-Mills, Frances. Unpublished memoirs. Author's collection.

Caroline Bancroft

Notes

1. Olga Curtis, "The Battling Historians," *Denver Post Empire,* January 16, 1972, p. 14.

2. Sandra Widener, "A Walk Through History with Caroline Bancroft," *Denver Post Magazine,* May 19, 1985, p. 14.

3. Letter to the Editor, Leadville *Herald Democrat,* July 9, 1957 (and subsequent issues for responses).

4. Patricia Wilcox, interview by author, Lakewood, Colo., 1997.

5. Patricia Wilcox, interview.

Sources

Bancroft, Caroline. Collection. Western History Department, Denver Public Library.

Dallas, Sandra. Let's remember the real Caroline Bancroft. *Denver Post,* October 29, 1985, p. 22D.

Griggs, Marilyn. "Caroline Bancroft: Portrait of a Popular Historian." *The Center Programme* (publication of Denver Center of Performing Arts), August 1977 (vol. 2, no. 10): 4–9.

Wilcox, Patricia. Interview by author. Lakewood, Colo., 1997.

Antonia Brico

Notes

1. Gerald A. Elliot, "Success Didn't Come Easy for Conductor," *Grand Rapids Press*, February 22, 1978, p. 6C.

2. "Antonia Brico," in *There Was Light*, edited by Irving Stone (New York: Doubleday, 1970).

3. Joanna Palacas, interview by author, Lakewood, Colo., Summer 1997 and Summer 1998.

4. Palacas, interview.

5. Palacas, interview.

Sources

Brico, Antonia. "Antonia Brico." In *There Was Light*, edited by Irving Stone. New York: Doubleday, 1970.

Brico, Antonia. Papers and clipping file, 1945–1962. Stephen H. Hart Library, Colorado Historical Society.

Brico, Antonia. Listing in *Who's Who in America*. Chicago: Marquis Who's Who, 1900–.

Brico Symphony scrapbooks and correspondence with J. Sibelius, 1948–1982. Western History Department, Denver Public Library.

Frandsen, Betty. Interview by author. Jefferson County, Colo., Summer 1997.

Palacas, Joanna. Interview by author. Lakewood, Colo., Summer 1997 and Summer 1998.

"Renowned Conductor Brico Dies in Rest Home at Age 87." *Denver Post*, August 4, 1989, pp. 1B, 8B.

Mary Coyle Chase

Notes

1. Frances Melrose, "She Pulled a Million-Dollar Rabbit Out of Her Hat," in *The Women Who Made the Headlines*, edited by Nancy Peterson and Clé Cervi (Denver: Denver Woman's Press Club, 1998), p. 53.

2. Mark Barron, "Mary Chase Doesn't Act Part of Broadway Playwright," *Rocky Mountain News*, October 26, 1952, p. 48.

3. Barbara MacKay, "Mary Chase: Colorado's Lady of the Theater," *Bravo*, 1981, p. 19. Colorado Women's Hall of Fame files. Denver.

4. MacKay, "Mary Chase," p. 17.

5. Barron, "Mary Chase," p. 48.

Sources

Chase, Mary Coyle. Biographical information. *Bravo,* December 1981 (vol. 5, no. 12), p. 20.

Chase, Mary Coyle. Collection. Western History Department, Denver Public Library.

Coyle, Mary Chase. Letters to Caroline Bancroft. Bancroft Collection. Western History Department, Denver Public Library.

Harris, Eleanor. "Mary Chase: Success Almost Ruined Her." *Cosmopolitan,* February 1954: 99–104.

MacKay, Barbara. "Mary Chase: Colorado's Lady of the Theater." *Bravo,* 1981, p. 14. Colorado Women's Hall of Fame files. Denver.

"My Life with Harvey." *McCall's Magazine,* February 1951, pp. 53–54. Mary Coyle Chase clipping file. Western History Department, Denver Public Library.

Melrose, Frances. "Mary Chase, Colorado's Pulitzer Winner, Dies." *Rocky Mountain News,* October 21, 1981, p. 7.

Melrose, Frances, "She Pulled a Million-Dollar Rabbit Out of Her Hat." In *The Women Who Made the Headlines,* edited by Nancy Peterson and Clé Cervi. Denver: Denver Woman's Press Club, 1998.

Reef, Wallis M. "She Didn't Do It for Money, She Says." In *More Post Biographies,* edited by John E. Drewry. Athens: University of Georgia Press, 1947.

Jane Silverstein Ries

Notes

1. Robin Chotzinoff, "A Ripe Old Age; Sixty Years After Landscape Architecture School, Jane Silverstein Ries' Career Is in Full Flower," *Westword,* July 15, 1992, pp. 26, 29.

2. Julia Andrews-Jones, interview by author, Golden, Colo., June 27, 1997.

3. Andrews-Jones, interview.

4. Jane S. Ries, video interview for Colorado Chapter of American Society of Landscape Architects, 1989.

5. Ries, video interview.

6. Ries, video interview.

Sources

Andrews-Jones, Julia. Interview with author. Golden, Colo., June 27, 1997, and November 1998.

"Professional History of Jane Silverstein Ries, 1932–1982." Colorado Women's Hall of Fame files. Denver.

Ries, Jane Silverstein. Clipping file. Western History Department, Denver Public Library.

Ries, Jane Silverstein. Colorado Women's Hall of Fame files. Denver.

Ries, Jane Silverstein. Video interview by Colorado Chapter of the American Society of Landscape Architects, Denver, 1989.

Young, Barbara. Interview by author. Golden, Colo., June 27, 1997.

Genevieve D'Amato Fiore

Notes

1. Genevieve D'Amato Fiore, interview by author, Denver, June 10, 1997.
2. Fiore, interview.

Sources

Fiore, Genevieve. Interview by author. Denver, June 10, 1997.

Fiore, Genevieve D'Amato. Fiore Collection (papers, clipping file, trophies, awards; 156 boxes). Archives and Special Collections Department. Auraria Library. Denver.

Malkinson, Lynn. "Very Important Woman." Intermountain Jewish News, January 22, 1982, p. 10.

Oleta Lawanda Crain

Notes

1. Oleta Lawanda Crain, interview by author, Denver, June 17, 1997, and May 1998.
2. Crain, interview.
3. Crain, interview; and military biography of Oleta Lawanda Crain.

Sources

Cottman, Vaughn. "A Salute to Women in the Military." *Urban Spectrum,* November 1988: 4–5.

Crain, Oleta Lawanda. Interview by author. Denver, June 17, 1997, and May 1998.

Crain, Oleta Lawanda. Nomination letter and file. Colorado Women's Hall of Fame files. Denver.

Crain, Oleta Lawanda. Military biography, September 1942–June 1963. In author's possession.

"Oleta Crain Named to Colorado Women's Hall of Fame," *CTAC* (publication of Colorado Technical Assistance Center, Pikes Peak Community College, Colorado Springs), Fall 1988: 2.

Jean Jolliffe Yancey

Notes

1. Jean Yancey, interview by author, Denver, May 28, 1997.

2. Yancey, interview.

3. Marty Meitus, "Helping Businesswomen Earns White House Honor for Modern-day Grandma," *Rocky Mountain News*, February 11, 1982, Lifestyles section, p. 16S.

4. Yancey, interview.

Sources

Silvas, Sharon. "Profile: Jean Yancey—The Mother of Women Entrepreneurs— Celebrates 80th Birthday." *Modern Woman*, August 1994.

Spitzer, Judith. "Mentor Jean Yancey Looks Back, Looks Forward, and Looks Within." *Torch*, November 1994: 1.

Yancey, Jean. Clipping file. Western History Department, Denver Public Library.

Yancey, Jean. Interview by author. Denver, May 28, 1997; and by phone July 2, 1999.

Yancey, Jean. Scrapbook.

Hannah Marie Wormington Volk

Notes

1. *Denver Post*, June 9, 1968, Contemporary section, p. 11.

2. Sally Lewis Rodeck, interview by author, Denver, May 2, 1997.

3. "Dr. Marie H. Wormington Off for Archeology Talk in Russia," *Rocky Mountain News*, July 28, 1964, p. 23.

Sources

Leonard, Stephen J., and Thomas Noel. *Denver: Mining Camp to Metropolis.* Niwot, Colo.: University Press of Colorado, 1990.

Rodeck, Sally Lewis. Interview by author. Denver, May 2, 1997.

Sudler, Barbara. "H. M. Wormington: An Exceptional Archeologist." *Colorado Heritage News*, April 1983: 1.

Volk, Hannah Marie Wormington. Curriculum vitae. Colorado Women's Hall of Fame files. Denver.

Helen Louise White Peterson

Notes

1. Vine Deloria, Sr., speech at Native American Youth Conference, Denver, 1982.

2. Helen Peterson, typescript of interview by Chaer Robert, "50th Anniversary—Agency for Human Rights and Community Relations in Denver," June 13, 1993, p. 8. Colorado Women's Hall of Fame files. Denver.

3. Lucille Echohawk, telephone interview by author, 1997.

4. Owanah Anderson, telephone interview by author, July 1998.

Sources

Anderson, Owanah. Interview by author. Telephone. July 1998.

Butterfield, Nancy L. "N.W. Indian News Assoc. Holds Annual Conference." Indian Voice, November 1979, p. 10.

Peterson, Helen Louise. Interview by author. Telephone. Fall 1997.

Peterson, Helen Louise. Nomination application by Owanah Anderson for The Wonder Woman Awards, submitted June 1984.

Peterson, Helen Louise. Nomination letter. Typescript of interview by Chaer Robert. June 13, 1993. Colorado Women's Hall of Fame files. Denver.

Peterson, Helen Louise. Resume. February 1986. Colorado Women's Hall of Fame files. Denver.

Miriam Goldberg

Notes

1. Hillel Goldberg, interview by author, Denver, July 20, 1998.

2. Miriam Goldberg, interview by author, Denver, May 19, 1997, and July 1998.

3. Miriam Goldberg, interview.

Sources

"A Woman Who Cares." Colorado Editor, May 1984. Clipping file. Western History Department, Denver Public Library.

Goldberg, Miriam. Interview by author. Denver, May 19, 1997, and July 1998.

Goldberg, Miriam. Nomination letter. Colorado Women's Hall of Fame files. Denver.

Goldberg, Rabbi Hillel. Interview by author. Telephone. July 1998.

Ruth Small Stockton

Notes

1. "Boots" Stockton Beran, interview by author, Lakewood, Colo., June 2, 1997.
2. Stockton Beran interview.
3. Stockton Beran, interview.
4. Tilman Bishop, interview by author, Grand Junction, Colo., May 1998.
5. Bishop, interview.
6. Jeffrey A. Roberts, "Senate Does Windows; Former Sen. Stockton Honored with One by Appreciative Friends, *Denver Post,* December 9, 1986, p. 4B.
7. "Woman of the Year: Sen. Ruth Stockton," *Sentinel,* January 1, 1970, p. 25.

Sources

Bishop, Senator Tilman. Interview by author. Grand Junction, Colo., May 1998.
Jackson, Jean. "Ruth Stockton." In *Lakewood, Colorado: An Illustrated Biography,* edited by Patricia Wilcox. N.p.: Lakewood's 25th Anniversary Commission, 1994.
Stockton Beran, Alexe ("Boots"). Interview by author. Lakewood, Colo., June 2, 1997, and May 25, 1998.
Stockton, Ruth Small. Colorado Women's Hall of Fame files. Denver.
Who's Who in Colorado. Denver: 1984.

Rachel Bassette Noel

Notes

1. Rachel Bassette Noel, interview by author, audiotape. Denver, August 19, 1997.
2. Noel, interview.
3. Noel, interview.
4. Noel, interview.

Sources

Noel, Rachel Bassette. Interview by author. Audiotape. August 19, 1997.
Noel, Rachel Bassette. Nomination letter. Colorado Women's Hall of Fame files. Denver.

Elise Biorn-Hansen Boulding

Notes

1. Elise Boulding, telephone interview by author, Wayland, Massachusetts, August 28, 1997.
2. Boulding, interview.
3. As quoted in Leslie Sweeney, "Elise Boulding Nominated for Nobel Prize; Boulder Scholar an Advocate for Peace, Human Rights," *Boulder Daily Camera,* February 7, 1990, p. 1A.
4. Sweeney, "Elise Boulding," p. 9A.

Sources

Boulding, Elise. Interview by author. Telephone. Wayland, Massachusetts, August 28, 1997.
Boulding, Elise. Nomination letter. Colorado Women's Hall of Fame files. Denver.

Lena Lovato Archuleta

Notes

1. Lena Lovato Archuleta, interview by author, Denver, June 23, 1997.
2. Archuleta, interview.

Sources

Archuleta, Lena Lovato. Colorado Women's Hall of Fame files. Denver.
Archuleta, Lena Lovato. Interview by author. Denver, June 23, 1997.

Mildred Pitts Walter

Notes

1. Mildred Pitts Walter, interview by author, Denver, July 10, 1997.
2. Walter, interview.
3. Walter, interview.
4. Walter, interview.
5. Walter, interview.

Sources

Kozikowski, Thomas. "Mildred Pitts Walter." In *Something About the Author,* edited by Donna Olendorf. Vol. 69: 203–210. Detroit: Gale Research, 1992.
Walter, Mildred Pitts. Macmillan Children's Book Group. New York: Bradbury Press, 1993.

Walter, Mildred Pitts. Interview by author. Denver, July 10, 1997.

Walter, Mildred Pitts. Nomination biography by Oleta Crain. Colorado Women's Hall of Fame files. Denver.

Hendrika Bestebreurtje Cantwell

Notes

1. Henrika Cantwell, telephone interview by author, Summer 1997.
2. Cantwell, interview.
3. Cantwell, interview.
4. Cantwell, interview.
5. Cantwell, interview.
6. Cantwell, interview.
7. Donald Bross, telephone interview by author, February 1998.

Sources

Cantwell, Hendrika. Biographical sketch and resumes. Colorado Women's Hall of Fame files. Denver.

Cantwell. Hendrika. Interview by author and manuscript review. Telephone. Summer 1997.

Cantwell, Rebecca. Conversation with author. Denver, Summer 1997.

Joan Packard Birkland

Notes

1. Joan Packard Birkland, taped interview by author, Denver, July 22, 1997.
2. Peg Gibson, telephone conversation with author, July 1997.
3. Birkland, interview.
4. "Extra Bit of Concentration—An Interview with Joan Birkland," *Club Ties*, 1981, p. 12.
5. Birkland, interview.
6. Birkland, interview.

Sources

"A Smashing Success." *Club Ties*, 1981, pp. 39–40.

Birkland, Joan Packard. Taped interview by author. July 22, 1997.

Birkland, Joan Packard. Nomination letter. Colorado Women's Hall of Fame files. Denver.

Burris, Jim. "Birkland: Perhaps State's Best All-Around Athlete." *Denver Business Journal*, April 6, 1987.

"Extra Bit of Concentration—An Interview with Joan Birkland." *Club Ties*, 1981, p. 12.

Skyzinski, Rich. "People of the USGA." *Golf Journal*, July 1995, p. 48.

Anne Flick Steinbeck

Notes

1. Anne Flick Steinbeck, telephone interview by author, June 27, 1998.
2. Steinbeck, interview.
3. Steinbeck, interview.
4. Steinbeck, interview.

Sources

"Introducing President Anne Steinbeck." *National Business Woman*, August–September 1985: 6.

Steinbeck, Anne Flick. Interview by author. Telephone. Gunnison, Colo., June 27, 1998.

Steinbeck, Anne Flick. Nomination letter. Colorado Women's Hall of Fame files. Denver.

Dana Hudkins Crawford

Notes

1. Paula Moore, "Civic Group Tries History to Lure Visitors … ," *Denver Business Journal*, June 28, 1996: 3A.
2. Dana Crawford, audiotape interview by author, June 28, 1997.
3. Crawford, interview.
4. Langdon Morris, "The Larimer Square Historic District," in *Denver Landmarks* (Denver: Charles Cleworth, 1979), p. 167.
5. Crawford, interview.
6. Crawford, interview

Sources

Crawford, Dana Hudkins. Clipping file. Western History Department, Denver Public Library.

Crawford, Dana Hudkins. Interview by author. Audiotape. June 28, 1997.

Crawford, Dana Hudkins. Nomination letter. Colorado Women's Hall of Fame files. Denver.

Evans, Christina. "The Building Doctor," *Denver Magazine*, June 1982: 94.

Moore, Paula. "Civic Group Tries History to Lure Visitors ... " *Denver Business Journal,* June 28, 1996: 3A.

Moore, Paula. "Dana Crawford: The City's Queen of Adaptive Re-use." *Denver Business Journal,* April 24, 1998: 7A.

"One of 11 People Who Wield Power in Region." *Front Range,* November 1984 (vol. 3, no. 2): 13.

LaRae Orullian

Notes

1. LaRae Orullian, interview by author, Denver, July 27, 1997.
2. Orullian, interview.
3. Orullian, interview.
4. Orullian, interview.
5. Orullian, interview.
6. Orullian, interview.

Sources

Orullian, LaRae. Interview by author. Denver. July 29, 1997.

Orullian, LaRae. Listing in *Who's Who in the West, 1989–1990.* Chicago: Marquis Who's Who, 1949–, p. 515.

Orullian, LaRae. Nomination letter. Colorado Women's Hall of Fame files. Denver.

Silvas, Sharon. "On My Honor, I Will Try ..." *Colorado Woman News,* November 1990: 27.

Svaldi, Aldo. "Bank Founder Steps Down." Denver Business Journal, June 9, 1995: 3.

"Women's Bank Sold ..." *Intermountain Jewish News,* February 25, 1994, p. 14.

Elnora ("Ellie") Clausing Gilfoyle

Notes

1. Elnora Gilfoyle, interview by author, Fort Collins, September 4, 1997.
2. "Gilfoyle Named Colorado State University's Provost ... ," news release, Colorado State University, May 20, 1992.
3. Gilfoyle, interview.
4. Gilfoyle, interview.
5. Gilfoyle, interview.

Sources

Gilfoyle, Elnora. Interview by author and videotape. Fort Collins, September 4, 1997.

Gilfoyle, Elnora. Nomination letter by Albert C. Yates. Colorado Women's Hall of Fame files. Denver.

Dorothy Louise Vennard Lamm

Notes

1. Bartell Nyberg, "Dottie Lamm ... a Lot of Human Being," *Denver Post Empire*, February 14, 1982, p. 14.

2. Dorothy Lamm, interview by author, Denver, July 8, 1997.

3. Lamm, interview.

4. Lamm, interview.

5. Lamm, interview.

6. Lamm, interview.

7. Lamm, interview.

8. Chuck Green, "This Wild Hare Just May Run," *Denver Post*, July 13, 1997, p. B1.

Sources

Lamm, Dorothy. Interview by author. Denver, July 8, 1997.

Lamm, Dorothy. Clipping file. Western History Department, Denver Public Library.

Lamm, Dorothy. Colorado Women's Hall of Fame files. Denver.

Silvas, Sharon. "Feminism: The Issues Today. Interview with Dottie Lamm. Toward a Feminist Partnership." *Colorado Woman News*, March 1990: 14–15.

Marilyn Van Derbur Atler

Notes

1. Marilyn Van Derbur Atler, audiotape interview by author. September 19, 1997.

2. Atler, interview.

3. Atler, interview.

4. Atler, interview.

5. Atler, interview.

Sources

Atler, Marilyn Van Derbur. Clipping files. Western History Department, Denver Public Library.

Atler, Marilyn Van Derbur. Interview by author. Audiotape. Denver, September 19, 1997.

Atler, Marilyn Van Derbur. Nomination letter. Colorado Women's Hall of Fame files. Denver.

Atler, Marilyn Van Derbur. "A Story of Incest: Miss America's Triumph over Shame." *People,* June 10, 1991: 88–91.

Sumiko Tanaka Hennessy

Notes

1. Sumiko Tanaka Hennessy, interview by author, Denver, Summer 1997.
2. Hennessy, interview.

Sources

Hennessy, Sumiko Tanaka. Colorado Women's Hall of Fame files. Denver.

Hennessy, Sumiko Tanaka. Interview by author. Denver, June 30, 1997.

Hynes, Adrienne. Biography and update on Sumiko Hennessy. Interview by author. Telephone, 1997.

Prato, Janice. Interview of Sumiki Hennessy. *Network,* June 1986: n.p.

Patricia Scott Schroeder

Notes

1. Peter Blake, "Despite Tips, Schroeder Won't Change Image," *Rocky Mountain News,* September 10, 1989.

2. Patricia Schroeder with Andrea Camp and Robyn Lipner, *Champion of the Great American Family: A Personal and Political Book* (New York: Random House, 1989), p. 147.

3. Clara Bingham, *Women on the Hill* (New York: Times Books, 1997), p. 77.

4. Bingham, *Women,* pp. 77–78.

5. Patricia Scott Schroeder, telephone interview by author, New York, September 1997.

6. Schroeder, interview.

7. Eleanor Clift, "Schroeder's Last Stand," *Working Women,* April 1996: 42.

8. Claudia Smith Brinson, "Woman of the Year, Pat Schroeder," *MS Magazine,* January–February 1997: 56.

9. Schroeder, interview.

10. Ted Sorenson, Introduction in Schroeder, *Champion of the Great American Family,* p. 9.

Sources

Bingham, Clara. *Women on the Hill.* New York: Times Books, 1997.

Brinson, Claudia Smith. "Woman of the Year, Pat Schroeder." *MS Magazine,* January–February 1997: 56.

Clift, Eleanor. "Schroeder's Last Stand: Women Saw Her as Their Voice." *Working Woman,* April 1996: 42.

Range, Peter Ross. "The Quitters." *Modern Maturity,* September–October 1996: 36.

Roberts, Cokie, and Steve Roberts. "Mothers' Day in Congress." *USA Weekend,* May 9–11, 1997: 4.

Schroeder, Patricia, with Andrea Camp and Robyn Lipner. *Champion of the Great American Family: A Personal and Political Book.* New York: Random House, 1989.

Schroeder, Patricia. Colorado Women's Hall of Fame files. Denver.

Schroeder, Patricia. Interview by author. Telephone. New York, September, 1997.

Lenore E. Auerbach Walker

Notes

1. Lenore E. Auerbach Walker, audiotape interview by author, Summer 1997.

2. Walker, interview.

3. Lenore E. Walker, *The Battered Woman* (New York: Harper & Row, 1979), p. xv.

4. Walker, interview.

5. Walker, interview.

6. Walker, interview.

Sources

Walker, Lenore E. Auerbach. Interview by author. Audiotape. Summer 1997.

Walker, Lenore E. *The Battered Woman.* New York: Harper & Row, 1979.

Walker, Lenore E. *The Battered Woman Syndrome.* New York: Springer Publishing, 1984.

Walker, Lenore E. *Terrifying Love: Why Battered Women Kill and How Society Responds.* New York: Harper & Row, 1989.

Walker, Lenore E. Nomination letter by Janice Prato. Colorado Women's Hall of Fame files. Denver.

Wilma J. Webb

Notes

1. Alan Dumas, "The Wilma Factor," *Rocky Mountain News,* October 20, 1991, pp. 12–14.

2. Wilma J. Webb, audiotape interview by author, Denver, September 22, 1997.

3. Webb, interview.

4. Webb, interview.

5. Webb, interview.

6. Webb, interview.

7. Webb, interview.

Sources

Webb, Wilma J. Interview by author and manuscript review. Audiotape. Denver, September 22, 1997.

Cleo Parker Robinson

Notes

1. Cleo Parker Robinson, audiotape interview by author, Denver, October 6, 1997, and manuscript review.

2. Robinson, interview.

3. Robinson, interview.

4. Jim Schwartzkopff, "Cleo Parker Robinson Visits NYC," *Dance Magazine,* August 1994: 15.

5. Robinson, interview.

Sources

Gastineau, Janine. "Cleo Parker Robinson Dance Ensemble." *Dance Magazine,* January 1996: 110.

Robinson, Cleo Parker. Clipping files. Western History Department and Periodicals Department. Denver Public Library.

Robinson, Cleo Parker. Colorado Women's Hall of Fame files. Denver.

Robinson, Cleo Parker. Interview by author. Audiotape. Denver, October 6, 1997. Manuscript review.

Schwartzkopff, Jim. "Cleo Parker Robinson Visits NYC." *Dance Magazine,* August 1994: 15.

Silvas, Sharon. "Interview with Cleo Parker Robinson: Phantoms of the Spirit Overcome." *Colorado Woman News,* April 1990: 15.

Terri Helman Finkel

Notes

1. Terri Finkel, interview by author, Denver, August 13, 1997.
2. Finkel, interview.
3. Finkel, interview.
4. Finkel, interview and chapter review.

Sources

"Chimpanzees: Ultimate Long-Term Survivors?" *New Directions* (Journal of NIH Research), July 1993: 79.

Finkel, Terri Helman. Interview by author. Denver, August 13, 1997.

Finkel. Terri Helman. Nomination materials. Colorado Women's Hall of Fame files. Denver.

"Important AIDS Virus Discovery." *New Directions* (Journal of NIH Research), 1992.

Schneck, Lisha. "New Progress in Local Research." *Arthritis Observer,* Fall 1992: 1, 2.

"Two Center Researchers Take Rheumatology Awards." *Rapport* (publication of National Jewish Hospital), November 1990, n.p.

Nominations to the Colorado
Women's Hall of Fame

Nominations. The Colorado Women's Hall of Fame depends upon members of the public to nominate extraordinary women for induction into the hall. Nominations should be submitted on an official nomination form. Nominators should fully describe on the form how the nominee meets the induction criteria of the hall of fame.

Nomination forms can be obtained by calling the Colorado Women's Hall of Fame at (303) 904-4388 or on-line at the hall of fame's web address, www.cogreatwomen.org.

Induction Criteria. The Colorado Women's Hall of Fame inducts women who made significant contributions to Colorado (as a state or territory) and its national presence, and made ongoing efforts to elevate the status of women, and to open new frontiers.

Selection Process. A diverse group of Coloradoans are recruited to act as a Selection Committee. The Selection Committee reviews all the nominations, performs additional research if necessary, and recommends a minimum of two historical and two contemporary women for induction in the Colorado Women's Hall of Fame. The Board of Directors of the Colorado Women's Hall of Fame has the final authority to approve or not approve the work of the Selection Committee.

The Induction Ceremony. The induction ceremony is hosted by the Colorado Women's Hall of Fame on a regular basis (typically occurring once every two years). The inductees, the Colorado Women's Hall of Fame Board of Directors, volunteers, friends and family of the inductees, honored guests, sponsors, members of the media, and the general public attend the induction ceremony to publicly celebrate the inductees for their contributions to our Colorado community and to the world.

Alphabetical Index